T0390520

# JAZZ IN THE HILL

# JAZZ
## in the HILL

Nightlife and Narratives of a Pittsburgh Neighborhood

## COLTER HARPER

University Press of Mississippi / Jackson

The University Press of Mississippi is the scholarly publishing agency of
the Mississippi Institutions of Higher Learning: Alcorn State University,
Delta State University, Jackson State University, Mississippi State University,
Mississippi University for Women, Mississippi Valley State University,
University of Mississippi, and University of Southern Mississippi.

www.upress.state.ms.us

The University Press of Mississippi is a member
of the Association of University Presses.

An earlier version of chapter six appeared in *Jazz Perspectives*, 11, no. 1 (2018): 69–101.
Reprinted by permission of Taylor & Francis, https://www.tandfonline.com/.

Library of Congress Control Number: 2023045681
Hardback ISBN: 9781496849854
Trade paperback ISBN: 9781496849861
Epub single ISBN: 9781496849878
Epub institutional ISBN: 9781496849885
PDF single ISBN: 9781496849892
PDF institutional ISBN: 9781496849915

British Library Cataloging-in-Publication Data available

# CONTENTS

# JAZZ IN THE HILL

# PREFACE

From March 1991 to September 1999, Jazz at the Hill House (JAHH) brought together hundreds of musicians on Sunday evenings for a jam session in Pittsburgh's Hill District.[1] For younger musicians, it provided training in improvisation in front of a live audience. For older attendees, this gathering revived a tradition of listening to jazz in the Hill while also projecting possible futures in the storied neighborhood once widely known for its nightlife. On busy weeks, several hundred people filled the hall and dozens of musicians performed. Audience members entered free of charge, often bringing their own spread of food and drinks. The event was informal by design, evoking the mid-twentieth-century social scenes of Hill venues such as the Musicians Club (run by Local 471 of the American Federation of Musicians), the Crawford Grill No. 2, and the Hurricane Bar, as well as other neighborhood venues. With the exception of the Crawford Grill No. 2, the Hill's nightclubs and many of the buildings which housed them were gone by the 1990s. As the names of these venues filtered through conversations during JAHH, they symbolically mapped the neighborhood's history. The stories of these venues reminded younger musicians that the music they were learning was created not just by innovative artists, but also by networks of audiences, entrepreneurs, labor organizers, and educators who gathered in nightclubs.

JAHH did not feature a regular house band like most contemporary jazz jam sessions but rather relied on veteran bandleader Horace Turner to organize groups from the ever-shifting pool of volunteer musicians.[2] Turner chose songs and filled in as needed on piano, drums, organ, bass, and euphonium while his wife, Mary, registered musicians and made sure they had an opportunity to play during the evening. Around 6 p.m., audience members began to arrive, many of whom were from the neighborhood and old enough to have heard canonical musicians such as Abbey Lincoln, Max Roach, Art Blakey, and Jimmy Smith at their prime and in intimate settings. The shifting combination of more- and less-experienced musicians sometimes led to chaotic performances and a scolding

Figure P.1. Jazz at the Hill House in the Hill House Association's Kaufmann Auditorium. From left: Calvin Stemley (tenor saxophone), unidentified (tenor saxophone), John "Squirrel" Mosley (trumpet), Hillard Jordan (trombone), Roger Barbour (trumpet), Reynard Ford (alto saxophone), Horace Turner, Bunker Jones (piano), and Colter Harper (guitar). (Photo by Douglas Harper, 1996.)

from Turner. Mostly, the band powered through songs, held together by a shared repertoire and the guidance of more experienced players. At high points, the jam session welcomed renowned guests, including guitarist and vocalist George Benson, tenor saxophonist Stanley Turrentine, vibraphonist Johnny Lytle, drummer Pola Roberts, and drummer Joe Harris—artists who developed their early careers in fabled Hill clubs.

Young musicians, including myself, found themselves scrambling to piece together melodies and chord progressions for unfamiliar songs called out by Turner and other older musicians. Miles Davis's "Four," Thelonious Monk's "Round Midnight," Benny Golson's "I Remember Clifford," Stanley Turrentine's "Sugar," as well as American Songbook standards "Tangerine" and "All the Things You Are," were among the hundreds of compositions chosen on the spot. Grateful for the guidance, younger musicians studied the songs they heard to be better prepared the following week. My first time sitting in, I remember panicking and leaning over to the pianist Bunker Jones and saying, "I don't know 'Four'" as Turner was counting in the song. Jones responded casually, "Just listen." As I strained to follow the chord progression and find my way through the unfamiliar song, I became aware that I had to listen to the audience as well. While the auditorium was filled with people who were socializing, I recognized the high expectations of many

Figure P.2. Charles "Teenie" Harris, American, 1908–1998, Five-piece band performing, including Horace Turner on trumpet and piano, Jimmy Morris on electric bass, Jim Armstrong on alto saxophone, Specks Thompson on alto saxophone on right, and Mary Turner, wife of Horace Turner, on drums, c. 1955–1975, black and white: Kodak Safety Film, H: 4 in. × W: 5 in. (10.20 × 12.70 cm), Carnegie Museum of Art, Pittsburgh: Heinz Family Fund, 2001.35.1498, © Carnegie Museum of Art, Charles "Teenie" Harris Archive.

listeners, which registered in measured stares, clapping, or shouts of encouragement—reminders that the musical dialogue was not restricted to the stage.

As a teenager new to Pittsburgh, JAHH was where I first received lessons in the Hill's history. Within walking distance of Duquesne University and downtown Pittsburgh, the Hill bore a stigma of economic divestment that isolated it from surrounding neighborhoods and concealed its vibrant past. Through conversations at JAHH, I began to understand the Hill's importance in the region as the city's oldest African American community and destination for Jewish, Irish, Italian, Syrian, and Lebanese immigrants in the late nineteenth century, and following World War I, a steady influx of African American migrants from the South. A neighborhood in constant flux through the early twentieth century, the Hill was home to the *Pittsburgh Courier*, which provided a national platform for advancing racial equality while documenting the extensive contributions of the city's Black cultural, political, and social life. A departure of businesses and people that began with the neighborhood's redevelopment in the mid-1950s accelerated following the assassination of Dr. Martin Luther King Jr. on April 4, 1968. The trauma of the 1968 riots never fully healed, the aftermath obscuring the neighborhood's cultural history. While studying jazz at Duquesne University in the late 1990s, I found that the curriculum did not cover the Hill's contributions to the music though our classrooms were in sight of the neighborhood's St. Benedict the Moor Church, located across Centre Avenue from the civil rights monument named Freedom Corner.

Experiences at JAHH led me to examine how jazz performance intersected with processes of community formation, namely the creation of businesses, organizations of labor, pursuits of leisure, and the development of the city through public and private initiatives. As a part of what urban planners and social geographers call "placemaking," JAHH drew on a long tradition within the Hill's African American community of making hostile places into lived spaces.[3] Conveniently located for elderly audience members who lived nearby, the weekly jam was notable for engaging a neighborhood shaped by the struggle for social and economic advancement in African American communities during the first half of the twentieth century. JAHH was also a means through which outsiders experienced the Hill. By meeting in a community negatively portrayed through incessant reporting on crime and feared by those in surrounding neighborhoods, the jam session placed jazz performance at the center of continuing social and economic struggles. In the context of the Hill, jazz performance was an expression of the possible in what was widely viewed as a failed neighborhood.

It was around the time that I began attending JAHH that I first encountered the photos of Charles "Teenie" Harris (1908–1998). Photo vendor Dennis Morgan sold Harris prints amid the bustle of Pittsburgh's Strip District, and I purchased a portrait of guitarist George Benson. Initially unaware that they were at the center of a legal battle, I was thrilled to encounter these images that provided a look into the Hill's cultural past: bustling nightclubs and packed theaters featuring Billy Eckstine, George Benson, Ahmad Jamal, and Erroll Garner in their early careers. Morgan, a Hill District resident and devotee of its cultural history, had arranged to acquire and sell prints from Harris's extensive archive of negatives in 1986, though Harris initiated court proceedings to regain control of the negatives in 1998.[4] A court order returned the negatives to the Harris family in 2000, after which they were purchased by the Carnegie Museum of Art (CMOA) and housed in the newly formed Charles "Teenie" Harris Archive.[5] During my initial research, I used 173 photos, which were generously printed by research archivist Kerin Shellenbarger. In many ways, this study has grown from an extended engagement with Harris's photos and the cultural wealth his work has produced.

This book developed not as an attempt to tell the story of Pittsburgh jazz, but rather as a social history of several Hill District jazz clubs that existed between 1920 and 1970. I have sought to understand jazz as a form of community building and to explore how places were claimed and contested. Taking a "history from below" perspective, the musicians and other community figures discussed in this study are primarily those who spent their careers in Pittsburgh rather than those who left and gained wider recognition. By studying the venues, the lives of local musicians, club owners, listeners, labor organizers, and journalists come into focus, and we begin to see the extensive networks that jazz facilitated during the twentieth century as well as the continued relevance that nightlife and jazz venues have in our cities.

# INTRODUCTION

## Jazz, Nightlife, and the Hill District

Pittsburgh's Hill District is historically a multiracial and multiethnic neighborhood that fostered a vibrant jazz scene from the 1920s through the 1960s. Though the neighborhood has undergone an extensive and traumatic transformation that has muted its nightlife, the history of jazz in the Hill echoes through the city. Memorials dot the now significantly depopulated landscape of the Hill as reminders of how this musical tradition was fundamental to building its identity as a place of social experimentation and artistic innovation. The façade of the Legacy Apartments—a public housing complex built in 2007 on the main thoroughfare of Wylie Avenue—features the names of Mary Lou Williams, Erroll Garner, Earl "Fatha" Hines, Billy Eckstine, Art Blakey, Ahmad Jamal, George Benson, Stanley Turrentine, Roger Humphries, and Walt Harper—artists who had personal and professional connections to the Hill. These and many other artists are the most visible part of a musical lineage that continues to inform public discourse about the Hill's future as the heart of Black Pittsburgh.

Jazz has indeed shaped the Hill as a place and a way of life, with these connections speaking to larger political contexts, processes of urban development, and civil rights struggles. In delving into the history of jazz in the Hill, one discovers that jazz clubs reveal themselves not just as backdrops of remarkable careers, but also as sites of entrepreneurialism, placemaking, labor organizing and critical listening that contributed to the development of an African American community. In taking a broad approach to thinking about jazz clubs, I foreground the network of venues, patrons, business owners, and locally based musicians that were themselves the foundations of community building. This book aims to demonstrate how the clubs, as a nexus of music, politics, economy, labor, and social relations, supported the livelihood of residents and artists while developing cultures of listening and learning—characteristics that should guide current development visions for the Hill on the cusp of its remaking.

Through a close study of Hill jazz clubs, this book explores distinctive eras and issues of twentieth-century American urban history, including notions of "vice" during the Prohibition Era (1920–1934), "blight" during the mid-twentieth-century boom in urban redevelopment (1946–1973), and workplace integration during the civil rights era (1954–1968). In the 1920s and early 1930s, jazz cabarets were focal points in the struggle to define and enforce the color line in Pittsburgh. Colloquially referred to as "black and tan cabarets," these venues were places of interracial socialization as well as platforms for the emerging jazz scenes and Black political and economic power. These venues provided a foundation for the celebrated clubs of the Hill's jazz scene in the 1950s and 1960s, when the neighborhood became a destination for modern jazz musicians to perform for discerning audiences. It was in these venues that alternative visions of the city's development took shape and musicians advocated for their rights as musical laborers. Throughout the civil rights era, unionized musicians were one of many groups of laborers that faced the challenges of desegregation and the paradoxical consequences of integration. In this respect, the Hill is a valuable case study of how jazz intersects with political and cultural history, public policy, labor, law, and community formation.

The Hill District's central location and topography provide distinctive physical backdrops to the varied activities of music, urban development, and community organizing in Pittsburgh. Beginning a mile to the east of the convergence of the Ohio, Monongahela, and Allegheny Rivers, the Hill is adjacent to the city's downtown, referred to by Pittsburghers as the Golden Triangle, which contains the city's business and government district. Approaching the Hill from downtown, the land steadily rises into a series of rolling hills that reinforce the neighborhood's feeling of remoteness despite its proximity to adjacent neighborhoods. Wylie Avenue, the most prominent thoroughfare and a historic stage for the Hill's public life, was tagged as "The Street that Starts at a Church and Ends in Jail" in the column "Up and Down the Avenue" by Chester L. Washington (1902–1983) in the African American newspaper the *Pittsburgh Courier*.[1] The old Allegheny County Jail in downtown Pittsburgh, an imposing stone fortress completed in 1884, stood as a gateway between the Hill and Pittsburgh's seat of political power. A large Romanesque church completed in 1895, which was a site of Black worship, resistance, and political organizing, was two miles further east.[2] Thus the geographic and cultural boundary of the Hill District was established by the end of the nineteenth century.

The close proximity of Pittsburgh's business district had various implications for the Hill's nightlife scene, jazz clubs, and Black-owned businesses. In many respects, the Hill was culturally and economically self-contained. One resident who was interviewed for the 1991 documentary *Wylie Avenue Days* remarked, "There was practically every kind of business that you would want, especially to do shopping," implying an economic independence from downtown that bolstered a sense of community while strategically countering racial segregation.[3] In other respects, the Hill developed into a destination for people from downtown and Greater Pittsburgh seeking out nightlife and fostered diverse social scenes largely unique in the city. Much as New York City's Harlem and Chicago's South Side drew White entertainment seekers, Hill venues drew a steady stream of visitors to its clubs.

The neighborhood's jazz history is also intertwined with the Hill's identity as a working-class neighborhood that was a destination for African American families and workers from the American South. The Hill witnessed significant demographic shifts that were consistent with national trends of movement from the rural South to the industrial North. Though Pittsburgh's population was roughly one-sixth the size of Chicago's and one-twelfth that of New York City's, it was similarly impacted by the Great Migration.[4] In the 1910s, the percentage of the Hill's Black population increased from 25 to 54 percent in the Fifth Ward or the Middle Hill and from 17 to 40 percent in the Third Ward or the Lower Hill, reflecting the draw of Pittsburgh's steel industries.[5] Labor shortages during World War I led employers to hire more Black workers, though these jobs were often limited to positions as unskilled laborers or in highly toxic steel-making processes such as baking coke-grade coal.[6]

By 1930, the Hill District was Pittsburgh's most ethnically diverse neighborhood and home to the city's largest Black community.[7] At this point, the neighborhood was fast becoming what journalist Isabel Wilkerson called one of the many "forgotten islands" in US cities—neighborhoods where "the least-paid people were forced to pay the highest rents for the most dilapidated housing owned by absentee landlords trying to wring the most money out of a place nobody cared about."[8] Working for the Federal Writers' Project in the late 1930s, Fred Holmes and Abram Hall reflected on the lives and struggles of Pittsburgh's 54,983 Black residents, approximately twenty-five thousand of whom then resided in the Hill.[9] For these two Black writers employed by the short-lived Works Progress Administration program, the Hill District represented "the worst that a fiercely industrial city like Pittsburgh can do to human beings . . . . Its dominant note is squalor. Narrow streets are lined with tawdry houses, dingy red, their scarred doorways and tottering porches often reached by crumbling wooden steps."[10] This grim assessment captures the plight of the Hill's working class and also reflects a perception of the Hill as a place defined by poverty and a deteriorating infrastructure—a stigma that belied its influence on the city's cultural life and which provided justification for its development by the city. Yet the population density and housing challenges of the Hill also provided a sociocultural context in which Black-owned and self-determined sites of work and leisure provided a mutual support system and basis for community formation. Jazz clubs epitomized such spaces of self-determination that contributed to the Hill's value as a cultural center and place of business.

### Locating the "Crossroads of the World"

From the 1910s to the early 1950s, the intersection of Wylie and Fullerton Avenues was the heart of the Hill District—a site of convergence for its residents as well as an intersection between the neighborhood and Greater Pittsburgh. Chester Washington, who moved to the Hill in the mid-1920s from Pittsburgh's North Side, reflected in a *Courier* column on the intersection's unique contributions to the city's cultural landscape:

> The Wylie and Fullerton street corner last Saturday night reminded us of the title of Howard M. East's risqué sociological volume, *Mankind at the Crossroads*. Representatives of all races seemed to have gathered there. Two white cops stood jabbering on the lower right-hand corner, while a plainclothesman of color scrutinized the bustling, passing crowd carefully. In addition to being one of the most "excitable" corners in our Steel City, this intersection is one of the most valuable. The rich-looking, specially built Packard limousine belonging to the white man who owns the entire corner stands at ease down Fullerton Street a bit. The luncheon and confectionery establishment operated by foreigners on the corners does a rushing business. In front of the shop, on the curbstone, at least forty watermelons . . . were relaxing contentedly, waiting to be claimed by some admirer.[11]

Washington's sardonic reference to geneticist Howard East's 1924 book—one of many early twentieth-century eugenics studies that used social theory to incite White fears of interracial mixing and White erasure—positions the intersection whose site potentiality is defined by interethnic and interracial cohabitation. In East's writings, the crossroads represented a point of reckoning for White supremacists grappling with the question, "Who shall inherit the earth?"[12] For Washington, the intersection's night scene reveals the Hill as a place of emerging Black social life and alludes to the budding economic opportunities for the immigrant and African American populations.

In the following decades, the intersection of Wylie and Fullerton and the nightlife that it fostered became symbolically associated with the development of the Hill's Black community. Radio DJ and music promoter Mary Dee Dudley (1912–1964, née Goode) (figures I.1 and 5.1) popularized the intersection's nickname as "the crossroads of the world" during her music programs in the early

Figure I.1. Charles "Teenie" Harris, American, 1908–1998, Mary Dee at microphone in club with mirrored wall, c. 1946–1955, black and white: Kodak Safety Film, H: 4 in. × W: 5 in. (10.20 × 12.70 cm), Carnegie Museum of Art, Pittsburgh: Heinz Family Fund, 2001.35.2058 © Carnegie Museum of Art, Charles "Teenie" Harris Archive.

1950s. Drawing on her personal ties to the Hill and its nightlife, Dudley's tributes to Wylie and Fullerton challenged depictions of the Lower Hill as a center of vice and blight and claimed it as a source of pride. As a radio pioneer for Black women, Dudley used her programs to promote artists and create a new platform for Pittsburgh's African American community. Dudley joined the newly formed radio station WHOD on August 1, 1948, by hosting a fifteen-minute show called "Moving Around with Mary Dee."[13] Over the following seven years, Dudley also ran segments such as "The *Pittsburgh Courier* Newscast" with her brother and journalist Malvin "Mal" Goode and "The *Courier* Women's Page of the Air" with *Courier* columnist Toki Johnson. She also set up a broadcasting location on the corner of Herron and Centre Avenues in the Upper Hill, where she spun jazz, rhythm and blues, and rock and roll records, as well as interviewed public figures

# The Hill District

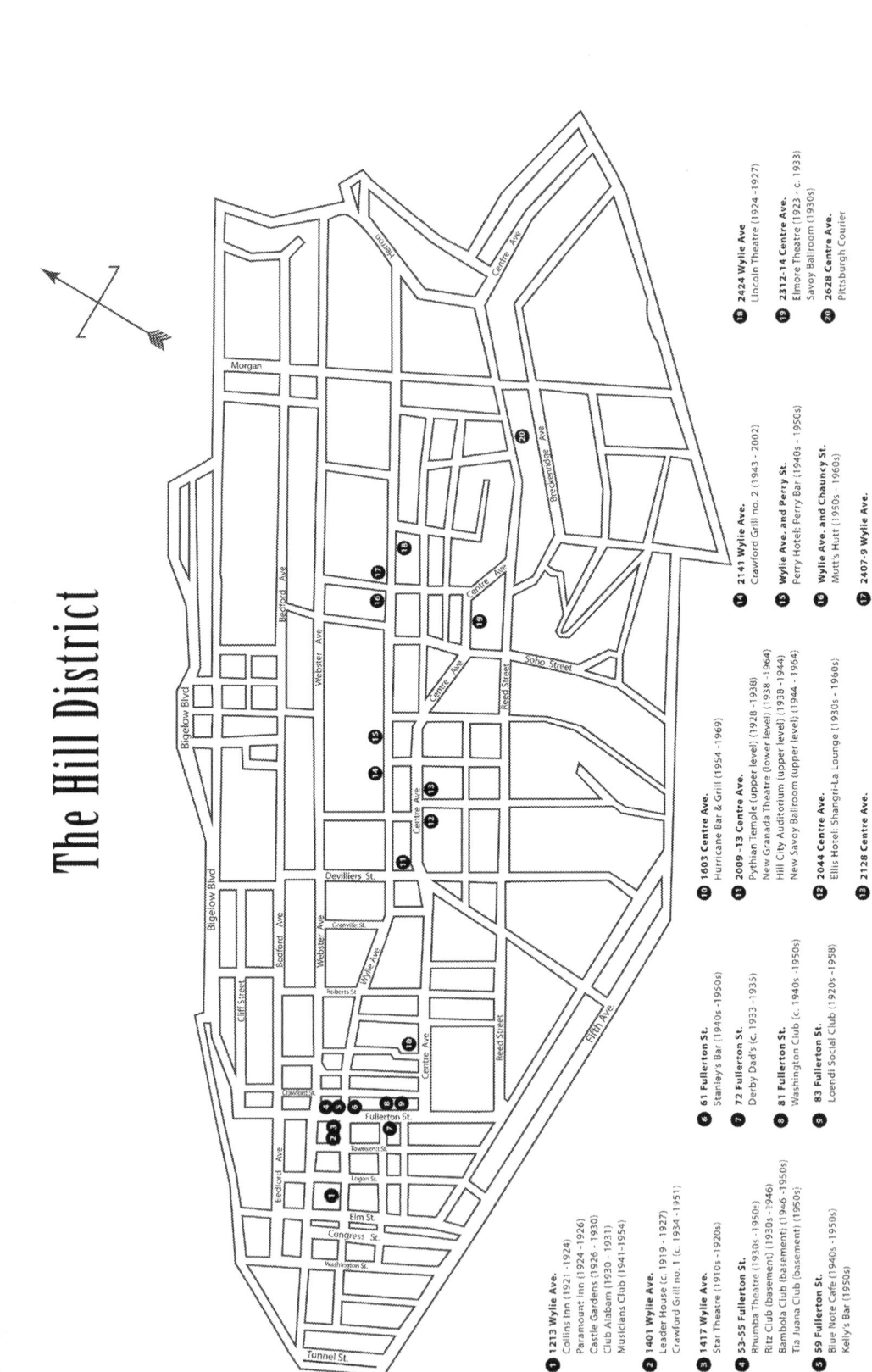

Figure I.2. The Hill District and locations of notable venues.[15]

**1** 1213 Wylie Ave.
Collins Inn (1921 - 1924)
Paramount Inn (1924 - 1926)
Castle Gardens (1926 - 1930)
Club Alabam (1930 - 1931)
Musicians Club (1941 - 1954)

**2** 1401 Wylie Ave.
Leader House (c. 1919 - 1927)
Crawford Grill no. 1 (c. 1934 - 1951)

**3** 1417 Wylie Ave.
Star Theatre (1910s - 1920s)

**4** 53-55 Fullerton St.
Rhumba Theatre (1930s - 1950s)
Ritz Club (basement) (1930s - 1946)
Bambola Club (basement) (1946 - 1950s)
Tia Juana Club (basement) (1950s)

**5** 59 Fullerton St.
Blue Note Cafe (1940s - 1950s)
Kelly's Bar (1950s)

**6** 61 Fullerton St.
Stanley's Bar (1940s - 1950s)

**7** 72 Fullerton St.
Derby Dad's (c. 1933 - 1935)

**8** 81 Fullerton St.
Washington Club (c. 1940s - 1950s)

**9** 83 Fullerton St.
Loendi Social Club (1920s - 1958)

**10** 1603 Centre Ave.
Hurricane Bar & Grill (1954 - 1969)

**11** 2009-13 Centre Ave.
Pythian Temple (upper level) (1928 - 1938)
New Granada Theatre (lower level) (1938 - 1964)
Hill City Auditorium (upper level) (1938 - 1944)
New Savoy Ballroom (upper level) (1944 - 1964)

**12** 2044 Centre Ave.
Ellis Hotel: Shangri-La Lounge (1930s - 1960s)

**13** 2128 Centre Ave.
Charles "Teenie" Harris Studios (1940s - 1960s)

**14** 2141 Wylie Ave.
Crawford Grill no. 2 (1943 - 2002)

**15** Wylie Ave. and Perry St.
Perry Hotel: Perry Bar (1940s - 1950s)

**16** Wylie Ave. and Chauncy St.
Mutt's Hutt (1950s - 1960s)

**17** 2407-9 Wylie Ave.
Flamingo Hotel: Joyce Bryant Rm (1950s)

**18** 2424 Wylie Ave
Lincoln Theatre (1924 - 1927)

**19** 2312-14 Centre Ave.
Elmore Theatre (1923 - c. 1933)
Savoy Ballroom (1930s)

**20** 2628 Centre Ave.
Pittsburgh Courier

such as Pennsylvania Supreme Court Justice Michael Musmanno and celebrity artists including Nat King Cole and Tony Bennett.

Dudley knew the crossroads as a place of opportunity and creativity, where the convergence of people gave rise to new possibilities. Though the crossroads did not feature the grand theaters of the city's downtown, it nonetheless drew together jazz musicians and listeners from throughout the country and exemplified the importance of nightlife to the neighborhood. In the early 1950s, the intersection was home to or near a number of nightclubs, including the Blue Note, Stanley's Tavern, the Bambola Social Club, the Rhumba Theater, the Crawford Grill No.1, and the Musicians Club, as well as the African American business associations the Washington Club and the Loendi Club. In the evenings at Stanley's Tavern, Dudley organized the long-running Celebrity Night for young entertainers to gain experiences in front of audiences. Her promotion of this corner of the neighborhood as a cultural hub had undeniable links to her family's involvement in the local business since Goode's Pharmacy, located opposite the tavern, was owned by her father, William W. Goode. Operating twenty-four hours a day, the pharmacy was an integral part of the Hill's commercial infrastructure and cultural life that made nightlife a more widely accessible cultural space.[14]

While Dudley was celebrating Hill nightlife during her broadcasts, her contemporary John Clark (1888–1961) wrote of the crossroads as a place that offered the freedoms and thrills of the night. In 1954 for his *Courier* column "Wylie Avenue," Clark described an unnamed World War II veteran from Washington, DC, who visited Pittsburgh shortly after the close of the war and ended up in one of the clubs at Wylie and Fullerton. After exiting an underground club, the veteran exclaimed:

> It was around eleven when we left and stepped right onto the "Crossroads of the World." It was greater than [Washington, DC's] Seventh and T [and] had more pimps, gamblers, hustlers and dope peddlers. What made this "crossing" so attractive was that it was surrounded with everything that any wild night-lifer wanted. We covered at least a dozen joints, never used my car, a taxicab or street car. Walked to every one within five minutes. Oh boy, that was the greatest spot I had ever seen in my twelve years of Army service, all over the world.[16]

Clark may have withheld the unnamed veteran's identity out of concern for privacy, or the character could have been an extension of his own musings on the neighborhood that he had been writing about for three decades at this point. In either case, the nostalgia is palpable in Clark's writing as he reminisces about nightclubs that were slated to be demolished as part of the city-led Lower Hill redevelopment that would start in 1955.

On the cusp of its destruction, this intersection's identity as a place of gathering and a hub of nightlife was thoroughly established in the minds of not only residents but among touring musicians. The grand evocation of the intersection as a "crossroads of the world" projected a sense of pride in the neighborhood and the achievements of its residents. Moreover, this phrase reflected the political and cultural need to legitimize nightlife in the Hill as part of an economically viable and artistically vibrant community—perspectives that counterbalanced the negative perceptions of blight and vice perpetuated by official sociological studies and public discourse.

### Narrating the Hill's Nightlife

The night has historically symbolized an opposition to the order and safety of the day, though as scholars have argued, it fosters times and spaces for creativity and freedom. If the day is dominated by the pressures of work and domestic life, the night offers leisure and temporary respite from these obligations and hardships. Historian Bryan Palmer conceives of nighttime as both a time and cultural space that introduce "theaters of ambiguity and transgression that can lead toward enactments of liberation."[17] Historian Robin Kelley grounds his theorization of the night in Black experiences where "actions that were otherwise choked back in public could find expression."[18] Both of these perspectives claim the night as an outlet for self-determination and resistance. The work of figures such as Mary Dee, John Clark, and Chester Washington demonstrates nightlife's importance in the Hill and provides a window into the jazz clubs in the neighborhood as important institutions of music, social life, and labor as a context for experiences of transgression, liberation, and creativity.

In looking at Hill venues, patrons, artists, and club owners, we see how journalists in the Black and White presses contested notions of Black nightlife and the roles of jazz clubs. Writers for the *Pittsburgh Courier*, including Clark and Washington, wove nightlife into narratives of the struggles and triumphs of the city's Black cultural, political, and economic life. Clark's column "Wylie Avenue," which ran from 1923 to 1961, and Washington's "Deep Wylie," "Walking Up Wylie," and "Up and Down the Avenue," which consecutively appeared between 1929 and 1939, ran weekly and, in five hundred to eight hundred words, delivered political commentary, arts and theater reviews, gossip, and humor. These narratives addressed both the famous and unknowns: politicians, pastors, sex workers, civic leaders, sports heroes, musicians, and racketeers. Their weekly commentaries documented the challenges and conflicts faced by the neighborhood's expanding African American community and used nightlife scenes to narrate the Hill's social life from the perspective of those who lived in the neighborhood. Both

Clark and Washington presented local and national readers with counternarratives to those found in the White press. In 1929, Washington remarked that a "misinformed public" most often associated the Lower Hill, known as "deep Wylie," with "tragedy," whereas his role was to present "both sides of the usually one-sided story."[19]

Columns in the White-owned press, such as "Pittsburghesque" by Charles Danver, predictably provided a running commentary of the Hill as a place of social decay and exotic experiences.[20] A quintessential "slummer," Danver relished visiting speakeasies along Wylie Avenue and describing the characters and scenes that he encountered. As an outsider, he took special pride in crossing the color line, remarking, "[T]he darkest sectors of Wylie Avenue accept the white stranger with quiet tolerance, if not respect."[21] Danver enticed curious would-be slummers with descriptions of Wylie Avenue as "fairly well behaved, if somewhat unconventional and at times rowdy," where interested "strollers who stare with frank curiosity at 'Little Harlem' are stared at in return, but not offensively."[22]

Born of his infatuation with the Hill and the privileges that his Whiteness afforded him there, Danver's descriptions reinforced an anonymity that served to undermine the community's cultural contributions. As opposed to the *Courier* columns, which focused on individuals and places, "Pittsburghesque" invoked common tropes that stood for those actually living in the Hill. In 1933, Danver described an unnamed Lower Hill nightclub: "The old-fashioned piano, its keys blackened with age, blazed away in one of the [H]ill [D]istrict's countless tiny hideaways. Between beers, set up by customers who liked music, a dark-skinned little fellow, his fingers in what seemed to be a frantic frenzy, pounded out everything from Beethoven to Berlin."[23] By removing the event from its setting, Danver creates stereotypes of the downtrodden genius and escapist barfly while the age-blackened keys of the piano cohabitate with the performer in an equal standing of object and human.

On the other hand, *Courier* writer Clark's "striking snapshots of life" speak to the experiences of its growing Black community.[24] Clark often included small vignettes of conflicts that defined Black life on Wylie as a public acknowledgment of the lived experiences of racism. In 1923, he opened one column with a short description of two policemen beating a Black man "insensible" before arresting him outside the Star Theatre in the Lower Hill.[25] Clark concludes with the statement, "[W]e are reliably informed that the unfortunate victim could not appear for a hearing the next morning."[26] With this and many other descriptions of police violence, Clark demonstrates that journalists were watching in protest of systemic anti-Black violence and had the political will to call for reform. The columnist's reference to the Star Theatre, one of several Hill District venues on the national Theater Owners Booking Association (TOBA) circuit, grounded the description of police violence in a site of Black entertainment and leisure that would have been familiar to many residents. Clark ends the piece with a call for police reform with the addition of Black police officers or a restructuring of the police force to emphasize social services over violent enforcement—demands that are achingly familiar a century later in the wake of the killings of George Floyd, Breonna Taylor, and many other people of color by police.

### Charles "Teenie" Harris: Visualizing Nightlife

Just as writers for the *Pittsburgh Courier* depicted aspects of the Hill's nightlife, photographer Charles "Teenie" Harris (1908–1998) created an invaluable visual record of the neighborhood's jazz clubs and nightlife scenes. In documenting every aspect of the community from the mid-1930s to the mid-1970s, Harris created a visual archive that centered on the experiences of the Hill's residents and contributed to the *Courier*'s documentation of the city's African American population. Now preserved in the city's Carnegie Museum of Art as a research resource, his photos show clubs as integral parts of the social and economic life of the neighborhood and offer jazz scholars a cultural record with layers of nuanced intimacies, everyday life, and unfinished narratives. These photos also provided a record of when, where, and with whom various events took place, as well as how nightclubs looked.

Practical details captured in Harris's photos helped musicians recall their experiences during my research interviews, which provided a guide for describing everyday experiences that were not otherwise documented. Drummer Cecil Brooks II noted after looking at a photo of himself performing fifty years earlier (figure 5.7), "A lot of this stuff I forgot because there was no need to remember. If you hadn't brought these pictures, I would have forgot about this. It helps a whole lot. You take this stuff for granted and you don't document it."[27] Brooks recalled small details of venues, audiences, repertoire, and interactions with older musicians and venue owners. In many other cases of photo-elicited interviews during my research, Harris's images helped musicians process and narrate the ways in which jazz functioned as a creative practice bound to the economic and physical conditions of the Hill's nightlife.[28]

Harris, a Hill native, was intimately familiar with the neighborhood, having worked and lived there most of his life. In the late 1920s and 1930s, he was active in local football, basketball, and baseball leagues and also worked as a "numbers man" collecting bets for the numbers lottery run by his brother William "Woogie" Harris (1896–1967) and William "Gus" Greenlee (1895–1952). Harris's interest in photography grew as a counterpart to his personal investment in the Hill and Black life in Pittsburgh, which he documented for several decades. In an interview with historian Ralph Hill in the early 1970s, Harris recalled that his love

Figure I.3. Charles "Teenie" Harris, American, 1908–1998, Billy Eckstine Orchestra performing with Eckstine on trombone on left, Marion "Boonie" Hazel on trumpet on left, Sarah Vaughan on right, and spectators Rita Ings Frazier wearing light colored flowers in hair and Tommy Turrentine wearing beret in background, at Hill City Auditorium (Savoy Ballroom), October 1944, black and white: Agfa Safety Film, H: 4 in. × W: 5 in. (10.20 × 12.70 cm), Carnegie Museum of Art, Pittsburgh: Heinz Family Fund, 2001.35.11509, © Carnegie Museum of Art, Charles "Teenie" Harris Archive.

for journalism drew him away from the numbers and encouraged him to open a private studio in the Hill while working for the *Courier*.[29] Harris was one of many Black photographers freelancing in the Hill District but was hired as the *Courier's* staff photographer in 1941.[30] A respected public figure, Harris cultivated an intimate relationship with the Hill community and developed a sense of mutuality with those he photographed. Patricia Parker-Reid, who worked for the *Courier* from 1958 to 1961, recalled how Harris's personality informed his photography: "Teenie was very good at taking pictures because he was like a comedian and he would make a lot of faces . . . . I think what happened was, as a result of how Teenie's antics were—with his eyes and smile over to the side—he elicited the faces. You can see it in his pictures. The people seem very relaxed and that was real because he was very quick at relaxing people."[31]

Harris's depictions of nightlife and jazz clubs can be characterized as what visual studies scholar Nicole Fleetwood terms "non-iconic" photos, which "resist singularity and completeness in narrative."[32] The "non-iconic" visual framework apparent

Figure I.4. Charles "Teenie" Harris, American, 1908–1998, Intersection of Wylie Avenue and Fullerton Street with Blue Note Cafe, Stanley's, Washington Club, Loendi Club, Bobby Hinton's, Goode Pharmacy, and Amoco Station, on winter day, Hill District, c. 1956 black and white: Kodak Safety Film, H: 4 in. × W: 5 in. (10.20 × 12.70 cm), Carnegie Museum of Art, Pittsburgh: Heinz Family Fund, 2001.35.6025, © Carnegie Museum of Art, Charles "Teenie" Harris Archive.

in Harris's depiction of jazz musicians emphasizes the context of performance and also bears witness to his own role in the scenes he captured. His approach to photographing jazz could be contrasted with renowned photographers such as Herman Leonard, Francis Wolff, and William Claxton, whose mid-twentieth-century photos of musicians focus on the individual performer's embodiment of artistic innovation and greatness. In his photos of jazz performers, Harris's presence behind the camera and familiarity with his community is also evident in the expressions, gazes, and relaxed demeanor of his subjects. Harris's "non-iconic" photographs help us see nightlife as both a network of places operating in a local entertainment economy and a space of community formation. Community, in this study, represents those aspects of collectivity and sets of relationships that are valued for their ability to sustain personal investments in places. In addition to creating visual documentations, Harris's photographs signal his own role as a listener-participant in the community formation underway in the clubs he frequented.

Harris could frame his photos widely knowing that the 4 × 5-inch negative from his Speed Graphic camera provided a great deal of detail and that *Courier* editors

Figure I.5. Charles "Teenie" Harris, American, 1908–1998, Intersection of Wylie Avenue and Fullerton Street with Blue Note Cafe and Goode Pharmacy, on foggy night, Hill District, c. 1945–1965, black and white: Kodak Safety Film, H: 4 in. × W: 5 in. (10.20 × 12.70 cm), Carnegie Museum of Art, Pittsburgh: Heinz Family Fund, 2001.35.3181 © Carnegie Museum of Art, Charles "Teenie" Harris Archive.

could later crop out what was not needed for the given story. As a result, Harris's photos are a rich source for understanding the social dynamics of jazz venues. For instance, many images capture the viewpoint of the musicians (figures 4.12 and 4.13). This involved sitting at a drum kit or perching on an elevated stage—a precarious place off limits to outsiders. We see the act of performing as well as the processes of interaction between listeners and musicians that grounded these events in their locale (figures 5.2 and 5.6). Even in figure I.3, which is a portrait of Billy Eckstine, trumpeter Tommy Turrentine stands in the background and studies the trumpet section as it plays through an arrangement. Turrentine's gaze directs our attention to the unseen scores that drew the dedicated teenage musician to the stage—a participant in this nightlife scene that existed to serve dancers and listeners.

Evident in two of Harris's photos (figures I.4 and I.5) from the late 1940s of the intersection of Wylie and Fullerton is a collective sense of place and an understanding of the night as a stage for the people, businesses, and events that comprised the scene. Harris reveals the crossroads as a boundary between daytime and nightlife, where entertainment and business intersected with everyday life. With the steel mills running around the clock, many businesses served food and drinks at any hour. In the daytime image of the crossroads, the nightclubs and businesses fade into the rows of brick buildings as pedestrians and cars trace daily routines.

The nighttime image tells a different story. A streetcar meanders up Fullerton past parked cars and low brick buildings, linking the Hill to the city's far-flung neighborhoods and satellite steel towns dotting the Allegheny and Monongahela Rivers. Those vehicles crossing the intersection leave only the traces of their headlights during the second-long exposure time of the camera. Sharply dressed men and women cut dark silhouettes against the welcoming glow of neon and storefront lighting, their relaxed stances revealing the sidewalk as an extension of the congregation and socializing taking place behind closed doors. All of these elements of Harris's image allude to the intersection as a prospective sanctuary to those who knew its nights. Those movements that the camera would not reveal in the daytime are apparent here under darkness as the glow of nightlife illuminates the social intimacies of the neighborhood. Just as this study is indebted to the writers who penned intimate experiences of the Hill, it is indebted to these images that narrate the living memories of jazz in the Hill.

### Regional Perspectives in Jazz Studies

In the time period that this book focuses on, between 1920 and 1970, nightlife served as a barometer for changing notions of vice, freedom, and even work, which has broader implications for the study of jazz beyond musical analysis and canon formation. In addition to the extensive use of historical newspapers, primary documents, photos, and interviews, I draw on a wide range of musicological, sociological, queer, and feminist studies for theoretical approaches to examining Pittsburgh's jazz scene in terms of the racial politics of the Prohibition Era, midcentury urban development, and civil rights struggles among unionized musicians. This interdisciplinary approach to writing jazz history grounds narratives in the contested nature of urban space and foregrounds the multiplicity of perspectives and experiences that shape the neighborhood's identity.

This book also contributes to the growing literature of regional jazz studies that have explored the relationships between jazz and communities outside major metropolitan centers. Jazz scholar and historian Eddie Meadows lists thirty-eight regional studies of jazz in his 1995 jazz research bibliography.[33] This list reveals a strong focus on New Orleans, with Kansas City, Chicago, and New York also treated extensively. Meadows also cites studies on Columbus, Detroit, Indiana, and cities on the West Coast, illustrating the expanding scholarship on jazz as an embedded cultural practice throughout the United States. Since Meadows's bibliography, scholars and historians have continued to contribute regional studies of jazz scenes that collectively speak to the importance of national networks of jazz clubs. These studies explore Kansas City (Driggs et al.), Detroit (Bjorn; Stryker), Los Angeles (Bryant et al.; O'Connell), and New Orleans (Charters), as well as previously unaddressed cities and states including Wisconsin (Dietrich), South Carolina (Franklin et al.), Minnesota (Goetting), San Francisco (Pepin), Washington, DC (Blair et al.), Boston (Vacca), Ohio (Watkins et al.), West Virginia (Wilkinson), and Indianapolis (Williams).[34] The emerging narrative of these studies emphasizes the role locally based artists and neighborhood venues play in establishing jazz as a global culture.

Pittsburgh's absence from scholarly jazz histories can, in part, be attributed to the relationship it has with its most renowned musicians.[35] In 1964, *Courier* journalist Phyl Garland acknowledged Pittsburgh's "reputation for spawning jazz greats who invariably had to go elsewhere to find success and acceptance."[36] In jazz scholarship, Pittsburgh often serves as a backdrop for biographies of artists such as Mary Lou Williams, Earl Hines, Erroll Garner, Billy Strayhorn, Kenny Clarke, Roy Eldridge, and Art Blakey.[37] These portraits offer glimpses of jazz performance in pre-World War II Pittsburgh through descriptions of the early lives of these artists as they struggled to establish professional touring careers. Pittsburgh is often depicted as a barrier that artists must overcome before gaining their due recognition. Pianist Mary Lou Williams, when stranded on tour as a teen, did not ask her mother for money since she expected that it would require her to "return to Pittsburgh and stay there."[38] David Hajdu's portrait of Billy Strayhorn finds that Pittsburgh's "provincialism had encumbered Strayhorn's arrival as an artist" while "in the more inclusive, cosmopolitan atmosphere of Manhattan, Strayhorn's musical success spurred his coming-of-age as an individual."[39]

This theme of Pittsburgh as a place of departure also appears in Stanley Dance's study of Earl Hines, where the young pianist is scolded by the older and more experienced pianist Eubie Blake: "If I catch you here again, I'm going to take this cane and wrap it around your head. Do you realize you can stay in Pittsburgh the rest of your life and still be the same boy you are now? You've got to get away from here."[40] In leaving for the cultural centers of Chicago and New York, these artists gained recognition that they could not have attained locally. However, they left behind communities and artists that, despite being outside of major metropolitan centers, played integral roles in developing jazz as an artistic practice and Black music labor. Nonetheless, this book fills a conspicuous gap in scholarly explorations of jazz in Pittsburgh, in particular focusing on venues and the infrastructures of nightlife to offer insights into the potential and challenges of community building in American cities.

Part I explores several of Pittsburgh's early jazz clubs located in the lower Hill District. The site of 1213 Wylie, which was home to the Collins Inn, Paramount Inn, and the Musicians Club, and 1401 Wylie, which was known as the Leader House before it became the Crawford Grill No.1, were two publicly contested nightlife spaces during the Prohibition Era. This decade provided opportunities for underground economies in bootlegging and the numbers street lottery, which provided capital to establish nightclubs. However, the racial politics of this time period were shaped by growing White anxieties over shifting urban demographics that coincided with the emergence of jazz as mainstream American culture. Black club owners faced the difficult and dangerous task of creating venues that could cater both to the Hill's expanding and diverse African American population as well as White patrons who were seeking new experiences in nightlife. These black and tan cabarets were focal points in vice wars that highlighted the overlapping of political corruption, nightlife, and White fears over, and at the same time, infatuations with, miscegenation. They also contributed to establishing the Hill as a center of cultural production in Pittsburgh and laid the foundation for small nightclubs in the coming decades.

Part II centers on the Crawford Grill No. 2 and the Hurricane Bar and Grill, two notable Hill clubs that developed into major destinations for experiencing modern jazz during the 1950s and 1960s. This part focuses on the social life and creative practices of these intimate listening spaces and explores these businesses as community-based developments. Against the backdrop of extensive redevelopment projects that were reshaping and redefining the Hill to serve the city's most privileged, club owners in the Hill were also creating social spaces that demonstrated alternative potentials for conceptualizing urban renewal. They were places of great creativity and also spaces in which Hill residents could find respite from the top-down rebuilding of the Lower Hill that represents a form of cultural and social erasure. These clubs grounded active listening, public discussions of modernity, cultural production, and musical innovation in the Hill, all of which demonstrated the importance of countervisions of city development. Compared to city- and corporate-driven narratives of development, active listening was a model of creativity that accounted for audience feedback and participation.

Part III focuses on Local 471—Pittsburgh's Black local of the American Federation of Musicians (AFM)—and the work of its members to advance civil rights struggles and address the challenges of desegregation in the workplace. Black jazz musicians organized to build collectivity on a local and national basis and to represent their interests within the AFM. In the Hill District, Local 471 established the Musicians Club, where members rehearsed, socialized, performed, and networked. During the civil rights era, members and leadership of 471 advocated for the rights of jazz musicians in Pittsburgh and negotiated with Local 60—Pittsburgh's White local—to determine the basis for their eventual merger.

The struggle resulted in the only legal case brought against a merged AFM local and revealed the difficulties in shaping the terms of integration following legal desegregation. This history of organized labor reveals the ongoing challenges faced by jazz musicians and African American communities to sustain places and traditions of musical study, economic development, political organizing, and socializing.

In Part IV, I close this book with a discussion of nightlife in the Hill during the era of urban crisis in the 1970s and 1980s. Here I connect continuing jazz performance with present-day struggles to rebuild and renew the neighborhood. As of this writing, the Hill has arrived at a new crossroads of development that raises many questions about how best to honor cultural heritage while repairing extensive destruction to the neighborhood's economic and social infrastructures. As jazz remains an important part of Pittsburgh's cultural landscape, performers face the challenges of memorializing ways of listening and gathering that sustain the music as a critical space of reflection and celebration.

# PART I

# DANGEROUS GROUND

## Black and Tan Clubs, Vice, and Prohibition (1920–1934)

# Chapter 1

# RACIAL AND SEXUAL POLITICS OF BLACK AND TAN NIGHTLIFE

Early on the morning of Tuesday, August 28, 1934, Pittsburgh police arrested nineteen patrons of the short-lived Hill District cabaret Derby Dad's, charging them with "visiting a disorderly house."[1] Three local newspapers revealed the raid's subtext in listing the racial and gender makeup of those arrested: "five white men, one white woman, seven Negro men, and six Negro women."[2] This was not the first raid on Derby Dad's, nor would it be the last. In March and again in August 1935, police descended on the club, arresting the White proprietors, Black employees, and racially integrated patrons. Located in the heart of the lower Hill District—a block south of Wylie Avenue on Fullerton Street—Derby Dad's was one of many music venues during the interwar years where nightlife seekers from greater Pittsburgh mingled with the neighborhood's ethnically and racially diverse population. Derby Dad's, billed as "Pittsburgh's Little Harlem," provided White patrons with a cozy and informal after-hours scene where they could unwind after downtown theater shows. It also drew traveling performers who delivered both Black and White patrons a taste of the jazz and theater scenes of Chicago's Bronzeville and New York's Harlem. With the club's growing popularity, affluent downtowners and famous White theater and film entertainers such as Joe Penner, Ben Bernie, Frances Williams, and Eddie Cantor brought in good business but also roused fears of interracial socializing.[3]

Though the late-night revelry provided justification for police raids, it was Derby Dad's reputation as the "hottest black and tan spot in Smoketown" that incited moral outrage among law enforcement officials and condemnation in local courts.[4] Modeling itself on the famous Harlem Cotton Club, Derby Dad's enticed patrons with its "exotic jungle murals" and nightly performances, including a "sizzling hot orchestra" playing "syncopated Harlemese," "veil dance" routines, an array of young vocalists, and Bobby "Beulah" Lewis, "Smoketown's favorite [female] impersonator."[5] Beulah, "tall [and] Nubian-like," shocked and awed audiences on the dance floor, "painted with yellow stripes, garbed mystically in jungle voodoo costumes, swing[ing] his long arms and kick[ing] like a witch doctor in true jungle fashion."[6] Duo Druscilla Drew and Jackie Johnson, previous headliners of the Washington, DC, and Cleveland Cotton Clubs, became a celebrated attraction during their extended stay for their singing, dancing, and comedy. Their repertoire reflected the varied expectations of their audiences ranging from Duke Ellington's introspective ballad "Solitude" to "Christopher Colombo," a vaudeville song and exercise in hyperbolic lewdness. Following another raid, Police Superintendent Jacob Dorsey commented on the cabaret's floor show: "It was indecent, vulgar and the most revolting thing I ever heard of. I don't see how human beings could stand for the filth."[7] Special Deputy Attorney General J. Alfred Wilner later echoed these sentiments while providing his "spicy testimony" in Criminal Court, where he described "obscene shows" and "ribald songs" in which Black entertainers "cavorted in a way that would make a waterfront habitué blush with shame."[8]

William G. Nunn, city editor of the African American newspaper the *Pittsburgh Courier*, was quick to challenge the police superintendent's charges of indecency against Derby Dad's Black performers, pointing out that the "filth" was in service of White patrons who "continued to pack the place, night after night, always coming back for more." Though the club welcomed both Black and White patrons, Nunn claimed that "[a]side from the payroll, [Derby Dad's] meant little to Negroes," adding that Druscilla Drew and Jackie Johnson had expressed to him that they were "disgusted with singing the [sexually explicit] songs. But these were the type of songs which would draw the dollars out of half-high, tuxedoed night-lifers and after all, they were working to make money." While the music was at the center of the charges of indecency, Nunn stressed that it was the presence of White women among Black men and "rumors of mixed couples enjoying themselves" that motivated the raids.[9] Nunn likely felt compelled to address accusations of indecency at the club publicly because he recognized it had a greater significance for Pittsburgh's growing African American community. Derby Dad's capitalizing on affluent White "slummers" was one of several examples of Hill District nightlife businesses that accommodated a mixed-race clientele during the 1920s and early 1930s. Nunn was well aware that public officials and White-owned newspapers regularly attacked these venues in an ongoing effort to enforce racial segregation in the city's public life.

Struggles over the representation of nightlife in black and tan cabarets were common in African American communities in the North during the 1920s and early 1930s. These venues were sites of racial politics where early jazz emerged entangled with fantasies of sexual liberation and conquest that played out between White and Black patrons and artists. In this respect, individuals in these venues both affirmed and transgressed existing power relationships. Entrepreneurs created spaces of entertainment and networking within growing Black communities while also being targeted for promoting interracial socializing. White men and women patronized Black nightlife though also encouraged Black exoticism. Black female entertainers developed solo careers yet also faced being reduced to objects of sexual desire and symbols of interracial sexual contact. Jazz came to express new creative freedoms while being targeted as a source of vice. Much as the social spaces of black and tans were rare for their racial diversity, jazz traversed its roles as dance, background music, and modernist artistic endeavor. As music that adapted itself to multiple uses and interpretations, it reflected the liminal characteristics of these contested spaces.

Nightlife—encompassing times of leisure, places of business, and spaces of the American musical imagination—created new social possibilities within the development of Black public spheres in northern cities. "Dangerous ground"—in the words of *Pittsburgh Courier* columnist John L. Clark—was the Hill District at night, where racial and sexual norms were challenged in the context of the Great Migration and the unfolding of the Prohibition Era's twisted political logic and power structures. Critical to an understanding of the establishment of jazz in the Hill District, these black and tan nightclubs engendered music that signified otherness and exoticism and fostered imaginaries of both racial harmony and transgression. More than backdrops to nightlife, the music of these clubs was a public expression of African Americans' claims to Pittsburgh. Young entertainers from throughout the country transformed small venues into popular destinations for experiencing the pluralism of migrant communities and contemporary Black culture. Black women entertainers singing popular songs from musicals and classic blues hits, in particular, found outlets for carving out careers. All the while, musicians pushed the creative boundaries of improvisation and expanded the possibilities of orchestration within small ensembles.

In this discussion (part I), I focus on the racial and gender politics of black and tans and examine several Black-owned nightclubs that emerged in the Lower Hill District during the Prohibition Era (1920–34) as homes for a nascent jazz scene. As sites of musical experimentation, these venues were training grounds for young musicians, places where local and traveling entertainers could find work, and informal settings where audiences could hear and take part in a range of popular songs, ragtime, blues, and early jazz. These intimate spaces were counterparts to the stage productions of Pittsburgh's booming theater scenes in the early twentieth century. Tucked into the close quarters of commercial brick buildings along Hill District avenues, the clubs greeted patrons from throughout the city who mingled with entertainers during late-night revelries. Those Black-owned venues became places of leisure and refuge for Pittsburgh's rapidly expanding African American population, sites of Black collectivity and political power, and transit points that connected creative scenes between Harlem and Bronzeville. These clubs would also lay the foundations for the Hill's jazz scenes of the 1940s, '50s, and '60s.

## Black and Tan Spaces of American Popular Culture

The term "black and tan," designating a site of interracial contact, socializing, or collaboration, was deeply embedded in the political and public life of the United States in the late nineteenth century. During the Reconstruction Era (1865–1877), "black and tan" appeared as a derogatory term for mixed-race Republican political conventions responsible for drafting state constitutions that would allow the former Confederate states to return to the Union.[10] The Republican Party, formed in 1854, emerged from the Civil War as an ally to emancipated African Americans. As Frederick Douglass stated in an 1872 public address in New Orleans to a Black national convention, the GOP was a "deck" on which Black political power could stand above the "sea" of the Democratic party.[11]

From November 1867 to February 1869, coalitions of African Americans, sympathetic White southerners pejoratively called "scalawags" and Northern Republicans derided as "carpetbaggers" rebuilt the political infrastructure of the defeated and occupied South. The resulting governing documents, which became known as "black and tan constitutions," were short-lived, though the conventions that had drafted them continued to symbolize the indignity of Union soldier occupation to Southern Democrats. The Jackson, Mississippi, *Clarion-Ledger* journalist E. H. Henry lamented in 1911, "Oh, if we could blot out the impression of those trying hours from memory, and forget the era of the saturnalia."[12] Henry's reference, while equating reconstruction with wanton rule, invokes the ancient Roman holiday of Saturnalia when social rules, including those that distinguished enslaved people and enslavers, were temporarily suspended during a prolonged revelry.[13]

In the early twentieth century, "black and tan" continued to be used in political contexts as a designation of Southern Black Republican party factions, though the term was also adapted as a contentious descriptor of sites of interracial socializing.[14] The term appeared in Black and White presses with both damning and approving connotations. In White-owned newspapers, the term most often appeared in stories referencing miscegenation and therefore tapped into deep-seated fears among Whites of fundamental societal change challenging White supremacy. Post-Reconstruction gestures to advance racial harmony or challenge segregationist policies triggered violent and visceral reactions; interracial social relationships, particularly those between Black men and White women, were reduced to narratives of sexual predation. On April 27, 1908, the Cosmopolitan Society of Greater New York organized an interracial gathering of a hundred people to discuss racial prejudice and solutions for the "race problem."[15] When reports revealed that organizer Hamilton Holt had advocated interracial marriages, newspapers throughout the South published a slew of condemning responses. Reprinted in the *New York Times*, an article in the *Richmond News Leader* berated the Society's dinner as a "black and tan festivity" that was "eminently disgusting."[16] The writer insisted to readers that such gatherings would serve "only to vindicate further among the Northern masses the policy of the South in dealing with the negro socially and politically" and "hasten the day of complete race separation, which is the only solution of the broader negro problem."[17]

References to black and tan cabarets reached their height in the 1920s as early jazz and Black entertainment drew White audiences to growing African American communities in cities outside of the American South. The common characteristic of these venues was that they facilitated various forms of cross-racial and -gender interaction around music, dance, and drinking. In many cases, there were interventions by police, local governments, citizen organizations, and White supremacist groups to regulate or close these establishments. An early example of black and tan policing occurred at a club known as the Black and Tan, located at 153 Bleecker Street in Manhattan and shut down in July 1885 after police arrested the proprietor, Patrick Mee.[18] Although Detective John Sullivan had failed to gain a warrant to raid the location on the grounds that it was "a place of bad repute . . . frequented by both white and colored people," he was able to gain a warrant to arrest Mee on the grounds of "keeping a disorderly house."[19]

In the context of nightlife, black and tan became shorthand for the societal upheaval and moral corruption perceived in Black music and dance in the 1920s. Jazz, a key element of sensationalist depictions of black and tan clubs, provided a substitute for the taboo subject of interracial sex, thus descriptions of music and dance figured prominently in attacks on integrated nightlife and identifications of vice. Both White and Black newspaper editors exploited the marketability of black and tan spaces and hyped-up stories of interracial love and so contributed to the mystique of these nightlife scenes.

In the *Pittsburgh Courier*'s first decade, chief editor Robert Vann resisted featuring stories of mixed-race affairs but by 1922 had come to adopt the explicit reporting known as "yellow journalism" in order to expand readership.[20] In September 1923, a *Pittsburgh Courier* article described a police investigation into Cleveland's "'black and tan' night life" as part of a "relentless police war on vice and immorality."[21] The article focuses on details of exploitation where "white girls are portrayed as selling their souls that colored slave masters might wax fat [get rich]." Music, in this context, is described as a soundtrack to prostitution, drug use, and exploitation:

> In one house, booze and cocaine form the chief article of trade, while rooms are provided as amorous retreats for visitors, some of the girls being mere school children not more than fourteen or fifteen years old. The "star boarder," a colored man, is an expert pianist, and it is said that he plays the instrument while some of the girls, ranging in age from sixteen to thirty, dance nude.[22]

The pianist of this narrative plays the role of the Pied Piper, enchanting innocent girls to follow him into a cave where indecency runs amok. The description of the females as "mere school children" underscores their innocence rather than portraying them as accomplices in the den of vice. Far from being a redeeming and wholesome endeavor, the music is targeted as a means of entrapment rather than lighthearted entertainment. Vann and other African American news editors were surely aware of the ramifications that such stories of interracial sex and sexual exploitation had on interracial socializing. The story of a raid in a nearby city may have served as a warning to the local readership. Above all, the fact that such stories were featured in one of the major African American newspapers of the era speaks to the pervasive notion of the black and tan as a site of vice and moral decrepitude.

Black and tan venues were both Black- and White-owned businesses that ranged from informal backroom cabarets with small bands to expansive nightclubs with elaborate floor shows. The most high-profile black and tans were located in Chicago and New York and run by businessmen, sports heroes, and gangsters. Heavyweight boxing champion Jack Johnson opened the Café de Champion in 1912 in Chicago's South Side, where interracial audiences gathered for extravagant parties. Famous black and tan clubs of Harlem included Black businessman Barron Wilkins's private club—operated for over a decade before Wilkins's murder in 1924—and the Cotton Club, which was opened in 1923 by Owen Vincent "Owney" Madden, a White gangster notorious in New York's bootlegging underworld. Both Wilkins's and Madden's clubs were known for catering to affluent White audiences while exclusively hiring Black artists and entertainers. In the case of the Cotton Club, artists were subjected to demeaning working conditions that included a plantation façade stage backdrop and performances of exoticized African dance.

Despite the exploitative working environment in an industry geared toward wealthy White "slummers," many Black musicians and dancers used such clubs as a place to develop their artistry. The most notable example was Duke Ellington, who was nurtured and educated in Washington, DC's middle-class Black community and found commercial success and a creative outlet working at the Cotton Club from 1927 to 1931. It was during this period that Ellington recorded "Black and Tan Fantasy," an enduring statement that spoke to a multiplicity of American perspectives and reflected on racial imaginations in American nightlife.[23]

Concurrent with the White vilification of interracial socializing in black and tans was the defense by writers, entrepreneurs, and artists of these venues as being important social institutions within the growing Black public sphere. While the majority of journalistic references to black and tan cabarets aimed to incite a moral panic in northern cities, there are examples of Black journalists who defended them as institutions of social and sexual liberation and rare examples of racial cohabitation—sites in a marginalized social world that historian Kevin Mumford calls "interzones" where "racial and sexual conventions were not merely transgressed but were inverted, mocked, or completely ignored."[24]

Although Black-owned newspapers certainly shared the widespread sentiment of black and tan clubs as dens of vice, as seen in the earlier example of the *Courier* article by Vann, it is more likely that they, rather than the White-owned press, would write of these venues in light of the struggles of Black club owners, musicians, and entertainers to create and maintain sites of Black cultural and social life. In 1920, an unidentified *Chicago Defender* columnist railed against public calls in the White press for the city administration to target clubs with mixed clientele:

> A fight for cleanly operated places of business is one thing and a fight against personal liberty is another. By what right has a newspaper, police officer or any public official to specify where any man or woman, regardless of race or color, shall spend either their time or money, providing that they do so in a decent and respectable manner in places conducted along the same lines?[25]

Chandler Owen, an economist, writer, and cofounder of the Harlem Renaissance magazine *The Messenger*, penned some of the strongest defenses of black and tans as sites of social and sexual liberation. In his articles "The Cabaret—A Useful Social Institution" (1922) and "The Black and Tan Cabaret—America's Most Democratic Institution" (1925), Owen celebrated clubs such as Chicago's Sunset Café and Harlem's Happy Rhone's as "destroying the hydra-headed monster of race-prejudice," a task Owen claims "the church, school and family have failed to do."[26]

Owen provided important counternarratives of social life in black and tan venues: "The break down in racial brotherhood was well-nigh complete except for the black and tan cabarets. Here white and colored men and women still drank, ate, sang and danced together. Smiling faces, light hearts, undulating couples in poetry of motion conspired with syncopated music to convert the hell and death from *without* to a little paradise *within*."[27] Owen's description of the dancers' "poetry of motion" conjures a utopian counterculture that challenged systemic racism in intimate urban corners. Chandler unequivocally embraced the black and tan, reducing the multiplicities of investments and experiences in these spaces to a narrative of Black male social and sexual freedom. His celebration of Black male liberation, however, circumvented discussions of the experiences of Black women in these liminal spaces and failed to reflect on the varying and uneven power relationships that comprised this sexual revolution of the early twentieth century.

Like White women, Black women of black and tan cabarets also became sites of male fantasies and dominance, though their exploitation did not incite the same moral outrage. In the *Courier*, theater writer Floyd G. Selson's account of Wilkins's Café in New York says that the sole woman vocalist takes on the role of striptease artist: "Soon a pretty brown-skin girl begins chirpin' the latest tunes . . . she raises her dresses far above the waterline and displays much of her expensive lingerie . . . a gentleman passes her a five dollar bill."[28] The lighter their skin, the more chance a singer or dancer had of working on the chorus line or as a featured "Creole" cabaret singer. Embedded in the favoritism of light-skinned Black women were embodied histories of racial and sexual violence in the US. As poet Caroline Randall Williams writes of her own body: "I have rape-colored skin. My light-brown-blackness is a living testament to the rules, the practices, the causes of the Old South."[29] The dominance of male prerogatives and fantasies in narratives of the black and tan—whether it is in newspaper reports or celebratory writing such as those by Owen and Snelson—privilege a historical lens that obscure Black female voices amid the spectacle of their bodies. As quoted in Heap's book *Slumming*, Will Marion Cook, the renowned African American composer, lamented these "degradations" of Black women that were common even in the most upscale Harlem black and tan clubs.[30] Critics of these dynamics were well aware of the predatory tactics of White men toward southern Black migrants: "[W]hite men were particularly guilty of exploiting the economic vulnerabilities of Southern black migrants, nudging them into lives of prostitution shortly after their arrival in northern cities or, at the very least, into casual encounters that encouraged them to treat white men with sexual favors in return for dinner, entertainment, or gifts of clothing."[31]

Snelson's narrative also introduces "Diamond Tooth Annie," who "specialized in the gorgeous high yallows [*sic*], which were a direct importation from the sunny south . . . for the white millionaires." She looms as the singular Black woman in a position of power within the black and tan. It is notable that she is only able to take on this role through the exploitation of younger nameless women. As a mythologized, larger-than-life character who doles out sex partners to rich White men, Annie embodies the corrupt figure in a social environment that complicates Owen's description of black and tans as valuable democratic institutions where racial inequalities were destroyed. Even as black and tans offered a place of leisure and escape from the drudgeries of domestic work, young Black women inhabited a perilous position under what was known as "wayward minor laws." Although the Mann Act of 1910 was wielded to protect White women, wayward minor laws enabled police to criminalize the social lives of Black women in public and private places. In this context, Annie played an intermediary role, a broker of White male fantasy.

Reframing waywardness from a feminist perspective, literary scholar and cultural historian Saidiya Hartman looks to black and tans as places of possibility amid danger. There, a "wayward" woman might savor "the joy of losing herself in the crowd,"[32] and music and dance might provide a professional context for her to pursue a career of her own and be acknowledged as an artist. Although few rose to canonical status in jazz history, most women who led professional lives in the performing arts were afforded some level of mobility and an alternative to the constraints of domesticity. Hartman's book title, *Wayward Lives, Beautiful Experiments*, acknowledges the importance of Black women's aesthetic expressions within and against a society that denied these pursuits. With a dearth of personal testimony from women patrons, employees, and entertainers in black and tans, Hartman looks to the legal and social systems of regulation that bore down on their lives and transformed their quotidian movement into acts of subversion. She considers how legal categories of waywardness criminalized Black women seen as engaging in "counter-conducts" or "different ways of conducting the self-directed at challenging the hierarchy of life produced by the color line and enforced by the state."[33] Embracing waywardness as a way of life and an "ongoing exploration of *what might be*," Hartman reveals the black and tan as a potential space in which economic, racial, and gender boundaries drawn across the social landscape were both enacted and enforced while subverted through the rituals of nightlife.

# Chapter 2

# CLAIMING A PLACE FOR JAZZ
## The Collins and Paramount Inns

During the Prohibition Era, an array of cabarets, speakeasies, hotels, restaurants, theaters, and private homes made up the infrastructure of the Hill District's nightlife. In the Lower Hill District, several venues, including the Little Paris, the Rathskeller, and Hotel Sutton, accommodated racially mixed audiences and therefore became targeted by police, city officials, citizen groups, and White-owned newspapers as "black and tans."[1]

The two most notable black and tan cabarets in Pittsburgh's Hill District—The Collins Inn located at 1213 Wylie Avenue and Leader House located at 1401 Wylie Avenue—were opened by African American entrepreneurs and became popular sites in the neighborhood's growing nightlife. The emergence of the two prominent Wylie Avenue nightclubs in the 1920s was tied to the sporting, business, and political life of the Hill in the early years of the Great Migration and reflected the importance nightlife and music had in shaping perceptions of the neighborhood in the following decades.[2] While drawing audiences from throughout the region and employing touring and local artists, these venues were also the center of struggles over Black economic and political power in Pittsburgh.

On the eve of Prohibition, African American business partners Harry Clark and George Bowles rented 1401 Wylie Avenue from Hill entrepreneur Abraham Fistell and embarked on the lucrative yet perilous path of running a speakeasy and cabaret. They named it the Leader House as a gesture of optimism and confidence in their abilities to provide one of the Hill's principal Black-patronized restaurants and nightlife spots where audiences could hear emerging styles of jazz and blues.

The location had a history as a restaurant and saloon that reached back at least twenty years. At the turn of the century, 1401 Wylie was operated as a restaurant run by a man whom *Pittsburgh Courier* journalist John L. Clark remembered only by the name of Glenn.[3] Tracing the building's storied past, Clark recalled that Glenn's restaurant was followed by a barber shop and then a seafood lunchroom owned by John "Kid" Bates, a Black Washington, DC, native who became a "political boss" praised in the *Courier* as "the most independent Negro leader Pittsburgh ever had."[4] After Bates, Hill entrepreneur Charlie Thomas opened a saloon at the location. In April 1911, Fistell purchased the property from Isaac Schwartz for $15,150, after which Fistell transferred his liquor license from the nearby 1214 Wylie Avenue saloon and invested $8,000 to develop a five-room addition to the building.[5] Fistell operated the location as a saloon until at least 1918, when he renewed his liquor license for the location, though he decided to rent the building soon afterward, possibly to get out of the saloon business in light of the impending passage of the 18th Amendment and the national ban on alcohol sales.[6]

The Collins Inn, a block and a half west of the Leader House, also developed into a successful venue for jazz that became the focus of public debates about race and vice in the city. Records show that African American entrepreneur Harry Collins (1881–1950) acquired a liquor license for the location before purchasing the three-story commercial building and a 24 × 109-foot lot for $18,000 in September 1921.[7] Clark noted that Collins was "one of the best-known men in Pittsburgh during the early twenties," though he would be remembered as "the man who made a fortune and lost it" in the Hill District.[8] Clark, a contemporary of Collins's, recalled that the businessman got his start in Pittsburgh operating a social club on Hazel Street in the Lower Hill in 1906, though he was a skilled boxer and avid sports enthusiast who invested in local athletes. He began by sponsoring a local football team that took the name the Collins Tigers, followed by managing lightweight boxer Eddie Carver and financing the Pittsburgh Giants baseball club.[9] Despite apparent losses in these endeavors, Collins had accrued enough capital in other business activities to open the Collins Inn as the Prohibition Era began. Like Clark and Bowles, Collins likely saw the potential of capitalizing on the underground economy of liquor sales as well as creating an upscale yet intimate nightclub in the Lower Hill.

It was not long after Collins opened his first-floor restaurant in the Collins Inn that he remodeled the second floor as a cabaret with table seating, a small bandstand, and a dance floor. As singer Lois Deppe recalled, "[B]lack-and-tan shows were a novelty then, just as they were in Harlem, and white people went where the good black talent was."[10] Collins's booking demonstrated an appreciation for innovative young dance bandleaders and musicians. Among the array of local and visiting musicians and entertainers that performed at the Collins Inn was the newly formed Broadway Syncopators led by twenty-year-old arranger

Don Redman. Pianist Earl Hines also worked at the Collins Inn with violinist Vernie Robinson and his group, including banjo player Harold Birchett and a singer he remembers only as Corinne. As Hines recalls, the band's income largely depended on the vocalists' ability to solicit tips from the patrons:

> The club had two rooms upstairs with a sort of a hallway in between. The bandstand was right in the middle, and [Corinne] would have to go around the stand to get to the people sitting on the other side. There were very small salaries at this place, so everybody had to depend on the tips. Vernie Robinson had the band and Corinne would sing in front, and she might end up with two hundred dollars in two fistfuls of bills, which she had to divide up, a hundred for herself and a hundred for us.[11]

This income for a night's work in the early 1920s would have been vastly higher than the average daily wage. Sociologist Abraham Epstein's 1917 study of African American migrant populations in Pittsburgh shows that, among those interviewed, 62 percent earned two to three dollars a day, with the average Black laborer paying twenty-four dollars a month for room and board.[12]

In its early years, the Collins Inn continued to draw diverse audiences while avoiding conflicts with city officials. On Saturday, July 23, 1921, a journalist for the *Baltimore Afro-American* visited the Collins Inn and was struck with the vibrant music scene.[13] The afternoon set featured the Elite Trio, an all-female group with pianist Vernetto Wilson, cornetist Alice E. Proctor, and drummer Jesse H. Byrd, after which another trio made up of pianist James Fellman, Russel Johnson, and vocalist and dancer Vivian Greenlee took over.[14] The journalist, celebrating the successful Black-owned business, referred to Collins as "progressive" and noted that he "[enjoyed] the endorsement of the city officials for the orderly manner in which he operates his place."[15] The commendation of the club's "orderly manner" may have been a reference to Collins's rule of only admitting couples to the second-floor cabaret.

Building on his initial success, Collins conceived of developing a booking agency that coordinated a network of cabarets and touring Black entertainers and musicians. As the visiting journalist would later report, Collins saw the potential for expanding and improving the Black cabaret entertainment circuit and envisioned an organization of Black club owners between Chicago and New York City. Collins proposed that this circuit would enable like-minded cabaret owners to minimize the expense of regularly rotating entertainers while ensuring them stable employment and providing audiences with new shows, adding, "If twenty-five of the sixty-odd managers in the territory enter into the arrangement . . . the business of all will be improved."[16] The article was reprinted in the entertainment trade magazine *Billboard*, which announced a call for club owners to contact Collins.[17] Though it does not appear that the organization materialized, Collins's efforts demonstrate his investment in improving the quality and working conditions of Black entertainers.

In addition to conceptualizing a wider network of Black-owned cabarets, Collins also used his business as a social pillar in the Hill District. On October 21, 1921, he hosted a banquet in honor of actor Charles S. Gilpin, who had come to downtown Pittsburgh's Pitt Theater as the star of the Eugene O'Neill play *Emperor Jones*. In 1920, Gilpin had become the first African American actor to perform the lead of a dramatic production in an all-White theater. Following widespread acclaim for his role in *Emperor Jones*, Gilpin received the Springarn Medal for distinguished achievement by the NAACP and was honored by the Drama League of New York.[18] For the event, Collins printed special menus with Gilpin's portrait and an inscription stating, "In a small and limited way, we have endeavored to show appreciation and honor to the greatest Negro tragedian, Charles S. Gilpin. If this will serve to inspire him and induce others to higher attainments, our efforts have not been in vain."[19] The event was attended by over one hundred individuals from Pittsburgh's Black community, including "doctors, lawyers, judges, tradesmen, bankers, preachers, and businessmen," who came for an evening of music and entertainment and to pay respects to Gilpin.[20]

Like the Collins Inn, the Leader House, though a relatively small venue, drew an array of local and visiting musicians playing ragtime and early styles of jazz. Pianist Earl Hines remembered his first trip to the Leader House as a revelatory experience. Though he was only a teenager, Hines's uncle and cousin brought him to the Lower Wylie for a taste of the Hill's nightlife, hiding his age by dressing him in a suit. Hines was an avid pianist who studied classical music and was delving into contemporary popular songs but encountered a new style of music at the Leader House that sent him on the path to becoming an influential innovator in jazz. As he recalled:

> I heard this strange music and I heard the feet and the beat and so much laughter and happiness I asked my uncle and cousin could I go upstairs and listen. They put a Coca-Cola in my hand and I did. Pittsburgh was a wide-open town and there wasn't such a ban on children going into clubs. A hunchback fellow named Toadlo was playing the piano. He was playing "Squeeze Me," and singing. His playing turned me around completely. It put rhythm in my mind, and I went home and told my auntie that that was the way I wanted to play.[21]

Toadlo, the nickname for Charles Johnson, was a pianist who journalist Chester L. Washington called the "prince of good little fellows, the soft-peddlin' piano king who reigns supreme in the musical world up Deep Wylie."[22] Johnson had come to Pittsburgh from Pueblo, Colorado, bringing a Western style of ragtime piano that would catch Hines's ear.[23] Inspired by what he had heard, Hines formed a trio with violinist Emmett Jordan and drummer Harry Williams called the Melody Lads and began playing parties in the city.[24] It was at a rent party that singer Lois Deppe heard Hines and was struck by the young musician's abilities. Later, during a visit to Hines's relatives, Deppe presented Hines with the sheet music for Irving Berlin's 1920 composition "I'll See You in C-U-B-A," a Prohibition Era song about escaping to Cuba where one did not have to hide away in basement bars to drink alcohol.[25] Again, Deppe was impressed with Hines's ability to quickly read through the piece.

Both the Leader House and Collins Inn would figure heavily in Deppe's career. After completing eight months in the army in April 1919 and a tour of South America and the West Indies alongside the renowned African American soprano concert artist Anita Patti Brown, Deppe found himself waiting tables in the Collins Inn restaurant.[26] Though Deppe was continuing his training as a concert artist in Pittsburgh, it was at the Collins Inn that he found his way into his career as a nightclub singer. Deppe took a request while serving drinks and sang Gene Lockhart and Ernest Seitz's popular 1918 ballad, "The World Is Waiting for the Sunrise." After Deppe made the rounds through the Collins Inn restaurant, he remarked, "I came back with my hands full of dollars, and I decided right there I was through waiting tables."[27]

Deppe left the Collins Inn and, following a short stint in 1921 singing with Dave Peyton at the Sunset Club in Chicago, approached Clark and Bowles about singing full-time at the Leader House. When they agreed, Deppe hired the young Hines rather than the club's house pianist Johnny Waters, whom Deppe criticized as being unable to read music or play in more than a few keys.[28] Hines, like Deppe, had studied classical music, but was drawn to the contemporary popular music of Black and White vaudeville and theater productions. As Hines recalled, he and Deppe were successful at drawing audiences to the Leader House because they kept their repertoire up to date by learning newly published scores. They worked at the Leader House and in the region for about two years, adding musicians and expanding the group into what would become Deppe's Symphonium Serenaders. In July 1923, the *Courier* published a photo of the ensemble with Deppe, Hines, Robert Seals (banjo), Harry Jackson (saxophone), Vance Dixon (director, clarinet, saxophone), Emmett Jordan (violin), and Fred Robinson (trombone) under the heading "Latest Picture of 'Pittsburgh's Pride.'"[29] The Serenaders' popularity grew, and they drew on connections at the *Courier* to play larger dances. As a preteen, pianist Mary Lou Williams sought out the Serenaders as part of her musical education. Hearing them perform in Pittsburgh's East Liberty neighborhood at the Arcadia Ballroom, she soaked up the group's arrangements as well as Earl Hines's own innovations on piano.[30]

Earl Hines recalled that the Serenaders was not the only jazz group that appeared at the Leader House through 1924. The Broadway Syncopators, an

Figure 2.1. "Pittsburgh's Pride": Lois Deppe's Symphonium Serenaders (1923). Standing from left to right: Robert Seals of Pittsburgh (banjo); Harry Jackson of Charleston, WV (saxophone); Lois B. Deppe (manager, vocals); Julius Franklin of Baltimore, MD (cello, C melody saxophone, baritone saxophone); Earl Hines of Duquesne, PA (piano), Vance Dixon of Parkersburg, WV (director, oboe, clarinet, saxophone); Emmett Jordon of Duquesne, PA (violin); Fred Robinson of Cleveland, OH (trumpet). Sitting from left to right: Harry Williams of Homestead, PA (clarinet, buck and wing dancer, drums, xylophone); Annetta Miller of Columbus, OH (mascot); and Thornton Brown of Washington, PA (coronet). "Latest Picture of 'Pittsburgh's Pride,'" *Pittsburgh Courier*, July 21, 1923, 9.

eleven-piece orchestra directed by clarinet and saxophone player Billy Page, was also an up-and-coming group that recorded with Okeh Records.[31] The group had previously been led by the West Virginian saxophonist and arranger Don Redman during his year-long stay in Pittsburgh, making them a strong competitor with Deppe's Symphonium Serenaders as the premier local jazz orchestra. Both groups began to travel and perform beyond Pittsburgh but returned for special dance events. In October 1924, Page's Syncopators returned from an extended residency in New York City's Palace Casino to perform for a dance organized by Black Pittsburgh promoter Sellers McKee Hall at the Labor Temple.[32]

The Leader House and Collins Inn catered both to Hill residents as well as patrons of downtown and Hill theaters. Pittsburgh's thriving industries and the region's booming population ensured that there was no shortage of theaters or devoted audiences during the 1920s. Factories serving wartime industries were expanded, and many Black migrant workers from the South found jobs as European immigration steadily declined.[33] At the time of US entry into World

War I in 1917, Pittsburghers were taking in a wide range of stage entertainment, including popular Broadway shows, ballet, opera, vaudeville, and "family burlesque" in theaters such as the 3,000-seat Grand Opera House, 2,183-seat Nixon, and 1,300-seat Gayety (now the Byham).[34]

Allegheny County's population, exceeding a million by 1920, ensured that theaters were flooded with patrons, with an estimated twenty-five to thirty thousand attending downtown theaters daily.[35] Several African American productions, such as Noble Sissle and Eubie Blake's musicals *Shuffle Along* and *In Bamville*, did appear in downtown theaters, though seating was segregated in the Gayety as well as the Nixon, which had a second balcony with a separate entrance from a side street.[36] Several smaller theaters that booked Theater Owners Booking Association (TOBA) productions and catered to Black patrons were established in the Hill District. The Star Theater was the first, opened in 1916 at 1417 Wylie Avenue, half a block from Fullerton Street in the heart of the Lower Hill and booked as part of the TOBA from 1921 to 1925.[37] A block-deep brick building on a 24×109-foot lot, the Star Theater could have, at best, accommodated three hundred patrons. The Star was followed by the Elmore Theater, located at 2312 Centre Avenue and opened in September 1923, and the Lincoln Theater, located at 2424 Wylie Avenue and opened in February 1924, both regular stopping points for TOBA productions.

Many patrons attending shows in Hill District and downtown theaters came to the Leader House, where musicians played from 5 to 7:30 p.m., floor shows ran from 8 p.m. to 1 a.m., and the dining room was open until 3 a.m.[38] As in New York and Chicago, nightclubs featured floor shows, bands for dancing, and late-night entertainment that catered to revelers leaving theater shows. Also known as cabarets, a term borrowed to evoke Parisian nightlife, these venues provided intimate settings for performance and marked the emergence of small clubs as middle- and upper-class social institutions. In 1927, *Courier* reporter Geraldyn Dismond wrote that such examples marked a notable shift from the 1910s, when the cabaret was closely associated with the working class. Patrons described a night out as "cabareting," a marked difference from previous decades where the "very daring and necessarily secretive escapade" into the "unattractive rear rooms where one could buy drinks and hear risqué songs" was referred to as "slumming."[39] The use of the term "bohemian" in promotional ads signaled a welcoming environment for artists and intellectuals as well as White patrons from outside the neighborhood. Clark and Bowles promoted the cabaret as the "Headquarters for Out-of-Town Guests" and catered to the city's "younger set" who were looking for a place to spend "idle hours."[40] Musicians from throughout the US appeared at the Leader House and were promoted in ads such as "FIVE PRETTY GIRLS accompanied by two clever boys direct from the Bohemian quarters and cabaret life of Kansas City, Indianapolis and Chicago and en route to Atlantic City to play the season there."[41]

The Leader House's popularity with local and visiting entertainers and musicians ensured that the festivities continued through the night. Visiting entertainers mingled with theatergoers and "after-dark pleasure seekers" to witness impromptu performances by rising stars of Black theater while ordering "chicken and waffles" or one of the featured "old-fashioned, home-cooked meals."[42] When *Shuffle Along* (1921), the first full-length Black-produced, -written, and -acted Broadway musical, came to downtown Pittsburgh's Pitt-Schubert Theater (former Kenyon Opera House) in September 1923, the Leader House hosted late-night after-parties celebrating the touring production and featuring performances by its cast.[43] Again, when *In Bamville* played at the Nixon Theatre downtown, members of the company would head to the Leader House after performances to mingle with local theater patrons, musicians, and entertainers while listening to Billy Page's Broadway Syncopators.[44] The Leader House's schedule often featured back-to-back events hosting notable Black performers and musicians. For example, during the last week of April 1926, the Leader House hosted members of *Come Along Mandy*, which was appearing at the nearby Elmore Theatre, as well as musicians Richard Mariney Jones, Willie Hightower, and Sonny Thompson's Syncopating Jazzers, who were performing at the Gayety Theatre in downtown.[45]

The Leader House and Collins Inn—both Black-owned businesses that city officials and private organizations targeted as black and tan clubs—were among the most popular small music venues in the neighborhood due to the presence of local and touring artists whose innovative conceptual approaches shaped early jazz. These clubs also nurtured Pittsburgh's Black public sphere, a space of discourse centered on struggles and aspirations within the local African American population. Ideas of Black cultural, economic, and political advancement as well as Black claims to public space filtered from the space of the club into journalism. For local musicians such as pianist Earl Hines, these clubs were a training ground, place of work, and platform for accessing Chicago's immensely larger music scene. For touring artists such as Laura "Baby Hines" Badge, these clubs were a stopping point in the midst of a career that took her to theater and cabaret stages across the US. Such artists, while seeking new musical directions and a viable existence in the music industry, made these clubs the destination of both Hill residents and "bohemian" theatergoing audiences from Greater Pittsburgh. The resulting social scenes were rare sites of interracial socializing in a rapidly shifting urban landscape where the growing African American population was asserting new spatial, political, economic, and cultural claims to the city.

## Women Performers at the Leader House

Saidiya Hartman's intimate reading of young Black women in early-twentieth-century New York captures the paradox of the female performer's hypervisibility amidst the anonymity of the chorus line. Writing from the perspective of Mabel Hampton in the musical comedy *Come Along Mandy*, Hartman reflects on the stage as an opportunity for economic independence as well as a physically dangerous workplace that stifled creativity:

> She was weary of the costumes and the silly songs; she was sick of being pawed and threatened and she worried about the rent because of uncertain work and unsteady wages. She no longer liked dancing, and if her option had been something other than the kitchen, she might have quit earlier. She tolerated what she had to, but refused to yield an inch more.[46]

Hartman's narrative, born from a close reading of historical documents, re-creates experiences of "minor figures" relegated to the backstage of dominant historical narratives but whose bodies were desired, policed, and studied. Hartman, while acknowledging the struggles of nightlife, also provides a feminist reading of the chorus line as "an incubator of possibility, an assembly sustaining dreams of the otherwise." This definition of the chorus shifts the analytical gaze from that of the critic or the audience to the women who comprise it. From their perspectives as Black women theater performers, the chorus provided another form of dissension against anonymity and the embodiment of desire. In Hartman's words, "The chorus is the vehicle for another kind of story, not of the great man or the tragic hero, but one in which all modalities play a part, where the headless group incites change, where mutual aid provides the resource for collective action, not leader and mass, where the untranslatable songs and seeming nonsense make good the promise of revolution."[47] Hartman's reading on the chorus foregrounds the unknown figures behind the lead actors—a collectivity representative of the highly visible yet muted women often harassed or arrested for their "wayward" existences. This acknowledgment of the chorus offers agency to those whose job was to perform in anonymity.

Hartman also provides a framework for critiquing privileged male perspectives that positioned the Black theater production as a progressive force. For example, Harlem Renaissance theater critic Theophilus Lewis, in his advocacy for the development of distinctly African American theater arts, "decried the overwhelming tendency for directors to cast only light-skinned African Americans in their productions."[48] In his lukewarm review of *Come Along Mandy*, Lewis found that the most notable element of the forty-five-minute musical comedy was that the chorus line was not exclusively comprised of light-complexioned women as was the norm.[49] He repeated this critique of colorism and praise for featuring darker-complexioned dancers in a subsequent review of the play *Stepping Out*—a perspective that nonetheless centers the bodies of women performers rather than their artistry.[50]

Many women performers, including famous recording artists Ethel Waters and Bessie Smith as well as lesser-known singers Babe Badge and Teddy Peters, came to Pittsburgh in the 1920s through a network of tour circuits that linked cities and towns throughout the United States. A midpoint between the country's largest African American communities in Chicago's South Side and New York City's Harlem, Pittsburgh's Hill District provided a welcome stop for musicians and entertainers as they toured through the northeast, midwest, and south. Many Hill cabarets, including the Leader House and Collins Inn, were connected to a national network of entertainers through their proximity to theaters that featured touring shows. Black vaudeville companies presenting an array of music, singing, dancing, comedy, and theater were booked by the Theater Owners Booking Association (TOBA) in venue circuits that linked distant cities, including Chicago, New York, Tampa, New Orleans, and Dallas.

The TOBA would connect many traveling performers to Pittsburgh venues such as the Leader House and Collins Inn, where they would perform alongside local musicians and earn income between tours. Established in 1921 and operating for a decade, the TOBA was affiliated, to its greatest extent, with over eighty theaters and was capable of booking productions for an entire season.[51] The *Chicago Defender* and *Pittsburgh Courier* regularly published surveys of touring TOBA companies to promote new productions as well as publicize newly added theaters. A survey of these listings includes a look into the extensive reach of the tours and the variety of entertainment they provided. In June 1921, the *Defender* listed Tim Moore's Chicago Follies at Nashville's Bijou Theater; Sidney Perrin's Company featuring Iris Hall at Memphis, Tennessee's Palace Theater; McGarr De Gaston's Ragtime Steppers featuring blues singer Mamie Smith in Detroit's Koppin Theater; Paul Carter's company in Pittsburgh's Star Theater; and seventeen other theaters active that month.[52]

Maud Woodson, who appeared at the Leader House in June 1923, was one of the thousands of performers who pieced together a living on theater and cabaret stages. Her stay at the Leader was short and was one moment within a steady touring life throughout the US. In April 1920, she performed at Josh T. Gibson's New Standard Theatre in Philadelphia as part of Sandy Burns's musical comedy *Hallo Sue*.[53] Burns's troupe also toured TOBA circuits through the South, including two-week stints at the 81 Theater in Atlanta and the Gay Theater in Birmingham, where Woodson was listed in the dancing chorus backing up the main acts.[54] In 1921, Woodson performed at the Regent Theater in Baltimore as one of several opening acts for Mamie Smith's Jazz Revue, where she "won a big hand for her toe dancing."[55] The show's main act, Mamie Smith and Her Jazz Hounds, had recorded "Crazy Blues" in August 1920, which sold seventy-five thousand copies in its first month after release and ignited a craze that ushered in the era of classic blues singers.[56] After leaving the Leader House, Woodson would become a regular feature at the famed Harlem black and tan nightclub, Small's Paradise, as part of Leonard Harper's revue. She later appeared alongside blues singer Bessie Smith and vaudeville star Cora Green at Harlem's Alhambra Theater before it was closed in 1932.

The Leader House provided a temporary break from traveling for performers such as Woodson. Touring life on the TOBA circuit was notoriously difficult as many artists were paid low fees, faced grueling working conditions, and were required to cover their travel expenses between engagements. In a 1928 *Courier* article, TOBA performer Clarence Muse denounced contract agreements that allowed theater owners to cancel events at will while penalizing artists for late or missed shows.[57] Pianist and Pittsburgh native Earl Hines recalled that attending Hill District TOBA shows were an important part of his early musical development, exposing him to new music and the difficult working conditions of theater entertainers: "Then theatrical people used to sit out back of the theatre on beer boxes and soda boxes. The sun would bake down the alley, and they'd fan themselves and fan the flies away. The dressing rooms were small and terribly hot, for there was no air conditioning then and few electric fans."[58] These conditions plagued traveling performers seeking a career in the entertainment industries and were characteristic of the struggles faced on the widest-reaching network of Black-patronized theaters.

Most full-time careers as a woman artist required balancing shorter residencies in cabarets with extended stints traveling theater circuits. Touring the TOBA with vaudeville troupes and cabaret performance provided a tenuous means of mobility and financial independence for women who sought new lives in northern cities and faced limited career options that made them dependent on their partners for financial support.[59] The life stories of female celebrities such as Josephine Baker, Alberta Hunter, and Ethel Waters reveal early decisions to abandon the drudgery of housework for the uncertainties of the road: Baker left St. Louis at thirteen with the Dixie Steppers vaudeville troupe; Hunter was also thirteen when she left Memphis to perform in Chicago; and Waters was seventeen when she abandoned domestic work for the stage in Philadelphia.[60]

On TOBA stages, Woodson and thousands of other performers would open for and cross paths with recording blues singers who stood out as rare examples of economic and social independence. Sharing these stages, less-experienced women performers witnessed and drew from various styles of femininity that centered on the individual voice and persona. In the Hill, audiences flocked to hear women blues singers, eager to witness displays of glamor intertwined with defiant heartache and sexual innuendo, as well as songs made familiar by local record dealers and the radio. In October 1923, singer Ethel Waters's week-long appearance at the Star Theater offered Hill residents an opportunity to hear the Black Swan recording artist in person. The main selling point of her performance in a *Courier* advertisement was her "gorgeous $5,000 'radio' dress," which was a misprinted description of her famous dress infused with radium.[61] Before the performance of "Whenever You're Lonesome Just Telephone Me," Waters would cue the theater electrician to abruptly cut the venue lights, at which point she would emerge before the startled audience in a glowing dress.[62] The following year, Bessie Smith, the "Empress of the Blues," opened the Lincoln Theater drawing a crowd that blocked traffic and left hundreds turned away. Smith, accompanied by pianist Irving Johns and violinist John V. Snow, was the featured attraction. The show also included the acting duo Tim and Gertie Moore, dancing team Mayo and Glenn, and Gennet Recording artist and vocalist Sammy Lewis. Demand through the week continued to the point that Smith's show was booked for a second week at the Star Theater with evening sets scheduled for 7, 8, and 10 p.m.[63]

Many more vocalists, far less known and without stardom, performed on intercity theater and cabaret circuits, where they honed their acting, singing, and dancing skills. Women performers looking to build solo careers turned to black and tan cabarets for opportunities that could lead to wider notoriety. For Black women entertainers, black and tan cabarets such as the Leader House provided a step forward from the obscurity of the vaudeville chorus line. The marketing of their youth, "Creole" complexions, and southern origins marked their bodies as sites of struggle and desire. While sexualized within the context of the black and tan, their exploitation incited little of the moral outrage reserved for even the suggestion of exploitation of White women by Black men. Yet these women were professional entertainers who had seen a great deal of the country from the stage and embodied a mobility that was in itself an affront to wayward minor laws.[64]

Following Hartman's call to reimagine the chorus as a vehicle for another kind of story, this study of black and tan clubs in the Hill includes an account threaded together from various published documents of several women performers. Those who found themselves in Pittsburgh on TOBA tours were often hired by local cabarets for extended stays. The Leader House was not unique in featuring women entertainers, though they were the most widely advertised part of the cabaret shows. Performers including Laura Badge, Maud Woodson, Nora Collins, Teddy Peters, Iona Hayes, Rosie Motley, and Georgia Davis found their way to Pittsburgh through the TOBA and sang a repertoire of popular songs from musicals as well as hits by blues queens Mamie Smith, Bessie Smith, Ma Rainey, and others. Though no monographic studies of their creative output exist, their contribution was foundational to the creation of a jazz scene and musical community in Pittsburgh and beyond.

Notable among these women entertainers, singer Laura Badge, who also performed under the names Babe Badge and Baby Hines, found the Hill to be a temporary home during her extensive travels. Badge, a native of Alabama, appeared with minstrel performer Hardtack Jackson's thirteen-member troupe between 1920 and 1922, taking on the roles of "soubrette" and "ingénue" for musical revues titled "45 Minutes from Nowhere," "Pedro's Long Chance," and "The Two Nuts from Brazil."[65] Early performances included stints at the Park Theatre in Dallas. By January of 1921, the group began to book shows in the Northeast, which brought Badge to Baltimore's New Lincoln and New Standard Theaters as well as Philadelphia's New Standard Theater.

Pittsburgh pianist Earl Hines met Badge in the Hill District sometime in late 1922 or early 1923 while she was performing as part of a show at the Star Theater. Hines portrays his role in Badge's life as paternalistic, helping book her into local cabarets, accompanying her and updating her repertoire and protecting her from those who would "destroy her future."[66] Missing from this narrative is Badge's own voice, though her professional life offers glimpses of a talented singer and independent and dedicated entertainer—characteristics that would likely have intimidated a young, upcoming artist such as Hines. Mary Lou Williams recalled hearing Badge when she and pianist Todd Rhodes would visit Wylie Avenue in search of jam sessions. The scene in the Lower Hill was a draw for visiting musicians—what Williams called a musical "paradise," though it was in a "notorious section of town which was held in dread by so-called decent people."[67] Badge's singing made a strong impression on Williams, who claimed that she "had paid little attention to singers" up to that point in her career: "Those days, when [Badge] began a number . . . the customers showered tips on her in appreciation—and I've seen 50- and 100-dollar bills among them. Her torch songs brought real tears to their eyes—as you can guess, for that kind of dough!"[68]

At the Leader House, Badge's appearances included a two-week run in July 1923, when she performed popular recorded hits such as "Who Did You Fool After All?" (1922) and "Running Wild" (1922), a song written from the perspective of a young woman who decides to flaunt her newfound independence after her partner ends their relationship.[69] A *Courier* ad notes that Badge and an unnamed "thrilling" pianist (likely Hines) performed "a large variety of swaying, sobbing, shouting blues, as well as many other sentimental and original numbers" such as "After All These Years," "I Know You Want Me Just as Much as I Want You," and "Who's Sorry Now?" a story of vindication by a jilted lover.[70]

Badge and Hines married spontaneously when they were asked to stand as witnesses for Lois Deppe's wedding, though they separated within a year because Hines claimed that Badge was unfaithful.[71] According to Hines's biography, he blamed Badge for being misled by those who promised a life of relative luxury rather than trusting his sincere love: "She thought it was something to be with people like that, who were living an easy life and running around in big cars."[72]

After Hines left for Chicago in 1925, Badge, having adopted the stage name Baby Hines, joined a forty-member troupe performing the musical comedy "Shufflin' Sam from Alabam."[73] For several seasons, they toured between Vermont and Missouri with Badge playing the role of Mandy, the love interest of a young city man who comes to the country and helps a farmer named Uncle Joe devise a plan for paying off his mortgage.[74] Snippets of news reports show that Badge's career continued through the following three decades and included collaborations with pianist Jennie Dillard and blues guitarist Lonnie Johnson in 1933; performances at New York's Café Society in 1942; a musical revue starring Bill "Bojangles" Robinson at the Philadelphia Shangri-La in 1946; the Frolic Show Bar in Detroit in 1947; and a four-year residency at the Lamplighter in New York City in the early 1950s.[75]

The mobility that defined the life of touring women artists was often an important element of their appeal to audiences. In Pittsburgh, they found themselves the subject of the northerners' fascination with the exoticized and mysterious Deep South. Like Badge, performer Edna Richards traveled widely and found a temporary home in the Hill. A Louisiana native, she had trained in Chicago under producer and actor Jerry Mills and worked in the chorus line in Flournoy E. Miller and Aubrey Lyles's musical comedy *Who's Stealin'* (1918) and performed in well-known cabarets such as Harlem's Nest Club and Chicago's Sunset Café.[76]

In Pittsburgh, the *Courier* gave special attention to Richards's southern roots, evident in her "rolling, full-throated drawl, which years of contact and association in the North could not eradicate," as well as her light complexion, which was representative of New Orleans's famed "Creole beauties."[77] In a portrait captioned "Creole Beauty Entertaining at Paramount Inn," Richards is depicted sitting on a piano bench, staring at the viewer with a discerning gaze. According to the review, Richards "ran away from a good home to heed the lure of the twinkling footlights" of the stage but remained nostalgic for her hometown. Her own words reveal that the difficulties of the performer's life provided freedom from her home life: "I have loved the stage forever, so it seems to me, and there was nothing else for me but to follow the path of least resistance."[78] At the Paramount, audiences heard her sing John Turner Layton and Henry Creamer's 1922 composition "Way Down Yonder in New Orleans," which renders the southern city as a paradise filled with exotic and inviting women and escape for northern men. Richards's choice of the song pays a nostalgic tribute to her home while reflecting on her own exploitation in the entertainment world as a racialized sex symbol and standard of Black beauty.

Figure 2.2. Vocalist Edna Richards, billed as the "Creole Beauty Entertaining at Paramount Inn" (1924). "Charming Entertainer at New Cabaret Comes from Town Famous for Beauties," *Pittsburgh Courier*, July 25, 1924, 10.

Other vocalists at the Leader also illustrate how young women entertainers drew on the nationwide network of theaters and nightclubs to piece together livelihoods in the entertainment industry. In December 1923, Badge double-billed with "Harlem Sensation" singer and dancer Teddy Peters, another traveling entertainer who was active on the TOBA circuit. In 1926, Peters would record "Georgia Man" for Brunswick Records following the company's creation of its race record division Vocalion and subsequent search for Black musicians and singers.[79] Peters remained on the road in Black vaudeville shows, filling the role of classic blues singer alongside jazz bands, comedians, and dancing choruses.[80] Detroit singer and dancer Iona Hayes appeared at the Leader House for two weeks in May 1924 amid performances by a local group named Sherman's Syncopators, singing team Rosie Motley and Georgia Davis "of Harlem fame," and Earl Hines.[81] Hayes's songs included Irving Kaufman's "Just a Girl That Men Forget" (recorded in 1923), Bessie Smith's "Haunted House Blues" (recorded in 1924), and Edmonia Henderson's "If You Sheik on Your Daddy, Your Mama's Gonna Sheba on You" (recorded in 1924).[82]

Nora Collins was another traveling vocalist and dancer who appeared at the Leader House and made Pittsburgh a temporary home. Originally from Los Angeles, Collins had made her way across the US with various stage shows and cabaret performances, including in Chicago as well as the Jazzland Cabaret in

Figure 2.3. Vocalist Nora Collins. "Out of the Golden West," the *Pittsburgh Courier*, August 11, 1923, 9.

Figure 2.4. Vocalist Rosie Motley. "Cabaret Favorite," the *Pittsburgh Courier*, May 24, 1924, 5.

St. Louis, Missouri. Like the Leader House, the Jazzland was a joint cabaret and speakeasy where patrons could find "a pre-[P]rohibition good time," and police raids and court fines for "keeping a disorderly house" were regular occurrences.[83] Appearing in the Leader House in August 1923, Collins was advertised as a "Creole Fashion Plate" and "The Girl From the Golden West," conspicuous titles that referenced the contemporary vaudeville personality Karyl Norman and the 1923 silent film *Girl of the Golden West*. Her repertoire included well-known hits of the blues royalty such as Clara Smith's "Every Woman's Blues," Ida Smith's "Bama Bound Blues," and Bessie Smith's "Yodeling Blues" and "Lady Luck Blues."[84] While in Pittsburgh, Collins would be featured alongside Deppe's Serenaders, including a dance in Pittsburgh's eastern neighborhood of Homestead where patrons could "see the 'Gay Night Life' of Chicago and New York transplanted to a beautiful suburban outdoor resort."[85] In 1929, she joined the touring vaudeville revue *Miss*

*Creola*, produced by Will Mastin and including entertainer Sam Davis Sr. as well as the toddler and emerging star Sammy Davis Jr.[86] Following the stock market crash and onset of the Great Depression, Mastin was able to keep *Miss Creola* on the road for at least a year before closing.

This overview highlights the extensive contributions of a largely unacknowledged section of the music industry to jazz's early development and diffusion throughout the US. Imperfect records, newspaper advertisements, and reviews provide some context to these struggles of Black women for independence, mobility, and artistry in a society that legally sanctioned their policing, exploitation, and exclusion from desirable work. The Leader House was not unique in the Hill for featuring women performers, though it did invest more in promoting this aspect of the club's entertainment. These performers, a small cross section of those caught up in the Great Migration, were points of contact for Pittsburgh audiences with southern culture, jazz, and Black theater. Within contexts of gambling and liquor bootlegging, these performers became visual cues of vice that led to backlashes against the venues.

### The Collins and Paramount Inns

Hill District entrepreneur Harry Collins faced the daunting task of navigating the city's racial and Prohibition Era politics while running his venue at 1213 Wylie Avenue. *Pittsburgh Courier* reporting suggested that he envisioned the Collins Inn as a place of leisure as well as a social institution that supported the economic and cultural development of the neighborhood's African American community. Collins's idea of a cabaret booking agency and hosting of social events for the Hill's Black elite illustrates the venue's potential impact beyond the local entertainment industry. The Collins Inn cabaret featured touring and local artists who drew in White patrons from outside the neighborhood, creating rare sites of interracial socializing. Coverage of the Collins Inn in the *Pittsburgh Press*, *Daily Post*, and *Gazette Times* tells a markedly different story in which the venue was a source of vice endemic to the Hill. The nightlife of this venue created a flashpoint in the city, which revealed the extensive backlash that mixed-race audiences received from police and citizens' groups. Driving public attacks on the Collins Inn was a notion of vice advanced in newspaper reporting as sexual predation across racial lines. So much did this concept undergird mainstream press coverage of the Hill that *Daily Post* reporters nicknamed Police Inspector J. P. Clancey "Black and Tan" in a three-page article accusing him of ignoring the "debauchery of the two races" in the Hill.[87]

Amid pressures from citizens' groups to reduce vice in the Hill, police often drew on Prohibition laws to close black and tan venues as empty gestures toward enforcing bans on alcohol—an underground trade that city officials directly benefited from. Prohibition laws provided local officials broad power to raid or close black and tan clubs under the guise of stamping out so-called vice or enforcing the federal liquor ban. In January 1920, the Eighteenth Amendment to the US Constitution and National Prohibition Act of 1919 (known as the Volstead Act) took effect, prohibiting the manufacture, transportation, sale, and consumption of intoxicating liquors. As historian Julian Comte notes, federal laws did little to deter alcohol production and sales in Pittsburgh between 1920 and December 1933, when the Eighteenth Amendment was overturned with the ratification of the Twenty-First Amendment.[88]

Rather than enforcing liquor bans, Pittsburgh's Prohibition Era mayors, William Magee (1922–1926) and Charles H. Kline (1926–1933), presided over powerful political machines in which law enforcement and elected city officials flaunted liquor laws and directly profited from the lucrative bootleg alcohol underworld. Those Pittsburgh politicians who openly supported enforcing prohibition laws found themselves at odds with the city's large working-class population. While campaigning for mayor in 1921, Magee made clear to constituents that city police would not actively enforce prohibition nor coordinate with federal agents. Magee's unsuccessful Democratic rival weakened his own campaign by promising to build a local police force that would "smash the booze traffic."[89]

Local opposition to funding and enforcing prohibition extended to the state level, with "wet" legislators actively undermining the efforts of Governor Gifford Pinchot, a devoted "dry." In Pennsylvania, Pinchot pushed through a prohibition law called the Snyder-Armstrong Act in 1923, only to have it underfunded by the state legislature.[90] The disjuncture between federal rulings and Pennsylvania's state laws created a legal gray area that enabled Pittsburgh nightclubs, saloons, and cabarets to continue acquiring liquor licenses in the early years of Prohibition. In March 1921, the Court of Quarter Sessions of Allegheny County received hundreds of applications from every city ward and county borough for retail licenses to "sell vinous, spiritous, malt or brewed liquors."[91] Entrepreneur Harry Collins, whose liquor license for 1213 Wylie Avenue was approved, was one of thirteen applications in the Third Ward or Lower Hill.[92]

Though the Collins Inn and other Pittsburgh venues were licensed to sell alcohol by the Quarter Sessions Court, federal agents were still expected to enforce the national liquor ban. In the afternoon of Friday, November 4, 1921, federal prohibition agents, assisted by three city detectives, raided the Collins Inn and confiscated a small amount of liquor comprising two quarts of whiskey, five gallons of wine, and a few bottles of other liquors. The agents also claimed to have found two tins of morphine hidden in the basement wall, which was valued at $1,000. As the *Gazette Times* reported, the agents also raided the Eagle Inn located a block east at 1312 Wylie Avenue and two Lower Hill confectionery stores on Webster

Avenue, seizing three quarts of moonshine and a pint of whiskey—drops in the sea of Pittsburgh's bootleg alcohol underworld.[93]

Far from a concerted effort to enforce liquor bans, raids by federal prohibition agents were often a feeble gesture of their responsibilities as well as ways to extract payments. Comte noted that corruption was endemic among federal agents, with nearly 9 percent discharged between 1920 and 1931 for violating the laws they were hired to uphold.[94] Collins's application for a renewal of his liquor license several months after the November raid signaled that saloon owners believed that the "wet" interests of Pittsburgh's political machine offered adequate protection.[95]

Collins found that despite Mayor Magee's lax stance toward enforcing prohibition, police and city officials employed federal liquor laws to target black and tan businesses. In September 1922, Magee's first director of Public Safety, George W. McCandless, accompanied by Superintendent of Police John C. Calhoun, visited the Collins Inn as part of an investigation prompted by complaints about vice conditions in the Hill District. McCandless would have been aware of the night-club since Collins had been arrested two months earlier in a police raid that was in response to his cabaret's violation of a contentious music prohibition order that banned entertainment after midnight.[96]

After visiting the Collins Inn at 1:30 a.m. on a Sunday morning, McCandless described it as "filled with Negroes and whites" with the band "in full swing and a Negress . . . doing an immoral dance."[97] McCandless stated to the press that he had underestimated the conditions described in complaints received by his office and would immediately undertake an extensive campaign to clamp down on offending locations. His refusal to identify the source of the complaints led a *Pittsburgh Gazette Times* journalist to posit that an outside citizen's organization had independently investigated the Hill's nightlife conditions and pressured McCandless into action under the threat of exposing police complicity in the bootleg alcohol trade.[98]

Several days after McCandless's late-night visit, federal prohibition agents raided the Collins Inn, confiscating whiskey, gin, and wine. When an angry crowd formed outside the venue, the outnumbered agents called in the local police for support as they completed their raid.[99] Notably, six other locations were raided the same day, including a well-known hotel and saloon in downtown Pittsburgh, though agents claimed no alcohol was found at these locations.[100] McCandless moved quickly on the heels of the federal raid by filing a petition with the Quarter Sessions Court to have Collins's liquor license revoked on the grounds that he was "[s]elling booze, a quantity of which is said to have been seized by Federal agents," failed "to observe the closing hour rule of the court," and allowed "disorder in the place."[101] The resulting court case centered on competing depictions of the club's social scene while lawyers gave only cursory attention to acknowledging the Collins's rights under conflicting local and federal liquor laws.

When the case was heard on November 9, 1922, a dozen African American witnesses testified that Collins maintained a respectable and "properly conducted" club that was a "necessity" for the Hill District's Black community.[102] The lead witness speaking on behalf of Collins was Attorney George H. White Jr., son of the Congressman and post-Reconstruction era civil rights advocate, who testified that he had been sitting with Collins and his wife in the cabaret when McCandless and Calhoun had inspected the location. White testified that he had heard McCandless tell Calhoun "to remember that whites and blacks were mixing in the cabaret," and this comment was directed to his own table though he clarified in court that "Collins' wife may have been mistaken by the director for a white woman, as she is of light complexion."[103] White's questioning of accusations of racial mixing suggests that while the cabaret audiences at the Collins Inn were interracial, the venue actively discouraged Black and White patrons from sitting or dancing with one another as the house policy. Such policies varied in black and tan cabarets in northern cities, with some adhering to a "racial double standard" that barred contact between Black men and White women while allowing White men to associate with Black women.[104] Further testimony revealed that the Collins Inn prohibited single men and women from entering the cabaret to ensure that tables were occupied by couples and, therefore, would likely not be racially mixed.[105]

Collins's approach to managing interracial socializing was viewed by the Quarter Sessions court as a violation of pervasive though legally unsupported segregationist policies. Pennsylvania's Colonial era antimiscegenation laws were overturned in 1780, and although politicians such as John Tener (the Pennsylvania governor from 1911 to 1915) supported passing new laws, there was no legal basis to deny interracial marriage.[106] Court testimony reveals that the liquor license, had been granted to Collins with an unwritten agreement that the nightclub would cater to African Americans though McCandless's observations, demonstrated that "Collins gave more attention to inducing white people, both men and women, into the place."[107] The case ended on November 9, with the judge ruling four days later to revoke Collins's liquor license on the grounds that he had violated the Eighteenth Amendment. Though charges could not be brought against interracial socializing, the subtext of the cabaret as a site where White and Black patrons collectively enjoyed music, singing, and dance underlay the case.

The revocation of Collins's liquor license coincided with a campaign that implicated him in drug trafficking charges that would lead to his imprisonment. Collins was arrested on October 23, 1922, by city detectives as part of a drug crusade led by Lieutenant of Detectives Edward J. Brophy.[108] Collins's bail was initially set at $30,000, "the largest ever asked in a Pittsburgh police station on a single charge," and he was charged with violating the Harrison antinarcotic law.[109] While no drugs were confiscated in the raid, police received testimony from Nellie Harding and Ollie Vaughn, two female African American residents from the Hill District, who claimed to be addicts and have regularly purchased morphine and cocaine from Collins.[110]

On November 11, Collins was indicted in District Court and a month later faced testimonies of addicts as well as a prohibition agent who had been involved in the November 1921 raid in which narcotics were confiscated from the club.[111] The most damning evidence came from the testimonies of William E. Davis, a federal narcotics inspector, who claimed Collins "struck a bargain with him to 'run' dope from Canada," and Isaac Delphi, a convict who claimed to have sold drugs for Collins.[112] On February 16, 1923, Collins was convicted on these charges, fined $1,000, and sentenced to three to five years in the Western Pennsylvania Penitentiary.[113]

Following the conviction, *Courier* journalists supported Collins, noting that he had drawn attention nationally for the "determined manner in which he fought his case."[114] In his weekly column "Wylie Avenue," John L. Clark reflected on Collins's conviction and the closing of the Collins Inn as a great loss for the Hill District's Black community. When the Collins Inn went up for sale in November 1923, Clark commented on "alleged law violations" that had brought the celebrated business to an end and reminded his readers to aspire to emulate Collins's contributions:

> Here stands a building, the result of determination and courage to take a chance. Almost over night [*sic*] it came into national prominence as one of the best con- ducted places of its kind in the country. Money was made there and some of it was used wisely. If a few of our Negroes with $20,000 or $30,000 Bradstreet rating had the business foresight of Harry Collins, over seven-tenths of the property in the Third and Fifth Wards would be owned by Negroes. Unfortunately, his adminis- trative ability was not as highly developed as his foresight. If he profits any at all by his present misfortune, Negro business will witness a wizard in the next ten years. Harry has the stuff—COURAGE.[115]

Collins was released in August 1924 from county jail, having served eighteen months.[116] Determined to continue his work as a cabaret owner, Collins arranged to move to Chicago's South Side—a decision that played an important part in the early career of Earl Hines. As Hines recalls, Collins invited violinist Vernie Robinson and his band to perform at his new club, the Elite No. 2, located on State Street in Chicago's Bronzeville District.[117] It was a moment of reckoning for the young pianist who was comfortable working as a celebrated local artist. Following the advice of fellow musicians to take the opportunity, Hines moved to Chicago, where he would gain national recognition as a recording artist and bandleader.

According to Clark, Collins returned to Pittsburgh in 1929, broke from the failed business venture. In the summer of that year, the *Courier* reported that

Collins opened a modern sandwich shop and hotel called IT a block away from the old Collins Inn. The article emphasized that Collins's new venture was neither a cabaret nor a location where alcohol was served, but that it was meant to provide the Black Hill residents an inviting social environment where the "patrons are not penalized for the atmosphere."[118] Collins left Pittsburgh in 1932, living in New York and throughout the East before settling in Chicago in 1944, where he ran his second Collins Inn until his death in 1950.

In the summer of 1924, while Collins was serving his sentence, Black entrepreneurs Thomas "Kid" Welch (1872–1935) and William "Gus" Greenlee (1895–1952) took over the management of the Collins Inn, remodeling the second floor in preparation of reopening the cabaret. Greenlee and Welch renamed the business the Paramount Inn, possibly to disassociate it from the legal woes of the Collins Inn. Greenlee, twenty-three years Welch's junior, was a young entrepreneur looking to capitalize on legal and illegal business opportunities in the Hill District and rise through the ranks of influential figures in Pittsburgh's Black community. Both men had moved to Pittsburgh from the South and developed the Hill District's potential for Black sports, entertainment, and political engagement.

Welch grew up in Washington, DC, where he worked in barber shops and pool parlors, sang in vocal quartets, and performed in theater productions.[119] In 1904, he moved to Pittsburgh and joined the Lone Star Quartet, remembered as one of the first and most highly regarded secular vocal groups formed by Black church members in the city.[120] In addition to his pursuits as a singer, Welch was an avid athlete and fan of baseball and boxing. His primary business activities appeared to have been in real estate, co-owning businesses including the Paramount Inn as well as a tailor shop, and running a pool room and barber shop on lower Wylie Avenue.[121] As Clark reminisced after Welch's death in 1935:

> Nobody has been found who truthfully knows just what Kid Welch considered his major hobby or business. He could be found at ball games, hockey games, was almost a religious follower of [the] Homestead Grays, yet seemed just as much at home in the card room as he did any other place or any other game. Surely, he was a partner with Gus Greenlee in opening the Paramount. But nobody seems to know in just how many other places he had his money invested.[122]

By 1924, Welch had been involved in a wide range of business and property investments as well as sports and entertainment ventures. In co-owning the Paramount, he likely saw the economic benefits in running a speakeasy as well as the creative potential of running a cabaret where he could continue his involvement and support of Black music and entertainment.

The Paramount Inn was the first of several Hill District nightclubs and restaurants that Greenlee managed or owned from the mid-1920s to his death in

1952. Sometime around 1916, Greenlee moved to Pittsburgh from Marion, North Carolina, and began working odd jobs as a shoeshiner, construction site worker, steel mill fireman, and taxi driver before enlisting in the military and deploying with the 367th Regiment to fight in the closing years of World War I.[123] Though Greenlee came from a middle-class family, his early experiences in Pittsburgh likely overlapped with those of Black migrant workers interviewed by sociologist Abraham Epstein in early 1917. Among the five hundred migrants who contributed to Epstein's study, only thirty percent had traveled with families, with most single men cramming into lodging houses; many rooms were hastily organized in homes as well as "attics and cellars, storerooms and basements, churches, sheds and warehouses" to accommodate the steady influx of newcomers.[124] Workers had to endure living quarters that were cramped and often dilapidated, with half of those interviewed by Epstein sharing rooms with four or more roommates.[125] After returning to Pittsburgh from active duty, Greenlee entered the bootlegging racket, using a taxi to deliver liquor to speakeasies throughout the city. In this way, Greenlee came to understand the social and economic context of the Hill District and Pittsburgh and developed the savvy to cultivate alternative economic models.

Searching for new business opportunities, Greenlee, along with his friend and cohort William "Woogie" Harris (1896–1967), began locally operating a "numbers game" or illegal street lottery. By 1924, twenty-year-old Greenlee was likely already to have started his numbers business when he joined with Welch to reopen Collins's once-popular club as his official venture. Within several months, they purchased the property for $23,000 in August, the equivalent of over $390,000 in 2023.[126]

The *Courier* review of the Paramount Inn's opening night enticed readers with an exciting yet urbane scene where patrons could experience "the very latest in entertainment features" while enjoying "high-class cuisine, served by waiters in shiny black Palm Beach suits and spotless white shirts, catering courteously and efficiently to the wants of the overflow crowd." The review went on to describe the two rooms that comprised the second-floor cabaret—one red, with "soft-glowing lights of dark-rose hue," and the other blue—filled with "nattily-dressed couples" dancing between mahogany finished tables to the music of Ellzey Young's jazz band, featuring Sonny Christian (drums, vocals), Ellzey Young (piano), June Roberts (banjo), and Harold Jackson (violin).[127] As the night wore on, the band was joined by entertainers Lola Jones of Philadelphia, Vivian Greenlee of Pittsburgh (no relation to Gus Greenlee), and vocalist Edna Richards of New Orleans.

Throughout 1924 and 1925, Greenlee sponsored and managed the Paramount Inn Orchestra, booking regular late-night performances for the cabaret, radio broadcasts, and regional dance halls. Starting in December 1924, the orchestra, comprised of Oscar Butler (piano), Harold Holt (violin), Julian Franklin (cello and saxophone), Frank Caine (bass), Charles Addison (trumpet), Sunny Christian (drums), and Elmer Turner (banjo), broadcast hour-long live performances on

Figure 2.5. Lloyd W. Scott and His Orchestra. From left, the musicians are William Hicks (cornet), Emerson Dickerson (cornet), Lloyd Scott (drums), William Dickie Wells (trombone), Hubert Minor Mann (banjo, guitar), Don Frye (piano), Cecil Xavier Scott (saxophone), Chester Campbell (tuba), Fletcher Allen (saxophone), and John Williams (saxophone). "Opened at Capitol Palace Club, New York City, Monday," the *Pittsburgh Courier*, August 7, 1926, 11.

Pittsburgh's WJAS on Friday evenings.[128] These broadcasts, occasionally featuring rising stars Earl Hines and Lloyd Scott, were some of the first to bring live jazz performances into the homes of Pittsburghers. Greenlee also booked the Paramount Orchestra in the city's dance halls that included a performance alongside Fletcher Henderson's Orchestra with arranger Don Redman and trumpeter Joe Smith at the Duquesne Gardens.[129]

Using the third floor of the Paramount Inn as offices, Greenlee established a music booking agency in partnership with Bill Cleveland, who had previously managed the Broadway Syncopators.[130] Within a short time, Greenlee and Cleveland found that the agency, which they created to provide quality entertainment to an "exclusive clientele," had more demand for orchestras than they had anticipated.[131] Among their clients were Cumberland Posey and Sellers McKee Hall, who hired the Paramount Inn Orchestra to perform at the Loendi Basketball Club's season-opening event in 1925.[132] Posey, who was the star player of the Loendi Club, named after the Hill District's most elite Black social organization, also handled its finances and promotion, using the opportunity to organize joint basketball and dance events for Black Pittsburgh.[133]

When Lloyd Scott, a jazz drummer and bandleader from Ohio, took up a temporary residence in Pittsburgh, Greenlee and Cleveland's booking agency sponsored his orchestra.[134] Before arranging a residency in Harlem's Capitol Palace in October 1926, Greenlee and Cleveland arranged tours for Scott's orchestra that reached through West Virginia, Ohio, and Kentucky, as well as dances in Pittsburgh's Liberty Gardens.[135] Though Scott was only twenty-four, his ambitions led him from Pittsburgh to New York, where he would produce groundbreaking jazz recordings, including "Symphonic Scronch" (1927).[136] Greenlee's warm welcome of the band when it later passed through Pittsburgh reflected his continuing support of the innovative group. Trumpeter Bill Coleman, who joined Scott in 1927, recalls Greenlee as a larger-than-life patron of Scott's orchestra:

> Gus . . . had a gambling place . . . and there was always $1,000 in silver dollar pieces stacked on the crapshooting table. Lloyd Scott was the only one in the orchestra who liked to gamble. He very seldom won anything. With Gus in our corner, we had nothing to worry about if we did not make much money working around Pittsburgh. He would lend the orchestra his personal car if we needed transportation and he would bail us out if we could not pay our rent in the hotel.[137]

Greenlee's support of the musicians reflected his taste for a lavish lifestyle and nightlife scene. With his primary income coming from numbers running, music management and promotion was a way to center himself in Pittsburgh's Black public life and help build an infrastructure for sports while creating a vibrant and popular cabaret in the Paramount Inn. A soundtrack to this life of gambling, racketeering, and nightlife entertainment, the music of these early jazz groups and their popularity with racially diverse audiences became closely associated with vice in the neighborhood.

As black and tan clubs became contested spaces in Pittsburgh, so did definitions of vice encompass a myriad of social conditions, including consensual interracial relationships, sexual predation, prostitution, gambling, bootlegging alcohol, police corruption, and dancing. "Vice," a term that took on a variety of meanings, served to identify apparent moral failures in city life that warranted private and public responses. Definitions of vice were shaped by the political and economic agendas of specific individuals and their personal relationship to the city. Efforts to control vice in the Hill brought together a range of individuals who often presented conflicting agendas. Protest committees made up of religious leaders, educators, business professionals, and private citizens from the Hill demonstrate the ways antivice campaigns brought together divergent perspectives on solving urban social problems and, more specifically, the role of black and tan clubs in the neighborhood.

In 1925, citizen groups and religious leaders made concerted efforts to pressure city officials into a campaign addressing vice in the Hill District. With little interest in reducing bootlegging and gambling, city officials found scapegoats in the Paramount Inn and Leader House, which White journalists depicted as dens of vice. The ensuing vice wars were performative in that they did not seek to reduce crime but rather used fears of miscegenation and interracial socializing to incite racial tensions and justify attacks on Black clubs.

Throughout Pennsylvania, citizen groups played an important role in Prohibition, providing funding and political will to enforce liquor laws. When Governor Pinchot's plans to uphold Prohibition laws were underfunded by legislators and undermined by ineffective federal agents, he resorted to hiring state police and undercover agents with funds raised by the Women's Christian Temperance Union (WCTU). An activist group that grew to forty-seven thousand members in the 1920s, the WCTU allocated $138,580 of their funds between 1923 and 1927 to Pinchot's special council that oversaw investigations and raids.[138]

On March 24, 1925, the *Pittsburgh Daily Post* reported that Mayor Magee was taking his first action in two years against the city's "wide-open reign of gambling, bootlegging, disorderly houses and redlight activities which [have] endured in Pittsburgh since the present administration went into power."[139] Magee instructed Superintendent of Police Edward J. Brophy to ensure that cabarets were closed by midnight, though the *Daily Post* reporter mused that this was more a reminder to the underworld "that they will have to 'kick in' more heavily than ever" to Magee's reelection campaign fund.[140] The reporter also noted private investigations undertaken by an organization led by Dr. Charles R. Zahniser, executive secretary of the Council of Churches of Christ. Zahniser, who had supported Magee's previous election campaign in 1922, had become increasingly dissatisfied with the mayor's inability to "end the reign of wide open vice."[141] While not a public ultimatum for the mayor, the reporter speculated that Zahniser threatened to withdraw the church's support of Magee unless he immediately closed the sites of gambling and bootlegging as well as dismissed those police and city officials who protected these places. Zahniser claimed his organization's private investigations had uncovered "unspeakable conditions" in dozens of Hill District "black and tan resorts" and cabarets where "indescribable orgies are carried on nightly."[142] In a particularly sensationalist excerpt, the article claims that "17- and 18-year-old white girls dance with Negroes and drink with Negroes almost within sound of the office [of] John J. Ford, inspector of the First police district."[143] The following day, Magee revoked the Paramount Inn's dancing permit, which the *Daily Post* asserted was "one of the most notorious resorts in the city" where "girls from 14 to 18 years old engaged in drunken orgies throughout the night" and "whites and blacks mingled freely and danced together frequently."[144]

The *Courier* wasted no time in denouncing the *Daily Post* and its "prejudiced reporter," "'cracker' city editor," and "exaggerated misstatement of many of the facts" that contributed to revoking the Paramount Inn's dance license.[145] The unidentified writer reminded *Courier* readers that previous depictions of the

Figure 2.6. The Paramount Inn as it appeared in the 1926 *Pittsburgh Daily Post* article "Hill, City's Worse Plague Spot, Runs Wild Even as Probers' Light Advances." (August 6, 1926, 8).

Collins Inn as a "notorious black and tan" led to its closing and Collins's arrest. The *Courier* also reprinted a large portion of the *Daily Post* article to illustrate that city officials were again pushing to close the popular Black cabaret.

In response to the *Daily Post* report, the *Courier* conducted its own investigation to illustrate the Paramount Inn's policy on race and to argue that the presence of White patrons in the cabaret was due to the quality of entertainment and not interracial sexual exploitation. In an attempt to avoid police raids and closure, Greenlee and Welch had, for a short time period, only allowed White patrons in the cabaret. They later adapted this policy to allow both Black and White patrons with the agreement that men could not enter without a guest and "no intermingling of the races was allowed, unless, perchance, the parties were man and wife."[146] Speaking in defense of the Hill's Black cabaret owners, the *Courier* journalist pointedly commented on the danger that sensationalist reporting posed to Black entrepreneurs:

> Local newspapermen with a vague idea of the notorious "black belts" in Chicago, New York and other cities, where the races mingle without police interference, have chosen this method to stir up racial animosity. The report that white girls of 17 and 18 summers dance and drink with their brown-skinned paramours is a gross exaggeration and a bitter injustice. The reporter has picked out the Caucasian's most tender spot—his womanhood—to strike a blow below the belt. The article is cleverly written, and is refuted in detail by owners and managers of every cabaret on the Hill. These men realize that they are the unprotected targets for just such vituperous articles as appeared in Tuesday morning's *Post* and take every means to protect themselves. This is the other side of the story. Just when the Paramount Inn will open, if it ever opens again, is not known but in justice to the management, these facts are presented to Negro readers from a Negro's angle.[147]

The racialization of vice by reporters and city officials to justify targeted attacks against Black-owned cabarets such as the Paramount Inn was but a small part of a larger campaign of police intimidation of the Hill's Black population.

These attacks were met with a move to solidify Black political power in the Hill and organize the Black population into a unified voter block that could shape local elections. In July 1925, Black Third Ward political leaders Clarence E. Webster and Mary Clark appeared before Pittsburgh's City Council to detail the pervasiveness of police violence against the Hill's Black citizens, including the "wholesale arrests, fining and lodging in jail of innocent Colored citizens; the beating up of prisoners and the unlawful and alleged barbaric methods of arrest." In one case, they described "an expectant mother, who was lodged in jail and during a night of her incarceration gave birth to a child, but was denied medical aid until the following day."[148]

The *Courier* reported that the Council, moved by Webster and Clark's speeches, ordered an investigation and "complete shakeup of lieutenants and patrolmen at the No. 2 Police Station in the Hill District. Building on these actions, Webster, as well as realtor S. R. Lewis and Attorney George H. White, organized a meeting of Black Hill citizens to form the Third Ward Voters' League in the spirit of rising as one against injustices. Unanimously elected as chairman of the League was Thomas "Kid" Welch, a position he would leverage in an ongoing struggle to run the Paramount Inn's cabaret.

Zahniser's campaign to expose vice and police corruption continued through 1926 under newly elected mayor Charles Kline. In August 1926, Zahniser joined with twenty-four prominent businessmen and religious leaders to form the

Citizens' Anti-Vice Committee with the aim of building a wider coalition that could pressure Kline into action.[149] In a letter sent to Kline, the Committee stated, "While we are interested in the conditions of the city as a whole, we are particularly interested in the conditions of our own district, the 'Hill District,' and we regret to say that the general conditions of vice are worse than ever before and growing worse every day."[150] The committee demanded that Mayor Kline pressure Superintendent of Police Walsh and Inspector J. P. Clancey to "rid his police district of vice and crime, gambling, prostitution, illegal manufacture and sale of liquor; to root out the hell holes: to raid them and raid them again, if necessary."[151]

In a meeting with Kline, Committee member Rev. Dr. Davis E. Cruea accused Director of Public Safety James M. Clark of inaction, stating, "I am in this vice crusade in Pittsburgh because I have a boy, aged 14. I am speaking to fathers now. If my boy should be enticed into one of those dens such as have been described to Director Clark, I would take a shotgun and clean up the City-County Building."[152] The threat of citizen violence was echoed by George Zitzman, a Pittsburgh resident and representative of the Ku Klux Klan, who threatened that if the committee was unsuccessful in pressuring Kline into action, the Klan would request that Governor Pinchot instate martial law in Pittsburgh "until the situation is changed for the better."[153]

Sidney Teller, committee chairman and director of the Irene Kaufmann Settlement House, also called for Inspector Clancey's removal if vice conditions were not improved in the Hill. Teller's focus, however, was on prostitution and police corruption tied to bootlegged liquor. Teller argued that even if the city's safety director and superintendent of police were working in good faith to reduce vice, the municipal court system, in which judges were elected by the mayor rather than elected by the general population, was such that those arrested and charged were often released with minimal fines.[154] Noting that the No. 2 Police Station in the Hill was understaffed, Teller recommended the formation of a "special squad" made up of Black and White members who would help reduce prostitution and other blatant violations of the law.[155] Seeing little interest in these ideas from the city, Teller turned to his own resources in the Settlement House and helped coordinate women volunteers to report on neighborhood conditions, sites of prostitution and gambling, and records of arrests. This operation was overseen by Anna Heldman, a Settlement House nurse who became known as the "Angel of the Hill District," whose years of dedication to public health in the neighborhood earned her the title.[156]

Director of Public Safety Clark showed little public support for the committee's claims of rampant vice and underpolicing, echoing Kline's statement that "the city is cleaner now than it ever was and is growing still cleaner."[157] As a public gesture, however, Clark targeted both the Paramount Inn, which was ordered to end its cabaret entertainment, and the Leader House, which was raided by city police who confiscated two slot machines.[158] A *Gazette Times* reporter noted that the Paramount Inn had "long been a source of trouble for the police" and was able to operate without a cabaret license—"running wide open, catering to mixed parties and providing liquor and risqué entertainment"—because of Welch's powerful political connections in the Hill.[159]

These connections were most likely overseen by John J. Verona, a rising political figure who served simultaneously as the Third Ward's police magistrate, Republican chairman, and alderman, and was steadily building opposition to Mayor Kline's own involvement in the city's lucrative vice underworld. Verona's power was derived from his ability to protect bootleggers and gamblers in the Third Ward using his own band of constables and the alderman's judicial power. In one instance, the *Daily Post* reported that Verona "turned loose fourteen gamblers arrested in the joint of his friend, Carmen Bevilaqua, 1009 Wylie Avenue early yesterday morning. To make things look good, he fined his friend $10."[160] Clark, illustrating the futility of his raids in the Hill, told the committee that Verona "was turning offenders loose as fast as the police arrested them," adding, "[S]o you see, my hands are tied: I have no power."[161]

In an affront to Verona, Clark used the city's administrative powers to require cabaret permits to be approved on a monthly basis through his office or be immediately closed.[162] With Clark's tight control of club licenses, Greenlee and Welch handed over management of the Paramount to John W. Sebilla and Roxie Nesta, Italian American bootleggers who could guarantee a close working relationship with Clark's office. The club was reopened as the Castle Gardens in November 1926 with the agreement that it would no longer be run as a black and tan cabaret.[163] Writing in April 1927, *Courier* journalist John L. Clark lamented the closing of Black-owned and patronized venues while the Castle Gardens continued to operate and serve exclusively White patrons. The journalist Clark, well-tuned to city politics, mocked Inspector Clancey's assertion that they were simply upholding the law in closing the Black-owned and patronized Leader House, Chili Parlor, and Entertainers' Comedy Club: "For, to presume that a cabaret can operate on the Avenue successfully, without violating a federal or state law or a city ordinance, is equivalent to believing that a wooden table leg can talk . . . or that Avenue politics is a science instead of a money-making system."[164]

That most clubs flourished or folded depending on elected officials and public servants was common knowledge. Journalist Clark's public denouncement of this system of corruption and naming of specific individuals involved, however, was less common in the press. He claimed that the closing of Black clubs was part of a power struggle between Clancey and Verona or Captain Tony Forrester over control of liquor sales in the Hill District. Clark reminded his readers that "[T]he Avenue . . . is the scene of many underhand tricks for small rewards and the practice of making 'political examples' of certain privileged ones is regular— with no organized protest."[165]

These blunt attacks on political corruption in the Hill prompted threats against Clark, which he confronted through his following column (below). Responding to an unidentified individual who said these criticisms were "dangerous business," Clark wrote:

> Maybe it is "dangerous ground." Probably we have incurred the dislikes of a few political gents who could "buy and sell" all those who criticize them . . . . But toying with "dangerous elements" is in no way a singular experience with Negroes. In the mills and factories he is liable to be "bumped off" for seeking or holding a job that a pale-face formerly held . . . . Politically, he courts danger every time he seeks an elective office, in preference to the privilege of choosing between mops, cuspidors, and gambling houses. His domestic habitat is safe only when located in the disease-breeding marshes or out of the way sections where natural light seldom penetrates. As though these handicaps were not sufficient in number, the Negro of the Avenue is ever liable to arrest for any crime committed in Frisco, or any other parts of the US. . . . "Dangerous ground," then, is not a new location for any Negro. There are those of course, who never take time to orient themselves, and continue to gibber about "our" healthy prospect—and what some white "scheme" is going to do for "the Negro race". . . . Comparing one individual above another, discovering virtues in a prostitute and vices in a social matron; efficiency in a gambler and ignorance in an "old Pittsburgh businessman"—and a multitude of other conditions, constitute dangerous ground—in one way or another. In the matter of Avenue politics, the column cannot "go along" with a system, which is so one-sided, discriminatory, unreasonable.[166]

The closing of the Paramount Inn and Leader House cabarets, however, did not permanently turn Greenlee away from music and entertainment promotion in the Hill, though it demonstrated the tenuous position Black nightclub owners held during the Prohibition Era. The continuous pressure on places of interracial socializing made it clear that creating Black public spaces required both economic and political development in the Hill's African American community. Greenlee's numbers-running revenue allowed him to withdraw from entertainment management and support Black political engagement. During Mayor Kline's reelection campaign of 1929, Greenlee financed the Third Ward Voters' League, which backed Kline and also attempted to replace Verona with Kline's ally Samuel J. Price as Third Ward alderman. While Kline was reelected, Verona remained in power and continued to exert control over Hill politics. When Greenlee and the Voters' League supported Dr. Roy T. Anderson as the first Black Third Ward constable in 1931, the *Courier* reported that Verona ensured that Hill police "got the orders to defeat the Negro candidate—at all odds and at any cost."[167] In a widespread campaign of voter intimidation, the *Courier* estimated that nearly half of the Hill's 6,278 registered Black voters were prevented from voting.[168] This struggle over the voting rights of Hill residents was but one way that black and tan cabarets became embedded in the city's political, economic, and cultural life. They were also essential for establishing future jazz clubs that provided local and touring musicians places for organizing, networking, training, and performing, as well as providing Pittsburgh audiences sites for interracial socializing around music.

## The Crawford Grill No. 1 (1934–1952):
## Building on the Legacy of the Black and Tans

The Hill District vice wars of the Prohibition Era demonstrated that black and tan clubs were important sites of socializing and innovation in early jazz as well as Black entrepreneurship in Pittsburgh. The nature of their impact on the neighborhood was also highly contested, with White fears of miscegenation undergirding attacks on these spaces. The arrest of Collins Inn proprietor Harry Collins and raids on the Leader House and Paramount Inn demonstrated the volatility of nightlife businesses in the Hill and the need for strong political and economic power for Black entrepreneurs to maintain control of their property.

Among those with power in the Hill was Gus Greenlee, who emerged from the Prohibition Era as the owner of the 1213 and 1401 Wylie Avenue buildings, both of which continued to play central roles in the city's nightlife and professional lives of Pittsburgh jazz musicians. Greenlee had bought the Leader House at 1401 Wylie in 1929, which would be his business headquarters for the following two decades.[169] In its early years, the location had been known variously as the Green Boot, The Avenue, and the C&G Club, but was renamed the Crawford Grill by Greenlee as a tribute to the Pittsburgh Crawfords baseball team, which he purchased in 1931.

Greenlee was among the first Black business owners to acquire a liquor license in the Hill District after the repeal of the Eighteenth Amendment and federal prohibition laws in December 1933 and quickly established a bar and restaurant that was touted for upscale dining while also providing a casual drinking spot where Black patrons were welcome.[170] The *Courier* praised Greenlee for giving Hill Residents "something besides swinging doors, stand-up bars, backrooms and free lunch," references to drinking spots for working-class men.

Greenlee's vision for the Grill required considerable personal investment and involved redesigning the interior with "a novel replica of a Spanish hacienda . . . painted in bright terra cotta and paisley frescoes of exotic design."[171] These efforts to increase the respectability of drinking and socializing made the Grill one of

Figure 2.7. Charles "Teenie" Harris, American, 1908–1998, Wylie Avenue with Crawford Grill No. 1 and Cramptons Drugs on left, Hill District, c. 1947–1951 black and white: Kodak Safety Film, H: 4 in. × W: 5 in. (10.20 × 12.70 cm), Carnegie Museum of Art, Pittsburgh: Heinz Family Fund, 2001.35.2495, © Carnegie Museum of Art, Charles "Teenie" Harris Archive.

Figure 2.8. Charles "Teenie" Harris, American, 1908–1998, Women and men, possibly including Jasper Washington on right, gathered in Crawford Grill No. 1 with neon signs reading "bar" and "grill" in the windows, c. 1938–1945, black and white: Agfa Superpan Press Safety Film, H: 4 in. × W: 5 in. (10.20 × 12.70 cm), Carnegie Museum of Art, Pittsburgh: Heinz Family Fund, 2001.35.2971 © Carnegie Museum of Art, Charles "Teenie" Harris Archive.

Figure 2.9. Charles "Teenie" Harris, American, 1908–1998, William "Gus" Greenlee with his arm around woman wearing herringbone coat and head scarf, in booth at Crawford Grill No. 1, c. 1940–1945, black and white: Agfa Safety Film, H: 4 in. × W: 5 in. (10.20 × 12.70 cm), Carnegie Museum of Art, Pittsburgh: Heinz Family Fund, 2001.35.3097 © Carnegie Museum of Art, Charles "Teenie" Harris Archive.

the Hill's most popular meeting places, drawing everyone from the "highest profession" to the "lowest rackets."[172] Historian Rob Ruck writes of the Grill in *Sandlot Seasons*: "An evening's crowd included both Blacks and whites, and Black customers were usually fairly representative of a cross-section of the city's Black population. Visiting Negro League ballplayers, members of Black Pittsburgh's elite, and workingmen unwinding after a shift could be found at adjoining tables, if not actually drinking together."[173]

The Grill served as a stage for Greenlee's extravagant public life as a racketeer, philanthropist, and sports management figure. In public, he played up the role of the high-class socialite with expensive cars and tailored suits, though he was a tireless worker behind the scenes. With his focus on the Negro National League (NNL) and the Pittsburgh Crawfords baseball team as well as managing boxer John Henry Lewis, Greenlee put less time into making the Crawford Grill a venue for jazz, though he would host many artists as honored guests. Within a month of the Grill's redesign and 1933's New Year's Eve party celebrating the end of Prohibition, Greenlee hosted the first meeting of the NNL, inviting team owners and representatives from throughout the East and Midwest.[174] Greenlee was already a leading figure in Black baseball, having financed the building of Greenlee Field in the Middle Hill District, which was the only Black-owned baseball stadium in the country during its existence from 1932 to 1938.[175]

The dearth of entertainment at the Grill in the 1930s could be the result of Greenlee's focus on sports as well as manager Frank Sutton's preference for recorded music. The Depression Era, while greatly reducing high-spending patrons, also ushered in new technologies that impacted the professional lives of musicians. Jukeboxes, which were first commercially available in 1927, became ubiquitous in the 1930s as post-Prohibition bars, restaurants, and lounges sought to draw in and keep paying customers while reducing the costs of hiring professional musicians. The proliferation of radio and sound films further marginalized musicians in the entertainment industry. As a consequence, "no other occupation in America had ever faced such a threat from technology" as that of the performing musician during the 1930s.[176]

For shrewd managers, recordings were a quick and easy way to create an inviting nightlife setting without the challenges of managing unpredictable or unprofessional musicians. When asked why he had installed a "coin music machine" that threw entertainers "to the discard," Sutton responded:

> That little machine plays your number straight through, does the very best it can and works just as long as you have coins for the slot. When the number is finished, records go back to their proper places, power turns off automatically and it awaits another request. It makes no demand for tips when a good number is played, and calls you no names if you fail to give a dollar for its services. It is always friendly, has no moods, and never comes to work drunk. It welcomes all patrons, good, bad, black or white. Does no gossiping about your character, or snickers if your hair is not of the finer kind. It is a good worker and easy to get along with.[177]

The decrease in vaudeville stage shows also adversely affected cabaret entertainment as fewer touring troupes brought new talent to the city. As a national infrastructure of venues and tour routes, the TOBA was integral to bringing young Black talent to new cities and bringing cosmopolitan sensibilities into cabaret entertainment outside of major metropolitan areas. The popularity of vaudeville entertainment in Hill TOBA theaters peaked in the mid-1920s and fell out of fashion in the following decade. By the end of the 1930s, audiences tired of stale rehashing of schticks, and tabloid (or "tab") musical comedies flocked to movie theaters. The Star Theater closed in 1926, with *Courier* columnist John L. Clark proclaiming that it "should have been 'padlocked' several years ago, not because they sold liquor . . . but because they sold a class of amusement that did more damage to the moral structure of our youth than the most poisonous hootch could do to our physical frame."[178] White proprietor Harry Tenenbaum sold the Lincoln in August 1927, which reopened as a moving picture house. While the Hill's Elmore Theater continued to book stage shows, it too was run primarily as a movie house after 1933.

Though the Crawford Grill was widely popular throughout the 1930s, music and entertainment were not the primary draw the way they had been during the Leader House days. The *Courier's* listings for entertainment at the Grill were sporadic, with few mentions of informal jam sessions or extended bookings of entertainers or musicians. The few references to live entertainment during the decade are largely due to Greenlee briefly reviving the cabaret tradition of the Leader House and hiring producer Billy Maxey to host parties and stage floor shows on the Grill's second floor. In 1935, the Crawford Grill's C&G floorshow featured a female dancing quartet, singers, and two entertainers from New York, including female impersonator Manhattan Pearl backed by Jack Spruce and his septet.[179] Other listings include the entertainer Bulee "Slim" Gaillard, who played at the Grill in 1939 with his ten-piece Flat Foot Floogie Orchestra. Gaillard's group—named after a popular composition of his—mixed dance numbers with physical and musical feats involving Gaillard playing the piano palm up or the guitar with his left hand over the top of the neck.[180] Like Louis Jordan and Cab Calloway, Gaillard gained wide appeal playing comedic "jump blues"-style songs, though he was also able to improvise lyrics and scat sing in the style of Louis Armstrong.

The Grill's management began booking solo pianists and small groups in the early 1940s, which signaled a shift to more economical live entertainment. Saxophonist Hosea Taylor noted that when he was starting out as a gigging musician in the early 1940s, the Grill was not a popular spot for music.[181] Taylor would often drop by the Grill after a gig for a meal but saw it primarily as a place where Greenlee relaxed with friends and hosted guests. In 1941, however, *Courier* columnist Lee Mathews observed that the Grill's hiring of pianist Ruby Young and vocalist Reva George established a policy of providing music without dancing, which could have been a conscious effort to distance the entertainment from the black and tan cabarets of the 1920s. Other local soloists and groups would follow, such as the duo of pianist Cozy Harris and guitarist Ted Birch, solo pianists George "Duke" Spaulding and Alyce Brooks, and a trio comprised of bassist Al Hinton, pianist John Hughes, and guitarist Bobby Dummit. Hughes had been working at an upscale after-hours club in Charleston, West Virginia, owned by an African American racketeer named Ed Hicks. When that club was raided for gambling and Hughes was left without a job, Hicks, a friend of Greenlee's, recommended the group for the Crawford Grill. Greenlee accepted the group on behalf of Hicks; Hughes, Dummit, and Hinton were hired to replace pianist Harris, who was leaving for Atlantic City.

Figure 2.10. Charles "Teenie" Harris, American, 1908–1998, Alyce Brooks playing mirrored piano in Continental Bar at Crawford Grill No. 1, c. 1945–1946 black and white: unknown safety film, H: 4 in. × W: 4 in. (10.20 × 10.20 cm), Carnegie Museum of Art, Pittsburgh: Heinz Family Fund, 2001.35.5695, © Carnegie Museum of Art, Charles "Teenie" Harris Archive.

The connection between club owners was essential for young musicians establishing themselves in Pittsburgh. Hughes recalled, "It was almost like people there were a welcoming committee," with saxophonist Leroy Brown arranging apartments, Stanley Turrentine's father inviting the band to dinner, and Greenlee providing regular gigs. Hughes remembered that "it was an advantage being hired by Gus Greenlee" because he "made sure I was welcomed into the Hill as a celebrity," which negated the need to build one's reputation "rehearsing in people's houses and all that." Working at the Crawford Grill also meant that one had connections to other venues in the Hill. With Greenlee as a contact, Hughes found that "you could work seven days a week" at other Black-owned and -patronized venues, including the Washington Club, the Loendi, Stanley's, and the Hilltop Club.[182] Able to maintain regular work, local musicians including Leroy Brown, Ruby

Young, George Spaulding, and Alyce Brooks bolstered Pittsburgh's jazz scene as well as advocated for jazz musicians as members and leaders of the city's Black local chapter of the American Federation of Musicians.

Though the term "black and tan" faded in the 1930s, interracial social scenes developed in jazz clubs of the 1950s and 1960s as the music continued to permeate American popular culture. Jazz clubs that followed in the footsteps of the first Crawford Grill, as well as black and tan cabarets such as the Leader House and Collins Inn, were integral to developing the neighborhood as a vibrant and valued cultural center in the region. In the decades that followed the repeal of Prohibition, venues were not subject to the legal struggles and policing of segregation that marred black and tan nightclubs of the 1920s. However, by the 1950s, moralistic calls to eradicate vice in the Hill District made way for the removal of so-called blight in an effort to modernize and restructure the city. The "dangerous ground," to use John Clark's phrase, on which Greenlee, Collins, and other Black club owners seeded the Hill's nightlife scene, continued to provide entrepreneurial opportunities to club owners, contexts of creative development for jazz musicians, and vibrant social scenes for patrons. The dangerous ground also continued to yield great challenges. The following chapters trace how the Hill District's celebrated jazz clubs of the 1950s and 1960s, specifically the Crawford Grill No. 2, the Hurricane Bar, and the Musicians Club, continued to shape public discourse and policy centered on the neighborhood.

# PART II

# PITTSBURGH'S RENAISSANCE AND JAZZ'S GOLDEN AGE (1945–1968)

# Chapter 3

# COMPETING VISIONS OF MODERNITY

Silence itself, in a place of worship, has its music.[1]

On August 31, 1953, Hill District entrepreneur Joe Robinson launched a week of festivities celebrating the renovation and reopening of his club, the Crawford Grill No. 2. *Pittsburgh Courier* reporter George F. Brown declared the club the "prettiest lounge in the East—and maybe the West" and congratulated the management "for having confidence that Pittsburghers appreciate the finer things in life."[2] On opening night, the club's resident band Leroy Brown and his Brown Buddies performed for a room "packed with well-wishers" that included locals as well as visitors from nine states.[3] Roses were given out to women attendees while *Courier* journalist Malvin "Mal" Russell Goode served as emcee and introduced speakers who celebrated Robinson's leadership as a Hill District businessman.

The night's honored guest was Mayor David L. Lawrence, a Democrat and key architect of Pittsburgh's post-World War II renewal projects. Also present was Paul F. Jones, a Hill District resident and Duquesne Law School graduate whom Lawrence was supporting to become Pittsburgh's first Black city council member. Lawrence, speaking from the Grill's stage, reflected on the importance of the night: "This is one of the finest places I've ever been in and I would not have missed the opening."[4] Lawrence used the event to promote city-led development projects and likened Robinson's business to the recently completed Gateway Center business complex in Pittsburgh: "I am as proud of this restaurant as I am of the big skyscrapers going up downtown. Small businesses are the lifeblood of Pittsburgh as well as the big industries. I salute Joe Robinson."[5] In attending the event, Lawrence aimed to bolster his reputation as both an able leader of the city's development and an ally to its African American community.[6] His statements spoke to the right of Hill's Black business owners to participate in the city's renewal and, by extension, realize the potential of creating places in service of the greater good.

This intersection of the political elite's vision of urban renewal with that of a renowned Black business leader during the Grill's reopening celebrations reveals a moment of shared potential. Although it would not be long before Hill District residents realized the failed promises of redevelopment, the Grill's reopening coincided with Pittsburgh's most ambitious construction projects to radically alter the city's public spaces. In 1953, the Lower Hill Redevelopment proposal was taking shape, and, when approved in 1955, forcibly relocated Hill District families and businesses in the name of collective progress. With support from minority voters, labor groups, and Republican business leaders, Lawrence won the November 1953 election for his third mayoral term and ensured his continued leadership of these projects.

The Lower Hill District, as the closest residential neighborhood to downtown, was most directly impacted by efforts to refashion Pittsburgh as an ideal modern city—efficient, clean, and economically prosperous. For Lawrence and his supporters, the clearing and reconstruction of the Lower Hill birthed a hopeful vision and potent symbol of Pittsburgh's future. For Hill District entrepreneurs Joe Robinson and his son William "Buzzy" of the Crawford Grill No. 2 and Anna "Birdie" Simmons Dunlap of the Hurricane Bar and Grill, their clubs offered alternative visions of Pittsburgh's modernity even as parts of their neighborhood were being demolished. Though minuscule in scale in comparison to the extensive city renewal projects, these clubs contributed to the construction of Pittsburgh's image as a modern city. While the Lower Hill's redevelopment dismantled the neighborhood's existing cultural infrastructure, Robinson's and Dunlap's businesses were predicated on the Hill's social networks and musical traditions that fostered a community of dedicated listeners and performers of jazz.

Part II focuses on the Grill No. 2 and the Hurricane Bar as important sites that emerged within the context of urban renewal and were notable for fostering a rare convergence of jazz performance, critical listening, and interracial audiences. As music scholar Travis Jackson reiterates in his work, stylistic developments in jazz are intimately linked to "developments in the *use of urban space*" (emphasis in original).[7] To better understand why jazz scenes grow and fade in specific locations requires a historical approach that "takes account of the built environment and human uses and representations of it as more than silent partners to presumably more vocal historical processes."[8] The French philosopher Henri Lefebvre's studies of urban life also provide a useful framework for examining ways in which Pittsburgh's urban renewal projects and the clubs' social scenes and physical spaces are embedded in the creative processes of jazz performance in midcentury Pittsburgh. The Grill and the Hurricane, as "uses" of the urban landscape, were symbolic spaces in which jazz musicians, audiences, and club owners cultivated ways of knowing the city.

Thinking about physical places as actors in social life requires delving into the complexities of the everyday within a landscape continuously reshaped by governmental policies and corporate interests. The way individuals experience a city is determined largely by where they live, work, and play, as well as the patterns of moving between these points. "Spatial practice," in Lefebvre's writings, centers on these quotidian routines as they are learned, repeated, and shared. It is "perceived" as one learns and repeats familiar pathways through the private and public spaces that link home and workplace. These contours of the urban environment are not passively created but rather "conceived" by those who study, theorize, and implement development plans that alter the city's paths, structures, and uses. This conceived space constitutes what Lefebvre calls "representations of space," which are produced by "scientists, planners, urbanists, technocratic subdividers and social engineers" and realized by those with the political will and economic power capable of implementing large-scale changes within short periods of time.[9]

In post-World War II Pittsburgh, few examples better illustrate Lefebvre's concept of "representations of space" than the Lower Hill Redevelopment project. With the support of federal public domain laws and an immensely powerful political and business coalition, Pittsburgh's renewal reified visions of modern life that required completely different uses of occupied land. Through spatial practice, inhabitants of the city perceive dominant, conceived space (such as the Lower Hill during its redevelopment) as buildings, sidewalks, roadways, and public transportation (or the lack thereof), which take on symbolic meaning over time. What Lefebvre calls "representational spaces" emerge from such spatial practice and comprise collective understandings of the conceived representations of space. Representational spaces embrace "the loci of passion, of action and of lived situations" and manifest the efforts to appropriate the "dominated" spaces of city planning.[10] One has only to invoke the memories associated with a familiar street, home, or business to understand how representational spaces give life to a city.

Figure 3.1 illustrates Lefebvre's "spatial triad"—how lived, conceived, and perceived spaces interrelate as applied to the social space of Hill District jazz clubs during the 1950s and 1960s. In this Lefebvrian model, officials draw master plans for a city while residents make sense of a place and carve out routes and spaces that, in turn, become imbued with shared memories and meanings. Overall, this dynamic process involving planners, builders, and residents constitutes a social space that is at once conceived and perceived as well as dominated and appropriated. In the Hill District, even as the Lower Hill was being demolished, many residents experienced jazz clubs as cultural landmarks on pathways from home to work. In these clubs, rhythms, both literal and figurative, shaped the daily lives of many Pittsburgh residents. The sound of these clubs extended outside the confines of the venue to sidewalks and streets, where they became embedded in the daily rhythms of city life. Patricia Parker-Reid, a *Pittsburgh Courier* staff member from 1958 to 1961, remembers:

> People would stand right beside the Grill on that side street [Elmore Street] and they'd have that door cracked right by the bandstand and you'd listen to see who was playing. If you'd hear someone like Chico Hamilton on drums, you'd just stand there for a while. You'd always check out the Grill and the Hurricane on your way home from work. Even if people didn't work on the Hill, they came through there to stand and see who was on that night. There would always be an unofficial doorman and you could just yell out the car window.[11]

Parker-Reid's description of the clubs gives insight into how a social space is produced in the triadic model; these clubs provided a means to navigate the city and linked work and home in a landscape undergoing rapid transformation. Important to keep in mind, however, is that the production of social space is not a process of equanimity, and powerful economic interests that determine an urban landscape on behalf of the public often do not align with the needs of the residents. This was regrettably the case for the Hill District in the mid-twentieth century. For psychologist Mindy Fullilove, who extensively studied the impact of the Lower Hill's redevelopment, appropriated spaces—or spatial practice that goes against the grain of conceived spaces—comprise an individual's "mazeways," which, when disrupted, can cause lasting mental and physical harm.[12]

The Grill and Hurricane are vivid examples of appropriated space. In addition to providing a place of respite for locals, the clubs were part of a larger network of businesses catering to Black clientele on a national scale. From 1937 to 1966, Hill District hotels, guesthouses, and clubs appeared in *The Negro Motorist Green Book*, a travel guide advertised as a means "for vacation without aggravation." *The Green Book* linked Black-owned or -friendly businesses throughout the nation to aid spatial practices that appropriated the country's highway system and gave symbolic meaning to a traveler's destination as well as the routes between them. The *Pittsburgh Courier* would often run short articles reflecting on visitors to the Hill from other parts of the country, and in effect, reinforce the importance of these networks of businesses. The 1946 *Courier* blurb "Westerners Make Stop in Pittsburgh" recounts one such journey:

> Raymond Pendavis of Chicago and Robert Halloway of San Francisco made a stopover in Pittsburgh en route to the Louis-Conn fight. While in the city they were house guests of Samuel Scott, owner of Scotty's Garage. The visitors were also

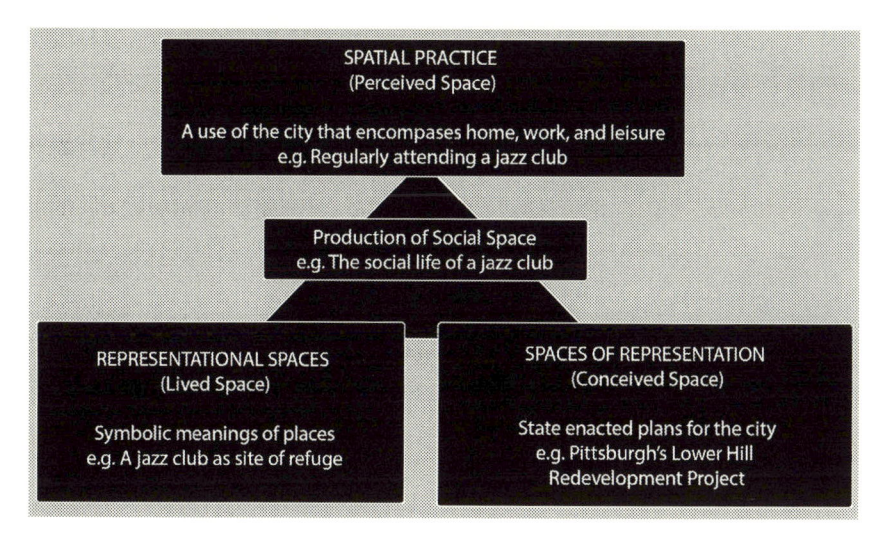

Figure 3.1. Henri Lefebvre's spatial triad as applied to the jazz clubs of Pittsburgh's Hill District.

entertained at Gus Greenlee's Crawford Grill No. 2. On their way back through town, the out-of-towners were entertained with a party at Counts, former M. C. at the Celebrity Club.[13]

The destination of the two travelers was the fight between Joe Louis and Billy Conn, a long-anticipated rematch that took place in New York City's Yankee Stadium on June 19, 1946. In 1941, in thirteen brutal rounds, Louis defeated Conn in the world heavyweight champion competition, one of many victories that made Louis a hero in Black communities throughout the nation. Louis's victory in the widely anticipated rematch drew hundreds of thousands of revelers to the streets of Harlem.[14] The *Courier's* tribute to the journey of two attendees reflects the symbolic value of their mobility and the importance of places such as the Grill that ensured their safe passage through racialized landscapes.

The role of clubs such as the Grill in structuring Black mobility should also be understood in the context of the nationwide federal program to overhaul transportation systems. The passage of the Federal-Aid Highway Act of 1956 under President Dwight D. Eisenhower and the subsequent creation of the Interstate Highway System represented a nationwide effort to improve driving conditions for truckers, commuters, and consumers. The construction of these highways in cities often took place in tandem with blight removal and the clearance of inner-city neighborhoods at a time when they were becoming increasingly populated by African Americans and lower-income Whites.[15]

Across the nation, mayors of urban centers sought increased mobility in and out of American cities that would simultaneously clear away densely populated

Figure 3.2. Charles "Teenie" Harris, American, 1908–1998, Car double-parked on Wylie Avenue, in front of Crawford Grill No. 2, Hill District, April 1967, black and white: Kodak Safety Film, H: 4 in. × W: 5 in. (10.20 × 12.70 cm), Carnegie Museum of Art, Pittsburgh: Heinz Family Fund, 2001.35.2366, © Carnegie Museum of Art, Charles "Teenie" Harris Archive.

communities and stem the exodus of the White middle class. As historians Eric Avila and Mark Rose state, these projects were guided by the hope that "[o]nce [a city's] downtown was easy to reach and looked safe and attractive . . . well-off urbanites would want to rent corporate space, move into upscale apartments, or perhaps just go shopping. . . ."[16] While clubs such as the Grill and Hurricane benefited from suburban visitors and interstate travelers, Hill District residents would witness the destruction of portions of their community to accommodate a new era in which pedestrian mobility was sacrificed for accessibility from the growing suburbs.

The representational spaces of jazz clubs—the associations and familiarities celebrated by patrons—emerged as both a defiance of the spatial politics of race in the United States and the active embrace of Black community formation. Musicologist Dale Chapman writes that jazz was often predicated on appropriated spaces, with jazz venues having "served as a crucial site for the negotiation of contested claims to urban space."[17] Mark Anthony Neal extends this notion of appropriation to a deeply rooted tradition in American Black society of creating a "covert social space" that "would provide the physical parameters in which to recover humanity, including the pursuit of pleasure, but also the space to develop more meaningful forms of resistance."[18] Chapman and Neal both offer the example of "rent parties," in which the private space of the home is appropriated to generate income to avoid eviction and to create shared spaces of leisure in segregated northern cities.

The emergence of the "Black Public Sphere," a collectivity "largely predicated on the realities of segregated housing" and reified in institutions as diverse as the Black church and the "juke joint," provided a means to critique and transform "notions of American democracy."[19] Neal's examination of "covert social spaces" echoes cultural theorist bell hooks's concept of "homeplace," which arises from Black women appropriating physical spaces to seek safety from the social spaces of racism. Such spaces of refuge are imbued with the radical power to forge new relationships with society at large. hooks's homeplace represents the convergence of physical location, spatial practice, and resistance in order to construct "a safe place where black people could affirm one another and by so doing heal many of the wounds inflicted by racist domination. We could not learn to love or respect ourselves in the culture of white supremacy, on the outside; it was there on the inside . . . that we had the opportunity to grow and develop, to nurture our spirits."[20]

These concepts of representational space, covert social space, and the homeplace undergird the concept of the "jazz house"—public performance venues, born of and against urban spatial and racial politics, in which musicians and audiences alike realized the collective potentials of jazz as both intellectual pursuit and spiritual catharsis. The jazz house is a physical place that marks one's path through the city. It is both a public venue and a social space apart from the public—a kind of homeplace in which dominant racial and class logics are suspended, at least to a degree, and where, in bell hooks's sense, there are potentials for growing, developing, and nurturing. In this respect, the jazz house inverts many of the associations and legal definitions of the "disorderly house" that were imposed on music venues, particularly black and tan cabarets of the 1920s.

The word "house" denotes a place in which the family as a social unit is produced. Policymakers, journalists, and law enforcement officials likely appreciated how these connotations of house and disorder would trigger deep-seated fears of social disarray in White mainstream society. As the term would later be appropriated in ballroom culture by queer people of color, "a 'house' does not [necessarily] signify an actual building," according to gender studies scholar Marlon Bailey; "rather, it represents the ways in which its members, who mostly live in various locations, view themselves and interact with each other as a family unit."[21] In mid-century Pittsburgh, the Grill and Hurricane attracted and helped form a community of diverse individuals who frequented the clubs as their house of jazz. This physical space not only mediated musical performances and fostered processes of listening, but also played a crucial role in forging deep social bonds within the Hill District and the city at large.

## The Lower Hill Redevelopment Project

In the summer of 1950, economist and photographer Roy Stryker set out with a team of photojournalists handpicked to chronicle a pivotal moment in Pittsburgh's history. City officials were poised to undertake one of the largest urban redevelopment programs in the US, which would reshape Pittsburgh's urban landscape and demographic makeup. Pittsburgh stood apart from other cities in realizing redevelopment projects because of a successful coalition between the private and public sectors. As Mayor David Lawrence's biographer Michael Weber points out, Pittsburgh's success drew delegations and reporters from throughout the country seeking "a magic formula for renewal."[22] What they found was a rare combination of business and political leaders who were able to forge cross-party alliances and reconcile personal and philosophical differences to envision and push through massive construction projects.

Pittsburgh at the time was choked by smoke from heavy industries, overrun by floods, crowded with substandard housing, and plagued by poor traffic patterns; an extensive urban redevelopment plan was the mayor's and business elites' cure for a "dying city."[23] In Lawrence's own words, spoken in 1960, the leaders of the redevelopment "had no book of rules to follow, no examples from which to learn," and so "the city itself was the laboratory."[24] Stryker, having implemented the federally funded Farm Security Administration's (FSA) nationwide photographic documentation of government responses to the Depression's human toll, was well prepared to take on the task of visualizing these ambitious changes. For the FSA project, he had carefully chosen photographers for creating the expansive documentation of American society, hoping to avoid the "sensationalism and condescension" of journalism that "reveled in poverty, criminality, and a penchant for the primitive."[25]

Stryker was enlisted by the Allegheny Conference on Community Development (ACCD) to build a visual archive for the newly established Pittsburgh Photographic Library (PPL). The PPL was envisioned to represent the city's varied community dynamics, social services, and redevelopment projects and drew on Stryker's devotion to photography's narrative power to create a citywide dialogue in a time of great change. From 1950 to 1953, Stryker's team of ten photographers contributed approximately eighteen thousand images, a small number of which were featured in exhibits and publications that sought to "educate Pittsburgh about itself" and visualize a model for urban renewal.[26]

The PPL and the images produced by Stryker's team were used to promote the ACCD's vision for a modernized Pittsburgh and the many public projects that collectively became known as the city's first Renaissance.[27] This visual campaign played an integral part in Pittsburgh's renewal, with the ACCD proclaiming that "Pittsburgh had the potential to become a case study of how a great city could rehabilitate itself"; furthermore, "promotional photographs could play a key role in focusing national attention on its improvements."[28]

Among those drawn to join the PPL team was a twenty-three-year-old photographer from rural Indiana named Clyde "Red" Hare. A curious newcomer to Pittsburgh and its cultural landscape, Hare was expected to create images that supported the ACCD's narrative of redevelopment as a beneficial, if not an inevitable, necessity. The difficulties of photographing the promise of change are apparent in Hare's 1952 photo (figure 3.3), which juxtaposes the dense low-lying buildings of the Lower Hill District with the nearly finished, geometric perfection of the aluminum company Alcoa's local headquarters. The use of a telephoto lens creates a visual trick where the aluminum structure takes on the appearance of a massive door closing on the sprawl of brick and wood buildings lining the Lower Hill's Webster and Wylie Avenues. Exceeding the frame of the photograph, the Alcoa building gives the impression of moving glacially from left to right, steadily replacing the old disorder of downtown's eastern edge with a new clean symmetry.

From the perspective of the ACCD's leaders, the image invokes a desire to extend Pittsburgh's business district and project an image of modernity and progress. For those in the Hill, this expansion represented the displacement and destruction of community, while also offering the promise of improved living and working conditions. Residents and organizations within the Hill had been calling on the city to intervene and address their neighborhood's housing crisis for years. In 1944, the Irene Kaufmann Settlement House organized the Hill District People's Forum to build a coalition of neighborhood figures who would address social issues such as housing, racial inequality, and waste management.[29] Led by the Forum's Social Action Committee and supported by the *Pittsburgh Courier*, citizens led a protest in Pittsburgh's City Council in 1946, demanding attention to the plight of impoverished Hill residents. A *Courier* photo essay, published in April 1946, documented living conditions marred by uncollected garbage, deteriorating structures, and the lack of running water. These conditions were compared to that of the Animal Rescue League, which the *Courier* quipped provided better accommodations to its dogs, horses, and cats.[30]

The ACCD's push for redevelopment was led by business magnate Richard King Mellon, who founded the organization with a coalition of regional Republican corporate leaders in 1943. Mellon saw redevelopment as a remedy for Pittsburgh's reputation as the nation's "smoky city"—a condition born of big industry but which threatened the city's growth as a business center. Mellon, one of four cousins who inherited the Mellon banking fortune, found it difficult to draw competitive business leaders to Pittsburgh during World War II because of problems in transportation, frequent flooding, constant smoke, and aging infrastructure. The city's image as crowded by working-class neighborhoods stained

Figure 3.3. Clyde Hare, American, 1927–2009, Overview: View of Alcoa Building and Hill District, 1952, gelatin silver print, H: 13 7/8 in. × W: 11 in. (35.24 × 27.94 cm), Carnegie Museum of Art, Pittsburgh: Gift of the artist, 1998.52.6 © Clyde Hare.

by the soot and smoke of steel mills and factories had made downtown anathema to the corporate elites who were "all too well aware of Pittsburgh's reputation as a city where automobile lights often were necessary at noon because of the smoke and where businessmen took an extra white shirt to work for a change before going to lunch."[31]

By 1949, Pittsburgh's wealthiest had joined with political leaders in a "corporatist-style regime" that was capable of realizing projects envisioned in the previous decade.[32] With extended powers of eminent domain granted by the Pennsylvania General Assembly's Urban Redevelopment Law of 1945, city officials could seize private property that they determined to be blighted or otherwise used in economically or socially undesirable ways. David Lawrence, Pittsburgh's mayor from 1946–1959, formed and chaired the Pittsburgh Urban Redevelopment Authority (URA) in 1946 and worked closely with the ACCD to implement the project.

In the spring of 1950, a crowd of two thousand gathered downtown with Lawrence and Pennsylvania Governor James Duff to watch a wrecking ball clear the first of many buildings as bands from the University of Pittsburgh and Carnegie Institute of Technology added to the fanfare. In the following decade, a thousand acres of businesses, warehouses, churches, and homes were cleared to make way for housing projects for those displaced from surrounding neighborhoods, highways connecting the city to the growing suburbs, the downtown high-rise Gateway Center business complex, and the Civic Arena.[33]

In 1955, after changes in housing legislation lifted restrictions on the uses of federally awarded redevelopment funds, the URA submitted a plan to the Housing and Home Finance Agency (HHFA) to redevelop the Lower Hill District. The neighborhood was in great need of rehabilitation of poor infrastructure and deteriorating buildings—physical remnants of the rapid industry-driven development that had sprung up in the late nineteenth century. Pre-Depression studies found that a third of the homes were either unfit for living or in need of major repair, with families sometimes sleeping six to a room.[34] The Depression compounded housing problems as widespread layoffs and pay decreases led to an increase in defaults on home mortgages. In the four decades leading up to its redevelopment, the Lower Hill saw the assessed values of properties decrease by 45 percent, which in turn hampered building maintenance.[35]

The 1945 Urban Redevelopment Law provided the legal conditions for acquiring and repurposing private property by broadly defining deteriorating living conditions as "blight." Blight could include premises with physical conditions deemed unsafe to children as well as properties that were unoccupied, tax delinquent, or otherwise posed a "public nuisance" due to violations of housing codes.[36] There is little in the 1945 law that details how properties are used other than addressing instances where properties enable "immoral and criminal purposes." Blight, so defined, was not a condition to be remedied, but rather a failure that had to be removed along with the underlying social landscape.

Redevelopment authorities showed little concern for replacing the Lower Hill's social and economic infrastructures, asserting that the "extension of the Central City as now represented by the adjoining Golden Triangle" would serve the city's modernization. Rather than rehabilitate the existing structures, the URA opted for complete demolition, stating that "the major objective of this project is the clearing of an area of massive blight which, due to a poorly designed street pattern,

# The Hill District

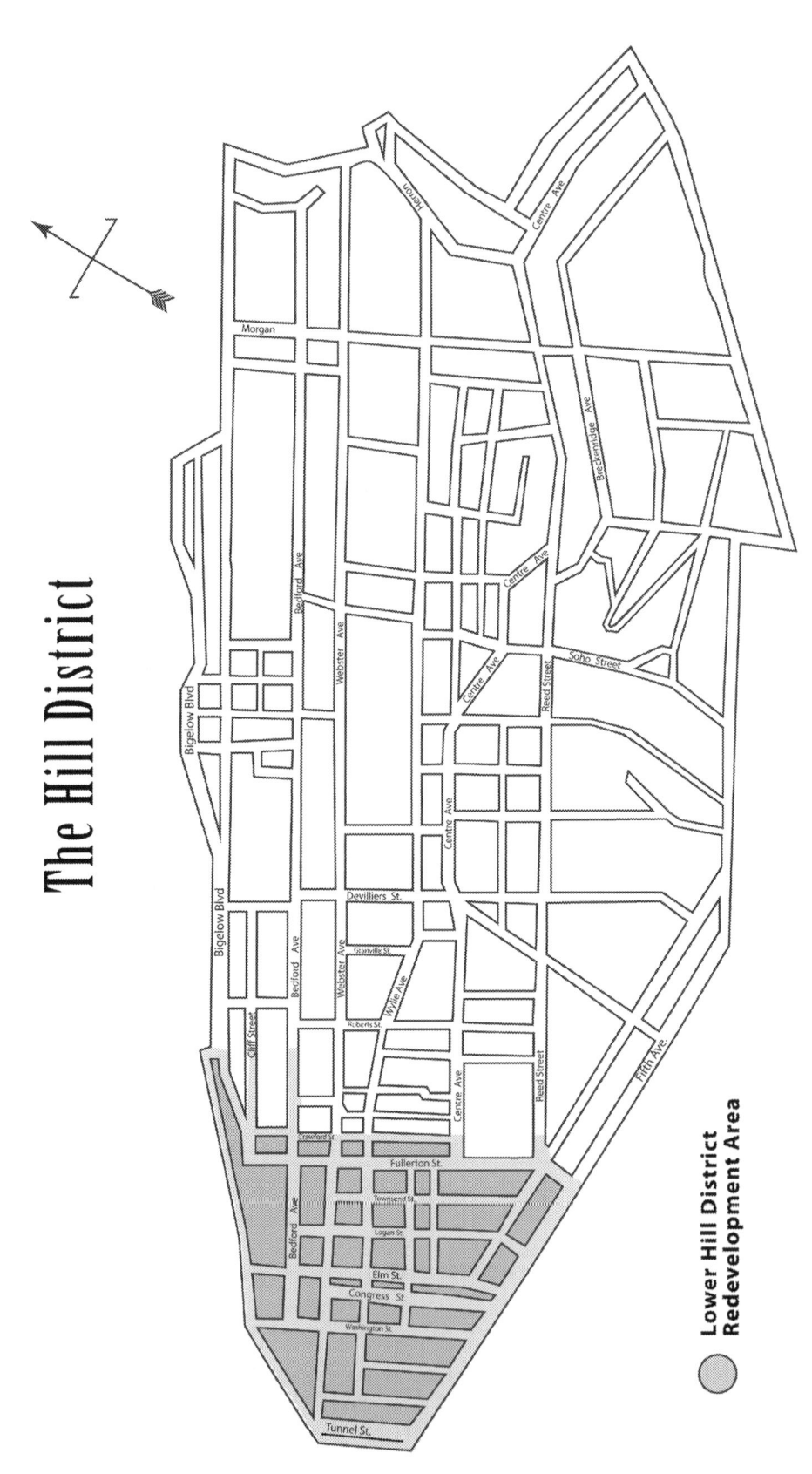

**Lower Hill District**
**Redevelopment Area**

Figure 3.4. The Hill District in 1950 with the Lower Hill Redevelopment Area marked in gray.[40]

Figure 3.5. Hill District Aerial View (ca. November 1967). An aerial photograph of Pittsburgh looking from the Middle Hill District towards the Lower Hill Redevelopment Area, Civic Arena, and Downtown. Harry Coughanour Jr. (1924–1989). Detre Library & Archives, Heinz History Center.

overcrowding, outmoded or completely lacking sanitary facilities, improper and mixed land use, has deteriorated beyond the point where rehabilitation would be conceivable."[37] A telling statement from the proposal frames the Lower Hill's problems as a collective responsibility to eradicate rather than to resolve: "Admittedly, it is a costly project. At the same time, it would be worth all its costs to secure the clearance of the Lower Hill District as it stands and to free the community from the burdens which such a concentrated area of sub-standard housing and depressed living conditions impose upon our common society and upon our individual conscience."[38]

In this statement, it is unclear whether it is the Lower Hill community that will be freed from the burden of poor living conditions or the business community that will be freed from the burden of the Lower Hill neighborhood's occupation of a coveted urban space. The use of the phrase "our common society" implies the right of the redevelopment's leaders to determine how the city best benefits an imagined community. City officials quickly approved the plan, setting into motion the city's largest urban planning project in both size and budget. Between 1956 and 1959,

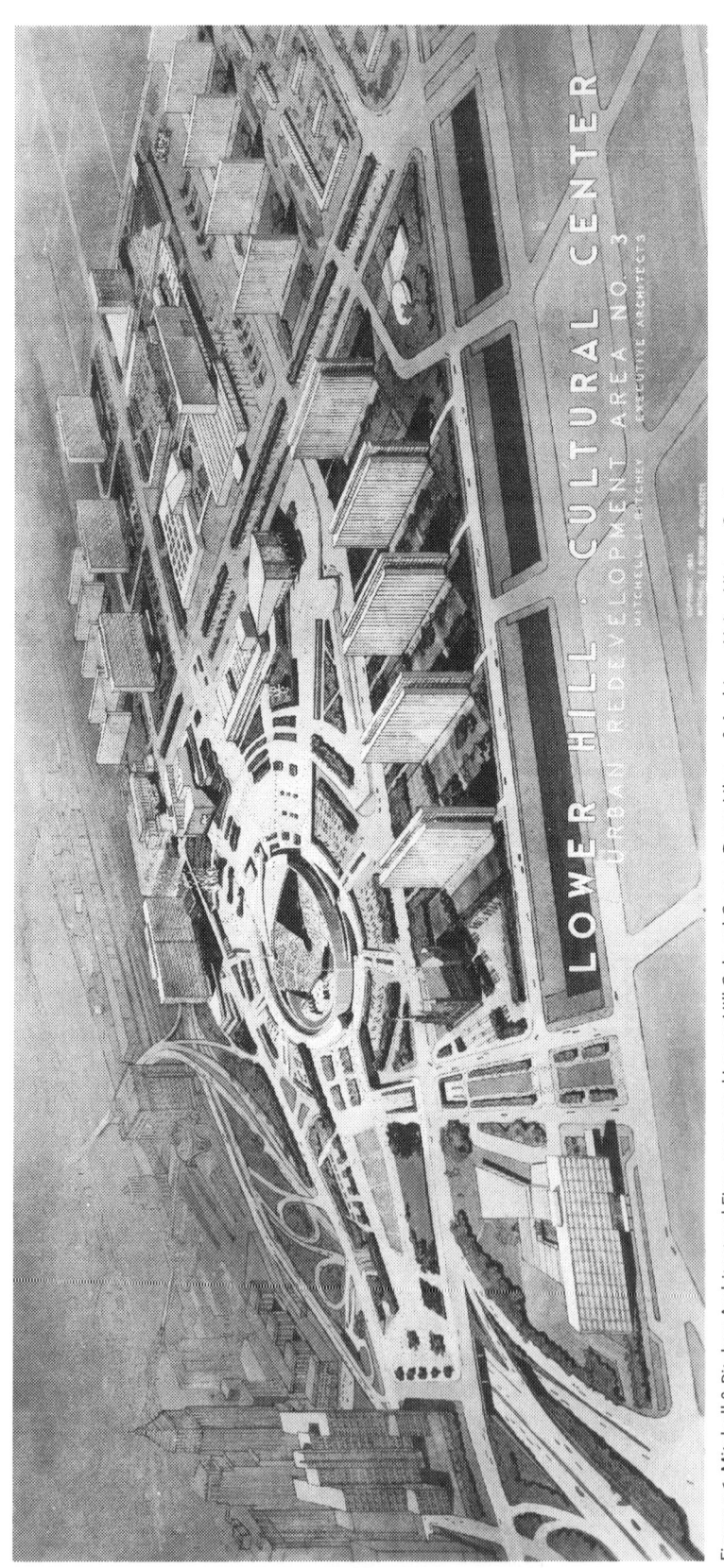

Figure 3.6. Mitchell & Ritchey Architectural Firm, proposed Lower Hill Cultural Center. Detre Library & Archives, Heinz History Center.

105 acres, including 1,324 buildings, were cleared, and an estimated eight thousand residents comprised of 1,239 Black and 312 White families were displaced.[39]

The redevelopment plan, in providing "new life to a dying section of the city" and extending the city's "Golden Triangle" for Pittsburgh's richest and the most powerful, reflected the spatial philosophy of the Modernist Movement, epitomized in Swiss French architect Le Corbusier's conceptions of the city. Lefebvre views Le Corbusier's logic as an attempt to align the rhythms of nature and everyday life dependent on an architectural landscape of preordained uses:

> As for Le Corbusier, as philosopher of the city, he describes the relationship between the urban dweller and dwelling with nature, air, sun, and trees, with cyclical time and the rhythms of the cosmos. To this metaphysical vision, he adds an unquestionable knowledge of the real problems of the modern city, a knowledge which gives rise to a planning practice and an ideology, a functionalism, which reduces urban society to the achievement of a few predictable and prescribed functions laid out on the ground by the architecture.[41]

Lefebvre's criticism of the reductive celebration of a few key pieces of architecture finds rightful targets in the Civic Arena and surrounding area. As the center of Pittsburgh's development plans, the Civic Arena promised the technical feat of mediating nature to the benefit of city residents: "The roof of the arena will pivot, permitting a starlight setting for the Civic Light Opera and other outdoor events when the weather is good, and folding quickly into a weathertight dome when it rains."[42] As Lefebvre argues about urban spatial rights, "The claim to nature and the desire to enjoy it [by some] displace the right [of others] to the city."[43]

Conflicting spatial logics emerge in comparing an aerial view of the Hill (figure 3.5) with the 1953 Lower Hill Redevelopment sketch by Pittsburgh architects James Mitchell and Dahlen Ritchey of the firm Mitchell and Ritchey (figure 3.6). In the architects' attempts to claim nature, the redevelopment model shows the replacement of the neighborhood's mixed-use patterning of street life, houses, and commercial properties with repetitive office and high-rise apartments. The extension of home and workspace upward and away from the street eliminates street-level neighborhood interactions. The regimented green spaces in the sketch hint at traces of nature that are to be viewed from windows and passing pedestrians. The arena, oriented toward the sky, is bordered by an expansive parking lot and concrete walkways that facilitate the passage of people and cars to and from the area while isolating the Hill's remaining business district from downtown. The boundaries of what the Urban Redevelopment Authority termed "our common society" emerge from this use of urban space along lines of class and race.[44]

Urban redevelopment, aimed at reducing poverty in the city, further isolated the Hill District and displaced businesses and residents, which precipitated the shift from an ethnically and racially diverse neighborhood into a largely working-class Black community. Guitarist and Pittsburgh native George Benson found the resulting displacement had benefits for those who received new housing yet carried the burden of a lost community. Benson, who had grown up in the Lower Hill, remembers that his early childhood home lacked electricity and required ice deliveries in the summer and coal in the winter. Benson reflected on the hardships he faced: "We didn't know what poor meant. We just lived our lives, and it was a good life, and being in the ghetto didn't matter one bit." Moving to new housing projects a short distance away in the Middle Hill, Benson found the new accommodations "affordable, safe, respectable housing for underprivileged families. The building was new, the hallways were pristine, and the apartments were spotless. For us, it was like we moved to heaven." Even so, Benson lamented the destruction of his home and street: "Nobody would call our neighborhood paradise, but it was our neighborhood, and when somebody takes something that's yours, regardless of how much you like or dislike it, it hurts."[45]

Displaced Black residents also moved east to Homewood and East Liberty neighborhoods, which had the effect of transporting impoverished communities farther from downtown, while "white flight" led to a general exodus from the city in a pattern that would be repeated across the country in the years to follow. The Lower Hill's community was once a dynamic mix of African American, Italian, Syrian, Lebanese, Irish, and Jewish families and businesses, and provided social conditions unique in the city. As Italian American drummer Chuck Spatafore remembers:

> I was born in the Hill and I think that's where I got my sense or feel for the blues because I used to go to revivals up the street from where I lived. Also, there was a Black church right on our corner on Bedford and Elm. We'd be playing outside and would hear the music and go in. It really gave you some sort of roots and direction. Where else would I have heard that type of music?[46]

Physical landmarks such as churches are integral to building a "mazeway" or collection of routine movements through which individuals engage their environment. Social psychologist Mindy Fullilove argues that a mazeway functions as an "external system of protection" that maintains a balance between the individual and their environment.[47] What Lefebvre termed "spatial practice" and resulting "representational space" are discussed by Fullilove from a psychologist's perspective of how individuals understand their relationship to social and physical environments. Constructing a mazeway is a spatial practice that involves incorporating symbolic places as they are registered by the collective psyche of the inhabitants. Disrupting these mazeways causes "root shock," which "disperses people to all the directions of the compass" resulting in a "profound emotional upheaval that destroys the working model of the world that had existed in the individual's head."[48]

Redevelopment plans failed to account for the importance of places for constructing the memories and social infrastructures that constitute a community. As Fullilove poetically states, "The cues from place dive under conscious thought and awaken our sinews and bones, where days of our lives have been recorded."[49] The displacement of eight thousand residents, about a fifth of the Hill's 1950 population of 38,110, compromised the community's mazeways as families looked for new homes and places of business, worship, and leisure spots.[50] Spataforc recalls how the city's cultural landscape was quickly destroyed as buildings fell and families resettled:

> Most of the Italians and Lebanese moved to Brookline, Beechview, and Dormont. I moved north. For the most part they moved in groups. The [Franciscan] church in the Lower Hill—St. Peter's—was torn down and it was political because they kept Epiphany Catholic Church. St. Peter's was a beautiful church. I was baptized there. There was an old woman [protesting] with a sign that said, "Save St. Peters." They taught Italian there when I was a kid.[51]

A pattern of resegregation emerged in resettlement that further entrenched racial divides in Pittsburgh.[52] Only a few of the Lower Hill's White families relocated within the Hill District; most chose to build communities in the city's suburbs. Many Lower Hill Black families found improved housing in projects such as Addison Terrace, Allequippa Terrace, and Bedford Dwellings.[53] By the late 1960s, the Hill District found that renewal had not delivered on its promise. Fears that the development would continue throughout the Hill to join downtown's business center with the University of Pittsburgh and Oakland neighborhood were met with protests by the remaining Hill residents on the corner of Fullerton and Centre Avenues, overlooking the Civic Arena. What would later be named Freedom Corner became a symbolic border that represented both the Hill District's struggle for spatial justice and gradual isolation from the city.[54] It was in this context of looming destruction and existential threat that the neighborhood's own business leaders Joe Robinson and Birdie Dunlap created their jazz house—a place of refuge, recharge, creative gatherings, and social relations.

# Chapter 4

# LIFE IN THE JAZZ HOUSE

The Crawford Grill No. 2 and Hurricane Bar

Pittsburgh's "Renaissance" of the 1950s and 1960s altered the physical landscape of the Hill District and disrupted the patterns of everyday life for many of its inhabitants. City developers admitted the Hill renewal led to the "disruption of daily habits" but insisted that the "promise of living on a more humane, spacious scale" and increasing land values would justify the experience of displacement.[1] For many Hill District residents, the sounds and sights of buildings falling were felt emotionally for years. Artist and Hill resident Carlos F. Peterson recalled, "Over the span of 16 years, I lived at 15 different addresses throughout the Hill, a love/hate relationship at best, never truly accepting the neighborhood as home. The Lower Hill was both a playground and plaything for me, but coming of age there during its downfall made it seem that I was born into a bad time, conditioned by it, raised by it."[2]

The visceral experiences of destruction also emphasized the importance of remaining spaces for maintaining a Black public sphere. English professor Derek Handley notes that because "formal places for deliberation on city matters that affected African Americans" were inaccessible to them, it led to the development of informal sites of public discourse within Black communities.[3] Jazz clubs provided a distinct place of leisure, entertainment, friendship, and quarrels where matters that affected the patrons could find expression among intimates and strangers.

Urban redevelopment in Pittsburgh coincided with the rise in popularity of the Hill District's most celebrated jazz clubs: the Crawford Grill No. 2 and the Hurricane Bar & Grill. As destinations for audiences from throughout the region, these clubs socially connected the Hill District to the city at large during a time of its otherwise increasing isolation. They also became celebrated locations in which to hear touring jazz artists. Focal points in the Hill's nightlife scene, these clubs fostered welcoming social atmospheres for music lovers and socialites alike. The Grill, located on the corner of Wylie and Elmore, and the Hurricane, located several blocks away on Centre Avenue, were important institutions that contributed to the social, economic, and cultural cohesion of the Hill during a time of upheaval. Performances in these spaces extended beyond that of interaction between musicians to include active listening by audiences, the musicians' negotiations of the club's physical and acoustic space, and the shared experience of urban renewal that was taking place immediately outside the clubs. These jazz houses were in fact informal sites of public discourse where Hill residents could openly engage in discussions of what was happening in their neighborhood.

The Crawford Grill No. 2 and Hurricane Bar were by no means the only small clubs to feature jazz in the Hill District during the 1950s and 1960s. Along Wylie and Centre Avenues, there were also the Ellis Hotel's Shangri-La Lounge, The Flamingo Hotel's Joyce Bryant Room, The Granville Hotel's Pine Room, Mutt's Hut, and Mason's Bar, among others. But along with the Grill, the Hurricane became a primary destination in the nightlife circuit, drawing many of the same socialites and dedicated listeners.

While the Grill was the most celebrated place for hearing the leading touring jazz artists epitomized by hard bop piano trios (e.g., The Wynton Kelly Trio) and saxophone- and trumpet-led quartets and quintets (e.g., Art Blakey's Jazz Messengers), the Hurricane shaped its identity by focusing on trios and quartets that included an organist. For this reason, *Courier* writers dubbed it the "house of organs." The complimentary music programming of these two clubs provided an exciting pairing with the diversity of artists that they collectively featured, drawing listeners from throughout the region. The few touring jazz artists who did play at both clubs, such as saxophonists Sonny Stitt and Lou Donaldson, had stylistic approaches that traversed hard bop modernisms while remaining rooted in the blues and R&B. Those who attended the Hurricane came to expect the lush sound of the organ paired with drums and soulful saxophonists. Organist Gene Ludwig remembers playing at the Hurricane: "Just swing. It didn't matter what you played as long as it was swinging. If you didn't swing, you wouldn't last."[4]

### The Hurricane Bar and Grill (1953–1970): Pittsburgh's House of Organs

The Hurricane held its grand opening celebration on November 5, 1953, three months after the Grill's celebrated reopening (see chapter 3). Charles "Teenie" Harris's photograph of the night (figure 4.1) shows the club owners Anna Simmons "Birdie" Dunlap and her husband William ("Shine") among the crowd

Figure 4.1. Charles "Teenie" Harris, American, 1908–1998, Crowd in opening night of Hurricane Club including Shine Dunlap on left wearing dark bow tie at bar, Gertie next to him wearing scarf around neck, Red in left foreground, and Anna Simmons "Birdie" Dunlap wearing light suit in foreground, with Ruby Young Trio performing in background, November 1953, black and white: Kodak Safety Film, H: 4 in. × W: 5 in. (10.20 × 12.70 cm), Carnegie Museum of Art, Pittsburgh: Heinz Family Fund, 2001.35.1166 © Carnegie Museum of Art, Charles "Teenie" Harris Archive.

while organist Ruby Young, trumpeter Chuck Austin, and bassist Bobby Boswell perform on the raised stage behind the bar. Though the business was a joint venture, Birdie took on the role of manager who, as *Courier* city editor and journalist Frank Bolden later recalled, "patrolled [the] place like a drill sergeant."[5]

Musicians and audience members recall a tough, professional, and elegant woman who rarely took a drink, smoked, or cursed. Her personality and presence were inseparable from the Hurricane's reputation as a warm and welcoming environment, though she did not tolerate behavior that she felt was inappropriate. Men who were being disrespectful to women or who used profanity were kicked out. Though there was never a cover charge, she may have removed those who were not purchasing drinks or food to make space for more lucrative customers. Dunlap was personally involved with seating, serving, and generally catering to her patrons. Relaxed and attentive in the photograph, she stands with the menu in hand, taking orders from a packed booth. At the same time, she looks over her shoulder to survey other patrons, possibly calculating where to seat new arrivals.

Shine, dressed in a tuxedo and sitting at the bar, observes Harris taking the photo of the scene while his wife remains engrossed in her tasks.

As with the Grill's founders, Joe Robinson and William "Gus" Greenlee, Dunlap was a popular Hill District native. Born in 1900, she had family roots in the city, reaching back to 1831.[6] At fifteen, she married her first husband, Bill Herbert, who worked for Sellers McKee Hall, an early promoter of Black music in Pittsburgh.[7] When Hall left for New York City in the early 1930s, Dunlap and her husband continued booking local concerts featuring renowned Black artists, including Louis Armstrong as well as Chick Webb's orchestra with vocalist Ella Fitzgerald. After her husband's death in 1938, Dunlap ran an after-hours club in the Hill and met Shine Dunlap, a handsome manager of the nearby Ritz Club, whose business dealings were entwined with the neighborhood's prostitution underworld. Shine and Birdie fell in love and married in 1945 after Shine promised to leave behind illicit occupations. The couple traveled often, and it was during a trip to Detroit that they visited a bar called Sonny Wilson's where musicians performed above and behind the bar—an arrangement that, Dunlap noticed, kept the listeners' attention focused on where they were more likely to buy drinks. Dunlap dove into building a successful business that reflected her own social values and musical tastes and recalls that her husband "left everything to me."[8]

Dunlap's vision for the Hurricane centered on creating an environment that intertwined the formality of high-class dining with the informality of neighborhood bars. Trumpeter Chuck Austin remembers that, in 1953, the Hurricane was a "novel new club" that distinguished itself with its mid-century modernist interior design and layout. The *Courier*'s promotional ads and reviews built anticipation for the grand opening with descriptions of the venue's "cozy air" and restaurant specializing in "beef steaks, milk-fed chicken, tasty shrimps and chops."[9] Columnist George F. Brown, who reported on Grill No. 2's reopening only a few months earlier, reviewed the Hurricane and celebrated its "exciting modern color scheme, the keyhole bar, the elevated bandstand, the cozy booths and the tete-a-tete tables" as well as the draperies that "lend a glamorous effect and class."[10] Brown concludes his review with a caveat for those who may construe the upscale setting as elitist or exclusive: "The Hurricane is a first-class spot for first-class people, but that doesn't mean that the place is trying to be snobbish. All people are welcome to come in and enjoy themselves in the way they wish to be entertained."[11] Brown's coded language positions the Hurricane as "first-class" to attract middle-class patrons seeking entertainment sans a "snobbish" environment that would discourage a more participatory social comportment.

By reconciling various spaces of leisure, the Hurricane grew from a tradition of Black public life and leisure. As Black studies scholar Katrina Hazzard-Gordon notes, Black-owned nightclubs that emerged after the Prohibition Era continued a tradition of "patrons as participants" from "juke joints," which were intimate and semiprivate places for drinking, dancing, eating, and gambling that developed in southern rural Black communities.[12] In Black nightclubs, patrons were both participants and audiences of a staged performance. Unlike White-owned venues, these clubs welcomed Black patrons and accommodated interracial socializing. Dunlap did not charge an entrance fee or set food and drink prices to discourage working-class patrons, ensuring that, within the limits she established, most would find a pleasant environment that they could regularly attend.

Dunlap created a culture of socializing and listening that both suited her personal tastes and realized her vision of a lucrative small business. She remembered, "I knew it would be a tough pull. It wasn't a large place, but it was up-to-date. The main thing was to be there every night and treat the people right."[13] Dunlap created a social environment that drew a steady stream of patrons and enough revenue to run the place and pay musicians. She worked constantly to maximize profits. As frequent client and former *Courier* staff member Patricia Parker-Reid remembered:

> No matter how crowded it was, [Birdie would] say, "Come on in! Plenty of room." You could hardly move your elbow and the waitresses were instructed by Birdie that someone had to be drinking something at all times. You could drink pop or liquor or whatever but she wanted to make sure that as fast as you finished that glass, she'd say, "Let me clean up, honey. You want something else?" She was a hustler. You were never turned down from going in there.[14]

Chuck Austin remembers that although she was always a courteous host, Birdie "had a little way of catering to money. If you sat around and weren't drinking nothing, then you weren't going to occupy this space" that could be used by a paying customer.[15] Because space was limited, Dunlap was known for introducing unacquainted patrons and seating them together in the small booths. On particularly busy nights, patrons would have to "sit with whoever Birdie sat you with. People would come from [the suburban neighborhood of] Mount Lebanon and she'd squeeze a fly in between a glass if she could. She'd make the people from Mount Lebanon sit with the guy from Wylie Avenue [in the Hill District] and it didn't make any difference to her as long as she made a buck."[16]

Regulars and performers alike learned that Dunlap's rule was absolute when it came to admitting patrons, though she was also accommodating to those who valued the music. Guitarist Tony Janflone Sr. remembers Dunlap allowing comedian Richard Pryor to perform during a twenty-minute intermission after he agreed to "keep it clean." After a few minutes of his act, "[t]hese two guys in suits came on either side of him and his feet never touched the floor. They just threw him out."[17] However, when aspiring underaged musicians sought out the clubs to listen to their heroes in person, Dunlap would occasionally accommodate their enthusiasm. Janflone recalls going to the Hurricane as a teenager and being confronted by Dunlap, who generally discouraged minors: "She wasn't going to let me in and I said, 'Tell me where to go to hear this kind of music and I'll go. I know I'm underage but I'm not underage to the point where I don't want to hear this kind of music.' So she gave me a big hug and I could go in there."[18] Pittsburgh legend George Benson also recalls Dunlap's support of his interest in the Hurricane as a place of musical education:

> When you'd step [into the Hurricane] they had a little cove right in back of the door. As a young person I used to stand there listening to music. I was too young to come in the place and I didn't have any money to spend anyway. I guess I was about fifteen years old when I started sneaking into that little cove. People knew who I was. I was always famous in Pittsburgh from the time I was a little boy and so Birdie would come over and say, "Stay in this spot here! Don't move from that spot!" That gave me the opportunity to hear some of the most talented people in America. Birdie's was very, very important as to my musical growth. I got the chance to see what it was like for musicians [such as Jimmy Smith and Johnny Hammond Smith] who were recording artists and I watched their fame progress. That's how I learned my art, by listening to what they were doing and checking out how they lived.[19]

Birdie chose a close friend, organist Ruby Young, to be the club's first resident artist. Young, an active member of Local 471 of the American Federation of Musicians, had worked floor shows with Pittsburgh drummer James Minor's band, Honey Boy Minor and His Buzzing Bees.[20] Though she had also worked extensively as a solo pianist and organist, Young hired Austin and bassist Bobby Boswell to accompany her for her stay at the Hurricane. Austin recalls that the group's sound was modeled after that of trumpeter Jonah Jones, whose understated interpretations of swing standards had wide popular appeal during the mid-1950s.

Austin, who had only been playing professionally for five years in the city, did not consider himself a modern jazz trumpeter. "In my early days I would play the melody and I was a good ballad player and had a big sound, pretty and all that. That's why Ruby used me. But in terms of being hip, I didn't know nothing about that."[21] Austin recalled that music in the Hurricane's early years was not the club's central focus but rather a complement to the décor, food, and ambiance. He reflected humbly on opening the Hurricane: "We really didn't draw that much [of a crowd] because the music really wasn't that great." Young's repertoire was comprised of popular songs and ballads such as "Indian Love Call," a sentimental love song from the 1920s Broadway musical *Rose-Marie* that became widely known through later film adaptations. Austin recalls that the focus on instrumental renditions of popular songs with little attention to improvisation, new arrangements, or newer compositions "was a drag for Boswell because he wanted to play [modern jazz]."

Young stayed at the Hurricane for eight months, eventually replacing Austin and Boswell with guitarist Calvin King and saxophonist Leroy Brown, who had recently finished an extended stay at the Crawford Grill with his quartet. In June 1954, the trio featured Pittsburgh trumpeter Roy Eldridge, who was home visiting family. Eldridge, famed sideman with the big bands of Gene Krupa, Artie Shaw, and Benny Goodman, was an important force in the stylistic development of jazz. A powerful player, he appears to have taken a restrained approach at the Hurricane: "Roy plays plenty of muted stuff and when he plays open horn he doesn't blast and this goes over [well] in the Hurricane."[22] The *Courier*'s review reveals the importance of the synergy between musicians and the audience as well as appealing to listeners who wanted a place where the music did not dominate the social environment. This dynamic would later shift as the Hurricane became a club known for the powerful and driving sounds of soul jazz and rhythm and blues.

Once the Hurricane's popularity was established, Dunlap began hiring out-of-town groups in July 1954. The first group was led by a relatively unknown Philadelphia organist who went by the name "King Solomon" and was accompanied by guitarist and vocalist Rose Lehman and tenor saxophonist Barry Calimese (figure 4.2). The *Courier* played up the group's reputation by citing a string of dates at northeastern clubs, including the Arlington Inn (Brooklyn), Pep's and Emmerson's (Philadelphia), Club Royal (Columbus), Carr's Beach (Annapolis), Comedy Club (Baltimore), and Del Rio Club (Binghamton).[23] Through the rest of 1954 and 1955, Dunlap introduced rhythm and blues groups featuring musicians such as Eddie Winters (drums), Ernie Ransom (guitar), Jackie Davis (organ), Buddy Griffin (piano) and Claudia Swann (vocals), Lindy Ewell (drums), Robert Banks (organ), Johnny Sparrow (tenor saxophone), and Al King (baritone saxophone).[24]

Songs such as Griffin and Swann's infectious vocal shuffle "I Wanna Hug Ya, Kiss Ya, Squeeze Ya," Sparrow's hard-swinging saxophone feature "When Your Lover Has Gone," and Davis's big band-inspired organ romp "It's the Talk of the Town" represented the diversity of styles that comprised rhythm and blues in the post-WWII years and signaled the Hurricane's shift to featuring foot-tapping music. However, a review by *Courier* journalist Hazel Garland shows that some listeners much preferred the more subdued sounds of musicians such as Johnny Sparrow over the hard-hitting soulful approach of saxophonist Wilburt "Red" Prysock, the brother of singer Arthur Prysock. Of Prysock, who would become a favorite at the Hurricane, Garland writes, "After listening attentively for an hour or so, I've come to the conclusion that this music isn't new at all. It's just the same old jazz and blues played with a louder but different beat. Take my word for it and don't get excited. This frantic so-called new music isn't really new."[25] Responding to criticism, she wrote a week later in her column, "I don't 'dig' it. So

Figure 4.2. Charles "Teenie" Harris, American, 1908–1998, Band with two women, possibly including Pola Roberts on drums, and two men, including one playing organ inscribed "King Solomon," and other playing saxophone, performing on stage at Hurricane Club, c. 1953–1965, black and white: Kodak Safety Film, H: 4 in. × W: 5 in. (10.20 × 12.70 cm), Carnegie Museum of Art, Pittsburgh: Heinz Family Fund, 2001.35.10099, © Carnegie Museum of Art, Charles "Teenie" Harris Archive.

perhaps I'm not 'hep.' But I really 'flipped my lid' over Johnny Sparrow's outfit at the Hurricane. Now he plays GOOD music. You can carry on a conversation as you listen to him. He's terrific."[26]

With its small space designed to accommodate as many seated patrons as possible, the Hurricane was not a place for dancing, yet it became renowned for featuring music driven by dance rhythms and high energy. Guitarist Tony Janflone remembers crowded nights when patrons filled the aisles between tables: "When [the band] played, everybody would sway back and forth. I'm not into dancing but you had to move because everybody else was. You were forced into it."[27] By focusing on bands rooted in rhythm and blues, the Hurricane invoked the culture and sensibilities of the Chitlin' Circuit, what Mark Anthony Neal describes as formal and informal music venues that gave rise to a culture of listening, dancing, and performing in Black communities.[28]

The environment of collective dancing drew on traditions of the juke joint where "core black culture—its food, language, community, fellowship, mate selection, music, and dance—found sanctuary."[29] At the heart of the aesthetics of the

Chitlin' Circuit were the sound of the tenor saxophone and Hammond B-3 organ, instruments capable of expressing a wide range of timbre and vocal qualities. Neal notes that small groups, epitomized by trios comprised of saxophone, organ, and drums, embodied "the economic and spatial sensibilities of the Chitlin' Circuit" where limits on space and budgets led to the development of a big band sound in a small package.

As a Black-owned club that was part of a touring network of small venues that featured Black performers, the Hurricane was a Chitlin' Circuit venue, though Pittsburgh musicians generally refrained from describing it as such. Saxophonist Harold Young emphasizes that the Hurricane was distinguished from the local Chitlin' Circuit, which included a string of low-paying and largely working-class clubs "up and down the rivers in Sewickley, Beaver Falls, Rankin, and Braddock."[30] Drummer Roger Humphries notes that the term "Chitlin' Circuit" was often used by musicians to describe venues that may not have been "as classy, where the décor inside wouldn't be the hippest or the most expensive, where maybe the ventilation wasn't as good and you could smell the grease" but where the music was cathartic.[31]

While the Hurricane was by no means a working-class bar, Humphries said it could be considered a "chitlin' joint" because "there was a whole lot of soul in there."[32] Chuck Austin associated the Chitlin' Circuit with southern networks of venues but admitted that the term could be applied to northern segregated tour circuits of Black-owned and patronized clubs in small towns around Pittsburgh.[33] Saxophonist Lou Stellute also distinguishes the use of "Chitlin' Circuit" to describe a southern Black entertainment network but associates it with the Black musical culture prevalent at the Hurricane.[34] Tony Janflone explains how the Chitlin' Circuit network extended across the northeast:

> The actual circuit was Pittsburgh, Washington DC, Baltimore, Philadelphia, Newark, and there were a couple scattered gigs in Connecticut. They would also call it the 500-mile circle. You could work all year but the only way you got into places like Newark's Key Club and the Cadillac Club was in the winter because they didn't want to take the chance of hiring big names and not being able to pay. You had to be a headliner to get a gig there in the summer.[35]

Dunlap's creation of a performance space that bridged the musical aesthetics of working-class Chitlin' Circuit venues and social sensibilities of the rising post-War Black middle-class illustrates the importance she placed on building a successful business that fostered the development of Black musical cultures. Dunlap's regular bookings of women instrumentalists also indicate a vision of nightlife as a place where women instrumentalists would play leading roles in the development of jazz and rhythm and blues. Following Ruby Young's extended stay after opening the Hurricane, Dunlap continued booking women jazz organists, including Sarah McLawler (1926–2017), "Lady Byron" Evelyn Childress (1930–2004), Shirley Scott (1934–2002), Dee Dee Ford (1936–1972), and Rhoda Scott (b. 1938). Dunlap's decades of experience in music promotion would have familiarized her with the plight of women entertainers relegated to chorus lines and marketed as "Creole beauties" in black and tan cabarets.

On the Hurricane stage, women organists could develop their profiles as bandleaders, promote their records, and hone their craft to compete in a field dominated by men. Shirley Scott, who was featured at the Hurricane at least six times between 1957 and 1965, was praised by *Courier* columnist Phyl Garland as "one of the most outstanding" stylists in an expanding field of jazz organists.[36] For Garland, Scott's approach was distinguished by her "sweet, subtle touch so elusive to those intoxicated by power at their finger-tips," an indirect dig at the characteristic bravado of male organists and claim to feminine prerogatives in jazz.

Dunlap's commitment to presenting a wide range of organ groups fostered a space in which listeners witnessed the subtle aesthetic convergences and divergences between rhythm and blues and jazz. Groups such as the Crazy Chris Columbo Quintet (figure 4.3), which played at least ten week-long engagements, and the Jolly Jax (figure 4.4), which Birdie booked at least thirteen times, brought a steady stream of hard-swinging blues, doo-wop, soul, and R&B. Columbo, a drummer known for his work with Louis Jordan and Wild Bill Davis, formed a quintet to feature his powerful performances.[37] Columbo's showmanship included sitting on a custom-built drum stool made from a motorcycle seat fixed to a spring, which allowed him to literally bounce to the beat of his drumming. His 1957 song "Oh Yeah" captures the energy of these performances as emphatic statements of an urban blues aesthetic. The song begins with Columbo yelling, "Oh yeah?" as a taunting response to an unspoken assertion or possibly to encourage the band to keep up with the drummer's insatiable energy. The band responds with an insistent "oh yeah!" and the call-and-response pattern is repeated until Columbo's ecstatic "oh YEAAAAAAH!" launches them into the song. Tenor saxophonist Jimmy Tyler's solo, drenched in full-throated screams and blues invocations, is a convincing statement of defiance to any who doubt his dedication to the music. These performances were honed in great venues of blues, jazz, and rhythm and blues, such as Atlantic City's Club Harlem. Columbo, who led Club Harlem's orchestra from the 1940s to its closing in 1978, relied on a heavy backbeat style unencumbered by virtuosic displays.[38]

The Jolly Jax was a Baltimore trio comprised of brothers Herman, Carroll, and Jerome Hill who promoted their act as "3 Talented Brothers who play SIX INSTRUMENTS!"[39] The group incorporated comedy, dance, and music into floor show-type revues and built a strong following at the Hurricane with its unusual and zany performance. The band peppered each set with antics such as

Figure 4.3. Charles "Teenie" Harris, American, 1908–1998, Danny Turner playing saxophone in front of a sign that reads, "Another Great Krazy Kris Kolumbo at the Hurricane and His Gentlemen of Swing" at the Hurricane Club, 1603 Centre Avenue, Hill District, c. 1953–1970, black and white: Kodak Safety Film, H: 4 in. × W: 5 in. (10.20 × 12.70 cm), Carnegie Museum of Art, Pittsburgh: Heinz Family Fund, 2001.35.10357 © Carnegie Museum of Art, Charles "Teenie" Harris Archive.

wearing Mexican straw hats and playing castanets to entertain audiences, but they would soon launch into parodies of hit songs or their own material. The *Courier* reported, "When the time comes to play serious music, the Jolly Jax cut out the clowning and get right down to the business at hand and keep performing in their own inimitable way."[40] Songs such as their 1959 composition "Love" feature standard R&B fare: a brisk shuffle, snappy lyrics extoling the powers of love, and a succinct guitar solo treading the well-worn path of blues and rock 'n' roll riffs.

Other songs, such as the Jolly Jax 1962 parody of Bobby Marchan's 1960 R&B Billboard chart-topper "There's Something on Your Mind," tested the limits of comedic license. In the 1960 version, the band dramatically drops out, leaving Marchan to emotionally describe the shooting of an unfaithful partner by a jilted lover. In their version, the monologue is reimagined as a grocery-list of gory details unleashed on the unfaithful lover.[41] Intended as a boundary-pushing parody on the popular musical trope of the scorned lover, the lyrics caused the record to be banned from radio play, prompting Carroll Hill to question why

Figure 4.4. Charles "Teenie" Harris, American, 1908–1998, Jolly Jax Trio, including Herman Hill, Jerry Hill, and Carroll Hill, performing on stage in Hurricane Club, c. 1959-60, black and white: Kodak Safety Film, H: 4 in. × W: 5 in. (10.20 × 12.70 cm), Carnegie Museum of Art, Pittsburgh: Heinz Family Fund, 2001.35.34912, © Carnegie Museum of Art, Charles "Teenie" Harris Archive.

the same standards had not been applied to singer Bobby Darin's 1959 murder ballad "Mack the Knife."[42] By regularly booking the Jolly Jax, Dunlap illustrated that she wanted a space that could accommodate music that drew from popular culture yet met high artistic standards. The band's antics, unlike that of Richard Pryor's, clearly did not exceed what Dunlap felt was appropriate. This inclusivity reflected her vision of the club as embodying elegance and refinement yet making space for edgy humor, irony, and wit.

Dunlap was quick to capitalize on the growing number of jazz organists who were realizing the instrument's potential and developing new approaches to ensemble dynamics and improvisation. Dunlap booked Philadelphia organist Jimmy Smith at least eleven times, providing Hurricane audiences an intimate environment to witness performances that would set the standard for generations of jazz organists. Smith's first week at the Hurricane in April 1956 coincided with the Charles Mingus Trio's stay at the Grill. Like Mingus, Smith had recently played at Café Bohemia, New York City's famed venue known for supporting innovative jazz artists.

Figure 4.5. Charles "Teenie" Harris, American, 1908–1998, Jazz band, with Jimmy Smith on organ, possibly Eddie McFadden on guitar, and possibly Donald Bailey on drums, performing in Hurricane Club, c. 1953–1965, black and white: Kodak Safety Film, H: 4 in. × W: 5 in. (10.20 × 12.70 cm), Carnegie Museum of Art, Pittsburgh: Heinz Family Fund, 2001.35.4863 © Carnegie Museum of Art, Charles "Teenie" Harris Archive.

Two months before his Hurricane appearance, Smith had recorded *A New Sound . . . A New Star*, the first of over twenty records he would release on the Blue Note label in the following five years. Though Smith was a relative newcomer to the Hammond organ, having purchased his first around 1953, he had forged an approach bridging the melodic language of bebop with gospel and blues harmonics and rhythmic sensibilities. Having studied both bass and piano, Smith developed an approach to the organ that encompassed their roles and allowed him to delve into modern jazz, gospel, blues, and R&B. Smith's approach, which infused the heavy block chord styles of Wild Bill Davis, Bill Doggett, and Milt Buckner with the melodicism of Charlie Parker, would be adapted and expanded by many other organ greats who played at the Hurricane throughout the 1960s. These included Jon Thomas, Shirley Scott, Johnny "Hammond" Smith, Rhoda Scott, Charles Earland, Don Patterson, Gene Ludwig, and Jimmy McGriff.

Though Smith was fast becoming a nationally recognized jazz star, he regularly returned to the Hurricane from 1956 to 1961. Dunlap extended his second visit in July 1956 to a month after the trio's success in drawing "standing-room-only crowds."[43] Smith's success also marked a shift in the *Courier*'s marketing of the Hurricane's music. *Courier* writer Brown's description of Ruby Young's trio as a "fitting backdrop"[44] in 1953 positions the Hurricane's music as a secondary draw to the club's bar and restaurant.

Within a few years, music became the central focus of reviews and advertisements. In a 1956 *Courier* advertisement for the Hurricane, Jimmy Smith's performance was celebrated for drenching the space in music: "They rock the plush confines of the Hurricane from front to rear, and every moment they're on the bandstand they're working."[45] When Smith returned in December for his third stay at the "House of Organs," the *Courier* warned that Dunlap "will not only have to batten down the hatches, but must also make certain that her Hammond has been wired for crazy sounds" since during the previous engagement, "Smith worked so hard that Birdie's organ caught fire and she was forced to send for a repairman."[46] The *Courier*, which, not long before, had celebrated the restraint of the venue's musicians, reveled in describing Smith's emotionally charged performances:

> When he becomes wrapped up in a number, begins grimacing, then breaks into his weird improvisations, bedlam breaks loose, perspiration streams down his face, his shirt becomes soaked and he's ready to really play. But enough of that. To read about this fellow and not see him is murder. Get down to the Hurricane in a hurry and have the treat of your life.[47]

Dunlap again invited Smith to the Hurricane for a month, during which time he played songs recorded on two recently released albums, *The Incredible Jimmy Smith, A New Sound—A New Star Vol.2* and *At Club Baby Grand*. Smith's solos on jazz standards such as "Sweet Georgia Brown" extended for ten minutes with nonstop flurries of single-note runs that would seem an exercise in self-gratification if the effect weren't so revelatory. Smith's extended stays at the Hurricane provided a nightly platform for him to develop the stamina and creativity to sustain his solos for long periods of time and create extended narratives that both enthralled and challenged listeners.

From 1956 to 1961, even as Birdie was building her reputation as the matriarch of the jazz house of organs, the sound of the Lower Hill being cleared and the Civic Arena being erected was a pervasive reminder to nearby residents of the city's redevelopment. The Hurricane, only three blocks from the edge of the development site, provided an alternative sonic space in the neighborhood. A 1957 *Courier* review reflected on these competing soundscapes:

> Birdie Dunlap's "House of Organs" is rocking in more ways than one this week as the Jon Thomas Trio continues to shake up the Hurricane patrons. Tremors in

the neighborhood during the past few weeks have been attributed to a variety of causes. Some have been blamed on the spectacular redevelopment project now going on a couple of blocks below the bistro. Others resulted from the recent appearance of one James (the Incredible) Smith . . . . However, this week's shakeup is being attributed to the fact that a 300-pound stud has been putting a whole lot of weight on the tiny stand behind Birdie's bar as he drums for the Thomas crew.[48]

While meant to be lighthearted, the review is evidence of the aural impact of the redevelopment on nearby residents as well as the importance of the Hurricane as a homeplace where "tremors," "rocking," and "shakeups" are transformed from noise to healing sound. In this juxtaposition, the humble site of the Hurricane's "tiny stage," strained under the weight of drummer "Big" Chick Farley, rivals that of the "spectacular redevelopment" that was swallowing 105 acres of the neighborhood. Such sensory experiences are muted in the photographs that document the destruction of the Lower Hill and Mitchell and Ritchey's architectural drawing (figure 3.6) of an idealized urban landscape. Studying the history of the Hurricane as a jazz house and a homeplace reclaims the importance of the sonic environment that it provided for Pittsburghers; the creative and constructive processes of artists in the jazz house offered real alternatives to the extensive destruction required in realizing Pittsburgh's vision of rebirth.

The redevelopment plan was predicated on the belief that it was replacing a "blighted" community that had deteriorated beyond rehabilitation. Celebrated by the city's business and political elite as "progress" and "renewal," "blight" removal was a statement to the community that it had failed and deserved to be eradicated. It was in this context that the Hurricane and Crawford Grill provided affirmation of the Hill community's "right to the city" by becoming sought-after destinations for not only local patrons, but also travelers from across the country, celebrities, and touring artists who demonstrated artistic excellence and innovation. In the case of the Hurricane, the development of the Hill's vibrant nightlife as a place of emotional healing and celebration was indebted to Dunlap's contributions as a Black woman, civil and business leader, and promoter of Black music. Her focus on organ jazz and rhythm and blues demonstrated her deep conviction in the importance of contemporary developments in Black popular music, which distinguished the Hurricane from the Crawford Grill as the Hill's venue for modern jazz.

### The Crawford Grill No. 2 (1943–2003): A Home for Modern Jazz

Business partners William "Gus" Greenlee and Joe Robinson opened the Crawford Grill No. 2 in 1943.[49] It was the last of Greenlee's Hill District nightclub ventures, which had included the Paramount Inn in the 1920s, the Harlem Casino in the

1930s, and the Crawford Grill No. 1 (1932–1951), and would become one of the Hill's most important institutions for jazz. The flood of internationally recognized jazz musicians started in April 1956—the same month that Birdie Dunlap hired Philadelphia organist Jimmy Smith and began building the Hurricane's reputation as Pittsburgh's "House of Organs." In its first decade, the Grill operated primarily as an upscale restaurant and bar that provided a comfortable alternative for Greenlee, Robinson, and other Hill figures to meet, relax, and talk business.

Into the late 1940s, the Grill No. 1, located in the heart of the Lower Hill, was Greenlee's primary business headquarters and location for booking musical acts, though a series of misfortunes made it an increasing business liability. In 1945, reports of leaking water lines were said to have nearly "doubled the normal cost of upkeep on the building," leaving Greenlee to request that the City Council reduce a $4,037 water bill that had accrued since the club's opening in 1932. Violence also marred the well-known spot. On a late Saturday in the summer of 1946, bartender Thomas O. West was stabbed by a customer. In a gruesome scene, West "ran into the well-filled main dining room . . . and toppled in the middle of the floor while blood gushed in torrents from the wound in his stomach."[50] West died shortly afterward, all reportedly because of a heated exchanged after he refused to serve the patron after hours.

Problems continued in 1950 when two individuals were injured on the property and filed lawsuits against Greenlee. The first involved a woman who fell after stepping on a loose grating outside while the second was brought by a soft drink salesman who fell down the cellar stairs after the top step broke under his weight.[51] The building, in need of renovation and typical of the deteriorating and underdeveloped infrastructure of the Lower Hill, was gutted by a fire in July 1951. Plans to rebuild the popular spot were preempted by the Lower Hill Redevelopment project, which slated the entire area to be cleared between 1955 and 1960.

As the Grill No. 1's time came to an end, the Grill No. 2 built on its name recognition and provided Greenlee and Robinson an opportunity to create a space more fully centered on music performance. Establishing the new Grill as a music venue took some years, however. Early promotion focused on its restaurant managed by chef Bill Norwood, who had served during World War II as the chief cook of the Bainbridge Naval Center's officers' mess.[52]

In the late 1940s, a raised stage was installed midway through the Grill's long, narrow space. Elevated four feet off the floor and positioned between the bar and restaurant seating, the bandstand became the central focus of the venue. While the small stage of the first Grill limited performances to solo pianists occasionally accompanied by vocalists, guitarists, and horn players, the new Grill's stage could accommodate jazz quartets and quintets. Initially, bands were a complement to the restaurant and bar business, entertaining guests who often requested popular songs. In the spring of 1948, Pittsburgh Hammond organist Sammy Nowlin

Figure 4.6. Charles "Teenie" Harris, American, 1908–1998, Crawford Grill No. 1 boarded up with old doors, and man seated in car in foreground, 1401 Wylie Avenue at Townsend Street, Hill District, 1956, 1956, black and white: Kodak Safety Film, H: 4 in. × W: 5 in. (10.20 × 12.70 cm), Carnegie Museum of Art, Pittsburgh: Heinz Family Fund, 2001.35.2362 © Carnegie Museum of Art, Charles "Teenie" Harris Archive.

began a regular series of gigs at the Grill that would extend for four years. In 1952, a *Courier* review of the Grill relegated the music as "a nice background for the prime steaks, chops, short orders and sandwiches."[53] In its early years before music became a central draw for the business, bands were booked for extended periods, and the location served as a place for the locals to socialize and have a good meal, as well as Greenlee and his business associates to meet informally.

Greenlee passed away on July 7, 1952, leaving the Grill to his business partner Joe Robinson and his son William "Buzzy" Robinson. As the sole proprietors of

Figure 4.7. Charles "Teenie" Harris, American, 1908–1998, Centre Avenue with Wash-A-Teria, and Chas. W. Lutz Choice Meats at 2145 Centre Avenue, at intersection of Elmore Street, with Crawford Grill No. 2 on Wylie Avenue, in background, Hill District, July 1957, black and white: Kodak Safety Film, H: 4 in. × W: 5 in. (10.20 × 12.70 cm), Carnegie Museum of Art, Pittsburgh: Heinz Family Fund, 2001.35.7798, © Carnegie Museum of Art, Charles "Teenie" Harris Archive.

the Grill, the father and son team built the Grill's identity as a music venue by presenting a series of well-known local jazz groups. The same month that Greenlee died, Nowlin was replaced with local alto saxophonist Leroy Brown and his Brown Buddies: pianist George "Duke" Spaulding, bassist William McMahon, and drummer Bobby Anderson. Brown's quartet was one of the most active and respected local jazz groups, distinguished by its versatility as well as professionalism. Brown, who had served as treasurer of the American Federation of Musicians' Black Local 471, was one of the first Black bandleaders to work an extended job in a downtown club.[54] The band's stay at this venue, called the Hollywood Showbar, started in 1944 and lasted for over a year.[55]

Local audiences also appreciated that Brown could "have written his own ticket to New York with big name bands" but preferred to stay in Pittsburgh. Defending his decision to pursue a local rather than national career, Brown stated, "I like the folks at home and they have been good to me. They deserve good music too and I have always tried to give it to them."[56] With the prospects of a long-term

Figure 4.8. Charles "Teenie" Harris, American, 1908–1998, Band with Bobby Anderson on drums, George "Duke" Spaulding on piano, Bill "Bass" McMahon on bass, and Leroy Brown on saxophone standing on stage, with audience looking on from below, at Crawford Grill No. 2, black and white: Kodak Safety Film, H: 4 in. × W: 5 in. (10.20 × 12.70 cm), Carnegie Museum of Art, Pittsburgh: Heinz Family Fund, 2001.35.10098 © Carnegie Museum of Art, Charles "Teenie" Harris Archive.

engagement at the Grill, Brown moved into the club's second-floor apartment with his wife Betty, who became "like family" to Robinson. This nurturing and supportive relationship between club owner and artist literally made a home of the "jazz house." As with Dunlap's social and business savvy and cultivation of a family of patrons, Robinson's relationship with the Browns signaled a deeper investment in the club's social networks. As Betty Brown recalled, on the rare occasions when her presence as a White woman in the Grill was questioned, Robinson would say, "[I]f they didn't like it, they didn't have to come to the Grill."[57]

Brown's style was rooted in the lyricism of the blues and repertoire of the big band swing era, such as popular arrangements by Fletcher Henderson and Benny Goodman, boogie-woogie and ballad requests, and occasionally contemporary crossover hits such as the 1952 Billboard topper "Blue Tango" by Leroy Anderson.[58] As saxophonist Hosea Taylor remembers about Brown, "That guy could play Mary's Little Lamb and I would love it. Just the way he played knocked me out. He had this beautiful tone. If he played fast, it was just beautiful."[59]

Taylor found that Brown was resistant to new directions in jazz exemplified by musicians such as Charlie Parker, however, and remained committed to the musical styles of the 1940s throughout his career. Nonetheless, Brown's approach to programming kept audiences engaged during nightly appearances at the Grill through the fall of 1953. A *Courier* review emphasized the band's restraint: "One reason that Leroy's outfit is popular is due to the fact that the boys never jump frantic. The people can always recognize the music. When the band plays jump numbers, the boys do not blow the patrons out of the place. It's cool. When Leroy plays, sweet, people listen and do not go to sleep. It's a happy medium."[60] The *Courier* also complimented Spaulding, a veteran of the local scene and dedicated Musicians Union member, who played the part of consummate sideman. The review described a musician who was "so unassuming that most fans miss his artistry. Duke is a team man and he doesn't reach for attention."[61]

After Brown's residency came to an end in early 1954, the Grill booked local bands led by pianist Alyce Brooks, guitarist Joe Westray, and pianist Walt Harper. Harper's band, at that time including his brother Nate (tenor sax), Bill Lewis (bass), Jon Morris (trombone), and Harold "Brushes" Lee (drums), was a staple of local dances and clubs and would be a celebrated regular at the Grill for the next ten years. Harper realized the potential of adopting standards into his repertoire as part of his musical identity. From his time at the Grill throughout his career, Harper always performed Duke Ellington and Pittsburgh native Billy Strayhorn's 1953 composition "Satin Doll," a song that exemplified Harper's preference for relaxed and easily danceable tempos and melodies that could be hummed by even the most musically challenged. Harper's repertoire focused on what was recognizable and relatable to general listeners, typically eschewing compositions emerging from modern jazz circles. Harper expanded his set with small band arrangements of contemporary hits such as Mario Bauzá's "Mambo Inn," George Shearing's "Lullaby of Birdland" as recorded by Erroll Garner in 1950, "Let's Fall in Love" from the 1933 film of the same name, Kitty Kallen's saccharine 1954 chart-topping "Little Things Mean a Lot," comedic lounge numbers such as "Hey, Mrs. Jones," doo-wop songs such as The Four Tunes' "Sugar Lump," and jump blues numbers such as The Treniers' tribute to the Giants' center fielder Willie Mays, "Say Hey."[62]

The musical pastiche of postwar American popular culture filtered through Harper's set was accompanied by visual cues of middle-class suburbia. Mondays at the Grill No. 2 featured Bermuda Shorts Night, when Harper's band was joined by local "celebrities" who joined in "sporting the latest in this new fashion."[63] Bermuda shorts, developed as tropical uniforms by the British military for officials in Bermuda and later adopted by American tourists, entered mainstream culture in the 1950s as the epitome of public leisure fashion. These shorts successfully melded the comfort and the casual look one might expect from private loungewear

Figure 4.9. Charles "Teenie" Harris, American, 1908–1998, Walt Harper's band, including Jon Morris on trombone, Bill Lewis holding eyeglasses, unknown man with arms around others, Nate Harper on saxophone, Howard "Brushes" Lee on drums, and Walt Harper, wearing Bermuda shorts and posed on raised stage in Crawford Grill No. 2, c. 1954, black and white: Kodak Safety Film, H: 4 in. × W: 5 in. (10.20 × 12.70 cm), Carnegie Museum of Art, Pittsburgh: Heinz Family Fund, 2001.35.11430 © Carnegie Museum of Art, Charles "Teenie" Harris Archive.

with the formality of military attire and in doing so broke a long-standing taboo against showing one's legs in public. The Grill's elevated stage contributed to the spectacle, creating a fashion runway for the musicians wearing the standard pairing of long socks with Bermuda shorts.

As a part of Harper's performance, Bermuda Shorts Night imbued the vaudevil-lian humor of Hill stage shows with a subtle appropriation of White middle-class culture in modern America through sartorial commentary. Though entrenched in swing-era sonic aesthetics, Harper's replacement of the traditional suit and tie with Bermuda shorts laid claim to cultural spaces outside of the Hill while playing with the odd juxtaposition of jazz musicians as British colonial administrators or American tourists in the Caribbean. The *Courier* praised Harper's first resi-dency at the Grill as an important milestone in his career, drawing crowds and introducing the "popular Bermuda shorts fad that has spread all over this part of Pennsylvania." As entertainment, the shorts contributed to Harper's success, and as a cultural signifier, they meant a participation in the social customs of middle-class America at a time when modernity and suburbs were largely reserved for the Whites fleeing the country's urban centers like the Hill. Robinson noted as Harper ended his first residency to pursue a tour of local colleges and proms, "Walt has drawn more people than any other attraction in the eight-year history of the Crawford Grill."[64] The end of Harper's residency marked a turning point for the Grill, which had been, up to that point, the supportive home for noted local performers and a place where jazz catered to rather than challenged the expectations of audiences.

The year 1956 was pivotal for the Grill, as it marked the beginning of regular appearances by musicians hailing primarily from New York, Chicago, Los Angeles, and Philadelphia and playing music that was promoted, and derided, as "modern" or "progressive." This shift was prompted by mid-1950s developments in jazz that marked new creative directions for small groups as well as a wider appreciation of the music as an important cultural phenomenon. From 1955 to 1957, Miles Davis's quintet with John Coltrane, Red Garland, Paul Chambers, and Philly Joe Jones shaped a range of expressive possibilities in jazz that greatly popularized listening to improvised instrumental music. The moment was ripe for presenting this and similar groups, well known through their growing recorded output, to audiences appreciative of jazz's artistic potential.

The demolition that year of the Crawford Grill No. 1 signaled the end of an era in the Hill, leaving the Grill No. 2, christened by the likes of Mayor Lawrence, as the new symbol of nightlife culture. By this year, Pittsburgh bandleaders Leroy Brown, Walt Harper, Alyce Brooks, and Joe Westray had established a tradition of nightly performances and, with regular reviews by *Pittsburgh Courier* staff, contributed to the Grill's popularity throughout the region. While these local bands had played extended engagements, incoming touring bands generally played week-long engagements with evening sets from Monday to Saturday, 9:30 p.m. to 2 a.m., and additional matinee sets on Friday and Saturday, from 5 to 7 p.m. Occasionally, engagements were extended to a second week if the artists were drawing a crowd and their schedule permitted, as was the case with Jimmy Smith at the Hurricane. These nightly performances helped keep the club crowded with a fast turnover of popular groups and allowed the musicians a brief respite from traveling. Audiences also had their choice of days and times that fit their preferences, and local musicians had the opportunity to stop by a matinee set before their own gigs.

With the influx of young jazz musicians from across the country came new aesthetic concepts and social practices of performance and listening. Grill audiences could hear in person new approaches in jazz that drew from familiar traditions yet challenged listeners to engage critically with the musicians' conceptual approaches. *Courier* writers often contributed to the discourse of modern jazz, providing their readers with frameworks for thinking about the music. Staff writer George E. Pitts recalled his amusement at hearing a confused listener define modern jazz as "whistling 'Yankee Doodle' through a keyhole. It may be hard to do . . . but what do you accomplish by doing it?"[65]

Pitts's fellow staff writer Harold L. Keith took on these perspectives more fully in his 1956 article "Who Says Progressive Jazz Is Doomed?" in which he positions critics of progressive jazz as "reactionaries of the jazz world" who "are against jazz breaking out of the straight-jacketed bounds . . . dictated by the staff, flats, and G-clef upon which music has been based since the so-called 'dark ages.'"[66] Keith argued that "reactionaries" reject modernisms in jazz on "the basis that it is hard to 'dig,'" that it "lacks continuity, has no melody, and defies the principles upon which harmony is based."[67]

In response to these criticisms, Keith reminded his readers that musicians such as Dizzy Gillespie and Clifford Brown were not rejecting the traditions of Dixieland and swing-era jazz but had developed creative approaches from contemporary experiences that required new ways of listening. So they could appreciate the music more fully, Keith encouraged listeners to focus on the ways drummers like Art Blakey, Kenny Clarke, and Max Roach "inspire" and "kick along" soloists as they depart from familiar melodies in extended, dialog-driven improvisations. Though this language of improvisation requires a critical perspective by listeners, Keith reminded readers that these developments were part of a larger creative struggle on the part of the artists, which connected jazz to the Black diaspora and positioned jazz musicians as a political force in the Cold War era:[68]

> Blakey, for example, has made an extensive study of African drumming. His beat has a definite Nigerian-Ebo thump. [Blakey, Clarke, and Roach] are well versed with Afro-Cuban rhythms . . . . The new jazz has already made a terrific impact overseas in such spots as Sweden, Great Britain, France, Denmark, and Norway. In fact, "Dizzy" Gillespie is America's latest goodwill ambassador and he is currently spreading the gospel of "Oop Bop Sh'Bam" in Egypt, India, Pakistan, and Europe. This tour is well calculated to win friends for the U.S.A. by inducing trauma overseas through Dizzy's "crazy" music and making alien "squares" more amenable to our propaganda.[69]

The example of Gillespie's deployment throughout the world as a representative of the US State Department's Jazz Ambassadors program, which began in 1956 and ran through the late 1970s, was for Keith a significant, though ironic, example of jazz's relevance. The contributions of jazz musicians in US diplomacy, despite the immediate struggles against state-sanctioned racial segregation, illustrate the music's potential as a progressive force with wide-reaching impact. All the more, jazz as a site of modern American progress—especially as a demonstration of the country's cultural advancement and racial harmony during the Cold War—becomes a contested battleground for musicians and cultural critics. Keith's article was a call for local jazz musicians to see themselves as cultural leaders contributing to the civil rights struggle.

In April 1956, the Grill auspiciously hired bassist and composer Charles Mingus, likely accompanied by pianist Mal Waldron, drummer Willie Jones, and saxophonist Jackie McLean. This two-week booking represented a conceptual shift in the club's programming and an investment in supporting new composers and visionaries in jazz. The year 1955 was a turning point in Mingus's career as he moved from working alongside jazz luminaries such as Charlie Parker, Bud Powell, and Art Tatum to leading ensembles that featured new approaches to composition and improvisation. Adopting the name "The Jazz Workshop" for his band, Mingus worked at Café Bohemia in New York City's Greenwich Village and explored extended song forms and methods for encouraging meaningful individual expressions grounded in the moment.[70] Café Bohemia, a club dedicated to progressive jazz, would feature artists such as Cannonball Adderley, Miles Davis, John Coltrane, and Randy Weston. During Mingus's gigs, audiences witnessed performed rehearsals where Mingus might stop mid-song to make changes or fire musicians mid-gig if he did not feel they were playing to his standards.

Mingus searched for creative devices to bring musicians into a new and uncharted space of performing, which, as comparative literature scholar Krin Gabbard notes, required new techniques of compositions: "At one point he asked his musicians to improvise on a drawing he'd made of a coffin."[71] Mingus's provocations of his musicians and audiences were driven by his desire to connect listeners and performers to the moment. As jazz studies scholar Scott Saul writes, Mingus's contentious demands on those around him contributed to establishing "jazz as music of psychological turbulence—music that probed the soul, stripped away the veneer of conventional decorum, and gave voice to the most knotty, and sometimes least articulate, of emotional states."[72]

Mingus was always searching for distinct creative voices that could join his Jazz Workshop. It was around the time of Mingus's Grill appearance that he met and played with Hill District pianist Horace Parlan who was a local fixture at that time. Parlan recalls, "[In 1956, we] had played together, and he was very impressed with my playing. He was putting together a new band, and he asked if I would be interested in joining. Naturally, I said yes."[73] In 1957, Parlan left Pittsburgh to join Mingus in New York and would soon be an essential contributor to his albums *Blues & Roots* (Atlantic, 1959) and *Mingus Ah Um* (Columbia, 1959). These records served as a launching point for Parlan's vibrant solo career as a recording artist, which in turn led him to be featured at the Grill with his own group in 1961.

Mingus's appearance at the Grill, though short, was highly anticipated among those following contemporary developments in jazz. For young jazz fans familiar with Mingus's recordings, a live performance would have been an opportunity to witness his experimental approaches in person. In January 1956, two months before appearing at the Grill, Mingus recorded *Pithecanthropus Erectus*, the first of five albums for Atlantic Records. The opening track of the same name, described by Mingus in the album's liner notes as a "jazz tone poem," extends over ten minutes and follows the path of the "first man to stand erect" through the stages of "evolution," "superiority complex," "decline," and ultimately, "destruction." The composition builds a linear narrative around the solos of Jackie McLean (alto saxophone) and Mal Waldron (piano), punctuated by melodic fragments and riffs that conclude in a slow unwinding of dissonance and chaos that simultaneously imagines the downfall of mankind while anticipating the sonorities of jazz in the coming decade.

Pittsburgh's culture writers anticipated Mingus's arrival at the Grill soon after this album's release. *Courier* columnist Pitts noted that Mingus's reputation preceded him, having received *DownBeat* magazine's 1954 "New Star" award.[74] A promotional *Courier* article for Mingus's upcoming performance also emphasized *DownBeat*'s praise, citing Nat Hentoff's description of Mingus's technical proficiency, conceptual innovations, and intensity in performance.[75]

Among Mingus's innovations was his use of songs as a way of cultivating spatial awareness through listening. His intention of having the listener attend to city soundscapes speaks to his appreciation of the rhythms of daily life as marked by the aural qualities of the city—a concept later echoed in Lefebvre's notion of "rhythmanalysis," which addresses the ways cycles link time and place and become rhythms of daily life. As Lefebvre argues, everyday life structures and is structured by "cyclical" rhythms of nature: "day and night, the months and seasons, and still more precisely biological rhythms," and "linear" rhythms of "the socio-economic organization of production, consumption, circulation and habitat."[76] A "rhythmanalyst" is one who can perceive rhythms in the noises and silences of social spaces and probe the unease underlying the collective experience in late capitalism of having cyclical rhythms subject to linear time—for example, the feeling of unvarying repetition in factory work days. Mingus anticipates some of this thinking in his 1956 recording of George Gershwin's 1937 composition "A Foggy Day," in which the band invokes the chaos of a busy street near a port full of vehicles vying for passage. In this album's liner notes, Mingus serves as a guide to the potentially confused listener:

> You might be tempted to laugh on first hearing—and a good, healthy laugh never hurt anyone—but on second hearing, try to imagine the tenor playing the melody as John Dow walking down Market Street to the Ferry Building, hearing the sounds of a big city on a foggy day—the rumble of truck, clang of cable car, scuffle of crowd, jumble of traffic, moan of fog horn, cop's whistle, car horn, the drunk left over from the night before who just dropped his last quarter, and that damned twelve o'clock whistle that used to wake me up! All these sounds make much music. I have tried to

reproduce some of them musically, and if you can see these pictures as you listen to the track—even to the ferry boat, amid the guiding fog horns, creaking to a stop at the docks (as reproduced by the bass)—then I have succeeded.[77]

The melody, played by Jackie McLean, floats amid the chaos of street sounds as if one were listening to it on a radio in the middle of a traffic jam. The effect is one in which the listener perceives the city as both a source and subject of musical expression. This orientation is key to what Lefebvre later called "listening out," where the rhythmanalyst perceives "a house, a street, a town as one listens to a symphony, an opera."[78]

Mingus's innovative approaches challenged listeners, including those who frequented the Grill, to reflect on the ways jazz performance could interrogate broader social issues. Listeners often resisted Mingus's demands to enter into uncomfortable spaces of listening. In September 1956, Mingus's "A Foggy Day" was met with stern criticism by Harold L. Keith in an ironic reversal of his previous defense of modern jazz. In a dismissive *Courier* review of the album *Pithecan- thropus Erectus*, Keith, who had defended progressive jazz five months earlier, takes a conservative stance toward Mingus's use of cityscape sounds:

> The group's work on "Foggy Day" is befogged by a lot of extra noise. Sound effects are unnecessary for good jazz because the good musician should be able to produce the mood that he wants with his instrument. Jackie McLean on alto and Mal Wal- dron on piano managed to surmount the distractions of fog horns and whistles to get the album a ½ [star] rating, but strangely, Mr. Mingus takes his own solo with- out said distractions . . . no whistle-tootin' for the boss? Mingus may talk of chord progressions and scale . . . "superimposed scales" within chords and the replacing of bars with "cues" but after hearing all this we beg to ask . . . is it really music?[79]

Keith's simultaneous rejection of Mingus's "A Foggy Day" and commendation of musicians such as Dizzy Gillespie for resisting "straight-jacketed bounds" is an example of multifaceted readings of modern jazz among *Courier* writers. Keith, who joined the *Courier* in 1946, was known for his critical writings on the role of labor movements in civil rights struggles as well as independence movements in Africa.[80] While Keith advocates the creative innovations of modern jazz and associates the contributions of Black music with contemporary societal struggles in the Black community, his conviction breaks down when he encounters Mingus's music. Keith scorned the contradiction of Mingus's modern jazz as embracing both a high art ideal and vernacular of the everyday; the imposition of city sounds in "A Foggy Day" collapsed the critic's concept of the music/noise divide.

When considering the growing din of noise from the Hill's redevelopment and the importance of jazz clubs as sonic spaces of respite, it is possible that Keith's criticism was rooted in a deeper unease with the imposition of urban soundscapes. As a Pittsburgh native and reporter engaged with the political and cultural life of the Hill District, he would have been keenly aware of the changes facing the neighborhood. Confronting the unnerving realities of redevelopment in the context of a progressive form of Black music was a contradictory experience of modernity—one that Mingus hoped to impart to his audience but also touched a nerve of a Black Pittsburgher listening to the record. The power of Mingus's music to demand that the listener radically rethink the familiar collapsed the uneasy boundaries that distinguish music from noise as well as reason from nonsense. In his spatialization of "A Foggy Day," Mingus appropriates city spaces and sounds and entices the listener to make meaning of urban chaos, which, at times, may very well have been painful to bear.

Even as the demolition and reconstruction of the Lower Hill were underway, the Grill would come to accommodate the ever-extending boundaries of modern jazz and to provide a space in which a multitude of conceptual and expressive approaches could be experienced, compared, critiqued, and celebrated. The steady succession of groups, presented nightly, contributed to the ever-shifting consensus among the Grill's audiences of what constituted modern jazz. Mingus was followed by tenor saxophonist Paul Quinichette, a former Count Basie and Louis Jordan sideman who was promoting his 1955 album *Moods*. The album, a mix of small group bop-infused swing and Afro-Cuban jazz, is notable as one of the first to feature the compositions and arrangements of Quincy Jones. Unlike Mingus's conceptual experimentations, the album's original compositions, which couch elements of bebop in subdued and recognizable stylistic settings, provide an alternative reading of modern jazz.[81]

Mingus's and Quinichette's short stays were immediately followed by Art Blakey and the first iteration of his Jazz Messengers, which included Horace Silver (piano), Donald Byrd (trumpet), Doug Watkins (bass), and Hank Mobley (tenor saxophone). As with Mingus, Blakey had recently finished a stint at Café Bohemia and was a rising star in New York's jazz scene. Blakey, a Pittsburgh native, had grown up performing in Hill District venues such as the old Savoy Ballroom and was a source of pride for the neighborhood. He had left for New York in 1942, where he played with Fletcher Henderson and later fellow Pittsburgher Billy Eckstine. Eckstine's big band, a cutting-edge experiment that bridged big band swing and bebop, brought together top players of the day, including Dizzy Gillespie (trumpet), Fats Navarro (trumpet), Miles Davis (trumpet), Charlie Parker (alto saxophone), Dexter Gordon (tenor saxophone), Sonny Stitt (tenor saxophone), and Sarah Vaughan (vocals). Touring with these artists provided Blakey an opportunity to develop a style with the power of big band drumming and the interactivity of small group bebop.[82] Blakey's music fused the technical virtuosity of bebop, sensibilities of gospel and blues, and an emerging harmonic language that broke from the standard progressions of the American Songbook. As a driving force of Thelonious Monk's early Blue Note recordings, Blakey's ride cymbal work and goading kick drum were integral to shaping the language of the modern jazz rhythm section.

In 1954, Blakey formed his first quintet that would lead to his career at the helm of the Jazz Messengers. The band's first records, *A Night at Birdland, Volumes 1 & 2*, were selections from the famous New York club and brought a balance of powerful drumming, new compositions, and melodic approaches that would define the era of hard bop. Pittsburgh drummer Cecil Brooks, who at the time had joined Walt Harper's band, remembers Joe Robinson saying that he was "taking a chance" by bringing in Blakey. The success of the shows, however, encouraged Robinson to continue booking touring modern jazz musicians. As Brooks recalls, this shift ensured the regular appearances of daring artists who represented the innovations of the New York jazz scene and "real jazz like Art was playing."[83]

Over the following four years, Blakey would bring various iterations of the Jazz Messengers to the Grill and build a close relationship with the venue and its audiences. In his role as a bandleader, Blakey saw the band not only as a means to feature new music but also to educate audiences on how to listen to jazz. The name "Jazz Messengers" represents this dedication to "spreading the word" of the music's importance by breaking down "barriers that exist between the jazz musician and his audience."[84] *Courier* columnist Pitts commented that this attempt to demand more of audiences—that they listen to the music with a critical and engaged ear—at times led to conflicts as the norms of socializing clashed with the expectations of musicians: "Some of the cats listening to Art Blakey . . . were insulted because they thought the drummer was talking down to them when he expounded on jazz and asked them to keep quiet and dig."[85]

Through the rest of 1956 and 1957, the Grill featured a dizzying array of small groups led by younger musicians, including Hampton Hawes (piano), Cecil Young (piano), Horace Silver (piano), Dodo Marmarosa (piano), James Moody (tenor saxophone), Eddie Jefferson (vocals), Julian "Cannonball" Adderley (alto saxophone), Sonny Stitt (tenor saxophone), Charlie Rouse (tenor saxophone), Julius Watkins (French horn), Chet Baker (trumpet), J. J. Johnson (trombone), Teddy Charles (vibes), Terry Gibbs (vibes), Chico Hamilton (drums), and Max Roach (drums).

Walt Harper, who performed at the Grill regularly throughout this period, reflected on the impact this flood of performers had on local musicians. In August 1957, on the eve of back-to-back bookings of Miles Davis, Art Blakey, and Max Roach, the *Courier* published an interview with Walt Harper about his own group's recent developments:

> Basically it wasn't a new sound, but we've tried to improve and modernize the sound that we've been getting and at the same time keep the swinging groove that

identifies the band . . . . We also have taken advantage of the fact that Pittsburgh, long considered a "square town" musically, is fast waking up and now has a more jazz-conscious public than ever before. This fact gives us a chance to play more contemporary numbers than we have in the past.[86]

Harper's statement reveals how modern jazz provided an aesthetic space where, as a bandleader, he felt comfortable with longer, more individualist soloing as well as presenting repertoire that might have been unfamiliar to listeners. In this respect, Harper—who had been playing popular tunes for dances and hosting Bermuda shorts nights—found that modern jazz was cultivating audiences that valued the music as a discursive space about modernity itself. His observation of the effect of touring musicians at the Grill is a testament to the club's burgeoning reputation as a nationally recognized jazz venue and its importance to the local community of musicians as a place to develop professionally. *Courier* reviews of the Grill regularly invoked the growing "jazz-consciousness" of "square" audiences as Pittsburgh abandoned its provinciality for New York City's progressiveness. *Courier* writers touted the Grill as Pittsburgh's "Birdland" and cited New York venues where groups featured at the Grill had recently played.

Performance reviews indicated that the Grill, despite regularly overflowing capacity, had become a place to appreciate the intimate dynamics of small groups. A review of drummer Chico Hamilton's jazz chamber group made up of cellist Fred Katz, bassist Carson Smith, reeds and flutist Paul Horn, and guitarist John Pisano celebrated their restraint and sophistication: "[T]he hep five put down the message in [a] nice, easy, expressive and modulated style, which kept the swank confines from sounding like a cross between a juke box [*sic*] and a boiler factory."[87] Hamilton, a Los Angeles musician and contemporary of Mingus, is underrepresented in historical narratives of jazz, possibly because his music confounds standard narratives of stylistic progress.

An understated drummer who developed an approach to bandleading that highlighted the group's sound and orchestral possibilities, Hamilton made over sixty albums between 1955 and his death in 2013. His first, *Chico Hamilton Quintet featuring Buddy Collette*, includes compositions drawn from the racially integrated band that combine guitar, cello, and saxophone in settings fit for a cinematic soundtrack.[88] Hamilton's "chamber jazz" concept would carry throughout his career even as he continued to incorporate elements of Afro-Cuban and African music as well as funk and shaped the solo careers of such jazz greats as guitarist Jim Hall, bassist Ron Carter, and saxophonists Eric Dolphy and Charles Lloyd.

Hamilton was one of the most regularly featured artists at the Grill between 1956 and 1965, making at least ten appearances with his first and second quintet. Hamilton's popularity with the Grill's audiences was possibly outmatched by that of drummer and bandleader Max Roach, who appeared at least eight times with vocalist Abbey Lincoln and various iterations of his quintet. Alongside drummers Kenny Clarke, Art Blakey, and Roy Haynes, Roach was a pivotal figure in the development of modern jazz and the dynamic possibilities of the jazz quintet. In 1954, Roach began a creative partnership with trumpeter Clifford Brown and created a series of live and studio records that set the standards for hard-bop aesthetics.

On June 26, 1956, Brown, pianist Richie Powell, and Powell's wife Nancy set out from Philadelphia to join Roach, bassist George Morrow, and saxophonist Sonny Rollins in Chicago, where the quintet was booked for a series of dates at the Blue Note. It was after dark and during heavy rains that Brown and the Powells were killed when their car skidded off the road and down a long embankment.[89] The news of the young musicians' deaths deeply affected Roach and the remaining band members. Roach felt responsible for the younger musicians, and their deaths manifested in a period of alcohol abuse that would plague him for years: "I got really strung out on booze. One night I was in a bar in Pittsburgh, and all of a sudden on the jukebox I heard Dinah Washington, who was like a mentor to Clifford and me, and she was singing [the song] 'Relax Max.' She was trying to bring me out of it."[90]

Following the accident, Roach continued to lead the group, adding trumpeter Kenny Dorham and pianist Ray Bryant. Roach's first Grill appearance in late 1957 likely included this group playing selections from *Max Roach Plus Four* (EmArcy, 1956) and *Jazz in ¾ Time* (EmArcy, 1957). These albums featured acrobatic modern jazz compositions such as George Russell's "Ezz-thetic" alongside American Songbook standards such as "Body and Soul." *Jazz in ¾ Time* is notable as the first jazz record comprised solely of waltzes, a conceptual development of exploring new time signatures that pianist and composer Dave Brubeck would more overtly expand on in his album *Time Out* (1959).[91]

Roach's exacting perfectionism and clean, hard-swinging style built a strong following for his appearances at the Grill. In February 1959, he returned to the Grill with a quintet comprised of trumpeter Booker Little, tenor saxophonist George Coleman, trombonist Julian Priester, and bassist Art Davis. In January, the band recorded *The Many Sides of Max*, an album that would not be released until 1964 but that highlighted Roach's talents as a composer and foregrounded the innovation of small ensembles free of a chordal instrument, a defining characteristic of many groups in the 1960s. In anticipation of his two-week stay, the *Courier* wrote: "In previous engagements at the Grill, Max has never failed to please. If anything, the opposite is the case. He has exhibited such a scintillating output of soulful diversions that Pittsburghers have come to appreciate this drumming wizard for the musical great that he is."[92]

Roach used this opportunity at the Grill to invite the Pittsburgh branch of the NAACP to the club, where he made an event out of his entire band becoming members (figure 4.10). Roach's activism would come to shape his career with

Figure 4.10. Charles "Teenie" Harris, American, 1908–1998, Men, including members of Max Roach's band, from left: Booker Little, Pittsburgh NAACP board member Matthew Moore, Max Roach, George Coleman, Art Davis, Julian Priester, posed in Crawford Grill No. 2, February 1959, black and white: Kodak Safety Film, H: 4 in. × W: 5 in. (10.20 × 12.70 cm), Carnegie Museum of Art, Pittsburgh: Heinz Family Fund, 2001.35.7057 © Carnegie Museum of Art, Charles "Teenie" Harris Archive.

musical statements such as *We Insist!—Max Roach's Freedom Now Suite* (1960), originally conceived as a piece to mark the Emancipation Proclamation's centennial but released earlier in response to the Greensboro sit-ins, and *Newport Rebels* (1961), a protest against the booking policies and culture of the Newport Jazz Festival.

Roach, a budding musical and civil rights hero, struggled with depression and the hardships of the touring Black American artist, conditions exacerbated by drinking and manifested in angry outbursts on stage. Though Joe and his son William "Buzzy" Robinson accommodated Roach as an honored guest, his emotional burdens occasionally marred his performances in the Grill. During a performance in the second week of February 1959, Roach began to berate his band on stage, and when the insults turned to the audience, Buzzy stepped in to send him home. As reported in the *Courier*, "Those close to Roach attributed his 'lip-flipping' to several causes, namely, his failure to get over the death of his former sideman, ace trumpeter Clifford Brown . . . his belief that all sidemen should be able to play like the late masters of progressive jazz, Charlie Parker and Brown, et al. . . ."[93] Columnist George Pitts, however, was forgiving as he later reflected on the struggles of the celebrated musician:

> The tragedy of Max Roach pains this corner no end after having come to know him as a personal friend. The drummer's drummer has been sent to Bellevue [psychiatric hospital] (New York) for observation, and his erratic conduct (especially in Pittsburgh) leads us to believe that this was no sudden thing. Max's tirades at the Steel City's Crawford Grill and Ellis Hotel will long be remembered. No matter, we hope it is only a temporary thing and he is back in order soon.[94]

Roach's contentious split with his band in the Grill led to a fortuitous collaboration when the bandleader drew from local talent to fill his roster. Joining Roach for the following years and at least seven studio recordings were brothers Tommy and Stanley Turrentine and bassist Bobby Boswell, a veteran Pittsburgh sideman who had also toured with Chick Webb, Billie Holiday, and Louis Jordan. The newly assembled band finished its engagement and, shortly after, proceeded to New York to record *Rich versus Roach* (1959), a concept album pitting Roach in a drum battle with famed bandleader and drum virtuoso Buddy Rich. The two bands involved in the session fade into the background as the drummers compete and trade solos: Rich flexing his power through a sustained wall of sound and Roach opting to juxtapose minimalism and grandeur, building tension with phrases of silence.

In July, the band recorded *Quiet as It's Kept* (1959), which gives the Turrentine brothers and Priester freedom to perform extended solos and layer "shout" chorus riffs behind each other's improvisations as Roach and Boswell revel in the open sound of their piano-less rhythm section. The album's standout track is the Turrentine/Priester composition "As Long as You're Living," a blues in 5/4 time driven by Boswell's metronomic yet hypnotic bass line and crowned with a repeating blues riff harmonized to discard traditional blues chord voicings.

Though released shortly after Brubeck's "Take Five," which is cited as introducing the 5/4 time signature to jazz, "As Long as You're Living" is a more adventurous statement of the possibilities of new rhythmic frameworks. It only introduces the melody as a closing statement, leaving the listener to focus on the interplay of the cyclical bass line, driving but lopsided swing pattern, and the soloist's negotiation of the new rhythmic landscape. When the melody does arrive, it is surprising in its novelty and serves to propel what might have become a monotonous pattern in lesser hands.

The band recorded the song three more times in 1959 and 1960: with vocalist Abbey Lincoln (*Abbey Is Blue*, Riverside, 1959); during a live concert in West Germany (released on *Long as You're Living*, Enja, 1984); and on Tommy Turrentine's only record as a leader (*Tommy Turrentine*, Time Records, 1960).

Lincoln's version features the lyrics of vocalist Oscar Brown, a tribute to the technique of vocalese developed by Pittsburgh native Eddie Jefferson, which involved writing lyrics to the recorded improvisations of notable musicians. Lincoln maintains a sense of ease while singing the words to the angular melody, bringing a conversational style to a decidedly difficult singing environment. Roach and Boswell provide steady support for Lincoln's understated vocal acrobatics, while Priester and the Turrentines either layer three-part harmonies on her vocals or interject subtle dissonant riffs among the lyrical message of self-determination and perseverance. These records reflect the wider impact of the Grill as a place where ideas were incubated and players' skills were tested. It was also a place where performance and social scenes intersected with political and social struggles as artists such as Roach explored the potential of community that can form through music.

Though Roach had parted ways with his Pittsburgh sidemen mid-1960, he continued to perform at the Grill throughout the rest of the decade with Lincoln. A July 1963 performance prompted the *Courier* report of the packed club at capacity:

> [The audience] responded to [Roach's] moods with deep speculative silence as he washed brushes delicately over the cymbals or with raucous applause to his fantastic press rolls and superhuman [precision]. These were some of the most appreciative audiences ever to pay homage to the stream of jazz greats who have played the Grill and they responded to Roach's artistry in a manner that has not been seen here in years.[95]

The special synergy of these performances was apparent in Roach's comment during an interview with Harold L. Keith: "All too often, the general public is of the opinion that jazz musicians are dope fiends, thugs, and assorted other things that have little to do with their art. Pittsburgh's Grill is one of the few decent houses that we have in which to play."[96] Roach expanded on his message in two Sunday appearances on the WZUM radio program, where he emphasized the importance of jazz musicians improving their professional treatment through the cultivation of their own social awareness and potential as community leaders. Calling for a national organization of jazz musicians that would unite their cause for greater recognition, Roach lamented that Black musicians were not actively engaged with processes of social change, nor were they developing a level of professionalism that would elevate jazz as a valued cultural contribution. Roach's denomination of the Grill as a "house" situates this social space as a bedrock of his activism and a larger cultural advocacy for Black Americans.

But Roach's status as a performer and activist would be scarred again by incidents in 1965 and 1966. During an anticipated week at the Grill in August 1966, Roach received the news that close friend and pianist Bud Powell had died.

Figure 4.11. Charles "Teenie" Harris, American, 1908–1998, Max Roach's band including Eddie Kahn on bass, Ron Mathews on piano, Clifford Jordan on tenor saxophone, and Max Roach on drums, on stage in Crawford Grill No. 2, July - August 1963, black and white: Kodak Safety Film, H: 4 in. × W: 5 in. (10.20 × 12.70 cm), Carnegie Museum of Art, Pittsburgh: Heinz Family Fund, 2001.35.9188 © Carnegie Museum of Art, Charles "Teenie" Harris Archive.

Powell, who had suffered from mental illness, died with little support or money in New York City on August 1.

Devastated at the loss of the great artist, Roach was driven to emotional outbursts that prompted two front-page *Courier* articles that described him throwing the acoustic bass from the elevated stage and shoving the piano against the wall.[97] Fearing further destruction, the Grill's doorman called the police, who arrested Roach and took him to a Hill District police station. After posting a small bail, Roach left Lincoln and the band and reportedly boarded a plane to attend Powell's funeral in New York City but was removed when his erratic behavior led to the plane landing in Johnstown, Pennsylvania. He continued his journey to attend the funeral and even returned to Pittsburgh to finish his contract at the Grill. Disturbed by the *Courier*'s coverage of his behavior, the chaotic scene it caused, and his arrest at the Grill, Roach threw another fit of rage at a nearby bar, punched through a window that severely cut his arm, and was arrested again.[98] Despite all the commotion, Roach repeatedly appeared in the Grill in the following two years, a sign of Joe and Buzzy Robinson's unfailing support of the troubled artist as well as Roach's investment in the club. In other words, the value of their social bonds far outweighed the convenience of their business transaction.

Throughout the 1960s, the Grill focused on booking leading figures of hard bop and cool jazz, including Art Blakey, Max Roach, Julian "Cannonball" Adderley, Illinois Jacquet, Slide Hampton, Ray Bryant, Red Garland, Wes Montgomery, Roy Haynes, John Coltrane, Les McCann, Kenny Burrell, Wynton Kelly, Art Farmer, Jim Hall, Bill Evans, Horace Silver, and Joe Henderson. It did not, however, shy away from occasionally presenting jazz musicians who were developing experimental approaches to small group jazz: what was called the "new thing," the avant-garde, and free jazz. In February 1960, alto saxophonist Ornette Coleman with trumpeter Don Cherry, bassist Charlie Haden, and drummer Billy Higgins played a week-long engagement on the heels of their 1959 release *The Shape of Jazz to Come*. Like Roach, Coleman was exploring a group performance concept that excluded piano, which marked a conscious shift away from explicitly stated harmonic progressions and provided an improvisatory environment where the drummer had a larger role in shaping the performance. While Roach's piano-less groups remained grounded in the hard bop style, Coleman's group broke with established song forms and tonal frameworks, propelling the music through stream-of-consciousness extrapolations of angular and soaring melodies stated by Coleman and Cherry.

Coleman's reputation preceded him, with his innovations cited as a benchmark in the development of jazz. The *Courier* reported the Grill's booking of Coleman: "Ornette Coleman, alto artist, is very definitely the most talented musician to arise on the jazz scene since the late Charlie Parker."[99] Responses in the Hill were mixed, however, with some in attendance finding the band's direction to be an affront to the listening culture of the Grill. Trombonist Harold Betters recalls going with fellow Pittsburgh musician Bobby Jones to hear Coleman's performance: "I couldn't understand him because he played all over. I couldn't stand him! I was with [jazz organist] Bobby Jones and he was saying, 'He's a bad motherfucker!' So I'm sitting there looking up and I heard that 'blip blop' and I wondered what the hell is he trying to prove? What's the feeling I get? I don't understand the picture."[100]

Betters's reaction to the group's new sounds was mirrored by others who felt it pushed too far beyond the boundaries of modern jazz. Pittsburgh vocalist Sandy Staley recalls of the band: "I don't know what the hell he was doing. I left because it hurt my ears. He was squeaking and squawking and it wasn't very pleasant so I only took a set and then left."[101] Drummer Chuck Spatafore, a proponent of the once-revolutionary style of bebop, confesses, "Twice I tried to listen to Ornette and I just couldn't do it."[102] Coleman's incorporation of new timbres such as pops, squeaks, and shakes into his solos was not new, however, as it had been used regularly by blues and jazz musicians for decades.

Coleman's emphasis on the "freedom" of the sounds and expressions of blues outside of recognizable formal structures challenged casual listeners and seasoned musicians alike to dramatically rethink the familiar. Coleman's extension of an understanding of blues as a "free music" could be read as an expression of Afro-modernism in which social and class divisions between blues and high art are collapsed.[103] As jazz historian and photographer Valerie Wilmer wrote, while Coleman's approach "did have its obvious precedents in rural blues, church music and field hollers . . . in terms of an actual concept, the freedom proposed by Ornette Coleman was entirely new."[104]

Coleman emphasized breaking down traditional song forms and cues challenging listeners to find new ways of hearing musical narratives. In an interview with Wilmer, drummer Ed Blackwell relayed Coleman's insistence that he break free from standard song forms and develop ideas that extended beyond the boundaries of four-, eight-, and twelve-measure phrases. This approach required abandoning common cues requiring listeners to focus rather on the melodic interplay of bass, drums, saxophone, and trumpet. The negative reaction of local musicians hinged on the emphasis and extension of these techniques as timbral studies in themselves, free from a grounding in familiar harmonic progressions or melodic figures.

Listeners may also have been exasperated by Coleman's use of an inexpensive plastic saxophone, which produced a brighter, thinner tone and perhaps did not look like the instrument of a serious professional. What his group offered was a collective process of abstracting the language of bebop and constructing improvised narratives that bridged the specific melodic and rhythmic ideas of musicians such as Charlie Parker into non-tonal territories. Both Mingus and Coleman drew extensively from the blues, though they took different approaches to reimagining its formal and stylistic qualities. That Mingus dismissed Coleman as belonging "to the category of instrumentalists who are incapable of interpreting a piece with chords and an established progression" speaks to the deep divisions wrought within the ranks of leading modern jazz musicians.[105]

These challenges to jazz's formal, harmonic, and melodic norms extended to the social norms of listening that had developed in the Grill. As music scholar Mark Anthony Neal argued, these conceptual developments in jazz, while forging new directions for the music's improvisatory potentials, also alienated core listening audiences in Black communities:

> As bebop presaged, the heady jazz of the 1960s, often devoid of swing and an accessible blues center, quite possibly represented the genre's final break with the black working class, who often valued it, like the blues and rhythm and blues, for its cathartic powers in the leisure spaces they inhabited. In this regard, the political agenda of critics and the personal choices of musicians were at odds with the

desire and pursuit of pleasure on behalf of some black audiences, particularly as pleasure often undermined, temporally at least, the realities of segregation, Jim Crow politics, and racism.[106]

Neal's emphasis on the relationship between stylistic innovation and embedded social norms of listening in Black communities, the working class in particular, highlights how Coleman's music complicated social cues that listeners used to emotionally engage in the music. While Coleman did not make another appearance at the Grill, the group made a deep impression on listeners as they were forced to decipher the music's "message." An unidentified *Courier* writer described the band playing "weird sounds to sparse audiences at the Crawford Grill" and remarked, "After attending the show opening night, which was Monday, we left completely frustrated because of our failure to understand the unconventional group. Nevertheless, we returned the following day."[107]

Confounded by what she was hearing at the Grill, the writer refused to dismiss the music outright and, in the spirit of the Grill's listening culture, encouraged his readers to experience the new music: "[W]e suggest you make it your business to see them. We assure you—you will have an unforgettable musical experience. Coleman and men possess a quality—without us being able to pinpoint it—that is exhilarating and very exciting."[108] As Don Cherry recalled, the group's conceptual approach and Coleman's playing often split audiences: "There was this thing when we played where there were those who really loved it, the growth of it and the spirit of it. And then there were those who didn't like it because they felt it was jeopardizing their position in life."[109]

Neal's observation of modern jazz's break from the aesthetic norms of the Black working class illustrates the fractures that emerged as musicians such as Coleman developed new creative approaches. This was certainly one of many reactions garnered at the Grill in a city known for its large working-class population. However, the Grill framed the divergent sounds of jazz as part of the continuity within the neighborhood's nightlife. The listening culture at the Grill developed shared values toward jazz performance that could complicate a consensus of what jazz's stylistic boundaries could be. The Grill's contribution to the discourse of modern jazz illustrates how the jazz house functioned as a listening environment in which audiences, writers, and musicians explored and problematized the boundaries between music and noise.

Critical listening revealed that these boundaries were not simply a question of discerning good from bad but also intertwined with constructing notions of modernity that resonated with Black political and social life. Modern life in America in all its contradictions filtered through the Grill as the demolition began in the Lower Hill, from Walt Harper's Bermuda Shorts Night to Mingus's "A Foggy Day," which grated on the ears of *Courier* editor Keith. As Dunlap sought to build the Hurricane as a homeplace, the Grill early on established itself as a cultural beacon where patrons and musicians were welcomed as family and even lived, as was the case with Leroy and Betty Brown. Events such as Roach's meeting with NAACP organizers in the Grill further speak to the club as a homeplace in which one could find a sense of belonging and a community of shared struggles. There, music was at once background, occasion, and primer for social relations. Listening in the Grill held the potential for connections and continuities that were of larger consequence to the Hill District neighborhood and beyond.

### The Art of Listening

In addition to providing a powerful political voice for Pittsburgh's Black community throughout the twentieth century, the *Pittsburgh Courier* was an important cultural forum where writers such as Phyl Garland (1935–2006), George E. Pitts (1925–1987), Harold L. Keith (1921–2002), and George F. Brown (1917–1975) distilled experiences of listening—characterized by intrigue, joy, frustration, and confusion—through their analyses of the music's cultural, political, and artistic dimensions.[110] With their office located in the Upper Hill District, the *Courier* journalists were regulars at the Grill. Their columns, reviews, and articles contributed to public discourse around modern jazz and fostered an environment that accommodated the ever-shifting tension between patrons expecting specific content and musicians developing new conceptual approaches.

Phyl Garland's column "Listen In," which ran weekly from 1964 to 1966, is one such example of a public forum that discussed artists who were testing the boundaries of modern jazz. Garland, daughter of *Courier* journalist Hazel Garland, was dedicated to developing critical understandings of jazz, blues, and soul. She wrote with passion about those whose music bridged artistic innovation and spiritual self-awareness and enticed her readers to hear the music within a larger cultural context. Her 1964 review of John Coltrane's *Live at Birdland* album illustrates her ardent belief in the potential of modern jazz as a progressive force in a rapidly shifting landscape of American popular music:

> With new artists emerging daily to add their own voices to the torment and joy of jazz, imitation is inevitable. Yet there are a few whose visions of new musical worlds are so clear that they seem to forge fresh musical paths with every note they play. Thank God for them! Otherwise, we would be left to wallow in an ocean of tired funk, the Beatles, and Al Hirt. Foremost among those who might be called saviors, in an artistic sense, is John Coltrane, whose saxophone statements, constantly, have provided the sound-delicacies for jaded ears. One has come to expect nothing less than excellence from this insatiable experimentalist.[111]

By distinguishing Coltrane among jazz musicians seeking "new musical worlds," Garland touches on the importance of critical listeners who engage meaningfully with modern jazz's creative directions. Garland's review positions Coltrane's music as a refuge for these listeners not only from popular culture but also from White mainstream music that was literally invading the Hill District. In September 1964, the Beatles drew a capacity audience of twelve thousand screaming teenage fans to the Civic Arena, which was completed and opened three years prior in the Lower Hill District. The zealous crowd prompted the venue's executive director to consider airlifting the band to and from the concert by helicopter.[112]

A year later, Garland found Pittsburgh's newly built Civic Arena's expansive stage far less accommodating to Coltrane's music. His appearance took place amid three days of back-to-back performances by jazz luminaries at the 1965 Pittsburgh Jazz Festival, produced by the renowned music promoter George Wein.[113] While the festival signaled the growing appreciation of modern jazz in American society, Coltrane's performance lacked the inspiration Garland had expected:

> Shades of his insistent, searing style were apparent, but the lines leapt too furiously to be consistent. He lapsed, at times, into chaos, offering shrieking, climactic utterances, for which no prelude had been presented. Furthermore, the usual unity of thought seemed to be lacking in the performances of his sidemen who, always, are so together . . . . Much of the audience became restless that night, which might account for the reason so many ladies suddenly had to go to the rest room. This, however, might be expected of a jazz festival crowd, where most come to hear a particular type of music, remaining immune to anything foreign to the taste . . . . Others, who would love him no matter what he did, realized that he might be tired and hungry, and disgusted at being required to play in a short period of time. He was too cramped to construct those formidable, extended improvisations which had earned for him a right to don the mantle of greatness.[114]

As an audience member, Garland expressed frustration at the disconnect between listeners and artists in a festival environment where many came for the spectacle of a large gathering rather than to listen intently. Aware of the limitations of such musical contexts, Garland asked her readers to seek other venues for listening and connecting to Coltrane's music: "I implore the resentful ones to understand a little, and to delve into his recorded efforts . . . . To appreciate it, one must approach it in the same spirit defined in the moving poem by Coltrane, which is to be found on the inner side of the album [*A Love Supreme*]: 'Help us to resolve our fears and weaknesses.'"

Informing Garland's review is the perspective of someone who worked in the Hill day in, day out, between 1956 and 1961 and witnessed the destruction and redevelopment of the Lower Hill and attendant changes to its cultural life. In the case of the Pittsburgh Jazz Festival, the Civic Arena provided a dramatically different context for listening to jazz that did not always serve the musicians' creative processes. In shifting blame for her disappointment from the artist to the performance context, she leads readers to question whether Coltrane and his renowned quartet would have played differently had they been better looked after and also had been allowed more time to develop their ideas. In accepting her own frustration, she acknowledges the important role of the venue and audience in shaping the performance.

While not explicitly citing the Crawford Grill No. 2 and Hurricane Bar & Grill, Garland's description of Coltrane's Civic Arena performance implies a yearning for the nearby clubs. Decades later, Garland reminisced about the Grill's welcoming social environment: "The magic of the Grill . . . grew from its unbeatable combination of a homey atmosphere, good food, extraordinary jazz, and attentive wait staff. The owner's warmth rivaled that of the musicians who would mingle with the crowd once they stepped down from the bandstand."[115] The Pittsburgh Jazz Festival, which drew approximately twelve thousand fans over three days, dwarfed the concerts held in the Grill and Hurricane, which accommodated 150 people at most. Whereas the Civic Arena was designed to draw fandom and host temporary communities of listeners, the Grill and Hurricane facilitated a sustained culture of listening shared by repeat performances and audiences.

The Grill and its weekly feature of touring musicians provided an informal environment that accommodated a wide range of patrons who came and went as they wished. Pittsburgh organist Gene Ludwig remembers stopping in on a Tuesday, a slower work night for the gigging musician, to hear John Coltrane with McCoy Tyner, Elvin Jones, and Jimmy Garrison during their April 1963 appearance. Coltrane's quartet, which remained together from 1962 to 1965, was one of the most important in the course of jazz history, as it collectively realized the potential of Coltrane's spiritually and theoretically driven musical visions. Ludwig found that the club was relatively empty, so he and his bandmates stayed for several sets. Because the Grill did not charge a cover, they had a few beers—"65 cents for a bottle of beer, 75 cents for premium beer"—and then went on their way.[116] Artist Thaddeus Mosley, an avid jazz listener and a longtime Pittsburgh resident, also attended a weeknight performance of Coltrane's group to avoid the weekend crowds. In the intimate setting, Mosley remembers Coltrane going to the Grill's cellar to continue practicing between sets.[117] Pittsburgh pianist Spencer Bey recalls the weekend scene of Coltrane's gigs being far more bustling: "Elvin Jones would be beating the shit out of those god damn [sic] drums. The place was jam packed [sic]. They had so many people in there that they had to lock the doors because they couldn't let anyone else in."[118] These divergent experiences throughout the week at the Grill shaped how listeners understood the creative processes of jazz musicians in relation to the hosting venue.

Listening in the Hill District occurred within a context of socializing that was as much a draw as the music for many patrons. The neighborhood clubs brought together a wide array of individuals to form what music scholar Guthrie Ramsey calls "community theaters"—public spaces that "provide [the] audience with a place to negotiate with others—in a highly social way—what cultural expressions such as music means."[119] The Grill and Hurricane welcomed patrons who were out to socialize alongside those who wanted to focus on the music. *Courier* staff writer Patricia Parker-Reid remembers the dynamic social life that framed the music:

> [As for] the atmosphere at the Grill, you were supposed to be cool. Everybody had their little walk-on and were dressed up in suits and ties. Ladies had their dresses. Some people preferred the booth to the bar. John Henry Johnson of the Steelers [football team] and [Pittsburgh Pirates' outfielder] Roberto Clemente would always be sitting at the bar. In the back were all the *Courier* staff. With the way it was set up, we would always sit in the back because we felt that we were closer to the bandstand because nobody would be walking in front of us except to go to the bathroom. The people who wanted action sat in the front because they wanted to see somebody and to be seen. We didn't care about being seen.[120]

Many who passed through did so as part of a social ritual that began Friday night and lasted through the weekend. Mosley distinguished himself as one drawn by the music rather than the nightlife scene, noting that many patrons "wouldn't know who was playing at the Grill because they had no interest." Weekend audiences included both a "core of people who went strictly to hear the music and a core of people who went out strictly on Friday and Saturday night."[121] With Pittsburgh's steel industry still alive in the 1950s and 1960s, workers would seek a social outlet as relief from a week of long shifts, moving from bar to bar and then to after-hours clubs. As a result, these clubs were places where industrial laborers and celebrities could rub elbows. In addition to the steady flow of featured bands, artists such as Duke Ellington, Count Basie, and Sarah Vaughn would stop in after performing concerts in Pittsburgh. Local sports legends such as former Steeler quarterback Bobby Layne would also come in. Stories circulated that Layne "put two crisp $100 bills in the saxophone of Big Jay McNeely as a tip" one night at the Hurricane.[122]

The Grill and Hurricane were also destinations for listeners from throughout the region and so provided rare contexts for interracial socializing. Racism plagued daily life in Pittsburgh's Black communities, exemplified by the front-page headlines of the *Courier* on July 11, 1964: "CROSS BURNED HERE: Independence Day Chosen to Warn Negroes," "[Black] Youth Slain by Cop Buried," and "Bombs Miss Auto of Teens."[123] Concerts in White communities remained largely segregated events, while Black-owned clubs generally welcomed White patrons. Parker-Reid reflects on this dynamic, also touching on the role of musical preferences in determining the racial makeup of musical events:

> Seemed like everyone, black and white, got along ok around music. There wasn't that big separation in the '50s. You'd see as many whites in the Grill as you'd see blacks. We weren't, as blacks, allowed to go to a lot of the white clubs. There was a place called the Holiday Inn in Monroeville. We could rent the place and all the blacks would be there but we weren't allowed in the club during "white night," as we called it. They'd have guys singing in there that we didn't care for anyway. They had second-rate crooners like Vic Damone.[124]

While an inclusive policy clearly aided business at the club, it was also a means for owners Joe and Buzzy Robinson and Birdie Dunlap to explore the possibilities of integration within the context of the civil rights era. As discussed in the next chapter, racial integration in places of work, education, and leisure, while a goal of civil rights leaders, presented challenges for social institutions and businesses in Black communities. In 1957, Carl Arter, president of Pittsburgh's Black Musicians' Local 471 of the American Federation of Musicians, defended his reluctance to rush integrating segregated Musicians Union locals in Pittsburgh. The question of how to "integrate on an equal footing" was of primary concern to Arter and other labor leaders who feared losing representation, independence, and connections to their communities.[125]

Those who relocated during the Lower Hill Redevelopment project often experienced forced integration in neighborhoods where White residents were not welcoming. In the Grill and Hurricane, integration occurred on the terms set by the Black club owners, who treated both Black and White patrons as valued guests. Within this context, collective listening provided a model for racial integration in which White patrons supported Black businesses as well as participated in the Hill's social life. The popularity of these clubs among White visitors also grounded discussions of segregation within the lived realities of Hill residents. The legacy of 1920s black and tan clubs would have lived in the memories of the Robinsons and Dunlap as they sought to build jazz houses that suited their needs as Black entrepreneurs in a predominantly Black neighborhood.

For Phyl Garland's mother, Hazel Garland, the popularity of these clubs was a source of pride in Black-owned businesses and their contribution to Pittsburgh's cultural life. At the same time, their wider appeal was also a reminder of the conditions of segregation that made them possible in the first place. In her weekly column "Things to Talk About," the elder Garland maps the racial landscape that Black and White patrons navigate in attending popular jazz clubs:

After making the rounds of some of the downtown niteries [*sic*], the column got to comparing them with some of the "name" spots in what they call the "Hill." In my opinion, the latter places have it all over the downtown spots. Take for instance, the Joyce Bryant Room of the Flamingo Hotel, the Hurricane, and Crawford Grill. Now there isn't a place downtown . . . where all of us are welcome . . . that can come up to those three places when it comes to cleanliness, beauty, entertainment and food. Not even [Lenny Litman's club] Copa where there is some question as to whether we are wanted or not, can top those spots above. And it seems as though I am not alone in my thinking. Word is getting around to those of the other race. Just like some of us are hurrying downtown, ofays are just as anxious to get uptown. There's certainly an awful lot of them making the rounds in the "Hill."[126]

Here, Garland reiterates to *Courier* readers the importance of Hill District clubs not just as convenient destinations for African Americans but as valuable sites of culture and entertainment—a stance that would echo through the music journalism of her daughter Phyl Garland. Addressing her readers with a familiar "we" as distinguished from "the other race" speaks directly to Black lived experiences in daily pursuits of leisure. Garland's observations of Black patrons venturing downtown in these pursuits are countered with that of Whites who are at liberty to participate in the Hill's cultural life. The word "ofay," a derogatory, early twentieth-century slang term used to identify Whiteness and White individuals, usually as encroaching forces within Black social contexts, further emphasizes the rift between Black and White understandings of nightlife.

The image of the jazz club as an entrée to Black social life was an established trope in popular culture in the 1950s and 1960s—the most celebrated literary example being Jack Kerouac's *On the Road*, published in 1957. In 1961, the Hurricane was chosen to stage a scene for an episode of *Route 66*, a television drama series that depicted two young, White American men as they traveled the United States in their convertible Chevrolet Corvette, searching for "a kind of niche" where they belonged.[127] The show, shot on location in various cities, aimed to connect character studies of remarkable and tragic individuals to urban and rural landscapes throughout the US. In the episode "Goodnight Sweet Blues," the two protagonists, Tod Stiles (played by Martin Milner) and Buz Murdock (played by George Maharis), set out from Pittsburgh to continue their journey when they narrowly avoid a collision with another car driven by an elderly and ailing African American woman. This chance meeting with Jeannie Henderson (played by singer and actress Ethel Waters) leads to Stiles and Murdock agreeing to gather members of her old jazz band scattered across the US.[128] Driven by the urgency of Henderson's failing health, the two men ultimately succeed in staging the band's last performance by her bedside in Pittsburgh before she dies. During their journey, the Hurricane's façade and interior are used to depict one of several fictional clubs where Stiles seeks the musician Hank Plummer (played by actor Bill Gunn).

On this fictionalized journey of self-discovery within America's cultural landscape, the Hurricane, as an archetype of a jazz club, embodies a space of redemption for the Black musician as well as the White protagonist in his vicarious search for friendship and social bonds. Gathered around Henderson's deathbed, Stiles and Murdock look on as Plummer confesses that the ailing singer was like the mother that he never had. As the other musicians gather, they too express similar sentiments of camaraderie and appreciation for Henderson as a musical matriarch. For Stiles and Murdock, *Route 66*'s protagonists, the Hurricane, and bedside jazz performance provide a temporary grounding in their own search for meaning. For the musicians, the reunion at Henderson's is a prodigal journey to a homeplace, a place of healing and affirmation of relations that were forged through years of performing and listening to one another.

In catering to younger White American audiences, *Route 66* centers on Stiles and Murdock as flawed yet well-intentioned participants experiencing the diversity of American life. In "Goodnight Sweet Blues," Ethel Waters's sage and gentle character realizes her personal redemption through the altruistic efforts of the White travelers, one of whom is a jazz aficionado. The story positions jazz as an underappreciated art form that requires White validation and support to realize its potential as a cultural force. Underlying this narrative is a reoccurring theme of a White search for Black authenticity as well as White anxieties over exclusion from Black culture.[129]

In the real Hurricane, jazz musicians also benefited from the patronage of White audiences, though it was within a social context and business infrastructure created by the matriarch Birdie Dunlap. In the context of the Hurricane, Dunlap's vision of integration and a music-oriented collectivity decenters rather than discounts White appreciation and participation in jazz. That Dunlap created a homeplace for Black cultural life within a besieged community while running a profitable business and fostering cross-racial socializing speaks more to her agency as a dedicated community leader than to the legitimacy of jazz in mainstream society. Dunlap, as well as Robinson in the Grill, was the ultimate arbiter who realized a vision of the musical commingling of integrated audiences and supporting the development of Black music within Black communities.

In addition to making space for listeners across the race line, Robinson and Dunlap strove for a level of musical commitment with nightly performances at the Grill and Hurricane, which provided steady work for musicians to hone their skills, build performance stamina, and develop new approaches. The frequent opportunity to hear music also helped listeners develop their own critical listening skills. One could hear the same group across several nights, taking notice of less-inspired performances and reveling in the convergence of various factors that made some nights exceptional. Listeners could also compare a range of jazz artists and maintain a critical framework for assessing a given artist's level of dedication to the moment.

Parker-Reid reflected on the importance of the clubs for developing discerning listeners: "I think Pittsburghers have a greater ear for music as a result of those days. Just your average, everyday worker had a better ear for musicians. We were very critical. Many times I got tired of George Benson, thinking, 'He's just messing around,' and just walked out. They had to really perform here to keep your attention. They had to be good." For Parker-Reid, the music unfolded as part of the social scene, but it also depended on an engaged audience striking the right balance between talking to a friend and focusing on the musicians. In this context, the audience members were not passive recipients of the music:

> Sometimes, Miles Davis, he could get way out there. What you would notice around you was that people would just continue to talk, drink, and eat. But if it was somebody who really was on target [there was] complete silence. Even if you were talking to someone you'd say, "hold up" and you're going to listen and then if they'd start getting way out somewhere you'd say, "As I was saying." The musicians could see that because they were that close to the people. Just up a few steps. They'd know instinctively where to go then [in their solos]. They'd say, "They were listening when I did this" so it gave them a gauge too. You didn't mind them going out there but they had to come back into that base tune that was recognizable.[130]

Parker-Reid's mention of Miles Davis losing her attention by playing "way out there" signals a discord between performer and audience—a departure from a collectively understood process or musical narration. Discerning listeners might react to this discord by shifting their focus to a conversation with another audience member only to refocus their attention on the musicians following certain cues, such as dynamic shifts. Dunlap, an avid music fan, found ways to interject nonverbal support for inspired musical moments. As saxophonist Lou Stellute recalls, "When she liked your solo or something, she would get a glass or a saltshaker and tap on the bar and that meant that she wanted you [the musician] to respond." Stellute, who was playing with the John Bartel Quartet, an all-White jazz group from Pittsburgh, recalls that Dunlap encouraged the band to "do your thing," adding, "I know what you do, so don't come in here and think that you have to play like Sonny Stitt."[131] In this example, Dunlap, as a dedicated listener, realized the importance of supporting artists so they felt welcomed and comfortable, as well as the diverse range and background of the performers that reflected the community that she helped coalesce at her club.

Figure 4.12. Charles "Teenie" Harris, American, 1908–1998, Men and women waving handkerchiefs in front of bar, including bass player Dan Lely wearing moustache and eyeglasses, and Billy Kimes on right, with band on raised stage behind bar, including Rhoda Scott on drums, at Hurricane Club, c. 1953–1965, black and white: Kodak Safety Film, H: 4 in. × W: 5 in. (10.20 × 12.70 cm), Carnegie Museum of Art, Pittsburgh: Heinz Family Fund, 2001.35.13237, © Carnegie Museum of Art, Charles "Teenie" Harris Archive.

When bands were not playing to the audience's expectations, listeners might actively guide musicians with positive feedback. Trombonist, educator, and jazz historian Nelson Harrison recalls hearing a band at the Grill that was not connecting with the audience. After the group finished a song, "[t]here'd be total silence and the looks on [the listeners'] faces would say, 'Are you going to play something or what?'" Noticing that the musicians were unable to get a reaction from the audience, Harrison "clapped to give them some feedback because they were scared to death." This gesture gave the musicians some confidence, which in turn improved their playing. As more listeners clapped in appreciation, the band improved, so that "by the time they were done with the set, they played something really good and the people were responding."[132] Harrison found this process to be central to the culture of listening and the demands that it placed on performers: "What made the music great were the audiences that knew whether you were playing or not. If you *weren't* playing, then they'd be looking

Figure 4.13. Charles "Teenie" Harris, American, 1908–1998, Women and men crowded in newly redecorated bar in Crawford Grill No. 2 with alternating checkered block floors, bronze marching band sculpture on wall, and upholstered booths, August 1953, black and white: Kodak Safety Film, H: 4 in. × W: 5 in. (10.20 × 12.70 cm), Carnegie Museum of Art, Pittsburgh: Heinz Family Fund, 2001.35.19642 © Carnegie Museum of Art, Charles "Teenie" Harris Archive.

at you [silently] and if you *were* playing, they'd be shouting at you. That's what made you play."[133]

With discerning listeners, these clubs provided valuable contexts to young musicians who were learning how to play jazz and interact with an audience. For drummer Roger Humphries, the experience of sitting in with his heroes Max Roach and Art Blakey at the Grill was formative to his creative development. In his teen years, Humphries attended Friday and Saturday matinees accompanied by a relative so that he could both learn and gain exposure for future work as a sideman. Humphries acknowledges that while audiences were not there to hear younger musicians sit in, they were understanding and supportive when they saw that he was already an advanced player engrossed in the musical styles of Roach and Blakey. These opportunities, though small gestures of support from renowned jazz musicians, were nerve-wracking and emotional experiences that Humphries learned to master with time: "It was a funny thing because I would get so nervous when I would go up there and sit in. I would be fine until I got

Table 4.1.

| Chorus | Description | Chorus | Description | Chorus | Description |
|---|---|---|---|---|---|
| Chorus 1 (00:44) | Riffing (Repeated patterns) | Chorus 11 (02:26) | Blowing | Chorus 21 (04:11) | Block chord riff with brighter timbre setting |
| Chorus 2 (00:54) | Riffing | Chorus 12 (02:36) | Sustained note with counter melody | Chorus 22 (04:21) | Continue… |
| Chorus 3 (01:05) | Blowing (Improvising linear ideas) | Chorus 13 (02:46) | Continue… | Chorus 23 (04:31) | Continue… |
| Chorus 4 (01:15) | Riffing | Chorus 14 (02:56) | Continue… | Chorus 24 (04:41) | Continue with variations… |
| Chorus 5 (01:25) | Blowing | Chorus 15 (03:07) | Blowing | Chorus 25 (04:51) | Rhythmic riff with non-tonal sounds |
| Chorus 6 (01:36) | Riffing | Chorus 16 (03:17) | Blowing | Chorus 26 (04:01) | Block chords riff |
| Chorus 7 (01:46) | Riffing | Chorus 17 (03:27) | Sustained note with counter melody | Chorus 27 (05:12) | Sustained note and rhythmic hits |
| Chorus 8 (01:56) | Blowing | Chorus 18 (03:37) | Continue… | Chorus 28 (05:22) | Rhythmic riff with non-tonal sounds |
| Chorus 9 (02:06) | Riffing | Chorus 19 (03:47) | Continued… | Chorus 29 (05:31) | Continue… |
| Chorus 10 (02:16) | Blowing | Chorus 20 (04:00) | Continued… | Chorus 30 (05:41) | Continue with variations… |

Table 4.1. A chorus-by-chorus outline of Jimmy Smith's solo on "The Champ" as recorded on Live at the Village Gate (1963). Each chorus consists of a twelve-bar blues progression.

home and when I came home, I felt like I was going to die. I had that at an early age and the doctor said that I would grow out of it."[134]

Compared to sociologist Howard Becker's classic study of dance band musicians in *The Outsiders*, where musicians might erect physical barriers to keep "unhip" audience members from interfering with the performance, the physical space of the Grill and Hurricane brought musicians and audiences as close as possible.[135] Italian American saxophonist Don Aliquo Sr. recalled the impact of playing the Grill early in his career: "They would let you know either with their body motions or their yelling or their appearance [in] some way." After the set was over, "you would get off the bandstand and everybody would come over—at least the ones who liked you—and talk to you to get some kind of feedback as to what you are all about, which would make you feel pretty good. The recognition always gave you some incentive to get better."[136] These encounters with actively listening audiences brought about a "rude awakening that you had to get better. I learned what I needed to do to improve myself and to please audiences. You had to play more artistically so that you could gain recognition."[137]

Organist Jimmy Smith honed this approach in his own extended solos, which led listeners through carefully constructed musical narratives. An unidentified *Courier* writer praised Smith's abilities to move beyond the listener's expectation and comprehension of the music while keeping them captivated:

> Smith, whose organ ramblings not only are entertaining, but at times downright baffling, has the unusual knack of injecting into his playing seemingly impossible improvisation. One of the highlights of the group's performance is when they sail into a tune called "The Champ," parts one and two, giving vent to all their individual know-how and simultaneously coming together on common ground after taking solo trips to "outer space."[138]

Smith's 1963 live recording of "The Champ," an up-tempo twelve-bar blues by Dizzy Gillespie, offers a look into this process of traveling to "outer space" as part of an extended musical narrative.[139] Smith begins his solo using a simple repeating "riff" to draw the listener in while interspersing choruses of linear melodic ideas, or "blowing," to provide a contrasting musical texture. As the solo develops, Smith then introduces the technique of sustaining a high note, which he carries across several choruses as a method of building tension and playing with the expectations of the listener. In the last third of his solo (choruses 21–30), Smith experiments with the organ's timbre settings to produce percussive noises, which he exploits with fast repeating rhythmic patterns. This progression leads the listener to hear discordant "trips to outer space" as part of a narrative continuity with familiar riff-structured playing common in blues (table 4.1).

Music innovations and improvisatory explorations of musicians such as Jimmy Smith were more than intellectual feats to be admired. Musicians and listeners alike describe the emotional impact of an inspired performance as having a healing impact and imparting a sense of peace and social connectivity. Harrison touches on the importance of music in these clubs as more than a backdrop to drinking and socializing: "People came there to get fed. That music enabled you to go out there and face life. When times were the hardest, you could go get healed with the music and you could face anything."[140] These sentiments are echoed in Stellute's reflections on performing at the Hurricane:

> I feel sorry for anyone who didn't go through that experience. When they liked you, the audience really fed the performance, and it was an important thing. That's the element of spirituality of this whole era. And there was a great element of spirituality involved in all this . . . . There was an extra spark when you start to receive that energy. It builds you up. You are enriching their lives and as a result they are enriching your life."[141]

To be fed by music so that one can go out and face the world is a powerful declaration of the role that the jazz house played in the 1950s and 1960s Pittsburgh—a city undergoing physical and socio-economic changes in the name of progress. With the help of a dynamic range of musicians, the Robinsons and Dunlap nurtured a unique community of cross-class and integrated listeners at the Grill and Hurricane. Collective listening provided a means of recentering narratives of cultural changes, racial harmonies and dissonances, and urban "renewal" within Black social contexts. With sounds of jazz still in their ears, the patrons of the clubs had to step out and make sense of the rhythms of urban life under duress from many development projects that threatened existing modes of the neighborhood.

Listening, however, is a skill that can be honed to enable one to navigate a city as well as to appreciate a musician's artistry. French sociologist Henri Lefebvre, who was also an avid pianist, urged scholars to listen to cities as one would a symphony and cultivate aural sensibilities that enabled them to build a "polyrhythmic" awareness of the overlapping rhythms of daily life. In the jazz house, listening cultures created a space in which audiences could subvert what Lefebvre calls the "linear," "oppressive" rhythms of work and experience how new rhythms produce "a time that forgets time, during which time no longer counts (and is no longer counted)."[142] In light of Lefebvre's attention to the lived consequences of urban policy, Mayor Lawrence's image of harmony between state-driven development projects resulting in skyscrapers, arenas, and highways and a small jazz club in the Hill District takes on additional significance. Was Lawrence's 1953 speech at the Grill an attempt to build support for the city's domination of public space including that of the Hill District? Or was it an acknowledgment of the right of citizens to develop their own spatial practices? Likewise, was Robinson's inclusion of Lawrence as an honored guest in the Grill's celebrations a sign of support for the city's development programs? Or was it a pointed assertion of the Hill's potential for realizing its own renewal?

Lefebvre depicts the relationship between state and citizen as a cycle in which "political power dominates or rather seeks to dominate space" while citizens "appropriate this space in a non-political manner" and resist the state by imposing new uses of time.[143] In their long tenure as successful businesses and musical institutions, the Grill and the Hurricane became cultural cornerstones of Pittsburgh, building a community of critical listeners and contributing to the livelihoods and creative development of jazz artists. Adopting this position of citizens developing their own sense of place in the Hill, the space of the jazz house reveals ways of appropriating the city and realizing possible urban futures built around collective listening.

# PART III

# THE PARADOX OF PROGRESS

Jazz as Black Musical Labor (1908–1977)

Chapter 5

# CIVIL RIGHTS AND THE MUSICIANS UNION

Do I really want to be integrated into a burning house?[1]

In his allegorical tale "Space Traders" (1992), law professor Derrick Bell unfolds a dystopian Afrofuturist vision aimed to lay bare the inextricable existence of racial inequality within constitutional law in the United States. Re-created as a segment within the 1994 HBO movie *Cosmic Slop*, the filmic version—hosted by the floating three-eyed head of funk legend George Clinton—treads the thin line between wry irony and deadpan seriousness in telling a story in which the United States government trades its Black citizens to space aliens who, in exchange, promise to solve the country's looming economic and environmental catastrophes.

Bell, a Hill District native, served on the front lines of civil rights legal battles in the wake of the 1954 ruling of *Brown v. Board of Education*. Following the 1964 Civil Rights Act and the ensuing struggles to create equitable working conditions, Bell and others produced scholarship that addressed their disenchantment with the implementation of legislative victories, giving rise to the field of Critical Race Theory. Bell, like the invented African American professor Gleason Golightly of "Space Traders," argued that the protection of White supremacy at the expense of Black inequality was perpetuated through legal and constitutional powers engrained in the nation's founding principles as well as by Whites' resistance to sacrificing their privilege. Bell understood that the challenges of civil rights laws and implementing new rights for African Americans lay both in overcoming White resistance to sharing positions of power and preserving Black political, social, and economic structures born of segregation. In Pittsburgh, these tensions were at the heart of a court case involving Bell's nephew George Childress and other Black unionized musicians struggling to maintain representation in the newly integrated union. For many of the city's Black jazz musicians, the fight for representation as musical laborers was rooted in their hopes of preserving jazz as a part of the Black public sphere.

The landmark ruling of the 1964 Civil Rights Act included provisions that restructured organized labor throughout the country and rooted out the most visible remnants of segregation. The 1964 Act asserted rights that had been guaranteed to African Americans a century earlier under the 13th, 14th, and 15th Amendments to the Constitution but which had been undermined through Congressional Acts known as Jim Crow laws that enabled states to enforce racial discrimination in public life, including unionized work. Faced with an ultimatum to desegregate, labor unions immediately undertook the task of integrating local segregated chapters that for decades had their own elected officials, memberships, bylaws, and properties. The process of bringing together separate locals would test the realization of affirmative action in practice. President Lyndon Johnson, who had signed the 1964 Act, gave the 1965 commencement address at Howard University, during which he emphasized that civil rights legislation required additional considerations to be successfully implemented. In his case for affirmative action, Johnson insisted that "equal opportunity is essential but not enough" and addressed those disadvantaged by racism while avoiding the topic of economic sacrifice for Whites:

> You do not take a person who, for years, has been hobbled by chains and liberate him, bring him up to the starting line of a race and then say, "You are free to compete with all the others," and still justly believe that you have been completely fair. Thus it is not enough just to open the gates of opportunity. All our citizens must have the ability to walk through those gates.[2]

The realization of equal opportunity would be tested in union offices as labor leaders negotiated the terms of integrating segregated labor union locals, and courts reviewed cases in which integrated unions failed to undo systems of discrimination.

For Black unionized musicians, integration posed immediate challenges common to Black workers in other trade unions: how to gain and maintain representation in newly integrated unions, ensure fair hiring practices for new jobs, and fight failures in these practices within the union system and, if necessary, in the courts. Musicians, however, faced unique challenges due to being highly skilled workers dependent on the social networks of their respective communities and their own clubs that served as union halls, training centers, and performance spaces. In part due to the bond between musical laborers and their communities, many Black labor leaders resisted mandatory integration requiring that they negotiate the terms of a merger with the larger White locals. Black labor leaders in Pittsburgh saw these merger proceedings as a less effective alternative to their own efforts in promoting interracial workplaces by accepting White members. Labor organizing among Black musicians in the first half of the twentieth century thus left many invested in hard-won positions of power despite their marginalized status within the American Federation of Musicians (AFM). The unionization of Black musicians within the AFM was part of participating in the Black public sphere.

Local 471's operations in the decades preceding the 1966 merger and the continued struggle for union representation by 471 members bridge considerations of jazz as an artistic endeavor with the conditions of it as musical labor. As Martin Stokes argues, the role of money tends to be avoided in ethnomusicological studies despite the discipline's commitment to "understanding music materially."[3] Stokes sees the emergence of perspectives during the Romantic period that would position music as "an antidote to the cold world of commodity exchange"—a sacred space or "secular religion" endangered by capitalist systems of exchange. This anxiety over music's conditions as both aesthetic expression and work has given form to nostalgic readings of precapitalist musical cultures that extend into the modern and contemporary world—what Stokes has identified as ethnomusicologists' tendency to emphasize the "disenchantment of commoditized musical worlds."[4]

Popular music scholars have engaged with the intersections of music's aesthetic and commercial functions to further complicate this division between music and money. In 2012, Marina Peterson and Jesse Shipley edited an issue of the *Journal of Popular Music Studies* dedicated to music, labor, and value, in which they critique approaches to music that "fetishize aesthetic practices as exceptional."[5] As much as Stokes critiques nostalgic stances toward music aesthetics that exclude the role of money, Peterson and Shipley "engage with the longstanding dichotomy that opposes aesthetics to productive labor."[6] Exploring this dichotomy, ethnomusicologist Jennifer Ryan argues in her study of blues and tourism that the perceived distinction of music as either art or labor justifies underpaying folk musicians and "fetishizing poverty" for the purpose of attracting tourists with disposable incomes.[7]

Jazz studies scholars have focused on documenting artists' creative achievements for which economic considerations are often a backdrop. Invoking jazz's "golden age" implies a period of widespread innovation and codification of individualized approaches to improvisation, composition, arrangement, and expressivity, not of wage increases, increased labor rights, or job security. However, some newer scholarship has bridged celebrations of musicians' artistic achievements and the contexts and conditions of their work. Ingrid Monson's study of the "golden age" of modern jazz emphasizes the importance of intellectual and creative innovation in establishing "aesthetic standards" even as it remains committed to the economic, social, and political contexts that comprised the lived experiences of the musicians:

> The musicians of jazz in the 1950s and 1960s engaged just as intensively in music itself as they did in the political debates that raged around them. If the comfortable narratives of jazz heroism, triumph, and celebration have sometimes flattened the political and social struggles that musicians faced in pursuing their craft, so too have the jazz pedagogy books of the last three decades flattened the intense interplay between musical theory and practice that is one of the hallmarks of this golden age of modern jazz.[8]

Pittsburgh's Local 471 was one of nearly fifty AFM locals throughout the country that recognized Black musical labor as highly skilled and necessary to the socioeconomic well-being of a community.[9] These efforts reach back to the turn of the twentieth century when Black musicians in the urban north organized for better working conditions. Historian David Gilbert, in his study of Black musical labor in New York City in the 1910s, explores composer James Reese Europe's impact on both the "professional value" of improved working conditions and the "cultural value" of changing attitudes toward Black music and musicians.[10] According to Gilbert, Europe realized the importance of having an institution through which to coordinate artists as well as a common space in which to organize and rehearse. Europe founded the Clef Club of New York in 1910, which acquired its own building on West 53rd Street. Within two years, the Clef Club had over two hundred members and provided a space in which these members could perform, acquire work, socialize, rehearse, and set artistic standards for performances as well as pay scales for jobs.[11]

Establishing a physical hub for organizing Black musical laborers was equally important for Local 471. Named the Musicians Club, 471's headquarters from 1941 to 1962 provided a context for building professional networks that bolstered jazz's presence in the city. Much of the personal investment and collectivity of the mid-century 471 members was forged in the Musicians Club, a tradition which was abandoned following the 1965 merger with Local 60, the AFM's first Pittsburgh local. Though BMOP's subsequent lawsuit against Local 60-471 specifically sought to address the lack of Black board membership and the merged local's hiring practices, it should also be read within the context of the end of a central institution in Pittsburgh's Black public sphere.

### Local 471's Early Years of Labor Organizing

Local 471 was supported by a small but vibrant African American musical community that had roots in the early nineteenth century. In the New Deal-funded report "Arts and Culture," author Frances Weller briefly outlines a local Black music tradition with roots in both the American North and South. As a stopping point on the underground railroad, fugitive enslaved people brought plantation shout and breakdown dances and songs to Pittsburgh—traditions that could be heard as late as the 1930s.[12] Minstrelsy, musical comedies, and vaudeville were widespread in theaters, with spirituals, choral traditions, and orchestras supported by churches, fraternal orders, and social clubs. A concert brass band tradition reached back to the mid-nineteenth century and grew to include at least five ensembles by 1891. Ragtime and early jazz reached Pittsburgh as musicians traveled up the Mississippi and Ohio Rivers from as far away as New Orleans. Local 471, though born from musicians largely trained in concert and orchestra traditions, would be shaped by jazz's emergence in the 1920s as a dominant form of popular culture and music and, by the 1940s, would serve as the city's platform for representing and organizing jazz musicians.

Pittsburgh's Local 471 was the second of fifty-three locals formed by African American musicians and chartered by the AFM between 1902 and 1952.[13] Local 471 members held their first meeting on January 6, 1908, electing a president and board and setting out the goal of "inducing all the colored musicians in the city to join the organization."[14] The first board included Pittsburgh musicians in dance and concert orchestras who wished to establish a support system and fight for better working conditions for those excluded on the basis of race from joining Pittsburgh's Local 60, which was chartered in 1897. Despite racial discrimination within the AFM, the founders of Local 471 realized the potential of organizing within a national labor union—efforts that would contribute to the development of intercity networks of Black musical laborers during the first half of the twentieth century.

For its entire existence, Local 471 struggled to maintain its administrative autonomy and provide Black musicians access to the local music industry. Local 471 maintained its own board, officers, national convention delegates, and venue. Its jurisdiction was limited by Local 60, which controlled access to jobs in the city's downtown theaters, concert halls, public parks, and White-patronized clubs. This arrangement was codified in a document called the "Afro-American Agreement," signed by the officers of both locals in 1908, which required Local 471 to accept a subsidiary status to Local 60.[15] This agreement required Local 471 to follow the mandates of Local 60, particularly as they pertained to venues where Black musicians could perform. By the 1950s, Local 471's jurisdiction included the Hill District and East Liberty neighborhoods as well as areas within Pittsburgh's North Side.[16] Local 471 contracts that pertained to Allegheny County venues outside these neighborhoods, such as downtown Pittsburgh, the South Hills, Mount Lebanon, Brookline, Squirrel Hill, or other predominantly White areas, generally required approval by Local 60.

The small group of musicians that founded Local 471 was drawn largely from Pittsburgh's Black middle class, which had greater access to higher education and jobs as skilled workers. These families gravitated to the eastern neighborhood of Homewood as well as the Upper Hill District known as "Sugar Top," both of which provided some isolation from the dense, bustling Lower Hill, where many immigrant workers and families from the American South settled during the first wave of the Great Migration. Though there was a class distinction between the established "Old Pittsburghers"—as they came to refer to themselves—and the thousands of migrants seeking work in the industrial north, there were often efforts to address collective struggles that faced Pittsburgh's African American population as a whole. Early Local 471 members were among those who helped bridge these gaps and coordinate collectivity.

The scant records of the early 471 administrators nonetheless tell a story of educators and professionals who were able to traverse a wide range of musical contexts and styles, including European orchestral works, American folk and marching band music, and contemporary dance music. Also notable was their dedication to volunteering in support of organizations that served Pittsburgh's growing and diversifying African American population. Early members who served in administrative roles included William A. Kelly, Harry C. Waters, Albert Robinson, John Beatty, and Frederick "Fritz" D. Hawkins (1888–1934)—all of whom led orchestras that performed for local social events and fundraisers. Elected to the first board, Kelly's brief mention in Weller's report hints at a self-made figure who was able to escape industrial work and establish a music career in Pittsburgh. Upon returning to Pittsburgh, Kelly, "who had been a coal miner, studied for a term at Oberlin, returned to the mines, and then completed his work at Oberlin," formed an eleven-piece orchestra and founded one of the first musical studios in the city for African Americans where he kept a piano, violins, cellos, horns, and an organ for students who could not afford to buy their own instruments.[17]

Waters, who served as the first secretary, had founded an African American orchestra in 1903 and also led a marching band with fifty members.[18] His public service work included directing a band in the Coleman Industrial Home for Colored Boys, an organization founded in 1908 by philanthropists Samuel A. and Luella Coleman and first located at 2816 Wylie Avenue, where orphaned African American boys were housed and educated.[19] Among these children was future jazz drummer and bebop innovator Kenny Clarke who lived and played in the home's band from approximately 1919 to 1923.[20]

Like Waters, Robinson also performed in and conducted large ensembles. He led an orchestra in a November 15, 1908, recital of African American concert artists in the Hill's Continental Hall (2157 Centre Avenue) that featured fellow 471 members performing Ferdinand Hérold's "Zampa" (1831), Robert Schumann's "Träumerei" (1838), and Benoit Constant Fauconier's "Elegie."[21] Robinson also performed for local African American organizations, including the Nabisco Club (founded by Black employees of the National Biscuit Company), the Masons fraternal order, the Industrial Home for Colored Girls, and the annual balls of Local 471.[22] Often performing opposite Robinson's orchestra was Beatty's own twenty-piece ensemble, which advertised itself as the "BEST dance orchestra in Pittsburgh."[23]

One of the most active early Local 471 members was Frederick Hawkins, whose career exemplified the challenges Pittsburgh-based musicians faced in establishing sustainable careers as performers and conductors in the early twentieth century. Around 1914, Hawkins, a Baltimore native, completed a Bachelor of Science degree in Chemistry at the University of Pittsburgh—one of six African Americans to do so before 1930.[24] For the last twenty years of his life, Hawkins worked during the day as a chemist in a laboratory of the Crucible Steel Company. During nights and weekends, Hawkins dedicated himself to music. Despite his studies and demanding career, he developed as a conductor by leading his own orchestra in local musical theater productions and also became well known as a concert violinist who was featured in fellow 471 member Albert Robinson's orchestra. During the 1920s, Hawkins served as 471's president, a period when he was also the director of the pit orchestras for stage productions that appeared at the Hill's Elmore and Roosevelt Theaters. At these venues, he worked behind leading jazz, blues, and vaudeville artists, including Ethel Waters, Adelaide Hall, Josephine Baker, Clarence Muse, Lincoln "Stepin Fetchit" Perry, Irvin C. Miller, Edith Spencer, and Lottie Gee.[25] In addition to playing dance music, Hawkins remained an active classical performer and oversaw a concert honoring the African American classical composer Samuel Coleridge-Taylor in 1925 on what would have been his fiftieth birthday.

As 471's president, Hawkins was criticized by *Pittsburgh Courier* journalist John L. Clark, who claimed that the local charged members fifty cents a month but had not standardized pay rates for members, was not keeping membership records or booking jobs, and punished musicians with a twenty-five-cent fee when they did not have their membership card during a performance.[26] Clark was also incensed by the injustice of 471's subsidiary status under Local 60, which required, among other indignities, that 471 members have radio broadcast performances certified and paid through Local 60's offices.[27] Regardless of the criticisms, Hawkins continued to be elected as president and was praised at the local's twenty-second annual recruiting event for providing members with five-hundred-dollar life insurance policies as well as establishing a high level of professionalism in union orchestras.[28]

Hawkins faced the difficult task of building membership and operating under Local 60's limitations. Like other Black AFM local presidents, Hawkins also faced the difficult task of organizing laborers whose careers often developed from personal relationships and networks rather than employment in a factory or company. In its early decades, Local 471 kept various headquarters in the Lower Hill and would also hold regular meetings in the Masonic Hall, though unlike other trades, unionized musicians would most often contract jobs on their own.[29] Bassist William McMahon recalls that many unionized musicians still relied on informal hiring practices:

> If you went down on the corner of Fullerton and Wylie on a Wednesday or Thursday, different proprietors would come up, and if they saw a musician they knew, they'd ask him if they could get him for a certain club for a certain number of nights. A lot of times the guys would stand there on the corner with a horn under their arm, hoping someone would come up and say, "Hey, buddy! Can you play? Can you play that horn?" He might get a job, and it would last for a week or maybe a month.[30]

Hawkins, versed both in classical and contemporary popular music, led Local 471 when musicians faced a professional landscape hostile to early jazz. In 1921, Local 60 President William L. Mayer warned local White AFM members against the "musical immorality" of pursuing the growing "Jazz-craze." Mayer derided jazz as a short-lived fad appealing to the basest of tastes and denigrating the basic tenets of musicianship:

> The fiddle whines and wails . . . . The saxophone bawls periodically like a lonesome cow; the clarinet yelps occasionally as if a healthy brogan had descended on the tip of Fido's tail; the trombone heaves up spasmodically like the fellow who has imbibed too freely of boot-legging moisture; the muted cornet sounds like a cross between a cackling hen and a hare-lipped tenor with a cold in his head; the bass drum and crash cymbal recall what Flanders field must have been like immediately prior to the armistice, and the piano—poor thing—is pulverized with argeggii [sic] and chromatics until you can think of nothing else than a clumsy waiter with a tin tray full of china and cutlery taking a 'header' down a flight of concrete steps.[31]

While Mayer heard noise and chaos in jazz, his description of jazz dance revealed a racist and primitivist conceptualization of the music. Drawing on his experiences at the 1893 Chicago World's Fair, Mayer connected jazz dance with the "Dahomeyan village" exhibition, including "a dance by about 40 African females clad mostly in a piece of coffee bagging"—a performance he found "ridiculous" and which he believed should never have been re-created in an "enlightened country."[32]

In the early 1920s, Local 60 members could easily encounter these new sounds and dances at the Collins Inn and Leader House, two popular black and tan clubs on lower Wylie Avenue. It was there that Local 471 members played floor shows with entertainers and singers and led late-night jam sessions for the city's "bohemian" after-hours crowds. A Local 471 roster from 1922 lists 211 names, including Symphonium Syncopators members Earl Hines (piano), Vance Dixon (clarinet), and Emmett Jordan (violin); Broadway Syncopators members Billy Page (leader, reeds), Don Redman (arranger, composer), and Joe Smith (trumpet); and Paramount Inn Orchestra members Harold Holt (violin) and Elmer Turner (banjo).[33]

Hawkins died in 1934 at the age of forty-six following the onset of an unnamed illness attributed to the strain of overworking. The next 471 president to serve for an extended period was Henry Jackson, who led the local from 1938 to 1954. Jackson, a bassist who joined Local 471 in 1910, had previously served on the executive committee and gave up performing to devote his full attention to union obligations when elected president. Jackson used the opportunity to challenge 471's subsidiary status and assert greater autonomy within the AFM. Jackson viewed the "working agreement" between the city's two locals as a condition of the AFM policy rather than one of race, claiming, "Had we been the first local, the same condition would have prevailed with their having to secure our permission to be chartered."[34] Despite the lack of solidarity between White and Black musical laborers, the AFM provided support for workers' rights that Jackson viewed as a means of self-determination:

> 471 has complete autonomy, and is in no way obligated to report any of its activities to other than national headquarters. Elections of the officers of this local are held yearly, each member in good standing is at liberty to decide who shall govern him. Full representation at the national convention is enjoyed and exercised in order to protect our membership.[35]

Despite the deep inequities between Pittsburgh's Black and White locals, Jackson's statement, whether true in practice or not, reflects his support of musicians working within the union system. While no Black musicians had chartered AFM locals before their White counterparts, Jackson's hypothetical condition where Local 471 gained its charter twelve years earlier reflects his willingness to work within a union system that both upheld segregation and recognized certain rights of Black musicians. This perspective captures an important aspect of musical workplace segregation, one in which Black musicians valued the power to organize as workers yet faced discriminatory practices from fellow musical laborers.

### The Musicians Club

By the 1940s, Local 471 had come to represent the region's jazz musicians and would be a contact point between local and touring artists over the following two decades.[36] The central institution that facilitated this was the Musicians Club, where members built on the neighborhood's musical history, provided one of the city's most important small venues for jazz, and continued organizing Black musical labor in Pittsburgh. The Afro-American Agreement's racial coding of musical labor reflected the racial politics of live music in Pittsburgh. There existed a one-way road where Black-owned venues welcomed White musicians and patrons across color lines, while downtown and White-owned venues remained hostile to Black musicians. Local 471 member and trumpeter Charles "Chuck" Austin remembers:

> Before the civil rights struggle, you could go into some of these [downtown] clubs if a white guy took you in or vouched for you. You may walk in and have the same green dollar as the next guy but conditions were of such here that you were not welcome. You could feel it though they would not actually say to you "get out." But they would treat you in such a way that you knew you weren't welcome even though it was downtown Pittsburgh. Because of the [Local 60's] stronghold over the entertainment venues, it just was that way.[37]

Local 471 President Henry Jackson established a headquarters and began hosting regular events in early 1941 at 1213 Wylie Avenue, in the heart of the Lower Hill District, to provide its members with a meeting and performance space as well as a place for hosting guests. The building, owned by William "Gus" Greenlee, was the previous home of the Paramount Club, Greenlee's Prohibition Era black and tan establishment that drew integrated audiences and featured innovators of early jazz. In November 1941, the Club received a liquor license and soon began operating a bar for 471 members. In his weekly *Courier* column "Swingin' Among The Musicians," Lee A. Matthews celebrated the news that "Uncle Sam has opened up his big heart and granted Local 471 . . . their liquor license" since "[t]his old burg has been at a standstill; no place to go for real entertainment, but it will be a different story from now on."[38] To expand the club's bar business, Jackson authorized associate membership to provide access to nonmusicians. Local 471 issued cards to individuals who were endorsed by a 471 member and voted in by the local's executive committee. Associate membership also helped subvert the legal restrictions on hours of operation by maintaining its status as a private social club that could also generate funds for the operation of the local.

The Musicians Club was located at the edge of downtown and drew musicians, both White and Black, from throughout the region. Trumpeter Chuck Austin recalls that "it was a melting pot for musicians; North Side, East Liberty, Homewood, Braddock, Rankin, and Sewickley."[39] During weekdays and evenings, musicians used the space for rehearsals, jam sessions, band auditions, and meetings. Figure 5.1 shows Local 471 officer and saxophonist Leroy Brown with members

Figure 5.1. Charles "Teenie" Harris, American, 1908–1998, Musicians Edgar Willis, Calvin King, unknown woman, J. C. McClain, possibly Boots Swan, Mary Dee, George "Duke" Spaulding, Leroy Brown, and Ruby Young Buchanan, posed in old Musicians Club, 1213 Wylie Avenue, Hill District, January 1950, black and white: Kodak Safety Film, H: 4 in. × W: 5 in. (10.20 × 12.70 cm), Carnegie Museum of Art, Pittsburgh: Heinz Family Fund, 2001.35.1554 © Carnegie Museum of Art, Charles "Teenie" Harris Archive.

of his quartet, as well as local radio DJ Mary Dee and pianist Ruby Young, in the Musicians Club. Evident in the photo, the club provided musicians, officers, and patrons with the time and space to relax and socialize outside of performances. For many musicians, the club represented a home away from home. As Austin recalls:

> That's all I knew. In fact, all of us, that was our thing. Outside of the Musicians Club, we didn't have a life. We knew that to go to the club was . . . I won't call it a ritual, but you had to go to the club. I felt honored to be part of this group. Belonging to the union was totally different than it is now. All these guys were union members. We had to be. We couldn't play these clubs if we weren't in the union . . . and these clubs cooperated with the union to make our existence happen.[40]

From its inception, the Musicians Club was a destination spot for jam sessions where musicians would gather after theater or club jobs to meet with touring artists and challenge one another musically. By 1943, weekly sessions were held on Wednesdays, Saturdays, and Sundays with Jackson and Vice President Claude Fisher hosting guests including Benny Goodman, Gene Krupa, Jimmy Lunceford, Shep Fields, Duke Ellington, Erskine Hawkins, Sammy Kaye, Artie Shaw, Russ Morgan, Fletcher Henderson, Clyde McCoy, and Edgar Clyde "Skinnay" Ennis, some of whom were in town to perform in downtown Pittsburgh's Stanley Theater.[41] The stage could accommodate a small ensemble with singers and entertainers performing on the dance floor and among the tables.

Throughout the 1940s, Local 471's executive board continued to build the Musicians Club's reputation through events such as "Celebrity Night," which featured touring musicians and entertainers performing with 471 members. With claims to have the "first call on the services of traveling artists in this territory for appearances as celebrities," the Club provided an informal and intimate setting where traveling and local musicians could socialize and perform.[42] Organist and 471 Secretary-Treasurer Ruby Young remembered the popularity of the Musicians Club for traveling celebrities: "We invited them and would go for them in cabs and bring them up. We had all the stars. None turned us down and it would be packed. We did that for years."[43] In the spring of 1950, singer Wynonie "Mr. Blues" Harris, considered a founding father of rock and roll and well known for "dirty blues" Top 10 hits such as "I Like My Baby's Pudding" (1950), was a featured celebrity at the Club after headlining a revue at the Hill District's Roosevelt Theater. A week later, singer Larry Darnell, whose recording of "For You My Love" hit number one on the Billboard as a best-selling R&B record, performed in the Club to a "packed house."[44] On weekends, "floor shows"—performances made up of a convergence of music, theater, and dance—drew in audiences looking for popular R&B hits, dancing, and comedians.

Local 471 officer and saxophonist Leroy Brown was a mainstay at the Club and a celebrated traditionalist who played hard-swinging jazz and R&B with his band and various floor show acts. Figure 5.2 shows Brown on the small stage on the Club's second floor—his back turned as an entertainer dressed in a zoot suit, polka-dot tie, and large cap engages the audience with a dance routine. Pianist and longtime sideman to Brown George "Duke" Spaulding (figure 5.3) remembers that the Club became very popular: "Most of the time you couldn't get in there. Even the whites would come from the white clubs, anytime from 10 to 11 o'clock on till about 4 in the morning." Reflecting on the photos, Spaulding commented, "I never smoked but back then the smoke would be from the ceiling three-fourths of the way down to the floor."[45]

Gus Greenlee, who owned the building, was a longtime supporter of musicians in the Hill, having run the Paramount Club and booking agency in the 1920s (see chapter 1). Until his death in 1952, Greenlee lent financial support to Local 471, which, at times, did not "make enough money to even pay the rent."[46] Despite his

Figure 5.2. Charles "Teenie" Harris, American, 1908–1998, Man clapping on stage with band in background, including Bobby Anderson on drums and possibly Leroy Brown facing away on right, in old Musicians Club, c. 1938–1950, black and white: unknown safety film, H: 4 in. × W: 5 in. (10.20 × 12.70 cm), Carnegie Museum of Art, Pittsburgh: Heinz Family Fund, 2001.35.2968 © Carnegie Museum of Art, Charles "Teenie" Harris Archive.

backing, the building had fallen into disrepair by 1950. As a teenager, saxophonist Hosea Taylor remembers auditioning at the club for Wil Hitchcock's dance band in the mid-1940s and finding that the club's appearance did not match its reputation. From the street, Taylor found that the club was "nothing more than an old dilapidated row house" in which "the banister was nice and shiny on top and appeared to be in O.K. repair but it sure as hell wasn't . . . to be mistaken for a means of support. It had seen its last days while the remainder of the building was in the process of doing the same."[47] At times, performances on the second floor would strain the old structure. Drummer Joe Harris recalls hearing a

Figure 5.3. Charles "Teenie" Harris, American, 1908–1998, Male vocalist, possibly Floyd performing at microphone, with George "Duke" Spaulding on piano, and Leroy Brown on saxophone behind him, in old Musicians Club with sign on wall reading, "Talent Nite and Jam Session every Friday from 10 to ?", c. 1948–1955, black and white: Kodak Safety Film, H: 4 in. × W: 5 in. (10.20 × 12.70 cm), Carnegie Museum of Art, Pittsburgh: Heinz Family Fund, 2001.35.2048, © Carnegie Museum of Art, Charles "Teenie" Harris Archive.

young Erroll Garner one Saturday night: "Garner got his groove going and the floor was actually [moving] and I said this building is going to fall down because that's Garner's style. It makes you [tap] your foot. Everybody was yelling 'Yeah Garner!' and the floor was actually bouncing. It was an old building. Nowadays they wouldn't allow people in there."[48]

The building's dilapidated state and the looming city-led Lower Hill Redevelopment plan made it apparent in the early 1950s that the Musicians Club would

Figure 5.4. Charles "Teenie" Harris, American, 1908–1998, Count Basie and Stan Getz seated with two unknown men, in Musicians Club with band performing in background with bass and trumpet, c. 1940–1960, black and white: Kodak Safety Film, H: 4 in. × W: 5 in. (10.20 × 12.70 cm), Carnegie Museum of Art, Pittsburgh: Heinz Family Fund, 2001.35.11651 © Carnegie Museum of Art, Charles "Teenie" Harris Archive.

have to be relocated. In the summer of 1953, *Courier* reports showed that Local 471 was seeking a new location in the Upper Hill, and in December, it reported that 471 Officer George Childress was attempting to apply a mortgage on the Club to the purchase of a new building on Upper Wylie.[49]

In December 1953, Local 471 held general elections that replaced much of its board, including President Loraine "Stoney" Gloster and Secretary Leroy Brown, both of whom had served since 1946. The new board included Carl Arter as president, Ruby Young as secretary-treasurer, and Jim Baldwin as vice president.[50] The new leadership abandoned plans to relocate within the Hill. One of Arter's first moves as president was to relocate the Musicians Club and office to 6500 Frankstown Avenue, four and a half miles east in the Homewood-Brushton neighborhood. Arter's decision to move Local 471 out of the Hill District was likely informed by the proximity of his own work as a teacher and performer in Homewood, though the relocation did offer more space, the facilities to run a restaurant and bar, a stage, and a reputation as a place of entertainment. The previous occupant of the building ran a club called the Famous Door that featured floor shows, concerts, and dining for Pittsburgh's Black community. The *Courier's* review of the new Musicians Club hinted at those who were discontent over its relocation from the Hill but emphasized the advantages of a larger central seating area with a clear view of the stage, "whereas in the old Musicians Club, some members were on the first floor, some were in the back bar on the second floor and still others were in the main room where the shows were staged."[51]

The Club's relocation to Homewood coincided with the exodus of thousands of Hill District residents, many of whom were displaced by extensive redevelopment projects of the 1950s. By 1960, movement from the Hill and "white flight" led to several neighborhoods becoming predominantly African American. Homewood experienced one of the most dramatic shifts as the "black population increased from about 13 percent in 1940 to an estimated 70 percent in 1960."[52] Pittsburgh's African American population became concentrated in small, isolated pockets scattered throughout the city. Rapid demographic shifts and the instability of housing prices led to rising resentment and conflict within these communities. Within the rapidly changing Homewood neighborhood, the Musicians Club remained one of the few sites of fraternal contact between Locals 60 and 471. As Arter remembers, other than the few integrated local bands, the "bulk of social contact was on our premises. Some members of 60 did come with wives and girlfriends [who] represented a small amount of the [white] musicians—mostly jazz musicians. They came there after jobs. They found out they were welcome there and they would come with entertainers."[53] Younger White musicians seeking a jazz education were also welcome in the Musicians Club to learn their craft, though not without having their dedication to the art form tested. Organist Gene Ludwig shared:

> The first time I went there I had been playing organ maybe a year and was just getting a feel for the instrument. The Turrentine brothers were there, Stanley and Tommy, and Ducky Kemp, and Pete Henderson. They had a band and were playing on the bandstand. So somebody mentioned that I played organ so they invited me up to play. We were playing a blues and I wasn't even two choruses into my solo and they picked me up off that organ and slammed me up against the wall and said, "Boy! Go home and practice! What do you mean coming up here with us and trying to play." Now, young musicians have balls like watermelons but back then, if you weren't happening and you went on somebody's gig or a session they'd embarrass the hell out of you. So next week I came back and Stanley Turrentine came up to me and said, "Listen man, did you practice this week? Let's hear what you got." So I got up there and the same thing happened. It really gave me the spark and incentive to dig in and learn and practice and get my craft together. I went home, I don't know how many nights after being embarrassed, and I would say, "Man, I want to get this shit together if it kills me." So I kept pluggin' at it, getting' records, listening to juke boxes [*sic*], takin' down notes of tunes and looking

at books for tunes. I would practice and surround myself with good players so I could draw off of them. That really helped me in my starting years working with guys like Randy Gillespie and Jerry Byrd.[54]

Throughout its existence, 471's membership included a remarkable number of jazz artists who would gain international recognition. Early members included Don Redman (1900–1964)[55], whose arrangements were performed by Fletcher Henderson, Paul Whiteman, and Count Basie; pianist Earl "Fatha" Hines (1903–1983), whose illustrious career began as musical director for Louis Armstrong in the late 1920s; pianist Mary Lou Williams (1910–1981); and trumpeter Roy Eldridge (1911–1989). Later members included singer and bandleader Billy Eckstine (1914–1993), pianist and arranger Billy Strayhorn (1915–1967), drummer Kenny Clarke (1914–1985), drummer Art Blakey (1919–1990), pianist Erroll Garner (1921–1977), bassist Ray Brown (1926–2002), trumpeter Tommy Turrentine (1928–1997), pianist Ahmad Jamal (1930–2023), tenor saxophonist Stanley Turrentine (1934–2003), guitarist George Benson (b. 1943), and guitarist Jimmy Ponder (1946–2013).[56] While Pittsburgh's music economy nurtured the early careers of these innovators, it could not sustain their development as recording and touring artists. Celebrated for their advancement of jazz as an art form, they sought management, booking, press, and recording opportunities in New York, Chicago, and Los Angeles to build careers as solo artists. Often, they maintained links to Pittsburgh through Local 471, which served as an anchor for playing with locally based musicians.

For Pittsburgh-based jazz musicians, the union provided a means of navigating local working conditions while providing a welcoming home for visiting artists. The Musicians Club became an important place for seasoned musicians to jam with locals. Top billing jazz big bands that came through Pittsburgh most often played the Stanley Theater downtown but would come to the Musicians Club on their off time. Drummer Joe Harris recalls that after the shows were finished downtown, "they'd come up [to the Musicians Club] and we'd have drinks for them and food and then we would play and jam."[57] With the constant flow of local and touring musicians, the environment was rich in creative interaction. Pittsburgh jazz musicians rehearsing for a gig might be stopped by a musician from New York, Chicago, New Orleans, or Kansas City and shown a new way to voice a chord, phrase a melody, or approach a rhythmic feel. In informal jam sessions, competition contributed to high levels of musicianship. Stories tell of young Pittsburgh musicians catching national players off guard. As saxophonist Hosea Taylor remembers, "Everyone went to the Musicians Club whether you were a musician or into nightlife. I saw a number of national musicians go there and get [shown up] by Pittsburghers in the forties. A lot of national players were afraid of Tommy Turrentine and it brought them down a peg."[58]

## Divergent Careers in Jazz: Walt Harper and Tommy Turrentine

Local 471 and the Musicians Club influenced generations of Pittsburgh musicians as they faced the daunting task of carving out careers in western Pennsylvania. The examples of pianist Walt Harper (1926–2006) and trumpeter Tommy "Teen" Turrentine (1928–1997) illustrate the diversity of what constituted musical labor within the context of the AFM's Black Local. Harper's approach to bandleading embraced the aesthetics and economic concerns of "commercial" jazz, which sustained his lifelong career as a Pittsburgh-based bandleader. Meanwhile, Turrentine dedicated his career in Pittsburgh and later New York to developing virtuosic improvisational skills and pushing himself and others to approach jazz as artistic self-expression. These two musicians provide a case study for examining Black musical labor in Pittsburgh as it was shaped by tensions between economic viability and artistic innovation.

As a jazz musician who did not relocate to a larger city, Harper was faced with the challenge of securing or creating steady jobs within the region and developing a range of nonmusical skills to secure bookings, organize rehearsals, and work with promoters. While Harper has not been recognized as an artistic innovator alongside Pittsburgh contemporaries and pianists Billy Strayhorn (1915–1967), Erroll Garner (1921–1977), and Ahmad Jamal (1930–2023), he sustained a lifelong performance career and played an active role in Local 471. Those who worked with him praised his business savvy and ability to break the color line for booking lucrative dances. The same musicians also lamented Harper's commercially successful formula as creatively restrictive and unchanging over his six-decade career. Raised in the Upper Hill District, Harper came from a musical family—his mother was trained as a concert pianist, and his brothers Ernie and Nate were musicians. He began performing at house parties in his early teens. At fourteen, Harper would "sneak out of the house around 1 or 2 in the morning" to play after hours at the Bambola Club, noting, "Later on in life, my late mother, who was dying, says, 'You know what? You thought you were fooling me, but I know you were sneaking out of the house.'"[59] At these gigs, Harper met and worked with other young Pittsburgh jazz musicians and would shape a musical sensibility influenced by local bandleader and future 471 President Joe Westray. Harper's central musical tenet was reflected in conversations with Count Basie and Duke Ellington, who told him, "If it doesn't swing [and] you don't sit and pat your feet, you're in trouble."[60]

Harper focused on maintaining a dance band that could build a local identity and secure steady work. At seventeen, Harper was encouraged by 471 President Hence Jackson to join the local, where he rehearsed his first band for a graduation dance at Fifth Avenue High School. In figure 5.5, a teenage Harper sits at the piano in the Musicians Club and rehearses his band—young artists in the

Figure 5.5. Charles "Teenie" Harris, American, 1908–1998, Walt Harper playing piano, Nate Harper on tenor saxophone, Hosea Taylor on alto saxophone, Tommy Turrentine on trumpet, Billy "Stinky" Davis on trombone, and Joni Wilson on drums, performing in old Musicians Club, with radio in background, c. 1940–1946, black and white: Agfa Safety Film, H: 4 in. × W: 5 in. (10.20 × 12.70 cm), Carnegie Museum of Art, Pittsburgh: Heinz Family Fund, 2001.35.11413 © Carnegie Museum of Art, Charles "Teenie" Harris Archive.

process of becoming professionals. It was here that Harper first faced the task of programming a night of music and rehearsing a new band. Harper recalls, "They had a Duke Ellington book and I went to Volkwein's [Music Store] and got the book and copied about twenty numbers [because] someone told me you need twenty numbers to play a job."[61] Popular big band swing arrangements of Billy Strayhorn's "Take the 'A' Train" and Ellington's "Love You Madly" and "Satin Doll" became staples of his repertoire throughout his career. As saxophonist George Thompson recalls of "Satin Doll," "Walt played it so much that people thought he wrote it."[62]

Harper's success as a bandleader required a practical perspective of audience expectations and the perfection of what jazz musicians called a "commercial" approach to programming a performance. Few musicians were inclined to lead their own groups due to the range of responsibilities that came with the position.

Hiring and rehearsing musicians required steady members, while some felt the pull of travel, touring, and recording careers. Renowned Pittsburgh bassist Ray Brown, who rehearsed with Harper's early group, was exposed to a range of touring musicians who would visit the Musicians Club while the band was rehearsing. Harper remembers touring musicians being struck with the young bassist's originality and virtuosity and that it wasn't long before Brown was touring with Snookum Russell. Building a public identity for Harper's group required them to look professional in order to gain support from venues, the *Pittsburgh Courier*, local radio, and older union members. Repertoire and performances had to fit the tastes of young dancers who expected popular songs performed with familiar arrangements. For sidemen, playing "commercial" gigs required them to avoid trends of bebop musicians—extended solos that foregrounded individual virtuosity, fast tempos, and complex reworking of popular songs—and play music that was restrained, grounded in swing, and familiar to the widest selection of listeners. During the 1940s, Harper programmed his sets to include radio hits recorded by artists including Nat King Cole and Erskine Hawkins and routines that fostered an interactive environment between the band and the audience. Taylor remembered that these routines made the gig "a real thrill" when "at the end of the gig [Harper] allowed the horns to go out to dance and he'd play 'After Hours' by Avery Parrish. It was a real funky song and everybody would go out on the dance floor."[63]

Harper's approach was what sideman George Thompson called "understandable jazz," noting that "he stuck right with the way it was written—no deviation and don't get wild."[64] This led to tensions in the band as Thompson recalled that Harper "stayed right with the way the record came out. He even wanted [his brother] Nate to play the solos the same as they were on the records. After a while, the guys started rebelling and I played what I wanted to play when it came to my solo. When it comes to the solo, that's me. Now when your arrangement is there, I'll play it exactly the way you want it played but I want the freedom to be able to play." The tension between bandleaders cultivating a recognizable sound and sidemen experimenting with more challenging modes of playing also appears in sociologist Howard Becker's study of White musicians in late 1940s Chicago. Becker shows that the dance musicians' professional life required the constant negotiation of their own creative interests and those of their audiences and employers. Musicians valued modern jazz because it was "produced without reference to the demands of outsiders" yet made sacrifices for economic reasons:

> The most distressing problem in the career of the average musician . . . is the necessity of choosing between conventional success and his artistic standards. In order to achieve success he finds it necessary to "go commercial," that is, to play in accord with the wishes of the nonmusicians for whom he works; in doing so, he

Figure 5.6. Charles "Teenie" Harris, American, 1908–1998, Walt Harper performing outdoors with members of his quintet wearing plaid tuxedos with Jon Morris on trombone, Nate Harper on saxophone, and Harold "Brushes" Lee on drums for an audience at Carnegie Tech's annual Spring Festival, May 1959, black and white: Kodak Safety Film, H: 4 in. × W: 5 in. (10.20 × 12.70 cm), Carnegie Museum of Art, Pittsburgh: Heinz Family Fund, 2001.35.11426 © Carnegie Museum of Art, Charles "Teenie" Harris Archive.

sacrifices the respect of other musicians and thus, in most cases, his self-respect. If he remains true to his standards, he is usually doomed to failure in the larger society. Musicians classify themselves according to the degree to which they give in to outsiders; the continuum ranges from the extreme "jazz" musicians to the "commercial" musician.[65]

Harper's ability to sustain his band relied on establishing the group as a regular feature in dances in both Black and White communities. Taylor recalls that Black high school students in integrated schools attended their own dances, and in 1945, Harper performed a Black prom dance at the Cottage Inn, a dance hall in the eastern neighborhood of Homewood. Harper's success at this and other dances led the *Courier* to praise him as the "pride of the bobby-soxers."[66] Harper's success led to regular performances at college dances and country clubs in White communities. As trumpeter Roger Barbour remembers, Harper "found the right ingredient to cross the color line. Before Walt, most of them wouldn't hire Black bands."[67] This formula found strong supporters in two key figures: Gulf Oil executive Roy Kohler and manager Evie D'Andrea.[68] Kohler arranged Harper's first performance for the Pittsburgh Press Club, an exclusive private organization of newsmen that hosted events for the city's political and business elites. With access to these networks, Harper was, by the mid-1960s, playing between forty and sixty proms and concerts during the summer months. Bookings took the band to universities including Penn State, Carnegie Tech (Carnegie Mellon University), and Brown, with the band reputed to once having "performed the phenomenal task of completing seven jobs in just two days."[69]

Playing commercial styles of jazz and R&B was often seen as a creative sacrifice for bebop musicians struggling to build their own appreciative audiences. Harper's drummer Cecil Brooks II remembers, "[A]t the time I played with him, my heart was in jazz and bebop was out then. Walt didn't play bebop. He called the band in the later years 'Walt Harper and All That Jazz' but jazz could come in all kinds of forms. But he really wasn't playing real jazz."[70] The Musicians Club provided younger musicians who were interested in bebop one of the few places to develop the style. Saxophonist Hosea Taylor remembered, "Very few people could play true bebop. Just because a guy plays moderately fast, that doesn't constitute bebop. To me, bebop was a lifestyle. Guys wore those horn-rimmed glasses, and everybody tried to grow a goatee and get themselves a tam [hat]. In the winter, there was a coat they called the 'bear coat' with this big lapel. It was a lifestyle and it was fun. Everybody was going around [saying] 'bebop, bebop, bebop.'"[71] Musicians playing the new style met with criticism from dancers, listeners, and older musicians. Italian American guitarist Joe Negri remembers, "As beboppers, we were discriminated against by the [older] musicians" who saw the music as a trivial exploration and would remark, "What are you doing? You're just flattin' those fives, that's all you're doing."[72] Taylor also experienced a backlash from swing musicians "too old to switch over to our musical thoughts" who would insist on playing a song "like it was written." Ideological conflicts, at times, threatened to break out into physical conflict. As drummer Joe Harris recalls, at one point on Wylie, "I looked around and some of the older cats had pulled out their knives and we had picked up bricks and rocks [laughs]. We were getting ready to do a battle of the streets because they had said, 'You can't play that bebop!'"[73] Though the new music created some tension, it drew together a small group of younger musicians seeking new directions and challenges in jazz. Brooks remembers that early in his career, bebop brought together a diverse group of musicians interested in understanding the new style: "One thing about musicians, back when all the prejudice and all that stuff was going on, there wasn't none of that stuff with musicians. There was new music that had come out and everybody was trying to learn how to play it and it was just exciting then."[74]

Leading among Pittsburgh's bebop musicians was trumpeter Tommy Turrentine, who was a fervent practitioner of the idiom as a teenager. In figure 5.7, Turrentine plays at the back of the small stage in the Musicians Club, seated next to drummer Cecil Brooks II. With his beret hung over the bell of his trumpet as a makeshift mute, Turrentine's position nestled among the rhythm section and demeanor speak to his rejection of the swing entertainer persona. Turrentine inspired young jazz musicians in the Hill District to seek technical virtuosity on their instruments and embrace new concepts of chromaticism. Saxophonist George Thompson recalls that at Musicians Club jam sessions, Turrentine would write down the chords to a new song and instruct the other musicians, "Goddammit, I want you to know this next week."[75] This pushed Thompson and other musicians to "write those changes down" and start "thinking about changes because before we were playing by ear. He was the one horn man who knew the changes and he helped us so much." This new style of learning reflected the sentiment of trumpeter Howard McGhee: "With bop, you had to know—not feel; you had to *know* what you were doing."[76]

For Taylor, bebop's novelty lay in the challenges it posed, both to musicians and audiences who didn't appreciate it: "Even today, they don't understand. Today, you don't find many people understanding bebop or even listening to it. It was so hard to play." Soon, young musicians around Turrentine began to speak of swing as the "main thing" or "commercial jazz" while they were into the "new music." With many bebop songs being composed on the chords of older swing songs, musicians experimented with interjecting new approaches into live performances. Taylor remembers that Turrentine compromised little on swing gigs: "Turrentine, he didn't care. He would go on a commercial gig and play [Dizzy Gillespie's 'Groovin' High'] while everybody else played 'Whispering.' He wouldn't be there the next time. He didn't care whether he was there or not." Taylor remembers, "Leroy Brown's personality was the opposite of Tommy Turrentine's. Where Tommy didn't care, Leroy did. I never heard them play together, but I don't think they would get along. Tommy was aggressive and modern and contemporary where Leroy wasn't. They were both beautiful players but in different contexts. Different realms."[77]

Local 471, which depended in part on patrons to supplement its income, made the Musicians Club selectively available to Turrentine and other young musicians who wanted to play bebop. Bebop posed a dilemma for clubs looking to draw audiences. Thompson remembers older 471 members who worried that average listeners "wouldn't understand what we were playing" and would "only let us have a jam session on Wednesday because they said if we played on Saturday night, we'd run all the customers out of there."[78] On slower nights, "anyone who

Figure 5.7. Charles "Teenie" Harris, American, 1908–1998, Three musicians, with unknown on piano, Tommy Turrentine on trumpet with beret covering bell, and possibly Cecil Brooks on drums with initials "CB" and "WH," performing in Musicians Club, c. 1945–1950, black and white: Kodak Safety Film, H: 4 in. × W: 5 in. (10.20 × 12.70 cm), Carnegie Museum of Art, Pittsburgh: Heinz Family Fund, 2001.35.1791 © Carnegie Museum of Art, Charles "Teenie" Harris Archive.

wanted to come and play could," though on Friday and Saturday, Local 471 hired an "organized band or a group that played things that people wanted to hear." During the bebop jam sessions, patrons would often come in, "look around [and scowl] and take the steps. They wanted to hear that funk and move and dance and whistle. When you're running up and down the horn . . . they knew you were good musicians, but they couldn't understand what you were doing." Likewise, Thompson remembers feeling distanced from the culture of swing and blues. Playing repertoire such as Fats Navarro's "Ice Freezes Red" and Charlie Parker's "Now's the Time" gave them a sense of superiority. Thompson admits, "We thought that we were a little bit above the average." As for blues musicians: "We didn't allow them around us and it wasn't until later on that I started appreciating it."[79]

The careers of Harper and Turrentine illustrate tensions that were shared by both Black and White musicians. In his study of White Chicago musicians, Becker asserts that their careers are primarily defined by the dilemma that "one cannot please the audience and at the same time maintain one's artistic integrity."[80] These musicians struggle to achieve the freedom to create music free of demands from audiences and venue owners and, as a result, are defined by their opposition to "outsiders" or "squares" who do not appreciate music in the same way. The concept of outsider status examined by Becker among White musicians takes on new dimensions when applied to Local 471's musicians who grappled with traversing commercial jazz and bebop within a context of segregated working conditions and communities. As Black musicians, their status as "outsiders" within a White-dominant society subsumed the conflicts over the limitations of commercialism on artistic integrity. While commercial interests shaped artistic directions, programming, and the management of the Musicians Club, Local 471 accommodated, to some degree, musical outsiders among their ranks and provided a context for developing artistic aspirations. In this respect, 471 defended Black musical laborers in their pursuit of jazz as both work and art.

# Chapter 6

# CHALLENGING DISCRIMINATION, RESISTING MERGER

In the decades preceding the 1966 merger of Pittsburgh's Local 471 with its White counterpart, Local 60, the region's unionized Black musicians worked within the AFM's grievance system to challenge workplace discrimination and develop new performance opportunities for local and touring musicians, including jazz artists both Black and White. But the merger created a paradox of progress in the wake of the 1964 Civil Rights Act that resulted in many Black jazz musicians withdrawing from union involvement. In 1971, when it became apparent that integration was reducing Black representation and political power in the AFM, veteran Pittsburgh bandleaders, musicians, and union activists George Childress, Clyde Jackson, George Spaulding, Ruby Young, Charles Austin, Thomas "Doc" Miller, "Ducky" Kemp, and Leroy Brown formed the activist group Black Musicians of Pittsburgh (BMOP). In 1974, a representative of BMOP lamented the failed promise of civil rights legislation for the city's Black musicians: "We are in a worse position now.... At least [before 1964] we had some leadership positions, our own hall and more work."[1] This statement reflects the frustrations of two decades of concerted efforts to maintain Local 471 members' autonomy in the AFM while attempting to set the terms of integration.

Carl Arter, Local 471 president from 1954 to 1962, used his position as president to address discrimination cases that directly impacted the members. Black AFM locals were considerably outnumbered by their White counterparts, which compromised their political power on both the local and national levels. By midcentury, Pittsburgh's Local 60 was the tenth largest in the AFM, with 2,353 members.[2] As of Arter's presidency, Local 471 had ninety-nine members, which was average for the majority of the fifty-three Black locals.[3] This power imbalance made negotiations with Local 60 an uphill battle and tested the resources of 471.

In January 1954, Local 60 President Hal Davis invited Arter to a meeting with the ostensible purpose of congratulating him on his recent election. During this meeting, Davis presented and reviewed the terms of the "Afro-American Agreement," which stated 471's subsidiary status under Local 60 and limited their working jurisdiction along racial lines. Unfamiliar with the agreement, Arter proceeded to interview former 471 officers concerning their knowledge of its existence and legality. Finding that no previous officers were aware of the agreement, Arter called for a meeting at Local 60's headquarters that would include 471 members Leroy Brown, Stoney Gloster, board member Thomas Miller, and Local 60 Secretary Nick Cassett, President Hal Davis, and Vice President James Camarata. It was at this meeting that Arter rejected the terms of the agreement that Davis believed still dictated the relationship between the two locals. Seeking a decision from the AFM's national office, Arter traveled to Newark, New Jersey, to present his case.

The Federation's secretary Leo Klugman subsequently organized a hearing in which Local 60 and 471 representatives would defend their cases in front of the National Board committee led by James Petrillo, who served as the AFM president from 1940 to 1958. During the hearing, both Pittsburgh local presidents sparred over the agreement's validity. Davis's claims that the Afro-American Agreement had never been nullified were met with Arter claiming that previous AFM President Joseph Weber (1900–1940) had abolished subsidiary locals in the late 1920s. Arter's appeal to the authority of the AFM's national policy and Davis's claims over the local's rights to administer that policy invoke a common tension in the civil rights struggle between constitutional and executive powers and states' rights. As Arter recalled, during the hearing, Davis used the phrase "the tail does not wag the dog" to imply that an established hierarchy existed between the two locals that would be nonsensical to overturn.[4]

Petrillo and the AFM board ultimately ruled in favor of Local 471, effectively removing 471's subsidiary status and discarding the Afro-American Agreement that had previously allowed Local 60 to dictate to 471 the limits of its jurisdiction.[5] Petrillo had seen many cases addressing the relationship of Black and White locals before the 1954 hearing, with his position shifting in relationship to rising pressures from the civil rights movement. As president of Chicago's AFM Local 10 from 1922 to 1940, Petrillo faced challenges to racist policies brought by Local 208, the AFM's largest Black local. In 1931, Local 208, under President Alex Armant and Secretary George Dulf, had presented a plan for merging the segregated locals, which Petrillo's board unanimously rejected on the grounds that the "present arrangement" had proven "satisfactory over a period of years."[6]

During Petrillo's time as president of the AFM, pressure mounted for action on the question of segregation in the union. Petrillo used his position as president to remove the subsidiary status of twelve Black locals and grant them "the same autonomous rule and charter that the white locals enjoyed."[7] Petrillo used the 48th Convention of the American Federation of Musicians to grant these rights to subsidiaries, a political move that provided a defense against criticisms of the Federation's discriminatory practices while also addressing "cut-throat competition" between Black and White unions over wage scales in "white territory" venues.[8] By strengthening the rights of Black locals, Petrillo indirectly resisted calls to force locals to merge.

The NAACP's continued calls for the AFM to abolish segregation among its locals drew legal strength from President Roosevelt's wartime executive orders No. 8802 (1941) and No. 9346 (1943), which established the Fair Employment Practices Commission (FEPC) and declared that "[t]here shall be no discrimination in the employment of workers in defense industries and in Government, because of race, creed, color, or national origin."[9] The NAACP's attacks on segregation in the AFM were complicated by resistance from Black locals who feared losing autonomy: a stance that Petrillo drew on to justify abolishing subsidiary statuses and addressing individual demands of Black locals as cases presented themselves. In a 1944 *Billboard* magazine article, Petrillo was cited responding to NAACP secretary Walter White's demands for desegregation in the AFM: "[S]eparate charters were especially asked for in that way . . . [and were] entirely satisfactory to the colored membership."[10] Petrillo also claimed that while the AFM's original bylaws state that locals cannot discriminate on the basis of race, the national office lacks the power over these locals to implement their policies concerning segregation.

For Pittsburgh's locals, the conflict over subsidiary status strengthened Local 471's resolve to pursue self-determination over a merger. Under Arter's new leadership as 471's president, both locals voted on and fully rejected a merger.[11] Yet 471 encouraged both White and Black musicians to join its ranks following the removal of its subsidiary status. When confronted about 471's new promotion of racial integration by Petrillo, Arter argued that it should be a case of preference and not a racial requirement, adding, "I think this would be the first step we could have toward any type of communication between the musicians, Black and white, in this town. If there [are] going to be two locals there, rather than working towards polarization, I think the best thing would be to leave both doors open."[12] Arter envisioned a process in which the artistic and personal preferences of musicians could create working environments in which integration was determined by individual union members.

Arter's pro-integration and antimerger stance led to a public debate within Pittsburgh's Black community in which 471 was accused of having regressive politics. In a series of open letters and articles published by the *Courier* in 1957, WILY DJ Bill Powell accused 471's leadership of being "inept, in that they are . . . not interested in the perpetuation of the union's welfare as a whole . . . they do not seem to be aware that integration is both desirable and practicable."[13] In defense, Arter responded, "This little situation would probably have been solved much easier had Powell had to deal with white officials. He would have understood it more clearly and probably cooperate much easier if approached by some member of the Caucasian race. We will integrate when we get good and ready, and it will be done intelligently when we can integrate on an equal footing without any handkerchiefs on our heads."[14] The public conflict led to Local 471 placing Powell on an "unfair list" on the grounds that he was hiring nonunion musicians for his "record hop" events. This prompted Powell to publish a letter signed by Petrillo stating that the AFM's national office had not added him to any "unfair list." Powell's affront to 471's local authority exposed the ill will that criticizing an antimerger stance engendered within the Black community.

The basis for Arter's antimerger stance was rooted in the political power that independent local status provided Black musicians in Pittsburgh. The ruling that continued Petrillo's policy of abolishing the subsidiary status of Black locals did not lay out policies and procedures for how the Pittsburgh AFM locals should proceed in terms of booking jurisdictions following the removal of the Afro-American Agreement. These terms were rather fought on a case-by-case basis as 471 asserted its rights to book musicians across the color line. Two cases involving White-owned clubs demonstrate that 471 faced an ongoing struggle that required an extensive effort from its president to work within the union grievance structure at the local and national levels to challenge workplace discrimination.

The first jurisdiction dispute between Locals 471 and 60 began shortly after the AFM ruling when Local 471 member Arthur Barnes secured a contracted job in a White-owned downtown venue. Opened in 1954, the New Nixon Supper Club on 6th Street and Penn Avenue was managed by James Martire, a previous coworker of Barnes in the Pittsburgh offices of United States Steel Company. Martire informed Barnes that he was looking for artists for the new venue and subsequently signed a contract that included the unionized musicians' names and Local 471's approved pay scales. Problems arose on the second night of performances, when Barnes and his group encountered picketing representatives from Local 60 joined with American Federation of Labor (AFL), Local 188 Bartenders, and Local 237 Hotel and Restaurant Employees.[15] At the picket line, Local 60 officer James Camarata informed the 471 musicians that, as AFM members, they were required to leave the job since Local 60 had not approved the contract.[16] Barnes broke the picket line and stood by his Local 471-approved contract, seeing the engagement through. The *Pittsburgh Post-Gazette* reported that Martire opened a $150,000 lawsuit against the picketing unions the morning of December 2 and, by the day's closing, had signed agreements with them. Though the case was quickly settled between Martire and the protesting locals, the outcome of whether Local 60 accepted that the New Nixon would continue booking 471 members remained unclear.

Barnes's experience testing the color line as a 471 member had a long-lasting and demoralizing effect. As Barnes later stated during court testimony, shortly after breaking the picket line, he received a letter from the National Union offices stating that he had been suspended from the AFM and fined $500 for disobeying Local 60's call to boycott the New Nixon. Though Local 471 officer George Childress encouraged Barnes to appeal his suspension, the experience at the Nixon discouraged him from further conflicts and he instead chose to pay the fine, which took ten years. As Barnes stated, "At that time . . . I was disgusted with the whole musical setup," which led him to avoid regular union work as a musician rather than fight Local 60.

This and other incidents led to further meetings at the AFM's national offices, which demonstrated that while the Afro-American Agreement had been discarded, discrimination was still entrenched in local practices. In 1960, a dispute arose around Local 60's attempt to invoke the now-nullified agreement in a contract presented to Ralph Mastrangelo, owner of the Chateau Lounge, a jazz club located outside of the city proper. The contract announced planned increases in union pay scales and included a clause that stated, "These scales are predicated on at least 75% local employment [members of Local 60] when music is used," effectively requiring Mastrangelo to hire mostly White Pittsburgh musicians with the remaining employment reserved for touring artists.[17] Though a largely White-patronized venue, it featured both Black touring and local bands. Jazz drummer Cozy Cole, whose recording of Benny Goodman's "Topsy II" reached No. 3 on *Billboard* magazine's Hot 100 in 1958, played a stretch of shows at the Chateau in June 1960. Later that year, *Courier* writer Harold Keith included the Chateau on his list of notable Pittsburgh jazz venues alongside the Fallen Angel, the Crawford Grill, the Hurricane Bar, The Riverboat Room of the Penn-Sheraton Hotel, the Stardust Lounge, and The Duke.[18] Rejecting Local 60's contract on the principle that the venue was identified as a place for jazz and hence would draw from 471 members, Mastrangelo worked with Arter to sign an agreement with Local 471 that guaranteed the same wage scales and excluded the "75% clause." Though the new contract did not exclude Local 60, it resulted in threats from Local 60 President Hal Davis to place the Chateau Lounge on the union's "unfair list," which would have barred it from employing any AFM musicians. Had this ban been implemented, it would have forced Local 471 into the precarious position of either honoring the hiring ban enforced by the national office or ignoring the ban and supporting a club owner that had refused a discriminatory contract.

To avoid a conflict with the AFM's national office, Arter appealed to AFM President Herman Kenin to back 471's contract with Mastrangelo:

> It is Local 471's firm opinion that the contract signed with Mr. Mastrangelo represents a fair and equitable agreement. It is non-discriminatory toward musicians belonging to Local 60, Local 471 or any other local in the Federation. We do not believe that either our local or Mr. Mastrangelo has engaged in any unfair practices. Consequently, we respectfully submit that you take no action to change Local 471's contractual agreement with Mr. Mastrangelo.[19]

Insisting on a hearing with the AFM, Arter, again, traveled to national headquarters with Mastrangelo to present the case against Local 60. In a particularly contentious meeting, Arter asserted that Local 60's actions were the "Afro-American Agreement de facto."[20] With the AFM failing to rule on the case, Arter continued to discuss the case by phone with the AFM's lawyer, threatening to take the issue to the floor of the AFM's convention and then to civil court if needed. Following this pressure, the AFM compromised by requiring Mastrangelo to sign contracts with both locals and include the "75% clause" that clearly stated that musicians be hired from both Locals 60 and 471.

Though Arter had successfully challenged the "Afro-American Agreement" and fought its ingrained legacy in Pittsburgh's venues, most of the lucrative jobs remained in control of the larger and more influential Local 60. Early in his role as 471's president, Arter realized the importance of expanding the local's professional offerings in hopes of accessing public concert bookings. In 1954, having discovered that Local 60 was booking municipal concerts paid for by the city of Pittsburgh and the AFM's national office, Arter formed a concert band with 471 members to extend the Black local's offerings beyond "be-bop, jazz, swing, and mambo." As the *Courier* reported,

> The story behind the new concert band, as related by some of the musicians who say President Arter is too modest to take the credit, is that Arter launched an investigation to find out why none of the concert work in the city parks was being given to Negro bands. After an investigation by George Childress, which included an interview with City Councilman Paul F. Jones, it was learned that Negroes weren't getting any of the work because they hadn't asked for it. More than $35,000 is allotted each year by the city just for band concerts in public parks alone. Pittsburgh's Musicians' Local 60 had been getting this work and augmenting it with money from the Musicians Union's national treasury. It is said that Negroes will get some of this work in the future.[21]

The work of expanding 471's professional offerings was continued by Joe Westray, who succeeded Arter as Local 471 president in January 1962. When Westray's requests for positions performing at the County Fair were rejected, he presented the issue to the Board of County Commissioners, Dr. William B. McClelland, after which the city intervened on behalf of Local 471. The *Courier* celebrated the move and advertised in 1964, "For the first time, a Negro band will be among the musical units featured at the Allegheny Country Fair at South Park, as a result of action taken by Local 471 of the Musicians Union. Appearing daily, from September 3 to 7, on the patio of the Buffalo Inn, will be the Joe Westray Jazz Quintet, which will alternate with Benny Benack's Dixieland Combo and Slim Bryant's Wildcats."[22]

The actions of Carl Arter and Joe Westray illustrate the importance of building Local 471's political power and challenging institutionalized practices of discrimination. Though many AFM locals had voluntarily merged by the mid-1960s, the prospects of merging offered few incentives for 471 members. A merged union would have a ratio of approximately one Black to six White members, so board positions would prove impossible to win for former 471 members without general goodwill and mutual support. Hal Davis stated in 1960 that he believed that this disadvantage would fade as White members learned to vote on abilities and not color. But as *Courier* writer Harry Brooks remarked, "How long this 'liberal' attitude would take to develop is another question."[23]

## Mergers and Transitions (1965–1971)

In the years leading up to the 1964 Civil Rights Act, Local 471's board continued to focus on strengthening its independence, with few believing that a merger would grant more access to venues in White communities or allow for continued representation with the union. In 1959, *Courier* columnist George Pitts noted that many AFM locals had voluntarily merged in cities including Miami, Wichita, Des Moines, Asheville, and Jacksonville. New York's Local 802, which had technically been integrated since its establishment, as well as the merged locals of Los Angeles and Chicago, demonstrated that Black musicians could maintain some political autonomy and representation within an integrated local. Pitts also noted that Local 471 musicians remained deeply skeptical about merging: "We would be outvoted for top offices . . . and I doubt that we would get as much work as we are now getting. If most of the good jobs go to the white boys now, a merger would make them get all of the good gigs."[24] Three years later, Pitts found that the situation was largely unchanged when interviewing a 471 member: "Even today in Pittsburgh, few Negro combos are making their sole livelihood playing music. The big spots—Holiday House, Twin Coaches, Town House, Ankarra—and others, have all white house bands and have never entertained the idea of giving steady employment to a Negro group."[25]

Leading up to the merger, the relation of Locals 471 and 60 was fractured with the question of integration mired in past struggles. In 1962, the two locals

# CO-HOST LOCAL No. 471
*Chartered 1908 in Pittsburgh, Penna.*

## "We Are Keeping Music Alive"

JAMES A. BALDWIN
Vice President

JOSEPH WESTRAY
President

RUBYE L. YOUNGE
Secretary-Treasurer

ALICE BROOKS
Board Chairman

JAMES E. MINOR
Board Member Local 471
Chrm. Convention Comm.

WALT HARPER
Board Member

JACQUES GRAMBRELL
Board Member

### We wish to extend GREETINGS

*to President HERMAN D. KENIN and Officers*
*of the AMERICAN FEDERATION of MUSICIANS,*
*the INTERNATIONAL EXECUTIVE BOARD,*
*DELEGATES and GUESTS attending the*
*65th ANNUAL CONVENTION*

# LOCAL No. 471

915 LINCOLN AVENUE (East Liberty) PITTSBURGH 6, PA.

Figure 6.1. Local 471's president and board. This image was printed in the guide for the American Federation of Musicians' 65th Annual Convention, which was held in the Civic Arena in June 1962. American Federation of Musicians, Local 60-471, Pittsburgh, PA, Records, 1906–1996, AIS.1997.41, Archives & Special Collections, University of Pittsburgh Library System.

cohosted the 65th Annual Convention of the American Federation of Musicians in Pittsburgh, which drew 1,236 delegates from the US, Canada, the Virgin Islands, and Puerto Rico. The conference provided a platform for bands led by 471 board members Ruby Young, Alice Brooks, James Minor, and Walt Harper to perform for other locals. Westray, in his keynote address, avoided the issue of merging, emphasizing that 471 maintained the "best of relations" to Local 60 and that the separate locals were "a real example of democracy in action." Emphasizing that the two locals maintained the same pay scales, Westray went as far as to state, "[A]lthough we work the same territory, we never have any conflict."[26] Westray's illusion of harmony, possibly presented to prolong 471's independence, would quickly dissipate with the passing of the 1964 Civil Rights Act, which made the conditions of separate locals illegal.

Two years after Locals 471 and 60 hosted the AFM's national conference in Pittsburgh, the Civil Rights Act of 1964 was passed. In that year's AFM annual conference, Petrillo spoke strongly on the issue of segregation in the union and the urgency of merging the approximately forty remaining segregated locals. AFM President Kenin appointed Petrillo as head of the union's civil rights division to oversee the integration of what was one of the most segregated of all United States labor unions.[27] The locals that had merged before 1964 offered insights into the complexities of negotiating equitable terms that provided new working opportunities for Black musicians while maintaining leadership roles and opportunities to support music in Black communities.

Two examples demonstrated that the outcome of these mergers was also determined by the working conditions of musicians in those cities as well as the degree of collaboration or animosity between the locals throughout their existence. The merger of Los Angeles Locals 767 and 46 in 1953 far preceded other mergers. This was driven by Black musicians seeking access to new jobs and facilitated by a coalition of members from both locals who had the political will to support such a merger. In 1951, members of Local 767 began pushing for a merger that would potentially open access to film industry jobs for Black musicians. Bandstands that had included both 767 and 46 members had built lasting relationships, and though there was resistance from both locals, a collective of Black and White musicians was able to build support for the merger.

Local 767 member Marl Young was key to organizing support between both locals, formulating a merger proposal, and negotiating with Local 46's board. By creating a pro-merger coalition within 767 and running for office seats, Young was able to bring about a vote within both locals that supported the merger and then take the case for moderation to the AFM's national board under Petrillo. As recalled by Young, the primary points of negotiation included transferring services such as the death benefit, which covered the cost of funeral services, and seniority rights, which exempted those who had earned a life membership from paying further dues.[28] At every step of the process, Young provided amendments to the merger terms that took into consideration the bylaws of both locals and the national organization. For Young, his fundamental belief that segregation was socially and morally wrong drove him to resist backlash both from White musicians who feared the loss of jobs and Black musicians who valued their hard-won independence within the Federation. Once the terms of the merger were agreed on in the Federation's New York offices, AFM President Petrillo appointed Herman Kenin to oversee the merger in LA, where his comments struck Young as prophetic: "This will probably be the first of many mergers in the AF of M as far as black and white locals are concerned."[29] Though Young continued to fight discrimination within the merged local—including the practice of marking Musicians Union documents of Black members so they wouldn't be hired—he reflected on the merger as a victory for interracial organizations on a local level.

Following the Los Angeles merger was that of Seattle's Locals 76 and 493 in 1956 and San Francisco's Locals 6 and 669 in 1960. Detailed in Miller (2007), the merger agreement of San Francisco's locals extended the rights and coverages of Local 6's 5,500 members to the incoming four hundred members of Local 669, with temporary positions reserved in the merged Local's administration for an executive board member and the secretary-treasurer and business agent of 669. Within the year, locals in Denver and Sioux City followed with their own mergers, despite deep reservations over the loss of their independence and trepidation about their future roles in the merged locals. In San Francisco, the 1960 general board elections signaled a warning when none of the three former Local 669 members were elected. The following elections yielded better results, with former 669 member Vernon Alley winning his campaign for board member, which promised a small preservation of Black political representation in the AFM.

In Pittsburgh, merger negotiations between the boards of Locals 471 and 60 began in March 1965 at Local 60's downtown offices. Hal Davis, who served as Local 60's president from 1948 to 1970, was a Duquesne University graduate and percussionist who worked in the region's theaters and as a staff musician for local radio stations KDKA and WCAE.[30] Davis had clashed with 471 Presidents Carl Arter and Joe Westray in the previous decade, yet entered the meetings with a conciliatory tone, recognizing the need to "meet on common ground" so as to "effect an agreeable merger."[31] As a career union administrator, Davis had a strong presence in the Federation and would succeed Kenin as the AFM president in 1970, where he would fight for improved contracts for symphony musicians.

Joe Westray was, as evident from his AFM convention speech, still wary of a merger. While Davis was a well-connected union administrator, Westray had built his reputation as a respected bandleader, arranger, mentor, union representative, and businessman during the previous two decades. Alongside local Black bandleaders including Stoney Gloster, Thay Whiteley, Donald Woods, and Will

Hitchcock, Westray was an integral part of Pittsburgh's jazz scene and took pride in the professional training of Pittsburgh musicians, some of whom would go on to gain international recognition.[32] Saxophonist Stanley Turrentine began working with Westray at age thirteen and recalled how the elder musician invited him to join Local 471 and hired him for his first gigs touring in the surrounding mill towns.[33] Other distinguished Pittsburghers whom Westray employed and guided were singer Dakota Staton and pianist Erroll Garner.

At the time of the merger, Local 60 consisted of two thousand members with a president's yearly salary of $10,000, while Local 471 reported 324 members with a presidential salary of $2,100 a year.[34] Vocal in their concern about Black jobs, representation, facilities, and collectivity, 471 members lacked some of the advantages that larger Black locals had in bargaining within the merger negotiations. For example, Local 471 only had $2,429 in cash assets and did not own its own property, as was the case with the Black locals of Los Angeles, Chicago, and Philadelphia—all cases in which this equity would provide a focus for bargaining. Local 60 did own its own building in downtown Pittsburgh and reported a 1964 budget balance of $60,374.

Though the merger opened on friendly terms, the lingering resentment from previous disputes soon became apparent in the negotiations, with meeting minutes revealing themes common to merger negotiations throughout the country. Local 471 drummer Thomas Miller stated at the first merger meeting, "We are doing something in 1965 that should have been done in 1908 . . . . It is my understanding [that] in 1908 we were a subsidiary local of the Federation because you did not want to accept us as musicians and black people."[35] Westray and 471 proposed permanent representation on the board and delegateship as well as that "the merged union employ at least one Negro member who was employed in the same capacity, on the office staff at comparable salary." These conditions prompted comments from Local 60 members such as, "[T]here is no vacancy on the office staff of Local 60, and to create a new job, so to speak, is unwise and expensive."[36] The pervasive resistance to the idea of removing White members from positions of power led to Local 60 dismissing 471's attempts at enacting affirmative action as "segregation in reverse."[37] In addition to rejecting a system that would guarantee permanent representation for former 471 members, Local 60 also proposed restricting officers from performing. With 471 board members Westray, Secretary Ruby Young, and union officer Walt Harper leading active careers as performers, this policy took aim at the place of jazz in the newly merged local.

Locals 60 and 471's final merger agreement was ratified and signed on May 17, 1965, and became effective January 1, 1966. The newly named Local 60-471 would include three former 471 members on their extended board for a five-year transitional period. In 1970, the board would reduce to its original size, and general elections would be held. Westray, George Childress, and Ruby Young were chosen to fill the temporary spots on the expanded board alongside six Local 60 members. In addition to the expanded transitional board, two of the four delegate positions to the AFM's annual convention and one of two assistant positions to President Davis were reserved for former 471 members. Delegate positions were important, as they provided opportunities to travel and network with musicians in new cities. Ruby Young recalls: "I went to about fifteen national conventions for the musicians' unions. I was a delegate going to Vegas, Seattle, Portland and a lot of places I wouldn't have normally gone."[38]

The merger negotiations in Pittsburgh exposed the challenges of quelling resentments and negotiating for labor conditions that served both Black and White musicians. It was expected that members would build new relationships and political alliances in the five years following the merger. For Chuck Austin, socializing and creating goodwill within the new merged local was complicated by the closing of the social club in the downtown headquarters. Austin remembers:

> Local 60 had the same social environment in their Forbes Avenue musicians club because in the basement they had a bar where the guys would go after a gig. Sometime in 1965 they decided to dispense with the social atmosphere at the Local 60 club because, 'Hey, those guys from 471 are coming down in January so we don't want them speaking, looking at, dancing with our wives, daughters, and sisters.' The reputation with us was that we were womanizers and whoremongers so they closed the club. Who did they hurt: [trombonist] Joe Dallas, [guitarist] Joe Negri, [pianist] Bobby Negri, and the guys who wanted to jam. There were possibilities of drawing from the best of both locals, but they didn't look at it that way.[39]

Pittsburgh's merger was initially less contentious than those playing out in Buffalo, Chicago, Washington, DC, and Philadelphia, where negotiations failed to produce an agreement and the national office had to intervene.[40] Each merger would inform others as local musicians tried to determine the best ways to proceed within the short timelines determined by the AFM. Chicago's Black Local 208 and White Local 10 merged in 1966 after a tumultuous three years of negotiations. Local 208, with a membership of 1,700, was the most powerful Black local in the AFM, though its members were deeply divided on the issue of integration. Local 208 member Red Saunders built a coalition of Black musicians who were unhappy with the old-guard Black union leadership and wanted to "destroy the mythology that said Black musicians were satisfied with segregation and with dependency on union leadership for jobs."[41] In March 1963, Saunders and two hundred Local 208 members calling themselves "the Chicago Musicians for Harmonious Integration" demanded membership in Local 10. Under the advice of lawyers, Local 10 granted them membership.[42] Local 208 members continued to defect in this way throughout the year, while the Black union leadership enacted retribution against its "dissident" members. Though under pressure from the AFM's national office to merge, negotiations between Locals 208 and 10 came to a standstill a year after Saunders's demands to join Local 10. Petrillo and the AFM intervened and drafted an agreement that would guarantee that 208 members received full membership rights as well as two elected board members in the merged local. Local 10's rejection of these terms led the national board to place both locals into a trusteeship to complete the merger agreement that would ensure former 208 members a place on the board for six years—a period of time deemed adequate for "the members of Local 10 to be made aware of the intelligence of Negroes who might seek an office in the merged local."[43] Reflecting on the merger nearly three decades later, former 208 member Lefty Bates lamented the merger terms not guaranteeing Black representation: "[F]orever, or for a life time [sic] because there is not a single person to represent us down at Local 10-208 today."[44]

The minutes of the March 26, 1966, merger meeting between Buffalo's Black Local 533, headed by President Perry Gray, and White Local 43, headed by President Salvatore Rizzo, reveal the resistance of both parties to presenting the terms of agreement and environment of inaction created by fears from both parties.[45] For Gray, Local 533 did not oppose merging but didn't want to do so as a sacrifice of their way of working within the union. When pushed by Local 43 board member Vincent Impellitteri to clarify whether Gray wanted to obey the AFM national mandate and proceed with negotiations, Gray responded, "What do we have to gain?"[46] Local 533 Secretary-Treasurer Lloyd Plummer reflected Gray's stance and implied that delaying the merger would put pressure on the Federation's national office to intervene: "We should tell the Federation that we'll merge later on down the line. We should tell Petrillo that if we aren't moving fast enough to suit him, then he should do something."[47] Local 533 Board of Directors member Victor Einach questioned the basis for the directive to merge: "By what authority does Petrillo give this as a directive? Is it law? If it is, then we'll have to do something. Are we defying the law of the land as such? By what authority does this filter down, and what is the meaning of it?"[48] Two subsequent meetings between the merger committee members and Petrillo, in September 1966 and May 1967, demonstrated to the national office that little progress had been made. This prompted AFM President Kenin to write to both locals demanding a merger by the end of the year. Hal Davis, then vice president of the AFM, was sent to Buffalo to help draft the merger agreement, which was approved by Local 533's board in March 1968 yet rejected shortly afterward by Local 43's board on account of the work due rates. Further negotiations stalled the process, prompting Kenin to place the locals under national control and set the conditions of a merger that would take effect in 1969. The terms of the merger included a five-year period in which former 533 members would occupy the roles of administrative vice president, assistant secretary-treasurer, two of six director of the Board positions, and one of four delegates to AFM conventions.[49] As in Pittsburgh's case, Buffalo's merged local, renamed Local 92, established its headquarters in the previous White local's offices. Creative collaborations and socializing were curtailed because this space did not accommodate performances and was farther from Buffalo's East Side neighborhoods, where many former 533 members lived. In the general elections held after the five-year transitional board, no former 533 members were elected, effectively ending the Black representation of Buffalo's musicians. Gray's fear of the former Local 533's 125 members being outvoted by former Local 43's thirteen hundred members was realized.

Meanwhile, in DC, the three-year merger negotiations of Locals 710 and 161 in 1967 tested the argument against merging on the grounds that the Black local was already integrated. While Pittsburgh's Local 471 encouraged integrated enrollment, they added fewer than ten White members during Arter and Westray's presidencies. Local 710, however, touted approximately one-third White musicians among their 328 members.[50] Facing the insistence of the AFM head office to merge, Local 161-710 was formed with the agreement to reserve two executive board seats, two trial board seats, and one delegate seat of the merged local for Black members for a period of five years, after which general elections would be held. Within the merged Local, former 710 members would elect the vice president and one delegate from their previous membership. Despite the ability of Black musicians to maintain representation on the merged local's board after the transitional period, former Local 710 vice president Otis Ducker lamented in 1972 that general policy in Local 161-710 hurt the livelihood of jazz musicians, particularly the increase of wage scales, pension-plan costs, and the requirement of a minimum of twelve musicians in a contracted engagement. These stipulations favored symphony musicians and led many Black musicians who led smaller jazz trios and quartets to abandon union membership, which in turn led Black establishments to hire nonunion musicians. Having given up their own hall, Black musicians lost a central means of meeting and organizing. As Ducker noted, Black membership had dropped to around 80 members by 1972.

By 1970, the majority of separate locals had either negotiated their own merger or been forced to accept agreements presented by the AFM. Discontent over the conditions of these mergers had already surfaced in 1968 when Black musicians in New Haven and Chicago appealed to the AFM to have their separate charters reinstated.[51] White resistance in merged locals to Black leadership positions, policies that discouraged jazz musicians from joining, and the loss of musicians' clubs where union members could socialize and play were primary reasons for widespread disappointment. Philadelphia's Local 274 also rejected negotiations on the grounds that it was already operating an integrated local and that a merger with the White local offered no clear benefits. However, Local 274 would take a markedly different approach to the merger process, resulting in a rejection of unionized labor for Black musicians. With approximately nine hundred members, their own club and liquor license, and other assets, Local 274 was well positioned to continue to grow and to extend its membership to all interested musicians.

274 president James Adams's resolve to resist merging was strengthened by his awareness of the growing discontent of Black musicians in newly merged unions. In 1969, Adams called a general meeting of Black union musicians to meet in Chicago to discuss the creation of a national Black musicians' union that would be recognized by the AFM.[52] This plan did not garner enough support to proceed, so Adams focused on preserving Local 274's legacy within Philadelphia. To protect Local 274's assets against an impending merger or dissolution of their charter, Adams established a nonprofit in 1966 called the Philadelphia Clef Club of the Performing Arts, which included himself on the board of directors. The Clef Club accepted all 274 musicians as regular members and took over ownership of 274's building, liquor license, and funds. With Adams rejecting demands to merge, Hal Davis, then the AFM's president, revoked 274's charter in 1971 after a court hearing found their separate locals in violation of the 1964 Civil Rights Act. The Clef Club moved in to take over many of the 274's services, with Adams stating, "We wanted to keep what we had. It was our house. We built it, sweat, tears, and blood."[53] Adams's invoking of James Reece Europe's New York City Clef Club union speaks to the importance he placed on the social networks and physical institutions that comprised Black musical labor. In this endeavor, Adams worked to preserve the tradition of Black musical labor by fighting against a system that enforced workplace discrimination while maintaining its own political power— with or without the support of the Union.

## Black Musicians of Pittsburgh (BMOP) vs. Local 60-471 (1971–1977)

The five-year transition period of Pittsburgh's merged Local 60-471 ended in December 1970. As outlined in the transition agreement, the board reverted to six seats and general elections were held with no guaranteed positions for former 471 members. Ruby Young and Joe Westray, veteran 471 union officers, ran for the executive board, with Westray also running for a delegate seat. Both White and Black union officers publicly expressed the importance of electing a Black musician to the new board and proving that the merged Local would not revert to a de facto White local. Former 471 officer George Childress warned that without representation, Black musicians would lose faith in the union as an institution for overturning the long history of exclusion from radio and recording jobs, downtown venues, and city parks concerts. In the hopes of guaranteeing a permanent spot for former 471 members, Childress proposed a quota system based on membership. Preceding the election, Local 60-471 President Herb Osgood (1970–1993) wrote an open letter to the approximately two hundred Black and twenty-two hundred White members calling for the support of the Black candidates:[54]

> Some of the statements I hear that disturb me are; "why should we support a black person, they only represent a small minority. . . . Non-blacks can legislate and deal fairly with black people as well as black people can." I respectfully suggest to you that this king of archaic reasoning is what has led to some of the major problems, which confront our society today. This kind of reasoning has been in existence for well over 100 years and it is high time we start to face up to conditions as they exist today.[55]

Both Young and Westray received approximately four hundred votes, with no White candidate receiving more than eight hundred votes. With approximately half of the electorate voting, the results showed that a significant number of White members supported the former 471 candidates, though this was not enough to win the seats. The election demonstrated to the former 471 members that Black representation in the merged local would require either building more support among White members or organizing an intervention.

Shortly after the election, former 471 member and drummer Thomas "Doc" Miller wrote to the AFM's Executive Board requesting an extension of the transitional merger conditions and reinstatement of the three Black board members to Local 60-471. The AFM, led by former Local 60 President Hal Davis, responded that they found no "compelling reason" to extend the agreement and further pursue an affirmative action policy.[56] As stated later in court, Miller did not file a grievance since he believed that Davis would ignore these concerns. Seeing that there was little recourse to ensure their place in the union, former 471 members George Childress, Clyde Jackson, pianist George "Duke" Spaulding, Ruby Young, Chuck Austin, Thomas Miller, and vibraphonist DeRuyter "Ducky" Kemp formed the Black Musicians of Pittsburgh (BMOP) to fight what they saw as their erasure as organized musical laborers and the perpetuation of discriminatory practices addressed in the 1964 Civil Rights Act.[57]

BMOP filed suit against Local 60-471 on October 21, 1971, with Childress filing a charge of discrimination in hiring practice with the EEOC on December 13 of the same year.[58] The impetus to seek legal action grew from Childress's conversations with his uncle Derrick Bell who, in 1969, became the first Black professor tenured at Harvard Law School. Bell, born in Pittsburgh in 1930, attended Schenley High School, Duquesne University, and was the only Black student in the University of Pittsburgh's Law School upon his graduation in 1957. Working in the Pittsburgh office of the NAACP Legal Defense and Educational Fund, Bell would fight segregation in Pittsburgh's public recreational facilities before working on school desegregation cases in Mississippi.[59] Childress and Bell discussed

Figure 6.2. Charles "Teenie" Harris, American, 1908–1998, Musicians, from left: Clyde Jackson, George "Duke" Spaulding, Ruby Young Buchanan, Charles "Chuck" Austin, Thomas "Doc" Miller, "Ducky" Kemp, and Atty. William B. Gould, posed in Flamingo Club, January 1974, black and white: Kodak Safety Film, H: 2 1/4 in. × W: 3 1/2 in. (5.71 × 8.89 cm), Carnegie Museum of Art, Pittsburgh: Heinz Family Fund, 2001.35.9886 © Carnegie Museum of Art, Charles "Teenie" Harris Archive.

the merger of Pittsburgh AFM locals and the loss of political participation and job opportunities following the interim agreement. Bell contacted a then-thirty-four-year-old visiting professor at Harvard Law School, William B. Gould IV, who was at the front lines of antidiscrimination court cases, to consider taking on the case in Pittsburgh. Gould recalls being inspired by the sense of camaraderie among BMOP members and the urgent need to preserve aspects of how they had organized as Black musical laborers.

The case also represented a chance to set a precedent in legal fights aimed at both instituting affirmative action and undoing embedded systems of discrimination. As Gould recalls, courts had not intervened to extend the temporary affirmative action measures set by the AFM and its locals, which prompted him to try and "take the law to the next frontier. This inevitable tension [in] race consciousness which would preserve and guarantee the Black local representation beyond the five-year period and hopefully for an indefinite period of time and the elimination of racial barriers—this is the fundamental problem in all the civil rights cases."[60]

The challenge for BMOP lay in providing definitive evidence of previous racial discrimination in hiring practices and the perpetuation of that discrimination in the practices of the merged union. BMOP, a collective that was open to Local 60-471 members regardless of "race, color, nationality, or creed," represented approximately seventy previous 471 members who stated that they were "racially discriminated against in holding positions of union leadership and in union job referral practices" following the merger.[61] The legal basis for fighting discrimination was strengthened in March 1972, when Title VII of the 1964 Civil Rights Act was amended to give the Equal Employment Opportunity Commission (EEOC) the authority to sue. From the time of the passing of the Civil Rights Act in 1964 through 1972, only private plaintiffs could bring suits challenging discrimination, while the EEOC's role was to investigate complaints and provide reports that could be used in court. After Childress filed complaints, the EEOC investigated Local 60-471's hiring practices and submitted a report that supported BMOP's case. The main charges addressed by the EEOC centered on White Local 60-471 bandleaders who were "failing or refusing to hire black musicians because of their race; by maintaining hiring procedures and customs which tend to discriminate against that class because of race; and by failing to take affirmative action to eliminate the effects of past discrimination."[62] Tangible affirmative action, according to the EEOC, would have been apparent in continued Black representation and Black hiring by established White bandleaders.

The EEOC investigation provided the necessary support to bring a case to trial and hear the testimonies and examinations of previous 471 members Carl Arter, Arthur Barnes, Thomas Miller, Ruby Young, and Bobby Boswell. The nonjury trial opened in February 1975 and was presided over by Judge Barron McCune. Gould's opening statement focused on the flaws of a five-year transitional merger agreement, which did not provide sufficient pressure on Local 60-471's White members to bridge racial barriers. Gould argued that White musicians "knew that they had no real incentive to encourage the white membership to become personally acquainted with the blacks, to encourage social, personal contact which would give the blacks the prestige and respect which is necessary to win office in the large elections, such as those which existed after the transitional agreement."[63] This condition would be most immediately remedied through either reviving the transitional agreement for an unspecified period or installing two previous 471 members on the Executive Board as vice president and secretary-treasurer.[64]

To support Gould's "race-conscious remedies" in the service of ultimately eradicating racial barriers, he referenced other suits in which merged AFL union locals were found to have continued systems of discrimination and lacked personal contact and social exchange between Black and White workers. The previous year, Gould had worked on a civil rights case in which an organization of Black electricians formed the Betterment of Black Edison Employees led by Willie Stamps, which won four million dollars in damages from the Detroit Edison Company.[65] In the case of Local 60-471, Gould argued that the previous discriminatory practices of

Hal Davis as president of Local 60 and his rejection of BMOP's request to extend the merger agreement as president of the AFM was a sign of a systemic problem that required more than five years to undo. Gould described Davis as "the fox guarding the chickens" and pleaded with the court to intervene in the matter.[66]

Following four days of plaintiff testimonies and examination, McCune ruled in favor of the defendants Local 60-471, stating:

> First, both the plaintiffs and the EEOC . . . knew there was little evidence of discrimination available, and that the difficulties of the merged Local could be attributed as much to the plaintiffs as to the Local. Second, they knew that there was absolutely no evidence of disparate employment opportunities, and even if there were, there was no evidence that the Local had any effect on the hiring done, as it had no hiring hall and received at most, an insubstantial number of job referrals. Finally, the EEOC knew that the statistics offered as their case in chief were not conclusive and, in fact, substantially supported defendants' positions. In light of these conclusions, the EEOC's decision to pursue litigation on theories of membership and hiring discrimination was made in bad faith.[67]

The ruling implies that there were no provable cases of discrimination in hiring practices because the local's responsibilities were to set rates for wages and not hire workers. The court agreed that common music labor practice was to leave the hiring of musicians to bandleaders and individual contractors rather than the union officials—an arrangement not common in other labor unions.

McCune's charge that the EEOC and BMOP pursued their case in bad faith resulted from several statements given during the plaintiff's testimony. First, evidence of discrimination in some cases supported the defendants' case. Statistics showing improved wages for Black musicians after the merger harmed BMOP's case, as McCune's memorandum noted: "If you compare the overall class of black musicians in the area with white musicians, it looks like black musicians during the three years of the detailed tapes grossed more money. That quite candidly surprised us; we didn't anticipate that."[68] Secondly, bassist Bobby Boswell stated that members of BMOP requested that he withdraw from his candidacy for Local 60-471's Executive Board in 1974 because his success would weaken their case. Though Boswell could not withdraw from the election due to late notice, he did not actively campaign for support and narrowly lost by fifteen votes. Boswell stated during his testimony that he believed that Local 60-471 President Herb Osgood's support of his candidacy was motivated by a genuine interest in supporting Black representation in the local. Other BMOP members portrayed Osgood's support as an attempt to undermine their efforts to expose and address deeper structural problems in the local by allowing a position to be filled by a "token" former 471 member.

Though a small community of musicians, BMOP suffered from a lack of unity and strategic planning in its fight for racial and economic equality. The differing perceptions of Osgood's motivations and tensions between Black musicians over strategies for securing representation in Local 60-471 revealed the challenges of building the goodwill needed to realize an equitable system of integration. As Boswell testified, he believed that he would have won a seat on Local 60-471's board if not for reducing campaigning under pressure from other BMOP members. Those goodwill efforts put forth by Osgood to build friendships across racial lines were, as a testifying BMOP member admitted, not universally supported due to "a lack of interest on their part in trying to make the merger work."[69] These further challenged creating an environment for reconciliation.[70]

### Reflecting on the Paradox of Progress

Examining jazz musicians' roles as Black musical laborers imbues the jazz canon and genre-driven narratives of jazz history with practical struggles and visions of social progress that impacted the working lives of many musicians. As a means of articulating a Black public sphere, jazz performances are grounded in historically and geographically specific contexts shaped by the experience of segregation.[71] Pittsburgh's Black musical labor organizers drew on the social and business networks of their communities that, as Black studies scholar Mark Anthony Neal notes, allowed for "a diversity of interclass relations to thrive within their boundaries."[72] Within these communities, Black musical labor was shaped both by its resistance to the institution of White musical labor as embodied in the policies of Local 60 and collaborations with White jazz musicians as practiced in integrated Black clubs, bands, and Local 471 activities.

As these networks were disrupted during the 1960s by social unrest, urban redevelopment, the growth of suburbs, and labor integration, jazz musicians faced a crisis in the Black public sphere. Frustrations among Black musicians were exacerbated by the structural disintegration of Black economic and cultural institutions in Pittsburgh, particularly following riots incited by the assassination of Martin Luther King. The struggle to build workforces that reflected the equal opportunity goals of civil rights played out against a backdrop of rapid deindustrialization. In Pittsburgh, the looming collapse of the steel industry would eventually lead to the loss of 133,000 manufacturing jobs between 1979 and 1987.[73] The city's population was shrinking, and the economic foundation that had provided disposable wealth for Pittsburgh's nightlife crumbled.

Two decades after the Civil Rights Act of 1964, law professor Derrick Bell reflected on the effectiveness of legislation in removing overt forms of discrimination, such as the eradication of segregated schools, public facilities, and labor

Figure 6.3. Charles "Teenie" Harris, American, 1908–1998, Atty. Derrick Bell speaking during NAACP Youth Rally in Central Baptist Church, April 1960, black and white: Kodak Safety Film, H: 4 in. × W: 5 in. (10.20 × 12.70 cm), Carnegie Museum of Art, Pittsburgh: Heinz Family Fund, 2001.35.54401, © Carnegie Museum of Art, Charles "Teenie" Harris Archive.

union locals. Like other "freedom symbols" enacted by Congress, Bell argues that they are rendered powerless to change endemic discrimination: "Where civil rights enforcement inconveniences or even endangers the economic interests of whites, decisions in all but the most innocuous affirmative action cases sidetrack civil rights in a manner that differs more in style than in result from the white supremacist mindset that doomed the reparation plans for Blacks during the First Reconstruction."[74] For Black musical laborers in Pittsburgh and throughout the United States, the hard-fought victories of the Civil Rights Act of 1964 forced mergers between unwilling parties and the abandonment of Black institutions with the expectation of swiftly undoing previous systems of workplace discrimination. Within a merged union local, many Black musicians no longer felt that they had the means to represent their interests. Those disheartened by the loss of AFM representation, jobs, and a social club discontinued their membership and were officially barred from union jobs. As a result, Local 60-471 came to represent the interests of the region's symphony and society big band musicians.

Those few Black musicians who did stay with the merged union were often met with scorn from other former 471 members. Chuck Austin, who withdrew from the BMOP committee when he came to see their hopes for a settlement and compensation as unrealistic, was often the only Black musician in White bandleader Jack Purcell's big band.[75] These jobs came with the burden of being labeled as a traitor to those who had left the local. Austin recalls, "It hurt me that people I thought were my friends could say those things about me . . . but this was a step up in my career. I was fulfilling my dream of becoming a top musician, and I knew that I had earned the job. It wasn't given to me because I was black."[76]

The breakdown of union representation and collectivity once shared by Black musicians also impacted the working and social relationships of local and touring Black artists. Before the merger, Black artists from other cities could book bands through contacts in Local 471's offices. Following the merger, Local 60-471's hiring practices often favored White musicians, with the perceived weaker music-reading skills of former 471 members serving as a tacit excuse for exclusion. On occasion, a touring artist forced Local 60-471 to include Black musicians. Saxophonist Don Aliquo Sr. remembers, "I played the Lena Horne and Tony Bennett show at Heinz Hall in about '78. At the rehearsal, she looked at the band and there were no black players and she wouldn't play. Jack Purcell was booking and hired [former 471 members] Chuck Austin, Nelson Harrison, and Lee Gross. After that, she agreed to play."[77]

BMOP's lawsuit was aimed at breaking new legal ground in the wake of the 1964 Civil Rights Act by forcing Local 60-471 to address the lack of Black board and staff membership as well as White hiring practices. A deeper sense of loss— of ways of working and socializing—undergirded this case. The merger made structural changes to Black musical labor in Pittsburgh against a backdrop of immense challenges to Black communities—namely displacement, redevelopment, middle-class exodus, civil unrest, and relocation of businesses. Arter's service as president of Local 471 from 1954 to 1962 provided opportunities to improve the working conditions of musicians both Black and White. Though he successfully challenged many of Local 60's policies including the Afro-American Agreement, he saw that these achievements did not fundamentally change working conditions for Black musicians in Pittsburgh. These experiences of fighting discrimination to ensure workers' rights left him disenchanted with the union as a force for social change. When questioned during the 1974 court testimonies about why he had supported the efforts of BMOP, Arter's loss of resolve to continue fighting discrimination was apparent in his statement:

> I was not interested in getting into this fight any longer because I told [BMOP] that it was futile. I was not going . . . to try anymore. Do not ask me if one man could. I wouldn't be here now, but if I refused to be here, I could be subpoenaed. That is the only reason I am here now but I lost all interest when I [realized] that

there was no progress being made and [that] personal contacts and the essential things that I thought were necessary [were not being advanced].[78]

Though Arter was resigned to the failure of integration in Pittsburgh's AFM local, Chuck Austin continued to work as a unionized musician for decades to come. In 2000, at the age of seventy, Austin became the first former 471 member elected to Local 60-471's board in a long overdue gesture toward reconciliation. Having started his musical career at the Musicians Club in the Lower Hill District, Austin's involvement with the union through the merger is a testimony to his dedication to a career in music. Carrying on their tradition of activism and collectivity as jazz musicians, Austin and other former members of Local 471 incorporated the African American Jazz Preservation Society of Pittsburgh (AAJPSP) in 1996 and undertook an extensive interview-driven program to document their past struggles and experiences as Black musicians in Pittsburgh. By preserving the stories of musicians who lived through this tumultuous period, the AAJPSP belatedly fulfilled the role of reinstating a sense of community that was disrupted by the merger and court case. These efforts also helped build a collective memory of jazz in Pittsburgh. Though Austin and many other 471 members have since passed away, the AAJPSP continues to seek ways to engage the public through jazz.

# PART IV

# JAZZ AND THE COMMUNITY ARCHIVE (1968–2024)

# Chapter 7

# HILL NIGHTLIFE IN THE WAKE OF 1968

The Hill District, a point of convergence in the early decades of the twentieth century, had become a site marked by departure by 1970.[1] Those who remained in the Hill found themselves increasingly isolated within Pittsburgh and cut off from downtown due to the extensive Lower Hill Redevelopment Project of the 1950s. The Civic Arena, completed in 1962, stood as a monument for the modern city on the site of the displaced residential buildings and business corridors of the Lower Hill. The intersection of Wylie Avenue and Fullerton Street, once dubbed "the crossroads of the world," was submerged under the arena's expansive parking lot; this transformed the intersection into a "non-place" that accommodated car travelers and temporary gatherings around ticketed sports and concert events. The crossroads was no longer a point of entry into the Hill District, but rather a stopping point for those channeled into the arena and away from the streets and businesses of the Middle and Upper Hill District. Journalist, activist, and urban studies scholar Jane Jacobs argued that developers needed to address the social rupture caused by urban development projects and weave the Civic Arena site "back into the city fabric," if not on the eastern border with the Hill District, then possibly along the western downtown boundary.[2] Sprawling parking lots, street patterns, and the lack of new housing and commercial real estate ensured that this did not happen, and the arena site evolved into a buffer zone that discouraged foot and car traffic between the Hill and downtown. New highway interchanges threaded through the heart of the city, making the Arena easy to access from the suburbs but hostile to pedestrians.

Spurred by failures to envision programs of urban redevelopment that could sustain rather than marginalize the neighborhood, Hill residents dispersed throughout the city and into expanding suburbs. Between 1950 and 1990, 71 percent of Hill District residents left the area, with many African Americans settling in East Liberty, Homewood, and Penn Hills.[3] Over the same time period, Pittsburgh saw its Central City Black population increase from 82,000 to 105,000, while the city's total population dropped by 23 percent.[4] Rapid suburbanization, White flight, and the emergence of municipalities such as Monroeville were made possible by new highways, while growing employment in these areas drew jobs away from the city center.[5] Similar demographic trends in Rust Belt cities during the 1970s and 1980s coincided with the region's collapse in industrial output. From 1947 to 1972, Pittsburgh saw a loss of 22.5 percent of manufacturing jobs, the highest rate among urban centers in the Northeastern US.[6] In an urban crisis study of seventeen northeastern metropolitan areas, Pittsburgh was ranked fifteenth, scoring slightly better than Buffalo and Cleveland.[7]

Visions of an expanded and renewed downtown that would propel Pittsburgh's business leadership through the twentieth century were soon undone by the realities of economic disparities and social unrest in the country. Throughout the 1960s, American cities witnessed an unfolding crisis as experiences of poverty, systemic racism, and police brutality found outlets in mass uprisings and the destruction of large swaths of marginalized neighborhoods. In the US, 752 riots took place between 1964 and 1971 in which 228 died, 12,741 were injured, and nearly seventy thousand were arrested.[8] The Harlem riot of July 1964 was the first of hundreds of events that shifted public awareness of the civil rights struggles from the South to the northern cities.[9] The fruition of civil rights struggles was in part realized through the passing of the Civil Rights Act of 1964 and Voting Rights Act of 1965, though the Watts Uprising of August 1965 offered a stark rejoinder to the optimism surrounding these legislative victories. A glaring contrast to nonviolent resistance, civil unrest of the 1960s was a decentralized exercise of Black agency to displace White terror.[10] The crisis of northern cities was readily apparent to Martin Luther King Jr., who, in his 1967 speech "Civil Rights at the Crossroads," presented his Poor People's Campaign as a "last plea to the nation to respond to nonviolence."[11] It was a bitter irony that King's call to heed the warnings of impending uprisings was received as a threat by conservative politicians. Ohio Representative John Ashbrook pointed to King's plea as evidence that he was an "apostle of violence" who "has given credibility to one of the most dangerous dogmas that can be promoted in an orderly society."[12]

None of the 159 uprisings that came to be known as "the long, hot summer of 1967" reached Pittsburgh that year, though they nonetheless resonated in Pittsburgh's African American communities. In a series of articles published in the *New Pittsburgh Courier* in March 1968, Executive Editor Carl Morris wrote of a growing "black mood" in the city's neighborhoods "where frustration festers on the social sores of slum housing, unemployment, broken families, and inferior public education."[13] Black militants, Morris cited from inside sources, were inspired by what they saw as the liberatory "defiance of law and order" in Newark, Detroit, and Milwaukee and so were planning a "B-Day" or "burn day" for May 1968.[14]

These tensions were unleashed following the assassination of King on April 4, 1968. The Hill bore the brunt of arson that began on April 5 and lasted into the following week. Unrest, indicative of pervasive desperation, disillusionment, and anger, led to approximately five hundred fires, largely in the Middle Hill, which resulted in over $600,000 in damage.[15] On Sunday, April 7, the Hill's Mainway Grocery's windows were shattered, with residents carrying out food as the owner unsuccessfully pleaded for the building to be spared from burning. As one Hill resident remembers, the scene was one of chaos and despair:

> I listened to the twelve o'clock news and they [the owners] said, "[L]et people go in the Mainway Grocery store and tell them they can take anything they want. Just don't burn the place down." I grabbed my boys and walked all the way up Dinwiddie and got across from the Mainway and said, "You all stay here." I set them on the stoop and went in. People were snatching and grabbing and knocking shit all on the floor. They had one of these walk-in coolers and I went in there. They were stepping on more meat than they were carrying out. I had my little boxes and I came out and said, "Yeah, come on." We ate that stuff up damn near overnight.[16]

Later that day, civil rights activist and Pennsylvania House of Representative Kirkland Leroy Irvis attempted to dissuade a crowd from burning a paint store that was below his second-floor apartment. The crowd did not fully relent but offered enough time for Irvis to remove some of his belongings and load them into a truck before the fire consumed the storefront and his home.[17]

Much of the neighborhood's business infrastructure was destroyed in the upheaval, leaving the community fractured and further isolated within the city as merchants chose to close or relocate. Zola Hirsh, a second-generation Jewish Hill District business owner, commented on the destruction of his drycleaning business:

> The settlement that I wound up with was horrible and unbelievable. The final settlement for all of my business was $30,000. With my attorney's fee and outstanding debts on equipment, I wound up with $9,000. I had enough to start again but not enough to gamble another beginning on the Hill.[18]

Only in 2013 did a grocery store return to the neighborhood with the opening of a Shop 'n Save as part of a development project led by the Hill House Association

Figure 7.1. Charles "Teenie" Harris, American, 1908–1998, Men and women gathered outside Economart Market with broken windows, Rendezvous Shine Parlor, and Hogan and Mary's Bar-B-Q, with fire hoses in street, after riot, c. 1968, black and white: Kodak Safety Film, H: 4 in. × W: 5 in. (10.20 × 12.70 cm), Carnegie Museum of Art, Pittsburgh: Heinz Family Fund, 2001.35.7014 © Carnegie Museum of Art, Charles "Teenie" Harris Archive.

and Economic Development Corporation.[19] The Shop 'n Save would close five years later amid the Hill House's own financial crisis.

King's assassination had an immediate and long-lasting impact on the social atmosphere of nightlife in the Hill District. Trombonist Nelson Harrison noted of the Crawford Grill, "Before 1968, more than half of the patrons were white. If you wanted to go on an exotic date and you were in college, you went to the Grill."[20] After King's assassination, Harrison encountered widespread perceptions among previous White patrons that the Hill was unsafe and unwelcoming for White visitors, despite little evidence of actual violence. The pervasiveness of these opinions contributed to the Hill's isolation and perception as a hostile Black ghetto rather than welcoming the interracial and interethnic community.

Many White jazz musicians found that the isolation of the Hill and similar communities impacted how they professionally and personally engaged Black communities and Black clubs where they had previously performed, networked, and studied. Saxophonist Lou Stellute experienced similar isolation from the Black communities where he worked. Stellute was a member of an all-White quartet—alongside organist John Bartel, guitarist Larry O'Brien, and drummer

Jeff Marino—that found success locally in Black-owned venues and eventually branched out to tour throughout the northeastern US. Before April 1968, Stellute had encountered audiences that were supportive and appreciative of the group's dedication to learning and playing what was considered quintessential Black American music.

When King's murder was announced, Bartel's group was performing in a Black-owned venue in Columbus, Ohio. Stellute recalls, "We had to be escorted out with our equipment to our van and had to leave town because they were shutting the club down." In the following months, the group continued to play Black-owned clubs, but it quickly became apparent that "there was a new era coming in," leading Bartel to increasingly book performances in the "so-called 'white territory.'"[21] This new focus included rock clubs and festivals, opening slots for nationally touring acts such as the Mahavishnu Orchestra and Alice Cooper, and recording for the pop and rock label Capitol Records. The group stayed together until 1975 but split due to disagreements over the group's orientation toward rock.

The gradual movement by bands, such as the John Bartel Quartet, away from Black-owned venues and toward rock clubs and festivals impacted musical approaches and outlooks. Jazz musicians increasingly sought work in venues that catered to largely White audiences and found that they had to adapt their stylistic approaches to fit the expectations of White audiences. Singer Sandy Staley explains how this shift played out in her music:

> I could see the jazz thing ending when the Holiday Inn syndrome started. People wanted flash and Elvis suits. Every band had a name instead of [using the artist's name as with the] Bobby Negri Trio. We were one of the first jazz bands to do rock songs like "Green Apples," "By the Time I Get to Phoenix," and "Alone Again Naturally." We did stuff from *Jesus Christ Superstar*. "Everybody's Talking at You" from the movie *Midnight Cowboy*. We made up a fake band name, "Attila and Hon."[22]

For Stellute, the values and performative norms of clubs such as the Hurricane were no longer part of Bartel's music because "[a]fter the '60s, it was not so Black-centered. Basically, all the clubs we used to play were in the Black areas. It just wasn't happening after the riots. People weren't booking."[23] This shift marked the decline for many musicians—both Black and White—of a way of learning, performing, and experiencing jazz that was grounded in the social life of Black communities. As Stellute explains:

> When I came up, we learned by playing the music in its natural environment. No matter how technically excellent a musician is in school, there is still something missing when you are not in the midst of it. When you went to these clubs and played you learned directly from life. People who came into those clubs were

working people who had hard lives and came into those clubs to have a good time and you fed off of that. Through osmosis, it went into your being and you were inspired by that . . . . It was a great school. Those places were a great education. A lot of White people do not get a chance to interact with Black people in a real way and understand how they are. To see how they have really contributed immensely to the culture of this country and how willing Black people were in sharing this, though they have a great reason to be hostile to White people. Now, you almost have to teach in a university because the scene is gone. There are almost no places to learn how to play. There is something about passing it on verbally and being with the players that makes it a little bit different.

Those clubs in the Hill that continued after April 1968 saw a considerable drop-off of both White and Black patrons from outside the neighborhood. Though the Hurricane was not damaged in April 1968, the owner Birdie Dunlap received bomb threats and demands of protection payoffs from those angry with her White clients. Defiant and determined to maintain a welcoming environment, Dunlap hired an off-duty policeman to patrol the premises and deter petty theft.[24] Despite her efforts, business declined in the following year, reaching the point where "the bartenders started calling in sick because they weren't getting anything in tips," and she found herself "sitting in that bar and no one was there."[25] When an accidental fire damaged the Hurricane in April 1970, Dunlap initially planned to reopen and continue booking bands but soon decided to sell the club and retire from the nightlife business.[26]

Joe Robinson, the owner of the Crawford Grill No. 2, organized an evening to honor Dunlap's contribution to Pittsburgh's nightlife; Dunlap's illustrious career began with promoting Ella Fitzgerald with the Chick Webb Orchestra in the late 1930s and running a Centre Avenue bar named Birdie's Place and the Washington Club before opening the Hurricane in 1953.[27] The night featured a gathering of family and friends, with florist Edmond Prince providing a bouquet of three hundred red roses to Dunlap, to which she quipped, "It's really good to receive your flowers while able to see and smell them."[28] With Dunlap retired, Robinson was left to find a way to keep jazz in the Hill.

### "Oasis in a Desert": The Crawford Grill No. 2

The challenges facing the Hill District after 1968 were indicative of an urban crisis playing out across the United States in which civil unrest, rapid deindustrialization, and depopulation left entire neighborhoods physically and economically devastated. The exodus of businesses and residents, as well as a pervasive fear of the Hill among potential White patrons, made it increasingly difficult to sustain a

Hill nightlife scene that drew together jazz musicians and dedicated listeners. In an effort to preserve a space of critical listening within the Hill District, club owners Joe Robinson and his son William (aka "Buzzy") continued to bring touring and local jazz artists to the Crawford Grill No. 2, albeit on a much-reduced schedule.

Joe Robinson's continued investment in live music at the Grill was made possible because of his involvement in numbers running. In August 1973, Robinson was arrested after two detectives found numbers slips in the Grill kitchen.[29] Inspector Stephen Joyce claimed that Robinson employed between fifty and a hundred numbers writers who took in an estimated two million dollars a year through small daily bets. Consistent with the Hill's Black-owned nightclubs reaching back to the Prohibition Era, jazz venues in the Hill were often part of a larger network of businesses, rackets, and social and sports organizations.[30] The numbers, though illegal, generated profits that fed back into institutions such as the Crawford Grill No. 1 and No. 2, which served as entertainment establishments as well as informal focal points in Pittsburgh's Black political and sports life. Numbers running, in this respect, was an informal economic system that provided services not offered by White-owned banking and real estate institutions.[31] Pittsburgh entrepreneur Thomas Burley reflected on the Grill's economic model as a "neighborhood bar":

> Some of these places were fronts for other businesses such as the numbers business. Even the Crawford Grill, back in the day, before Buzzy Robinson had it, was a front for Gus Greenlee and Joe Robinson's numbers business. They didn't have to make it on the basis of the business because they provided a legitimate storefront for other things where the money was really made. A lot of clubs were tied to other businesses.[32]

From 1968 to 1983, the Robinsons drew on their extensive connections to journalists, politicians, artists, activists, educators, and musicians to continue a regular program of concerts, if not the busy schedule of the 1950s and early- to mid-1960s. Grill bookings continued to feature touring jazz artists, including Max Roach and Abbey Lincoln, Freddie Hubbard, Art Blakey, Johnny Lytle, Horace Silver, George Benson, Roy Haynes, Richard "Groove" Holmes, Kenny Clarke, Sonny Stitt, and Slide Hampton.[33] Grill events also included soul acts such as Ruby and the Romantics, Samson & Delilah, Chocolate Syrup, and Nate Evans and Mean Green. Locally based musicians, including Horace and Mary Turner, Gene Ludwig, Tim Stevens, Frank Cunimondo, Roger Humphries, Mike Taylor, Nelson Harrison, and James Johnson II, also contributed to keeping the Grill an active live music venue. For Johnson, the several months of residency at the Grill with veteran drummer Kenny Clarke in 1979 was one of his most important "qualitative educations about music and life."[34] Clarke, who lived with

Johnson's family during his time at the Grill, was dedicated to an artistic practice that advanced critical listening.

As newer generations of jazz musicians were playing larger stages for younger audiences and exploring the expressive potentials of rock and funk, the Grill continued to be a valued site for those seeking the listening experiences of the previous decades. *Courier* writer Greg Mims praised the Grill for maintaining a relaxed atmosphere where one could have an intimate conversation while listening to the band. Mims saw the Grill as a safe haven during "the age of *Clockwork Orange* and cheap contemporary plasticism [*sic*] decor" where the "realness" of an understated singer such as Arthur Prysock could be appreciated without the "strobe lit [*sic*] stages, rock operas, and a myriad of combined visual and aural assaults foisted upon all too accepting audiences as entertainment."[35]

Jazz artists such as vibraphonist Johnny Lytle maintained a close relationship with the Grill into the early 1980s. Lytle played at least eighteen times at both the Hurricane and Grill between 1959 and 1983, claiming that Joe Robinson once purchased him a new $4,000 vibraphone after his road-worn instrument collapsed on the Grill stage and nearly fell onto a nearby table. Lytle recalled that Robinson, rather than fire the musician for the state of his equipment, remarked, "Anybody who plays music as pretty as you can't be playing on an instrument like that."[36] A prolific artist who recorded over twenty albums as a leader, Lytle exemplified the career of the touring jazz artist integral to a network of local scenes, though absent from jazz histories and canons. His creative approach never deviated greatly from hard bop, with his music centered on his forceful, direct, and often virtuosic rendering of American songbook standards and contemporary soul tunes. One of his last albums, *Happy Ground* (Muse, 1991), pays tribute to the tradition of Hammond organ jazz that the Hurricane frequently featured. The title, the same as his second album released in 1961, memorializes places and nightlife scenes of the Hill and similar neighborhoods. In a genre often defined as a series of ruptures and evolutions, Lytle's career was an exercise in stylistic continuity that invoked collective spaces and ways of listening that were rapidly fading. As an artist whose creative development did not trace a narrative of innovation through jazz fusion, Lytle's dedication to performance styles rooted in clubs such as the Hurricane and Grill functioned as a community archive of those spaces and nightlife scenes—what, to Lytle, was "happy ground."

Though the Grill provided concerts throughout the 1970s, it was also a site of remembrance of the neighborhood's cultural history and a place of social gathering for African American community leaders. In May 1970, the Grill celebrated twenty-four years of live music with a month of events and parties thrown by *New Pittsburgh Courier* staff and week-long bookings of George Benson and Gene Harris.[37] Among those dropping in were political and business leaders of Pittsburgh as well as actor and singer Adam Wade, a Pittsburgh native who would

Figure 7.2. Charles "Teenie" Harris, American, 1908–1998, Louis "Hop" Kendrick presenting potted plant to Joseph Robinson, and woman in long dress, on stage with drum kit in Crawford Grill No. 2, c. 1960–1975, black and white: Kodak Safety Film, H: 4 in. × W: 5 in. (10.20 × 12.70 cm), Carnegie Museum of Art, Pittsburgh: Heinz Family Fund, 2001.35.3660 © Carnegie Museum of Art, Charles "Teenie" Harris Archive.

go on to host the CBS game show *Musical Chairs*.[38] In July 1974, Buzzy Robinson organized a night of honors for his father's public service as a club owner and patron of the arts.[39] Ruth Goode White of the Sickle Cell Foundation recited a poem about Joe Robinson's benevolent character that made the Grill a welcoming and safe space that drew people from throughout the region and the United States. Journalist Hazel Garland presented a plaque from the *New Pittsburgh Courier* praising his contributions to Pittsburgh's African American community while others spoke of his philanthropy.

Buzzy Robinson continued developing his father's vision for the Grill in the hopes that it would play a role in the Hill's return to prosperity. As Buzzy noted after redesigning the Grill in 1977, "I want this club to be like an oasis in a desert" where professionals and nonprofessionals alike met and socialized around live music as well as occasional performances by Black dance and theater companies.[40] Because White audiences had largely disappeared, Robinson asserted that this exposure to the arts and music depended on support from the Black elite of Pittsburgh, many of whom lived outside of the Hill. This call for support was part of his campaign to keep the Grill a point of convergence between the Hill, Greater Pittsburgh, and other cities.

Buzzy Robinson brought several small-scale theater productions that contributed to the venue's role as a place of Black community formation and critical cultural production. In May 1978, the Grill featured "Bitches Brew," conceived and choreographed by Robert Johnson. Johnson, a Brooklyn native, moved to Pittsburgh in 1969 to teach dance in the youth outreach program Project Self Esteem and, a year later, was offered a position in the University of Pittsburgh's newly established Black Studies Department (currently the Department of Africana Studies) where he taught until his death in 1986.[41] Johnson's work as head of the Pittsburgh Black Theatre Dance Ensemble centered dance to bridge African diasporic cultures and address issues facing African American communities. Productions such as "Bitches Brew" were an opportunity to reestablish neighborhoods such as the Hill as sites of innovative cultural production. As Johnson noted, "Most of our entertainment goes downtown, then out of there."[42] Johnson's commitment to bringing his dance production to the Grill was part of a collective effort to draw on the neighborhood's legacy and history as a living archive.

In addition to choreographing, acting, and directing, Johnson regularly toured as a dancer with Sun Ra's Arkestra. Sun Ra's influences are apparent in Johnson's approach in "Bitches Brew" in interpreting "the spiritual journey of black women as cosmic entities and philosophic notions in Africa's forgotten past, and in the western world as wives, lovers, blues-bearers and liberated women."[43] Borrowing the enigmatic title of his production from Miles Davis's 1970 album, Johnson's "Bitches Brew" featured dancers Janice Barron, Cynthia Robinson, Vivian Wright, and Linda Herring performing various notions of Black femininity. Dancer Robinson found the Grill a perfect setting because of its intimacy and the audiences that it drew from the neighborhood. Reflecting on her character created from aspects of both Bessie Smith and Billie Holiday, Wright commented, "I'm always nervous for that one. Most of the audience says, 'Get it Bessie!' or 'Go 'head Billie!' then I'm her. If you're doing it wrong, believe me, you're going to hear about that too." The audience's discerning reactions prompted Barron to remark, "That encourages you to dig deeper into yourself, to help them get more into what you're putting out. We like [the] feedback they give us."[44]

In 1979, dancer, historian, and Pittsburgh native Lenwood Sloan brought his musical *Three Black and Three White Refined Jubilee Minstrels* to the Grill for four nights.[45] The *New Courier* review of the Grill performance addressed the tacit question of why a minstrel show was appearing at the famed jazz club when many felt that the tradition was inextricable from racist historical narratives. Sloan's aim to reclaim minstrelsy as "an exuberant part of our common heritage" involved the difficult work of parsing its contributions to Black theater and American popular culture while addressing its history of constructing caricatures of Black life for White entertainment.[46] Through a period of study, Sloan learned that Black minstrels often held after-hours events at a "hoofer's club" that was distinct from downtown or mainstream performances.[47] The very constraints of blackface minstrelsy as a performance of Black masculinity and femininity could potentially be transformed by Black performers as a space of reclamation through humor and creativity.[48] It was in these late-night spaces that minstrelsy enabled "the joy of release among our own inverted shame into folk humor."[49]

Sloan's musical is set on the day of the death of Bahamian-born actor Bert Williams, who was one of the highest-paid American stage performers in the early 1900s. In order to pay tribute to Williams's legacy and tell a history of minstrel tradition, six minstrels hold a wake and perform songs and dances by composers including Williams, Scott Joplin, James Bland, Will Marion Cook, and Stephen Foster.[50] Sloan noted the importance of engaging the inherent paradoxes of minstrelsy, particularly in light of nostalgic musicals of the late 1970s, such as *Bubblin' Brown Sugar* (1976), *Eubie* (1978), and *Ain't Misbehavin'* (1978).[51] As Sloan noted, "I always say blacks have been denied a legacy and whites have been fed a myth."[52] By centering his performance on the career of another Black performer, Sloan claimed minstrelsy as a metadiscourse in which representation itself becomes the subject—what Henry Louis Gates would theorize a decade later as the reflexive African American tradition of "signifyin'." That the Grill hosted the experimental performances of Sloan and Johnson—theatrical and choreographic reflections on Black history and identity that may have been poorly received or misunderstood in downtown clubs—speaks to both Robinson's and the artists' continued efforts to make the Hill a site of critical listening.

Despite these bookings, the Grill struggled to remain an active jazz club and restaurant through the 1980s and 1990s, though it continued to symbolize the hopes for the neighborhood's renewal and broader political struggles for Pittsburgh's African American population. Joe Robinson's death on November 12, 1983, prompted writer Malvin Goode to write an opinion piece calling for a monument to be created for Robinson and lawyer Richard F. Jones.[53] Goode's vision for a monument was not a physical structure but rather the conditions in which Black Pittsburghers had political representation and paths to office. Citing other cities that elected Black mayors, Goode saw Pittsburgh's political leaders, including Mayor Richard Caliguiri (D) and Allegheny County Coroner Cyril Wecht, as unsympathetic to the advancement of Black leadership. Goode's hopes for a Black mayor in Pittsburgh would not be realized until 2021 with the election of Edward Gainey.

Efforts continued with Buzzy Robinson through the 1980s to rekindle the Grill as a destination in Pittsburgh. In 1982, singer and activist Tim Stevens was part of a group that formed the Committee to Support the Crawford Grill with the aim of promoting nightlife in the Hill and hosting social events that honored local and national Black civic organizations. With the perception that White fears of the Hill were decreasing, Stevens saw an opportunity to make the Grill "a focal point for a revitalization of the Hill" and counterpart to the downtown nightlife scene.[54] These efforts were unsuccessful in maintaining enough patrons to build a regular performance schedule. In 1988, disc jockey Ronald "Butch" Perkins promoted the renewed bookings of live music with appearances by Mickey Bass, Jack McDuff, Michelle Hendricks, and the Joe Harris Quartet.[55] Again in 1993, Robinson scheduled a recurring Friday evening jam session, citing familiar hopes for the neighborhood's renewal following the Crawford Square development, which brought a 375-unit New Urbanist housing complex to the Hill District. Throughout the 1990s, there were some signs of optimism about the neighborhood, with the *Post-Gazette* reporting, "These days in the Hill, the construction of homes and buildings, the rebuilding of lives, the recognition of rich history are taking head-on the blight of decades, the despair of the disenfranchised, the wounds of the past."[56]

Up to the time of its closing in 2003, the Grill drove narratives of the Hill's cultural legacy and drew people to the neighborhood in an effort to offset the pervasive myth that the area had only violence and poverty to offer the city. Once part of a dense grid of buildings that lined the Hill District's avenues, the Grill's three-story, early twentieth-century brick building remains standing in the neighborhood where other structures have been replaced with new housing, commercial sites, and empty lots waiting for development opportunities. Hill resident Louis "Hop" Kendrick's memories of attending the Grill in the mid-1950s touch on this historical moment: "The entire staff were professionals and it was more than an institute of jazz, especially to me; the customers were a cross-section of the entire Allegheny County, and it was my introduction to enhance my knowledge of people and things, the beginning of the kind of schooling that, if you pay attention, you can earn a PhD in Social Realities."[57]

Memories, such as those of Kendrick's, are drawn on by developers to provide a social backdrop for the neighborhood's revitalization. After the Grill's closing, the building was purchased by Crawford Grill Redevelopment LLC, though its revival as a place for music has yet to be realized. Plans to reopen the Grill beg the question of whether jazz musicians can again draw together enthusiastic listeners from throughout the region within the Hill. Do the creative and social possibilities of the jazz club still resonate in the building's walls and throughout the neighborhood's quiet spaces?

In 2010, four private investors and three nonprofits purchased the Grill. The public face of the project has been former Pittsburgh Steeler and football Hall of Famer Franco Harris (1950–2022), who has touted the importance of reopening the restaurant and nightclub:

This is a good corner. You stand here and your head just starts bopping up and down. This is such a historic site that the preservation and history of it has to live on. So the question is, how do we do that? Well, the first step is to buy this building—so we did. We had all these talented people who came from Pittsburgh like Ahmad Jamal, who I just saw at the first ever National Jazz Day concert here and though they went elsewhere to pursue their careers, they always came back and they were great ambassadors for Pittsburgh. Can we capture how things were and how they evolved? It will be hard, but we'll try to preserve that feel as closely as possible."[58]

When the Grill was originally purchased, there was no immediate plan to reopen it as a jazz club because the investors did not see the neighborhood as ready to support a venue. As the Hill continued to be developed through the 2010s with new housing and businesses, the group maintained the building and purchased surrounding lots while making plans for how to move ahead with developing the site. During the COVID-19 pandemic lockdown of 2020, vocalist and entrepreneur Jessica Lee and Harris conducted a series of virtual interviews with senior jazz musicians, including Judge Warren Watson, which inspired Harris, as the primary shareholder in the Grill, to push forward with reopening the venue, though he would pass away in 2022 before realizing this goal.

# Chapter 8

# THE COMMUNITY ARCHIVE IN PRACTICE

The history of Hill District nightlife and the venues that comprised its infrastructure discussed in this book illustrate the struggles that African Americans faced in establishing political, economic, and physical roots in Pittsburgh. Part I examines several Lower Hill nightclubs during the Prohibition Era (1920–1934) and the nascent jazz scene that they fostered. Because these venues were sites of interracial socializing, they were labeled in the White press as "black and tan"—a term that originated during the post-Reconstruction era and which was commonly used in the early twentieth-century discourses on vice. Within these subversive spaces of the night, dancing, listening to music, and drinking ignited fears, not just of miscegenation and its implications for White supremacy, but of broader coalitions across ethnic and racial lines. Part II traces the emergence of the Hill's jazz scene during the 1950s and 1960s, when jazz continued to draw an array of patrons into Black social spaces, and in doing so, positioned the challenges of integration and urban renewal as something that could be navigated within Black-owned institutions. Clubs such as the Crawford Grill No. 2 and the Hurricane were examples of entrepreneurial visions for developing the Hill District as a vital part of Pittsburgh's future—as businesses and cultural spaces that were of lasting value to the immediate neighborhood and supported by patrons from throughout the region. Part III focuses on labor organizing in the Hill and the paradoxes inherent to dismantling the legal basis for segregation that became apparent in struggles for improved working conditions for musicians. The dissolution of Black American Federation of Musicians (AFM) locals throughout the country, as seen with the merger of Local 471 with its White counterpart Local 60, greatly reduced Black representation in the AFM and further strained networks that supported nightlife in neighborhoods that included the Hill District. Within new racially integrated structures of labor came the end of institutions such as the Musicians Club of Local 471, which provided a platform for advancing jazz as Black musical labor.

While the Hill District community was not the sole site of jazz performance in Pittsburgh, it contributed significantly to jazz's broader development in the twentieth century and to establishing a tradition of jazz performance that has continued to shape the city's cultural life. As urban crises of the 1970s and 1980s curtailed the Hill's nightlife as a center of cultural development, the decline of Black-owned venues underscored the importance of maintaining jazz performances in situ and as a form of engaging the community archive. This sense of an archive is not that of a physical place of records, but rather a collection of memories that are stewarded by a group of people. Not bound to a place and often remaining unnamed, the community archive is fluid and mutable due to it being comprised of collective practices of transmitting knowledge, memories, and creative processes. Where a conventional archive caters to specialists producing research in academic disciplines, the community archive can be accessed and maintained by a wider range of individuals. Most importantly, a community archive comes into realization when it is collectively experienced and embodied.

Throughout this book, I drew on both the conventional and community archive to explore the Hill District's history through jazz. The Charles "Teenie" Harris Archive at the Carnegie Museum of Art has been a valuable source of visual records that have facilitated conversations connecting jazz with experiences and understandings of place. Yet this history of jazz in the Hill would not be possible without contributions from a rich community archive available in the networks of individuals dedicated to teaching, learning, playing, and listening to the music. In the context of jazz, a community archive can take an ephemeral form where musicians, organizers, and audiences engage in interconnected practices of teaching, active listening, and memorializing. In instances of gathering and performance, memories of venues and artists emerge as references for constructing a notion of community and history of the city. Though not every jazz performance engages the community archive, I argue throughout this book that the Hill District has left a legacy of jazz that is integral to a sense of collectivity necessary in the transmission of knowledge, values, and experiences in Pittsburgh.

An important community archive that has informed this book was Jazz at the Hill House (JAHH)—a weekly jazz jam session hosted by the Hill House Organization from 1991 to 1999. Evident in these gatherings were the desires to acknowledge jazz as a form of collective remembrance and the intention of connecting the music to the community of performers, organizers, and listeners. A printed pamphlet handed out at the event stated that the organizer's mission was to "reiterate jazz into the Hill District and recapture the significant jazz heritage of the community."[1] The narrative continued:

> There was a time when the Hill District was Pittsburgh's entertainment center. It was also the mecca of jazz. During the 1940s and 1950s, the jazz giants of the world would stop by The Musicians Club (at that time Local 471), The Crawford Grill, The Harlem Bar, The Roosevelt Theatre, Birdie's Hurricane, and many other places too numerous to mention. The jazz clubs were known coast to coast because they were open until the wee hours and most of the musicians that came to Pittsburgh played here.

Audience members who attended JAHH and were old enough to have experienced neighborhood jazz venues in their heydays understood their role in facilitating the younger musicians' process of learning jazz repertoire and ways of improvising. In this respect, they brought an experience as active listeners, which created a context for younger musicians to experience the spatial and social dynamics of mid-century clubs. During breaks, conversations often turned to experiences of hearing canonic performers in neighborhood clubs—a means of bridging the development of musicianship with an investment in place.

Events such as JAHH have helped sustain Pittsburgh's jazz scene as a multi-generational community of artists for whom the city's musical legacy remains a living tradition and form of community archive. Looking back on the past century of the Hill District's nightlife illuminates the many ways jazz performance intersects with broader struggles beyond the nightclub as it takes on roles of entertainment, artistic endeavor, labor, and placemaking. As new organizations and businesses draw from the community archive to create new contexts for the music, they face the challenge of finding locations that draw cross-sections of the city's population, establishing sustainable business or funding models, and nurturing a critically driven network of musicians. Institutions and individuals have approached memorializing and sustaining jazz in Pittsburgh through professional and artistic training, education on local history, scholarly engagement, concert programming, and nightlife entrepreneurship. Both formal academic programs and nightlife where learning happens in situ have strengthened the project of historical and critical reflection that centers on the Hill's community archive.

In the absence of the informal economies that supported Hill District venues such as the Crawford Grill Nos. 1 and 2, the Hurricane, and the Musicians Club, jazz found support in a range of nonprofit, nightclub, and university contexts. In 1969, Nathan Davis founded one of the country's first collegiate jazz programs at the University of Pittsburgh, which ushered in the era of jazz's institutionalization in higher learning. Davis used this platform to contribute to the scholarly study of jazz within a musicology department and create new contexts for the support of jazz artists. When Art Blakey and the Jazz Messengers returned to the Crawford Grill in 1970, Davis sat in with the group and decided to invite Blakey and the band to discuss their music with University of Pittsburgh students. Davis recognized the importance of bringing the community archive into a university context, so Blakey's visit became the first iteration of the Pitt Jazz Seminar. Meeting annually since 1970, this forum has brought veteran musicians to Pittsburgh to share their knowledge with and perform for local musicians, students, and audiences.[2] Similar programs emerged in music departments and conservatories throughout the US in the following decades to both codify and advance jazz as a creative practice.

Undergraduate and graduate student programs in jazz studies and performance continue at the University of Pittsburgh and Duquesne University. Previously chaired by pianist Geri Allen and flutist Nicole Mitchell, Pitt's PhD Jazz Studies program draws musician-scholars navigating the fluid and often ethereal professional landscapes of contemporary jazz performers. Nathan Davis, who developed and helmed Pitt's jazz program from 1969 to 2013, nurtured several generations of scholars focusing on jazz studies, including James Johnson II, Ken Prouty, Ken Foley, Yoko Suzuki, Alton Merrell, James Moore, and myself. While working on his dissertation titled *Enculturation in a Formal Setting: A Study of Problems and Prospects in Afro-American Music Education*, Johnson and his wife Pamela established the Afro-American Music Institute (AAMI) to develop programs of study and performance that are located within and directly serve the Homewood neighborhood. AAMI celebrated its fortieth anniversary in 2022. Other nonprofits centered on jazz performance and education include the Jazz Workshop, Inc., founded by Harold Young in 1973; the Manchester Craftsmen's Guild, which has presented jazz concerts since 1987; The August Wilson Center, a concert, arts, and cultural center opened in 2009; the Pittsburgh International Jazz Festival; and the City of Asylum @ Alphabet City, opened in 2016.

Over the past fifty years, there has been a handful of smaller commercial venues dedicated primarily to jazz. With the Hill District's business infrastructure heavily damaged and few prospects for rebuilding, downtown Pittsburgh became a center for new jazz clubs in the 1970s. Clubs such as Walt Harper's Attic, the Encore II, the Top Shelf, and the Crazy Quilt kept a steady stream of touring artists coming to the city.[3] Hill District native and pianist Walt Harper, building on his local popularity and support in corporate circles, pursued his aspiration of club owning and opened a 250-seat venue in Pittsburgh's Market Square Plaza in July 1969.[4] The second-floor space's décor included memorabilia one might find in an attic, such as trunks and household objects that evoked an earlier era. During the six years that it operated, the Attic was seen as an important boost to downtown Pittsburgh nightlife, providing both a home for Harper's own band and a venue to feature touring artists, including Herbie Mann, Carmen McRae, Ramsey Lewis, Cannonball Adderley, Joe Williams, Mongo Santamaria, and Buddy Rich.[5]

In 1971, real estate and restaurant entrepreneur Willard Shiner opened The Encore II, also in Pittsburgh's downtown. Shiner's first club, The Encore, was a popular jazz club in the eastern neighborhood of Shadyside where trombonist Harold Betters led the house band from 1960 to 1977.[6] The downtown-located Encore II, which remained open for fourteen years, was managed by local promoter Bobby Davis, who focused on providing working opportunities to both older and younger generations of jazz artists and filling "the void created by the demise of the Hurricane and other black jazz establishments."[7] Like Harper's Attic, the Encore II provided an intimate and relaxed atmosphere where audiences could listen to renowned artists such as George Benson, Stanley Turrentine, Arthur Prysock, Kenny Burrell, Shirley Scott, Sonny Stitt, Chico Hamilton, Ahmad Jamal, Mary Lou Williams, and Eric Kloss. Bobby Davis attributed the commercial success of the Encore II to booking acts that drew a range of demographic groups. As Davis noted, "Different acts attract differently. Eric Kloss might attract a majority white and younger following, whereas Arthur Prysock will attract a majority black clientele and somewhat older."[8] Amid bookings of jazz artists, Davis would also bring in reggae, R&B, and country and western bands to maintain a steady income and ensure that he could afford touring musicians.

The Balcony (1980–1998) in Shadyside, James Street Tavern (1987–2017) in the Northside, and Dowe's on 9th (2000–2007) in downtown Pittsburgh were the primary restaurant-style nightclubs that featured local and touring jazz musicians in informal settings. All three ran regular jam sessions that provided an important outlet for younger musicians to learn from veterans, including Roger Humphries, Don DePaolis, Dwayne Dolphin, Lou Stellute, and Jimmy Ponder. An important alternative space that featured hip-hop and jazz was the Shadow Lounge (2000–2013) in East Liberty, which drew younger audiences to the neighborhood when few businesses were operating in the area.

In the spring of 2019, chef Josh Ross, musician John Shannon, and manager Aimee Marshall opened Con Alma to provide Pittsburgh with a cozy and friendly bar and restaurant that featured live jazz six nights a week. Situated on the border between Shadyside, a long-established, affluent neighborhood, and East Liberty, a rapidly gentrified area of contested developments, the club benefits from its proximity to the city's young professionals but also draws a wide cross-section of fine-dining crowds, student and veteran musicians, and devoted music fans. On busy nights, the packed space buzzes with an energy that plays off the live music. Opposite the entrance is a small stage that fits a drum kit, Fender Rhodes keyboard, and space for a bassist or guitarist. Horn players and singers generally stand in front of the stage, an arm's length from the front tables. Photos by Charles "Teenie" Harris decorate the walls, and a record collection chosen by local musicians provides the background music between sets. During performances, there is little standing room between the tables and bar, though the close quarters feel cozy rather than cramped.

For Shannon, a Pittsburgher who returned home after years of touring as a solo artist and sideman, Con Alma was an opportunity to pay tribute to Pittsburgh's jazz history while supporting younger musicians and developing audiences for the music. The environment was designed to be inviting to both music aficionados and people seeking a relaxed nightlife scene, fine dining, and cocktails but who might gain an appreciation for live jazz. Like the Crawford Grill and Hurricane, Con Alma is a place without the formalities of a concert setting where socializing and performance overlap and, at times, clash. Unlike many revered jazz clubs in New York City, Con Alma does not insist that patrons refrain from talking during sets or that they pay by the set. While there is not a door fee, nominal charges are added to bills while the music is playing to offset costs to the musicians. At times, patrons close to the stage can be unaware of the give-and-take process of active listening in such an environment, though Shannon believes that silent listening should not be a hard rule: "Jazz is a social music. It's a good challenge for our musicians. Some musicians think people should just pay attention to them, but there's something you have to do to get the audience's attention that you can't be taught in school."[9] As was the case with the Hill venues, Shannon's perspective reveals an appreciation of listening as a self-reflexive process as well as a form of communication between musicians and listeners. He also makes a point of introducing sets with a short overview of the club's mission statement so that audiences will be made aware of the music's role as a community archive.

How do performances in these various contexts—classrooms, clubs, and even concert halls—recall places, times, and experiences of nightlife in neighborhoods such as the Hill District? What is remembered and forgotten? Many Pittsburgh jazz musicians actively compose new works and arrange contemporary popular songs through a canon of standards that are expected to be common knowledge at jam sessions and continues to inform many performances. Performing songs such as Horace Silver's "Song for My Father" (the original recording features drummer Roger Humphries at twenty years old), Stanley Turrentine's "Sugar," Clifford Brown's "Daahoud," or Jimmy Ponder's arrangement of "All Blues," while providing a context for sustaining the music by developing and maintaining one's abilities to improvise, is also a reflective ritual that grounds the globalized genre of jazz in local contexts. Thus, this tradition of performance sustains a critical discourse around the locations and meanings of nightlife.

Reanimating these songs can reclaim places, both in existence and long gone, where they had been performed; they can also embed themselves in new locations. As a teenager, I heard standards common to Pittsburgh played many times by different musicians on the stages of the Hill House auditorium, the Crawford

Grill, James Street Tavern, the Balcony, and in a myriad of other neighborhood bars and restaurants. Each of these renderings mapped the city, linking my "mazeway"—a term psychologist Mindy Fullilove uses for our daily paths that help make the city familiar and welcoming—with musicians and audiences as we listened, played, and talked. Always challenged to find new ways of interpreting these standards, these performances inevitably led musicians to seek out the histories of the music, a telltale sign that they have become active participants in a community archive.

Each audience, whether intently listening or noisily chatting, taught us how these songs were always shifting in relation to the context. Those moments when the goals of the musicians and audiences aligned, regardless of how humble the context, could be revelatory. Within the repertoire, the twelve-bar blues occupies an important place as a vehicle for evoking the jazz house; the short repetitive form lends itself to musical dialogues and modes of riffing that cue a responsive audience to engage the band (see figure 4.12). As guitarist and bassist Dan Wasson remembers of learning how to play the blues:

> We might be playin' a slow blues. The crowd played it, not me. They could sense that I wasn't sure what to do. I might [play some aggressive, fast idea] and they would say, "Take your time . . . okay . . . do a little bit . . . Now hold up." It was like they were teaching me to drive. They were so responsive and very supportive. It wasn't so much "let's be nice" as it was "we got to get our shit off" so let's walk him through this so he can get us to where we got to go. It is what is needed. Everybody needs that.[10]

Moments like these—intimate exchanges in small neighborhoods far from the bustle of New York and Chicago—emphasize how this music has always existed at the crossroads, a place of gathering in spite of forces of dispersal and a space of perpetual freedom-seeking. As musicians continue to play this music, the difficulty is in choosing what to remember as well as how to invite others to this process.

# EPILOGUE
## To Honor and Repair

Cities across the US have approached the challenges of economic reinvestment in once-vibrant Black communities by attempting to bridge memorialization with extensive construction and investment projects. As an example, the Kansas City Jazz Museum, which opened in 1998 near the historical intersection of 18th and Vine Streets, initially held promise as the country's first major museum of jazz but was criticized by educators and musicians as a lost opportunity. Kansas City veteran jazz musician Eddie Baker, disappointed with the museum's size, rudimentary exhibits, and scope, saw it as a failure of a top-down conceptualization of a monument to the tradition.[1] Located within an area in which businesses and houses are interspersed among empty buildings, lots, and decorative facades, the museum pinned its success on its ability to invite further economic investment rather than its contribution to honoring and preserving the artistic achievements of jazz. The museum's collection began with then-Kansas City Mayor Emanuel Cleaver's purchase of Charlie Parker's acrylic saxophone for $140,000, leaving director Rowena Stewart to undertake further acquisitions with approximately $100,000.[2] This fetishization of relics highlights the challenges of creating new spaces that foster intergenerational and racially and ethnically diverse gatherings, generate revenue, and sustain a creative practice as demanding as jazz. If the museum does teach a lesson about jazz history, it is primarily that city- and investment-led tributes to the music often serve the interests of developers rather than those communities in which they are located.

Urban renewal of the 1950s, fueled by federal funds and directed by corporatist regimes, shaped cities into places that would entice business leaders and suburban residents. The redevelopment model of the past three decades has shifted to creating businesses, often with a cultural focus, that function as the source of economic improvement. Musicologist Dale Chapman's study of the San Francisco Redevelopment Agency's role in creating a "jazz-themed business district" within the Fillmore District reveals the ways urban development and social repair intersect, particularly in once-vibrant historically Black neighborhoods.[3] As Chapman argues, jazz has served at times as the public face of what has been termed "speculative urbanism" or urban development driven by investment strategies with projected returns. Despite well-intentioned investments, the goals of honoring cultural legacies and serving the interests of marginalized communities can often clash as with Yoshi's SF, a 28,000-square-foot jazz club and restaurant that opened as part of a mixed-use development on the site that was known in the mid-twentieth century as the "Harlem of the West." As Chapman notes:

> In any event, there is reason to believe that Yoshi's SF eventually became a victim of its own "effect." A high-profile jazz venue of this kind, in hock to the Redevelopment Agency for the significant startup funds necessary to get things up and running, and facing the steep rents endemic to the San Francisco real estate market, would find it difficult to achieve a booking policy that would allow the club to maintain a level of profitability commensurate with the financial demands placed on its ownership. Even after its decision to forgo jazz acts in favor of a more eclectic calendar of artists, and despite pulling in an average of $10 million in revenue per year, the Fillmore satellite of the established Oakland club continued to encounter financial difficulties, and ultimately closed in the summer of 2014.[4]

Apparent in both examples are the continued roles jazz venues play in attempting to honor, repair, and build community in the aftermath of a prolonged period of urban crisis. However, when drawing on jazz to identify lost economic prosperity, culture, and social well-being, the focus most often defaults to preserving physical locations and paying tribute to deceased artists rather than examining the roles entrepreneurs and social networks play in sustaining a vibrant nightlife scene. Jazz as a community archive also counters this impulse to root cultural heritage in place.

The Lower Hill redevelopment of the 1950s aimed to construct an image of progress that would counteract negative public opinion about the heavily industrialized city and, by extension, prevent the corporations from relocating their headquarters. The reality of the Civic Arena in Lower Hill redevelopment, one of the first and largest experiments in urban renewal, was a space as hospitable and acoustically inviting as an empty parking garage. Originally meant as the home for the Pittsburgh Civic Light Opera, the arena would be adapted to all manner of concerts, rallies, and sports events. Later nicknamed the "Igloo," the aging arena won fans during the meteoric rise of the Pittsburgh Penguins hockey team during the late 1980s with Stanley Cup wins in 1991 and 1992.

Thirty-five years after its completion, the retractable roof was largely inoperable, and the seating capacity maximized at 16,000. By 2001, it was apparent that it would cost approximately the same to renovate the forty-year-old Civic Arena (renamed the Mellon Arena in 1999) as it would be to build a new arena for the Penguins.[5] With the opening of the Console Energy Center (currently the PPG Paints Arena) a few blocks south in 2010, the Civic Arena was closed with pressure mounting for its demolition. The proposed plan for the twenty-eight-acre Civic Arena development area at that time included 1,191 residential units, a 150-room hotel, 298,750 square feet of retail space and 606,000 square feet of office space as well as a new system of roads that would "better connect the Lower Hill District with Downtown."[6] Those opposing the arena's destruction argued for its redesign and incorporation into new business developments, while those supporting its destruction expressed a need for a fresh start. Howard Graves, CEO of Graves Architects Inc., supported "tearing down the arena because it would make way for positive development, which would not occur if you kept it intact," noting, "The urban fabric would benefit immensely."[7] There can be little doubt that improved road systems, the development of public spaces, and a strengthened business infrastructure will improve the use of the Civic Arena site, but those who remember the promises of the 1950s redevelopment authorities will surely question the benefits it will bring to the remaining Hill District community.

In 2024, the Hill District stands at a crossroads, the future defined by struggles to increase the neighborhood's population and facilitate investments in housing and businesses without displacing existing residents. Current trends present a paradox for those pushing for the neighborhood's economic and population growth. Nine percent of Pittsburgh's Black population left for the suburbs or other cities between 2009 and 2018.[8] Pittsburgh's ranking as one of the most livable US cities has been complicated by failures to attract and retain young Black professionals and reports that the city is one of the lowest ranking in the country for Black women in terms of health, employment opportunities, housing, and a range of other factors that comprise a city's quality of life.[9] The sentiments of author and long-time Pittsburgh resident Deesha Philyaw expressed a perspective of Black Pittsburgh women that resonated with many: "As I consider where might I go that I could actually feel good about living, the answer could literally be *anywhere but here.*"[10]

The troubled legacy of Pittsburgh's 1950s Renaissance has continued to loom over twenty-first-century renewal projects in the Hill District. This legacy was still prevalent in 2014, when the Hill District was classified by the US Department of Treasury as a "severely distressed neighborhood" with unemployment rates at 20.8 percent, 44.5 percent of residents subsisting below the poverty lines, and the median household income just below twenty thousand dollars.[11] The Pittsburgh Urban Redevelopment Authority (URA), created to implement Pittsburgh's urban renewal in the 1950s, remains an active part of envisioning and implementing city development plans, though there have been a number of other organizations, including the Hill Community Development Corporation (Hill CDC), the Pittsburgh Penguins, and Buccini/Pollin Group (BPG), which have vested interests in the Hill District real estate and have become key agents in shaping its future. Hill residents have gained some representation within this multilayered network of government agencies, corporations, and nonprofit organizations, and there have been extensive negotiations between community groups and developers over how best to present objectives that will hold developers accountable for serving the interests of underprivileged residents.

The Hill CDC released its 144-page *Greater Hill Master Plan* (2011), which was created with input from community meetings and submissions through its Development Review Panel (DRP). The plan was a definitive statement defending the Hill's importance to the greater Pittsburgh region and reiterating the city's responsibilities to restore it as a vibrant African American neighborhood. It presented guidelines for "reclaiming" the Lower Hill, developing the Upper and Middle Hill with "non-displacement strategies," providing affordable housing and creating employment and entrepreneurial opportunities for residents.[12] In 2014, the Hill CDC published its *Community Collaboration and Implementation Plan* (CCIP), which called for leadership by the Penguins, URA, City of Pittsburgh, and Allegheny County to commit to implementing the Hill CDC's guidelines for job growth, housing, cultural development, and accountability in development projects.

In a five-hour virtual public hearing held by the Pittsburgh Planning Commission on May 4, 2021, the development company Buccini/Pollin Group (BPG) presented its plan for a twenty-eight-acre portion of the previous Civic Arena site. The first of several parcels to be developed in the Lower Hill would include a twenty-six-story building with a mix of residential, commercial, retail, entertainment, and food venue properties, as well as redesigned street patterns and pedestrian walkways that would reconnect the Hill District to downtown. Chris Buccini, copresident of BPG, positioned the plan as an opportunity to right past failures: "I find it even more compelling that this site was the first chosen in the nation to create urban redevelopment, and now we're back after seventy years to do it again on the same spot. It is my desire to get it right for myself and my family, my partners, the Hill community, and the city of Pittsburgh."[13] Planned tangible benefits to the Hill in the initial phase of development include fifty million dollars allocated to Upper and Middle Hill developments overseen by other organizations, support for small businesses, minority-led construction contracts, worker development programs, and the creation of community space.

Two Hill residents, developer Bomani Howze and American Studies scholar and activist Kimberly Ellis, worked directly on this plan and represent the primary point of community engagement for BPG. Ellis, acting as a BPG consultant on

Hill District history, spoke directly to the need for the redevelopment project to "honor and repair" the neighborhood through strategic investment, a rethinking of public space that facilitates a range of activities throughout the day, and prominent, visible markers that teach local African American history. Ellis spoke of Black settlements in the Hill as early as 1829 and the continuous presence and investment in the area by African American businesses and homeowners. She also reflected on the Lower Hill's redevelopment of Pittsburgh's first Renaissance and its exclusion of Hill community members, such as activist Frankie Pace (1905–1989), from contributing to the redevelopment plan and working for the construction companies. Howze looks forward to the Lower Hill in ten years as a place that he hopes will have grown past its "persistent pain," where one could walk up Wylie Avenue and find a grocery store and live music venues invoking the Hurricane and Crawford Grill.[14]

In an hour and a half of public testimony, critics of BPG's proposal were an outspoken minority. Longtime activist and Hill resident Phyllis Ghafoor expressed disapproval of other Hill residents employed by BPG for supporting a "black bourgeoisie project" and considered their involvement an empty gesture toward the neighborhood's working-class population. Felicity Williams, programs and policy manager of the Hill CDC, argued that BPG's proposal did not meet the conditions of the CCIP, which she saw as the measure of the project's success in ensuring equitable development. Specifically, Williams criticized the failure to guarantee that one in ten new hires would be Hill residents and the plan for outdoor seasonal kiosks rather than retail spaces that were being made available for local entrepreneurs. Daniel Armanios, professor of engineering and public policy at Carnegie Mellon University, also raised concerns that the plan was not committing to the CCIP's guidelines, was disregarding the ongoing Development Review Panel (DRP) process meant to facilitate resident input, and manipulating tax credit systems:

> Yet rather than working through these mechanisms, the investor group went behind the community's back to successfully lobby for a merger of two Hill District Census tracts. This allows this high-end development to exploit Opportunity Zone tax credits designed for the Hill's neighboring low-income residents, a tactic that developers have used across the country. Such projects should not be allowed to proceed until mutually agreed milestones are met to prevent circumvention of review processes.[15]

While these criticisms failed to block or require the proposal to include provisions, they left open the question of how a lengthy grassroots process of consensus-building such as the DRP could shape large-scale development projects. Brenda Tate, a seventy-two-year-old retired police officer and Hill resident, supported the project but spoke of the continued need for accountability and for developers to understand how urban space can shape the daily lives of residents in profound ways. Tate shared, "My hope is that this project gets it right . . . . I was a little girl when I tried to sneak into the opera tent down there and got shooed away. I don't want that big building down there to shoo away any young kids like I was shooed away."[16] As extensive renewal projects continue to reshape the Hill, concerns by residents such as Tate raise the questions of how the living memories of the neighborhood, including that of its people and places, will be stewarded and who they will benefit. If restorative projects can reclaim aspects of what made the Hill the "Crossroads of the World," the practice of jazz as building and maintaining a community archive will potentially provide a means to repair and honor the neighborhood.

# ACKNOWLEDGMENTS

I have many people to thank for helping me work through the various stages of research, writing, and editing that have produced this book. The initial seed for the idea to write about jazz in Pittsburgh was planted in 1996 at Jazz at the Hill House (JAHH). The audiences and musicians there introduced me to Pittsburgh's rich jazz tradition, and subsequent conversations about the Hill District began to unlock many stories of the city's past.

The experiences at JAHH led to playing and recording with many Pittsburgh musicians who have helped me continue to grow as a composer and performer. Many have also taken the time to share their experiences and insights, some of which appear throughout this book. Venues including the Balcony, James Street Tavern, Foster's Bar and Grill, the Crawford Grill No. 2, Too Sweet's Lounge, the Manchester Craftsmen's Guild, and many others provided the opportunity to listen to, play with, and learn from Don Aliquo Sr. (s), Don Aliquo Jr. (s), Jay Ashby (tb), Marty Ashby (g), H. B. Bennett (d), Jeff Berman (perc), Kenny Blake (s) Dave Budway (p), Maureen Budway (v), Don DePaolis (p), Dwayne Dolphin (b), Jeff Grubbs (b), Tania Grubbs (v), Dr. Nelson Harrison (tb), Lindsey Horner (b), Roger Humphries (d), Greg Humphries (d), Eric Johnson (g), Dr. James Johnson Jr. (p), Pamela Johnson (v), George Jones (perc), Ken Karsh (g), Mark Koch (g), Dave LaRocca (b), Joe Negri (g), Ben Opie (s), Jimmy Ponder (g), Bill Purse (g), John Purse (g), Spider Rodinelli (d), Lou Stellute (s), Eric Susoeff (g), Mike Taylor (b), Mike Tomaro (s), Horace Turner (t), Mary Turner (d), Judge Warren Watson (s), John Wilson (t), Leroy Wofford (v), and many more (see the appendix for a key on instrument abbreviations).

As I began to sit in at jam sessions, I was fortunate enough to also learn from musicians of my generation, including Howie Alexander (p), Brendan Bosworth (g), Tony DePaolis (b), Roby Edwards (s), Danielle Eva (v), Chris Hemmingway (s), James Johnson III (d), Hill Jordan (tb), Paco Mahone (b), Alex Peck (d), Nathan Peck (b), Carolyn Perteete (v), Skip Sanders (p), John Shannon (g), Paul Thompson (b), David Throckmorton (d), Chauncy Upson (ts), Tom Wendt (d), and Reggie Watkins (tb). I want to also thank Michael Glabicki, Liz Berlin, Patrick Norman, Preach Freedom, Dirk Miller, Larry Dawgiello, and Mike Hammer of Rusted Root for our time making music together. The band was central to my creative life as I completed the initial stages of this research, and so this experience seeped into my ideas about the communities we build through music.

As this research took shape, I was fortunate to have feedback and insights from professors and graduate students at the University of Pittsburgh. Saxophonist and ethnomusicologist Nathan Davis—a veteran jazz artist and founding figure in university jazz education—helped me think through ways of teaching American history through jazz. Historian Larry Glasco contributed his time and deep knowledge of Pittsburgh's African American history to shaping my writing and ideas through discussions and editing. Andrew Weintraub, Akin Euba, and Bell Yung have been great influences through seminars and discussions and continuously pushed me to engage in the theoretical rigors of ethnomusicology. Librarian and musicologist Jim Cassaro also imparted invaluable research techniques and was always available for further guidance. I am also thankful to my colleague Oyebade Dosunmu for his input and encouragement during our long writing sessions. He left us too soon.

Teaching at the University of Pittsburgh, the University of Ghana, and University at Buffalo has been an invaluable part of developing and sharing ideas and research that have filtered into this book. I've had the opportunity to develop classes on nightlife and popular music, advise students on research topics in music culture and composition, and be inspired by my colleagues.

An important part of my research included using photos from the Carnegie Museum of Art's Charles "Teenie" Harris Archive. Curator Louise Lippincott and photo archivist Kerin Shellenbarger enthusiastically supported my research, which began in 2006, and made time amidst the difficult work overseeing the collection's digitization to provide me with prints for my interviews. As my work progressed over the following decade, archivists Dominique Luster and Charlene Foggie-Barnett continued to support my research by providing images for use in presentations and publications. In 2016, I began having conversations with photo vendor Dennis Morgan, who has brought his own perspectives as a lifelong Hill District resident and community historian to thinking about the Charles "Teenie" Harris Archive. I express gratitude to Joeva "Del" Morgan for the many wonderful meals and conversations she treated me to.

My parents introduced me to photography as a way of seeing, inquiring, and remembering. I would watch my father, sociologist Douglas Harper, developing images in our home darkroom, and the process gave me a love of black and white photography. My mother's dedication to running a greenhouse business and painting kept me grounded in an appreciation of the natural world. I remember my father mentioning that we should write on jazz in Pittsburgh at some point, and the idea hung in the back of my mind for years. Over the years, their ideas, insights, and creative pursuits have guided my own work.

I owe a great deal to the University Press of Mississippi director Craig Gill, who has patiently guided me through the extensive process of completing the manuscript. Our conversations began in 2007, at the annual Society for Ethnomusicology conference, and continued over the following decade. UPM readers Christopher Wilkinson and Aaron Johnson provided much-needed critical feedback and graciously offered detailed editing. Editor Catherine Osborn also worked through the text at various stages to restructure my writing and work on the difficult process of clarifying this historical narrative. Musicians Dr. Nelson Harrison, Tony DePaolis, and Tom Wendt have also lent their deep knowledge of jazz history to checking the names, dates, and ideas in this study.

Most importantly, I have my partner Liz Park to thank for the support, conversations, editing, inspiration, and love. You have helped propel this book into existence, and I am forever grateful.

# APPENDIX

is list of bookings at the Crawford Grill No. 2 and Hurricane Bar and Grill was compiled from advertisements and columns published by the *tsburgh Courier*, *New Pittsburgh Courier*, and *Pittsburgh Post-Gazette*. The band personnel and the length of the engagement are included *en* available in the original advertisement or article. The addition of the asterisk (*) indicates a minimum length of stay, as this information s not always published. Gaps in the list do not necessarily indicate the absence of performers, but rather the lack of their documentation.

*e* Contemporary Recording column includes singles and LPs of the principal artists that were released near the time of their Pittsburgh *pearances*.

*trument* abbreviations are as follows: vocals (v), saxophone (s), alto saxophone (as), tenor saxophone (ts), baritone saxophone (bar), *e* (f), B♭ clarinet (cl), bass clarinet (bcl), trumpet (t), trombone (tb), French horn (frh), guitar (g), violin (vn), violoncello (vc), acoustic bass electric bass (eb), piano (p), Hammond organ (or), vibraphone (vib), accordion (acc), and drum set (d).

| Crawford Grill No. 2 | | | | Hurricane Bar and Grill | | | |
|---|---|---|---|---|---|---|---|
| Date | Length | Artist | Contemporary Recording | Date | Length | Artist | Contemporary Recording |
| 3/1948 | 4 years | Sammy Nowlin (or) | | | | | |
| 1/1952 | 1.5 years | Leroy Brown (as), George "Duke" Spaulding (p), William "Bass" McMahon (b), and Bobby Anderson (d) | | | | | |
| | | | | 10/29/1953 | 4 months | Ruby Young (or) Trio with Chuck Austin (t) and Bobby Boswell (b) | |
| /1954 | 4 months | Sammy Nowlin (or) | | 1/4/1954 | 2 months | Ruby Young (or) Trio with Julie Gardner (v, acc) and Cal King (g) | |

| Crawford Grill No. 2 | | | | Hurricane Bar and Grill | | | |
|---|---|---|---|---|---|---|---|
| Date | Length | Artist | Contemporary Recording | Date | Length | Artist | Contemporary Recording |
| | | | | 3/6/1954 | 4 months | Ruby Young (or) Trio with Leroy Brown (as) and Calvin King (g) | |
| 5/8/1954 | 2 weeks | Alyce Brooks (p) and Bobby Boswell (b) | | 6/21/1954 | 1 week | Ruby Young (or) Trio featuring Roy Eldridge (t) | |
| 5/31/1954 | 4 months | Walt Harper (p), Nate Harper (ts), Bill Lewis (b), Jon Morris (tb), and Harold "Brushes" Lee (d) or Cecil Brooks II (d) | Eddie Jefferson, *The Bebop Boys* (Hi-Lo, 1952) | 6/28/1954 | 1 month | Ruby Young (or) Trio with Leroy Brown (as) and Calvin King (g) | |
| 9/13/1954 | 4 months | Joe Westray (g, pedal steel guitar) | | 7/21/1954 | 3 months* | King Solomon (or) Trio with Rose Lehman (g, v) and Barry Calimese (ts) | |
| 11/1/1954 | 1 month | Four Jewels with Willene Barton (ts), Regina Albright (p), Hettie Smith (d), and Gloria Bell (b, v) | | 11/1/1954 | 1 week* | Eddie Winters (d) with Peggy Morgan (v), Earl Patterson (as), James Creighton (p), George Briggs (eb), and Earl Patterson (as, v) | |
| | | | | 12/31/1954 | 1 week* | Ernie Ransome (g) Quartet with Pete Martin (p), Skeets McClain (b), and Bill Jones (s) | |
| 1/2/1955 | 8 months | Walt Harper (p), Nate Harper (ts), Bill Lewis (b), Jon Morris (tb), and Harold "Brushes" Lee (d) or Cecil Brooks II (d) | | | | | |
| | | | | 1/24/1955 | 3 weeks | Eddie Winters (d) with Peggy Morgan (v), Earl Patterson (as), James Creighton (p), George Briggs (eb), and Earl Patterson (as, v) | |

| Crawford Grill No. 2 | | | | Hurricane Bar and Grill | | | |
|---|---|---|---|---|---|---|---|
| Date | Length | Artist | Contemporary Recording | Date | Length | Artist | Contemporary Recording |
|  |  |  |  | 2/14/1955 | 1 month* | Jackie Davis (or) with Kenny Dennis (d) | *Hi-Fi Hammond* (Capitol, 1956) |
|  |  |  |  | 4/4/1955 | 6 weeks | Buddy Griffin (p) with Claudia Swann (v) | "Please Come Back to Me" / "I Wanna Hug Ya, Kiss Ya, Squeeze Ya" (Chess, 1954) |
|  |  |  |  | 7/1/1955 | 1 month* | Lindy Ewell (d) Trio with Ellsworth Gooding (ts), Howard Whaley (or), and Ruth Mobley (v) |  |
| /19/1955 | 4 months | Leon Abbey (vn) Trio | "If You Only Knowed," *Clara Smith Vol. 3* (1925) |  |  |  |  |
|  |  |  |  | 9/26/1955 | 1 week* | Robert Banks (or) Trio with Hank Durand (ts) and Hank Walcott (d) | "Moonlight Serenade" / "Sentimental Journey" (Regent, 1956), and Mildred Anderson, *No More in Life* (Bluesville, 1961) |
|  |  |  |  | 12/5/1955 | 1 week | Buddy Griffin (p) with Claudia Swann (v) |  |
|  |  |  |  | 12/19/1955 | 1 week* | Lindy Ewell (d) Trio with Ruth Mobley (v) |  |
| /1956 | 9 weeks | Walt Harper (p) |  |  |  |  |  |
|  |  |  |  | 3/5/1956 | 1 week* | Johnny Sparrow (s) and His Bows and Arrows | "When Your Lover Has Gone" / "Sparrow in the Barrel" (Gotham, 1952) |
|  |  |  |  | 3/19/1956 | 1 week* | Al King (bar) and His Kingsmen with Jimmy Sigler (p), Charlie Bombay (d), and "Bat" Johnson (g) | *Thunderbolt! Honkin' R&B Sax Instrumentals 1952-1956* (Krazy Kat, 1983) |

| Crawford Grill No. 2 | | | | Hurricane Bar and Grill | | | |
|---|---|---|---|---|---|---|---|
| Date | Length | Artist | Contemporary Recording | Date | Length | Artist | Contemporary Recording |
| 4/2/1956 | 2 weeks | Charles Mingus (b) Trio | *Jazz Composers Workshop* (Savoy, 1956) and *Pithecanthropus Erectus* (Atlantic, 1956) | 4/2/1956 | 1 week* | Jimmy Smith (or) Trio | *A New Sound… A New Star…* (Blue Note, 1956) |
| 4/16/1956 | 2 weeks | Paul Quinichette (ts) | *Moods* (EmArcy, 1955) | 4/16/1956 | 1 week* | Monroe Chatman | |
| 5/7/1956 | 2 weeks | Art Blakey (d) and the Jazz Messengers with Horace Silver (p), Donald Byrd (t), Doug Watkins (b), and Hank Mobley (ts) | *Night at Birdland, Volumes 1 & 2* (Blue Note, 1954) | 5/7/1956 | 1 week* | Michelle (or) Trio with Sadie DeVigna, Arthur Daniels (ts), and Snookie Richardson (d) | |
| 6/25/1956 | 1 week* | Walt Harper (p) | | 6/25/1956 | 1 week | Pancho Villa (d) and the Bandits | |
| 7/9/1956 | 1 week* | Hampton Hawes (p) Trio | *This is Hampton Hawes* (Contemporary, 1956) | | | | |
| | | | | 7/2/1956 | 1 month | Jimmy Smith (or) Trio with Thornel Schwartz (g) and Donald "Duck" Bailey (d) | *The Incredible Jimmy Smith At Club "Baby Grand" Wilmington Delaware* (Blue Note, 1956) |
| 7/23/1956 | 1 week* | Bill Rye | | | | | |
| | | | | 7/30/1956 | 1 week* | Jim Wilcher (?) with Logan Cave (s), Jerry Evans (b), and Jean Evans (p) | |
| 8/6/1956 | 1 month* | Walt Harper (p) with Nate Harper (ts), Cecil Brooks (d), Jon Morris (tb), and Billy Lewis (b) | | | | | |
| | | | | 8/27/1956 | 1 week* | Robert Banks (or) Quintet | |
| 9/17/1956 | 1 week | Cecil Young (p) Quartet | *A Concert of Cool Jazz* (King, 1952) | | | | |

| | Crawford Grill No. 2 | | | Hurricane Bar and Grill | | | |
|---|---|---|---|---|---|---|---|
| Date | Length | Artist | Contemporary Recording | Date | Length | Artist | Contemporary Recording |
| | | | | 9/24/1956 | 1 week* | Pancho Villa (d) and the Bandits with Earl Ross (s), Lawrence Scott (p), and Sam Merriweather (b) | "Ain't That Bad" / "Progress" (Pee Vee Records, 1963) |
| 10/15/1956 | 1 week | James Moody (s) featuring Eddie Jefferson (v) | New Sounds (Blue Note, 1952) | | | | |
| 11/5/1956 | 2 weeks | Walt Harper (p) with Nate Harper (ts), Harold Lee (d), Jon Morris (tb), and Billy Lewis (b) | | | | | |
| | | | | 11/19/1956 | 1 week* | Cleveland Lyons (or), Al Dobbins (s), and Grassella Oliphant (d) | Cleve Lyons and His Trio, "Out of the Closet" / "Fantastic Mood" (Vik, 1957) |
| 11/26/1956 | 1 week | Art Blakey (d) and the Jazz Messengers | The Jazz Messengers (Columbia, 1956) | | | | |
| 12/3/1956 | 1 week | Chico Hamilton (d) with Fred Katz (vc), Carson Smith (b), Paul Horn (s, cl, f), and John Pisano (g) | Chico Hamilton Quintet featuring Buddy Collette (Pacific Jazz, 1956) | 12/3/1956 | | Quartones with Bass McMahon (b), Robert Head (p), Billy Anderson (d), and Ducky Kemp (vib) | |
| 12/10/1956 | 1 week* | Horace Silver (p) | 6 Pieces of Silver (Blue Note, 1957) | 12/13/1956 | 5 weeks | Jimmy Smith (or) Trio with Thornel Schwartz (g) and Donald "Duck" Bailey (d) | At Club Baby Grand (Blue Note, 1956) |
| 12/24/1956 | 1 week | The Jazz Modes with Charley Rouse (ts) and Julius Watkins (frh) | The Most Happy Fella (Atlantic, 1958) | | | | |
| 12/31/1956 | NYE | Teddy Charles (vib, p, d) | The Teddy Charles Tentet (Atlantic, 1956) | | | | |

| Crawford Grill No. 2 | | | | Hurricane Bar and Grill | | | |
|---|---|---|---|---|---|---|---|
| Date | Length | Artist | Contemporary Recording | Date | Length | Artist | Contemporary Recording |
| | | | | 1/21/1957 | 1 week* | Stanley Gaines and the Hurricanes featuring Eddie Piper (comedy group) | |
| 2/25/1957 | 1 week* | J. J. Johnson (tb) | *First Place* (Columbia, 1957) | | | | |
| 3/18/1957 | 1 week | Chet Baker (t, v) Quintet | *Chet Baker & Crew* (Pacific Jazz, 1957) | | | | |
| 3/25/1957 | 1 week* | The All-Stars | | | | | |
| | | | | 4/1/1957 | 1 week | Rusty Bryant (s), Harry Marr (or), "Mitch" Robinson (d), and Nancy Wilson (v) | "All Night Long" (Dot Records, 1955), "Kitty Hawk" / "Little Hawk Walks" (Dot Records, 1957) |
| | | | | 4/8/1957 | 1 week | Willis "Gator Tail" Jackson (ts) | *Please Mr. Jackson* (Prestige, 1959 |
| 4/15/1957 | 1 week | Roger Ryan (d) Quintet | | 4/15/1957 | 1 month | Eddie "Lockjaw" Davis (ts) Trio with Shirley Scott (or) and Charlie Price (d) | *The Eddie "Lockjaw" Dav Cookbook* (Prestige, 195 |
| 4/22/1957 | 1 week* | Julian "Cannonball" Adderley (as) | *In the Land of Hi-Fi with Julian Cannonball Adderley* (EmArcy, 1956) | | | | |
| 5/6/1957 | 2 weeks | Chico Hamilton (d) | *Chico Hamilton Quintet* (Pacific Jazz, 1957) | | | | |
| | | | | 6/10/1957 | 1 week | Jimmy Smith (or) | *A Date with Jimmy Smit Volume One* (Blue Note, 19 |
| 6/17/1957 | 1 week | Terry Gibbs (vib) Quartet with Terry Pollard (p) | *Terry Gibbs Quartet featuring Terry Pollard* (EmArcy, 1955) | | | | |

| | Crawford Grill No. 2 | | | | Hurricane Bar and Grill | | |
|---|---|---|---|---|---|---|---|
| Date | Length | Artist | Contemporary Recording | Date | Length | Artist | Contemporary Recording |
| | | | | 7/1/1957 | 2 weeks | Tiny Grimes (g) and His Rocking Highlanders | "Blues Round-Up" / "Tiny's Boogie" (United, 1954) and Tiny Grimes, *Blues Groove* (Prestige, 1958) |
| ?/22/1957 | 1 week | Walt Harper (p) | | | | | |
| ?/29/1957 | 1 week* | Johnny Hartman and His House Rockers Organ Quartet | | | | | |
| ?/10/1957 | 2 weeks | Walt Harper (p) | | 8/12/1957 | 1 week | Duke Jenkins (p) with Areline Taylor (d), Curtis Wilder (b, v), John Hunt (t), and Fred Jenkins (s) | "Something Else" / "The Duke Walks" (Cobra, 1957) |
| | | | | 8/19/1957 | 2 weeks | Jon Thomas (or) Organ Trio | *Hard Head* (Mercury, 1957) |
| ?26/1957 | 1 week | Miles Davis (tr) | *Cookin'* (Prestige, 1957) | | | | |
| ?2/1957 | 1 week | Jerry Betters (v, d) | "Caravan" / "Secret Love" (Gateway, 1963) | 9/2/1957 | 1 week | Tommy Mills Organ Quartet with John Jackson (vib, g) | |
| ?9/1957 | 1 week | Art Blakey (d) and the Jazz Messengers | *Hard Bop* (Columbia, 1957) | | | | |
| ?16/1957 | 1 week | Max Roach (d) | *Max Roach + 4* (EmArcy, 1956) | 9/23/1957 | 1 week | Eddie "Lockjaw" Davis (ts) with Shirley Scott (or) | *The Eddie "Lockjaw" Davis Cookbook* (Prestige, 1958) |
| | | | | 9/23/1957 | 3 weeks | Stan Gaines (b) | |
| | | | | 10/21/1957 | 1 week* | Hank Marr (or) Trio + 3 | "Tonk Game" / "Hob-Nobbin," (King, 1961) and *Teentime . . . Latest Dance Steps* (King, 1963) |
| ?28/1957 | 1 week* | Cannonball Adderley (as) with Nat Adderley (cornet) and Sam Jones (b) | *Sophisticated Swing* (EmArcy, 1957) | | | | |

| Crawford Grill No. 2 | | | | Hurricane Bar and Grill | | | |
|---|---|---|---|---|---|---|---|
| Date | Length | Artist | Contemporary Recording | Date | Length | Artist | Contemporary Recording |
| | | | | 11/4/1957 | 1 week* | Chris Columbo (d) with Jimmy Tyler (ts), Floyd Smith (g), and Gil Askey (t) | "Oh Yeah!" (King 1957) |
| 11/4/1957 | 2 weeks | Deuces Wild with Dodo Marmarosa (p) | *Pittsburgh, 1958* (2007) | | | | |
| 11/18/1957 | 1 week | Max Roach (d) | *Jazz in 3/4 Time* (EmArcy, 1957) | 11/18/1957 | 1 week | Milt Buckner Trio with Danny Turner (ts) | *Rockin' Hammond* (Capitol, 1956) |
| 11/25/1957 | 1 week | Art Blakey (d) and the Jazz Messengers with Jackie McLean (as) | *A Night in Tunisia* (Vik, 1957) | | | | |
| 12/2/1957 | 3 weeks | Walt Harper (p) | | 12/2/1957 | 2 weeks | Chris Columbo (d) with Jimmy Tyler (ts), Floyd Smith (g), and Gil Askey (t) | |
| 12/23/1957 | 1 week | James Moody (s, v) featuring Eddie Jefferson (v) | *Moody's Mood for Love* (Argo, 1957) | 12/23/1957 | 2 weeks | Duke Jenkins (p) with Areline Taylor (d), Curtis Wilder (b, v), John Hunt (t), and Fred Jenkins (s) | |
| 12/30/1957 | 1 week* | Sonny Stitt (ts) | *Personal Appearance* (Verve, 1957) | | | | |
| 1/6/1958 | 1 week | Stan Getz (ts) | *Award Winner* (Verve, 1957) | 1/6/1958 | 2 weeks | Jimmy Smith (or) with Donald "Duck" Bailey (d) and Eddie McFadden (g) | *Groovin' at Smalls Paradi...* (Blue Note, 19...) |
| 1/13/1958 | 1 week | Roger Ryan (d) | *Deuces Wild* (DW3864, 1958?) | | | | |
| 1/20/1958 | 2 weeks | Horace Silver (p) | *The Stylings of Silver* (Blue Note, 1957) | | | | |
| 1/17/1958 | 1 week* | Sam Hurt (tb) Quintet with Lee Gross (bar), Bobby Boswell (b), Eddie Russ (p), and David Lee (d) | | | | | |

| | Crawford Grill No. 2 | | | Hurricane Bar and Grill | | | |
|---|---|---|---|---|---|---|---|
| Date | Length | Artist | Contemporary Recording | Date | Length | Artist | Contemporary Recording |
| | | | | 1/27/1958 | | The Lou Bennett Organ Trio | *Amen* (RCA, 1960) |
| | | | | 2/3/1958 | | Jimmy Tyler (s) Organ Quintet | "Fool 'Em Devil" (Federal, 1955) |
| 3/3/1958 | 1 week | Oscar Peterson (p), Herb Ellis (g), and Ray Brown (b) | *At the Concertgebouw* (Verve, 1957) | | | | |
| /10/1958 | 1 week | Dakota Staton (v) | *The Late, Late Show* (Capitol, 1957) | 3/10/1958 | 1 week | Jon Thomas (or) Trio with "Big" Chick Farley (d) | "Hard Head" (Mercury, 1957) and *Big Beat on the Organ* (Mercury, 1958) |
| "17/1958 | 1 week | Max Roach (d) | *The Max Roach 4 Plays Charlie Parker* (EmArcy, 1959) | 3/17/1958 | 1 week* | Bill Carney and His Hightones with Howard Whaley (or) | "I Really Mean It" (Coral, 1962) |
| 24/1958 | 1 week | J. J. Johnson (tb) | *J. J. in Person* (Columbia, 1958) | | | | |
| | | | | 4/7/1958 | 1 week | Dottie Dudley (or) Trio | Leon Eason's "I'm in the Mood for Love" / "Lazy River" (Blue Note, 1959) |
| | | | | 4/14/1958 | 3 weeks | Johnny "Hammond" Smith (or) | *Have You Heard Johnny Smith* (Arrow Records, 1958) |
| 3/1958 | 10 days | Art Blakey (d) and the Jazz Messengers | *A Night in Tunisia* (Vik, 1957) | 5/5/1958 | 1 week | Gloria Belle (b) Quartet | |
| 2/1958 | 1 week | Illinois Jacquet (ts) | *Swing's the Thing* (Verve, 1957) | 5/12/1958 | 2 weeks | Chris Columbo (d) with Floyd Smith (g), Gil Askey (t), Stan the Man (or), and Jimmy Tyler (s) | |
| 9/1958 | 1 week* | Leroy Brown (as) | | | | | |
| 5/1958 | 1 week* | Terry Gibbs (vib) | *More Vibes on Velvet* (EmArcy, 1958) | 5/26/1958 | 1 week* | Willis "Gator Tail" Jackson (ts) Quartet with Bill Jennings (g), Orville Johnson (or), and Al Jackson (d) | *The Remaining Willis Jackson 1951-1959* (Blue Moon, 2005) |

| Crawford Grill No. 2 | | | | Hurricane Bar and Grill | | | |
|---|---|---|---|---|---|---|---|
| Date | Length | Artist | Contemporary Recording | Date | Length | Artist | Contemporary Recording |
| | | | | 6/2/1958 | 2 weeks | Jimmy Smith (or) with Donald "Duck" Bailey (d) and Eddie McFadden (g) | *Jimmy Smith at the Organ* (Blue Note, 1958) |
| | | | | 6/13/1958 | 1 week* | Milt Buckner (or) | *Send Me Softly* (Capitol Record, 1958) |
| 6/23/1958 | 1 week | Earl Bostic (as) | "Special Delivery Stomp" / "Earl's Dog" (King, 1960) | | | | |
| 6/30/1958 | 1 week* | Erskine Hawkins (t) Sextet | "After Hours" (Bluebird, 1940) | | | | |
| 7/4/1958 | 1 week | Horace Silver (p) Quintet | *The Preacher* (Blue Note, 1955) | | | | |
| 7/28/1958 | 1 week | Art Blakey (d) and the Jazz Messengers | *Art Blakey and the Jazz Messengers* (Blue Note, 1958) | | | | |
| | | | | 8/18/1958 | 2 weeks | Lou Bennett (or) Trio | "Googa Moog" / "Diggin' llen" (Dawn, 1958) |
| 9/1/1958 | 1 week | Hank Marr (or) Trio and Howard McGee (t) | Hank Marr Quartette *Live at the Club 502* (King, 1964) | | | | |
| 8/9/1958 | 1 week | The Dartmouth College Sultans with Mike Melvoin (p) | | | | | |
| 9/15/1958 | 1 week* | Dave Cook (d) Quintet | | 9/15/1958 | 1 month | Chris Columbo (d) with Floyd Smith (g), Gil Askey (t), Stan the Man (or), and Danny Turner (s) | |
| 10/20/1958 | 3 weeks | The Kelly Quartet with Gethro Spencer, Ducky Kemp, and Bobby Anderson | | | | | |

| | Crawford Grill No. 2 | | | Hurricane Bar and Grill | | | |
|---|---|---|---|---|---|---|---|
| Date | Length | Artist | Contemporary Recording | Date | Length | Artist | Contemporary Recording |
| | | | | 11/10/1958 | 2 weeks | Jimmy Smith (or) with Donald "Duck" Bailey (d) and Eddie McFadden (g) | |
| 2/15/1958 | 1 week | The Dartmouth College Sultans with Mike Melvoin (p) | | | | | |
| ?/23/1958 | 2 weeks | James Moody (ts) | *Last Train from Overbrook* (Argo, 1958) | 12/29/1958 | 1 week | Arnett Cobb (s) | *Blow Arnett, Blow* (Prestige, 1959), *Smooth Sailing* (Prestige, 1960) |
| | | | | 1/5/1959 | 2 weeks | Johnny "Hammond" Smith (or) | *That Good Feelin'* (New Jazz, 1959) |
| ?19/1959 | 1 week* | Horace Silver (p) | | | | | |
| 26/1959 | 1 week* | Walt Harper (p) | | 2/9/1959 | 1 week* | Bobby Green Quintet | |
| ?16/1959 | 2 weeks | Max Roach (d) Quintet with Booker Little (tr), George Coleman (ts), Julian Priester (tb), and Art Davis (b) | *The Many Sides of Max* (Mercury, 1964) | 2/16/1959 | 1 week | Dave Hill Six-Piece Combo | |
| | | | | 2/23/1959 | 2 weeks | Johnny Lytle (vib) Trio | *Blue Vibes* (Jazzland, 1960) |
| | | | | | | | |
| 2/1959 | 1 week | The Three Sounds | *Good Deal* (Blue Note, 1959) | | | | |
| 9/1959 | 1 week* | Bennie Green (tr) Quintet | *Walkin' & Talkin'* (Blue Note, 1959) | 3/9/1959 | 2 weeks | Eddie "Lockjaw" Davis (ts) with Shirley Scott (or) | *Jaws* (Prestige, 1959) |
| 3/1959 | 1 week* | Walt Harper (p) | | 3/23/1959 | | Jimmy Smith (or) with Donald "Duck" Bailey (d) and Eddie McFadden (g) | *Groovin' at Smalls Paradise* (Blue Note, 1957) |
| | | | | 3/30/1959 | 2 weeks | Chris Columbo (d) with Gil Askey (t), Floyd Smith (g), Jimmy Tyler (s), and Stan the Man (or) | |

| Crawford Grill No. 2 | | | | Hurricane Bar and Grill | | | |
|---|---|---|---|---|---|---|---|
| Date | Length | Artist | Contemporary Recording | Date | Length | Artist | Contemporary Recording |
| 4/6/1959 | 1 week | J. J. Johnson (tb) | *Blue Trombone* (Columbia, 1959) | | | | |
| 4/13/1959 | 1 week | Billy Taylor (p) | *Taylor Made Jazz* (Argo, 1959) | 4/13/1959 | 1 week* | Wild Bill Davis (or) with Brice Robertson (g) | "April in Paris" from *Wild Bill Davis at Birdland* (Epic, 1955) |
| 4/27/1959 | 1 week | James Moody (s, v) Sextet | "Love Walked In" / "Andrew Got Married" (Metronome, 1951) | 4/27/1959 | 1 month | Jolly Jax Trio | "Love" / "Honeymoonin" (Tina Records, 1959) |
| 5/4/1959 | 1 week | The Three Sounds | | | | | |
| 5/11/1959 | 2 weeks | Cal Tjader (vib) | *Mas Ritmo Caliente* (Fantasy Records, 1960) | | | | |
| 5/25/1959 | 1 week* | Billy Taylor (p) Quintet | | 5/25/1959 | 1 week* | Sil Austin (ts) | *Slow Walk Roc* (Mercury, 1957 |
| 6/8/1959 | 1 week | Lou Donaldson (ts) | *Light-Foot* (Blue Note, 1959) | 6/8/1959 | 2 weeks | Cootie Williams (t) Quintet | *Cootie* (Decca 1959) |
| 6/13/1959 | 1 week* | Benny Green (tb) Quintet | *Soul Stirrin'* (Blue Note, 1958) | | | | |
| 6/22/1959 | 1 week | Art Blakey (d) and the Jazz Messengers | *Olympia Concert* (Fontana, 1959) | 6/22/1959 | 1 week | Cleveland Johnny Smith Quartet | |
| 6/29/1959 | 1 week | The Three Sounds | | | | | |
| 7/4/1959 | 2 weeks | Charles Bell (p) Contemporary Jazz Quartet with Bill Smith (g), Allen Blairman (d), and Dick Miller (b) | *Another Dimension* (Atlantic, 1963) | 7/6/1959 | 1 week | Willie Love Quintet featuring Chuck Jackson | |
| | | | | 7/13/1959 | 1 week* | Sonny Til and the Orioles | |
| 8/10/1959 | 1 week* | John "Spider" Martin (s) with Roberta Perry (v) and Austin Cromer (v) | | | | | |

| Crawford Grill No. 2 | | | | Hurricane Bar and Grill | | | |
|---|---|---|---|---|---|---|---|
| Date | Length | Artist | Contemporary Recording | Date | Length | Artist | Contemporary Recording |
| 3/31/1959 | 1 week* | James Moody (s, v) Sextet | | | | | |
| 0/19/1959 | 1 week | Lou Donaldson (ts) | | | | | |
| 9/26/1959 | 1 week | Donald Byrd (t) and Pepper Adams (bar) Quintet | 10 to 4 at the 5 Spot (Riverside, 1958) | 10/26/1959 | 2 weeks | Jolly Jax | |
| 1/9/1959 | 1 week | J. J. Johnson (tb) Quartet | | | | | |
| /16/1959 | 1 week | Charlie Shavers (t) | "Nobody Knows the Trouble I've Seen" | 11/16/1959 | 1 week | Carl Sally Quintet | |
| /23/1959 | 1 week | Donald Byrd (t) and Pepper Adams (bar) Quintet | Off to the Races (Blue Note, 1959) | 11/23/1959 | 2 weeks | Dayton Selby (or) | There She Blows! (Hollywood Records, 1956) |
| 30/1959 | 1 week | Ramsey Lewis (p) Trio | Wade in the Water (Chess, 1966) | | | | |
| /7/1959 | 1 week | Gigi Gryce (ts) Quintet | Gigi Gryce (MetroJazz, 1959) | 12/7/1959 | 1 week* | Don Gardner (v, d) Quartet | Don Gardner and his Sonotones "Dark Alley" / "Up the Street" (Junior Records, 1957) |
| 14/1959 | 1 week | Charles Bell (p), Allen Blairman (d), Bill Smith (g), and Dick Hiller (b) | | 12/14/1959 | 1 week | Billy Madison (or) Trio featuring Joe Cook | |
| 21/1959 | 2 weeks | James Moody (ts, v) Sextet | | 12/21/1959 | 1 week | Chris Columbo (d) with Floyd Smith (g) and Gil Askew (t) | |
| 4/1960 | 1 week | Art Blakey (d) and the Jazz Messengers | | 1/4/1960 | 3 weeks | Jolly Jax with Herman, Carroll, and Jerome Hill | |
| 1/1960 | 1 week | Phineas Newborn (p) Trio | I Love a Piano (Roulette, 1960) | | | | |
| 8/1960 | 1 week | Julian "Cannonball" Adderley (as) Quintet | Cannonball Enroute (Mercury, 1961) | | | | |
| | | | | 2/1/1960 | 3 weeks | Jimmy Smith (or) Trio | |

| Crawford Grill No. 2 | | | | Hurricane Bar and Grill | | | |
|---|---|---|---|---|---|---|---|
| Date | Length | Artist | Contemporary Recording | Date | Length | Artist | Contemporary Recording |
| 2/15/1960 | 1 week | Ornette Coleman (as) | *Change of the Century* (Atlantic, 1960) | | | | |
| 2/22/1960 | 1 week* | Philly Joe Jones (d) | *Showcase* (Riverside, 1960) | 2/22/1960 | 1 week* | Frank Heppinstall Organ Trio | *Trio by Heppinstall* (Polyphonic, 1961) |
| 3/7/1960 | 1 week* | Art Farmer (t) and Benny Golson (ts) | | 3/7/1960 | 1 week | Willis "Gator Tail" Jackson (ts) | |
| | | | | 3/14/1960 | 1 week | Johnny Lytle (vib) Organ Group | *Blue Vibes* (Jazzland, 1960 |
| | | | | 3/21/1960 | 3 weeks | Dayton Selby (or) Trio | |
| 3/28/1960 | 1 week | Yusef Lateef (s, f) Quartet | *The Three Faces of Yusef Lateef* (Riverside, 1960) | | | | |
| 4/4/1960 | 1 week | Illinois Jacquet (ts) | *Illinois Jacquet Flies Again* (Roulette, 1959) | | | | |
| 4/11/1960 | 1 week | J. J. Johnson (tb) Sextet | | 4/11/1960 | 5 weeks | Kris Colombo (d) with Floyd Smith (g), Gil Askew (t), and Jimmy Tyler (s) | |
| 4/18/1960 | 1 week* | Jack Montrose (s) and Pepper Adams (bar) Quintet | *Arranged/ Played/ Composed By Jack Montrose With Bob Gordon* (Atlantic, 1955) | | | | |
| 4/30/1960 | 1 week* | Slide Hampton (tb) | *Sister Salvation* (Atlantic, 1960) | | | | |
| 5/2/1960 | 2 weeks | Ray Bryant (p) Trio | *Alone With the Blues* (New Jazz, 1959) | | | | |
| | | | | 5/9/1960 | 1 week* | The John "Spider" Martin (ts) Organ Quartet | *Absolutely* (Improv, 197 |

| | Crawford Grill No. 2 | | | Hurricane Bar and Grill | | | |
|---|---|---|---|---|---|---|---|
| Date | Length | Artist | Contemporary Recording | Date | Length | Artist | Contemporary Recording |
| 5/16/1960 | 1 week* | Charlie Marriano Quartet with Toshiko Akiyoshi (p) | *The Toshiko–Mariano Quartet* (Candid, 1961) | 5/16/1960 | 2 weeks | William "Cat" Anderson (t) Organ Quintet with Stan Hunter and Len Blackburn (tb) | *A Chat with Cat Anderson* (Columbia, 1963) |
| 5/23/1960 | 1 week | Ramsey Lewis (p) Trio | | 5/23/1960 | 1 week | Thornel Schwartz (g) Organ Trio | *Soul Cookin'* (Argo, 1962) |
| 5/30/1960 | 1 week* | The Gary Bartz (as) and Grachon MonCur Quintet | *Another Earth* (Milestone, 1969) | 5/30/1960 | 3 weeks* | Jolly Jax Trio | |
| | | | | | | | |
| 6/20/1960 | 1 month | Slide Hampton (tb) | | 6/20/1960 | 1 week | Pearl Reeves (g) Organ Combo | "You Can't Stay Here" / "I'm Not Ashamed" (Harlem, 1955) |
| | | | | 6/27/1960 | 2 weeks | Jimmy Smith (or) Trio | *Crazy! Baby* (Blue Note, 1960) |
| | | | | 7/18/1960 | 1 week | Johnny Lytle (vib) featuring Chuck Jackson (v) | *Blue Vibes* (Jazzland, 1960) |
| 7/25/1960 | 1 week* | Charlie Persip (d) Quintet | *Charles Persip and the Jazz Statesmen* (Bethlehem Records, 1961) | 7/25/1960 | 1 week* | Big Jay McNeeley (ts) Sextet and Little Sonny Warner (v) | *Recorded Live at Cisco's* (Warner Bros. Records, 1963) |
| 8/1960 | 1 week* | Mal Waldron (p) Trio | *Left Alone* (Bethlehem Records, 1960) | | | | |
| 8/2/1960 | 1 week | Yusef Lateef (s, f) Quartet | *The Centaur and the Phoenix* (Riverside, 1960) | 8/22/1960 | 1 week | Chris Columbo (d) Quintet | |
| 8/29/1960 | 1 month | Les McCann (p) Trio | *Les McCann Ltd. Plays the Truth* (Pacific Jazz, 1960) | 8/29/1960 | 1 week | Chuck Jackson (v) | *I Don't Want to Cry!* (Wand, 1961) |
| | | | | 9/19/1960 | 1 week* | Cat Anderson (t) Quintet | |
| | | | | 10/3/1960 | 2 weeks | Chris Columbo (d) with Gil Askew (t) and Floyd Smith (g) | |

| Crawford Grill No. 2 | | | | Hurricane Bar and Grill | | | |
|---|---|---|---|---|---|---|---|
| Date | Length | Artist | Contemporary Recording | Date | Length | Artist | Contemporary Recording |
| 10/18/1960 | 1 week* | Red Garland (p) Trio | *Alone with the Blues* (Moodsville, 1960) | 10/17/1960 | 1 week* | Jack McDuff (or) Trio | |
| | | | | 10/31/1960 | 3 weeks | Jolly Jax Trio with Jerome, Carroll, and Herman Hill | |
| 11/7/1960 | 1 week | Duke Jenkins Quintet | | | | | |
| 11/14/1960 | 1 week | Eddie "Lockjaw" Davis and John Griffin Quintet | | | | | |
| 11/28/1960 | 1 week | John Coltrane (ts) Quartet with Elvin Jones (d) | *Giant Steps* (Atlantic, 1960) | | | | |
| 12/5/1960 | 1 week* | The Three Sounds: Bill Dowdy (dr), Gene Harris (p), and Andy Simpkins (b) | *Moods* (Blue Note, 1960) | 12/5/1960 | 1 week* | Jimmy Smith (or) with Donald "Duck" Bailey (d) and Quentin Warren (g) | |
| 12/19/1960 | 3 weeks* | Slide Hampton (tb) Octet | | | | | |
| | | | | 1/2/1961 | 1 week | Chris Columbo (d) | |
| | | | | 1/9/1961 | 2 weeks | John Thomas Organ Quintet | *Heartbreak* (AB Paramount, 1960) |
| 1/16/1961 | 1 week | Eddie Russ | | 1/16/1961 | 1 week | Howard Whaley Organ Combo | |
| 1/23/1961 | 1 week* | Ramsey Lewis (p) Trio | *More Music from the Soil* (Argo, 1961) | 1/23/1961 | 1 week* | Lindy Ewell Trio | |
| | | | | 1/30/1961 | 3 weeks | Frank Heppinstall and the Allegros | |
| 2/6/1961 | 2 weeks | Bill Evans (p) Trio | *Sunday at the Village Vanguard* (Riverside, 1961) | | | | |
| | | | | 2/13/1961 | 3 weeks | Sarah McLawler (or) Trio with Richard Otto (vn) | *We Bring Yo Swing* (Vee J Records, 195 |

| | Crawford Grill No. 2 | | | | Hurricane Bar and Grill | | |
|---|---|---|---|---|---|---|---|
| Date | Length | Artist | Contemporary Recording | Date | Length | Artist | Contemporary Recording |
| 2/20/1961 | 2 weeks | The Three Sounds | *Feelin' Good* (Blue Note, 1961) | | | | |
| 3/6/1961 | 1 week* | Gene Ammons (ts) | | | | | |
| 3/13/1961 | 1 week | Junior Mance (p) Trio | *Junior Mance Trio at the Village Vanguard* (Jazzland, 1961) | 3/13/1961 | 2 weeks | The Dayton Selby-Wilena Barton Organ Trio with Pola Roberts (d) | |
| 3/20/1961 | 1 week* | Art Farmer (t) and Benny Golson (ts) Jazztet | | | | | |
| 3/27/1961 | 2 weeks* | Al Grey (tb) and Billy Mitchel (s) Sextet | *The Al Grey – Billy Mitchell Sextet* (Argo, 1962) | 3/27/1961 | 1 week* | Don Gardner (v, dr) Trio featuring Dee Dee Ford (or) | *I Need Your Lovin'* (Fire Records, 1962) |
| | | | | 4/3/1961 | 1 week | Sil Austin Organ Group | |
| 4/10/1961 | 1 month | Les McCann (p) Trio | | 4/10/1961 | 3 weeks | Jolly Jax with Jerome, Carroll, and Herman Hill | |
| | | | | 5/1/1961 | 1 week | Red Prysock (ts) Sextet | *Swing Softly Red* Mercury, 1961) |
| 5/8/1961 | 2 weeks(?) | Slide Hampton (tb) Octet | | 5/8/1961 | 1 week | Gene Smith and His 4 Notes | |
| 5/16/1961 | 1 week* | Chico Hamilton (d) Quintet | | 5/16/1961 | 1 week | Shirley Scott (or) Trio with Stanley Turrentine (ts) | *Hip Soul* (Prestige, 1961) |
| 5/22/1961 | 2 weeks* | Jazz Brothers Quintet | | 5/22/1961 | 2 weeks | John Thomas Organ Quartet | |
| | | | | 6/5/1961 | 1 week | Don Gardner (v, d) Quartet featuring Dee Dee Ford (or) | *I Need Your Lovin'* (Fire Records, 1962) |
| 6/12/1961 | 1 week | Montgomery Brothers Quartet featuring Wes Montgomery (g) | | 6/12/1961 | 1 week | Johnny Wilson's Troubadors [sic] Sextet | |
| | | | | 6/19/1961 | 3 weeks* | The Dayton Selby-Wilena Barton Organ Trio with Pola Roberts (d) | |

| Crawford Grill No. 2 | | | | Hurricane Bar and Grill | | | |
|---|---|---|---|---|---|---|---|
| Date | Length | Artist | Contemporary Recording | Date | Length | Artist | Contemporary Recording |
| 7/3/1961 | 1 week | Gene Ammons (ts) | *Boss Tenor* (Prestige, 1960) | | | | |
| 7/10/1961 | 2 weeks | Horace Parlan (p) Playhouse Four with Booker Ervin (ts), George Tucker (b), and Al Harewood (d) | *Speakin' My Piece* (Blue Note, 1960), *On the Spur of the Moment* (Blue Note, 1961) | 7/10/1961 | 2 weeks | Sarah McLawler (or) Trio with Richard Otto (vn) | *At The Break of Day* (Vee Jay Records, 1960) |
| 7/24/1961 | 1 week | Al Morrell Quartet | | | | | |
| | | | | 7/31/1961 | 1 week* | Red Prysock (ts) Sextet | |
| | | | | 8/7/1961 | 2 weeks* | Johnny Wilson and His Debonaires | |
| 8/14/1961 | 1 week | Jazz Brothers Quintet with Gap and Chuck Mangione | | c. 1/14/1961 | | | Route 66 filming of scene for "Goodnight Sweet Blues" |
| 8/21/1961 | 1 week | Chico Hamilton (d) Quintet | | | | | |
| 8/28/1961 | 1 week* | The Three Sounds with Gene Harris (p), Andy Simpkins (b), and Bill Dowdy (d) | | 8/28/61 (?) | 2 weeks* | Johnny Smith (or) Quintet | |
| 9/4/1961 | | Lennie Tristano (p) with Lee Konitz (as) | | 9/4/61 (?) | 1 week | Sonny Warner Sextet | |
| 9/11/1961 | 1 week | Ramsey Lewis (p) Trio | | | | | |
| 9/18/1961 | 1 week | Big Jay McNeilly (s) with Jackie Baldain (v) | *Big Jay McNeely* (King Records, 1959) | 9/18/1961 | 3 weeks* | Jolly Jax (fifth appearance) | |
| 9/25/1961 | 1 week | Terry Gibbs (vib) Quartet | | | | | |
| 10/2/1961 | 1 week | Art Farmer (t) and Benny Golson (ts) Jazztet | *Meet the Jazztet* (Argo, 1960) | | | | |
| 10/9/1961 | 1 week | Slide Hampton (tb) | | 10/8/1961 | 1 week* | Red Prysock (ts) Sextet | |
| 10/16/1961 | 1 week* | Chico Hamilton (d) Quintet | | | | | |

| Crawford Grill No. 2 | | | | Hurricane Bar and Grill | | | |
|---|---|---|---|---|---|---|---|
| Date | Length | Artist | Contemporary Recording | Date | Length | Artist | Contemporary Recording |
| | | | | 10/29/1961 | | Jack McDuff (or) Quartet with Joe Dukes (d) | |
| 1/13/1961 | 1 week | Wes Montgomery (g) Quintet | | | | | |
| 1/20/1961 | 1 week* | Jazz Brothers Quintet | | | | | |
| 2/4/1961 | 1 week* | Ramsey Lewis (p) Trio | | | | | |
| 2/18/1961 | 1 week* | Bobby Timmons (p) Trio | | | | | |
| | | | | 12/25/1961 | 1 week* | Jack McDuff (or) Quartet with Joe Dukes (d) | |
| 1/8/1962 | 1 week | Bobby Jones (or) Trio | | 1/8/1962 | 1 week | Lady Byron (p) Organ Trio with Evelyn Childress (or) | |
| 22/1962 | 1 week | The Three Sounds | | | | | |
| | | | | 1/29/1961 | 2 weeks | Rhoda Scott (or) Trio | |
| 12/1962 | 1 week* | Charles Bell (p) Contemporary Jazz Quartet | The Charles Bell Contemporary Jazz Quartet (Columbia, 1961) | 2/12/1962 | 3 weeks | Jolly Jax Trio with Jerome, Carroll, and Herman Hill | "There's Something On Your Mind" Pt.1 / "There's Something On Your Mind" Pt.2 (V-Tone Records, 1962) |
| 5/1962 | 2 weeks | Slide Hampton (tb) Octet | | 3/5/1962 | 2 weeks | Don Gardner (v, d) and Dee Dee Ford (or) Quartet | "Last Dance" / "Harlem Rock" (Sonet, 1965) |
| 6/1962 | 1 week* | Sonny Stitt (ts) | Rearin' Back (Argo, 1962) | 3/26/1962 | 2 weeks | Dayton Selby (or) and Willene Barton (ts) Trio with Pola Roberts (d) | |
| | | | | 4/9/1962 | 1 week | Lady Byron (p) Organ Trio with Evelyn Childress (or) | |

| Crawford Grill No. 2 | | | | Hurricane Bar and Grill | | | |
|---|---|---|---|---|---|---|---|
| Date | Length | Artist | Contemporary Recording | Date | Length | Artist | Contemporary Recording |
| 4/12/1962 | 1 week* | Chico Hamilton (d) Quintet | *Man from Two Worlds* (Impulse, 1964) | | | | |
| | | | | 4/16/1962 | 2 weeks | Shirley Scott (or) and Stanley Turrentine (ts) | *The Soul Is Willing* (Prestige 1963) |
| 4/23/1962 | 1 week | The Jazztet with Art Farmer (t) and Bennie Golson (ts) | *Another Git Together* (Mercury, 1962) | | | | |
| | | | | 4/30/1962 | 2 weeks | George Benson (g) and his All-Stars | "The Nearness You" / "Begin th Beguine" (Gon 1951) |
| 5/7/1962 | 1 week* | Johnny Lytle (vib) | *Nice and Easy* (Jazzland, 1962) | | | | |
| | | | | 5/14/1962 | 1 week | Jack McDuff (or) | *The Honeydripper* (Prestige, 1961 |
| 5/21/1962 | 1 week | Milt Buckner (or) | | 5/21/1962 | 2 weeks | The Johnny Wilson Debonaires featuring Carl Hall | |
| 5/28/1963 | 2 weeks | Bobby Timmons (p) Trio | *Dat Dere* (Riverside, 1963) | | | | |
| | | | | 6/4/1962 | 2 weeks | Frank Heppinstall Trio | |
| 6/18/1962 | 1 week* | The Three Sounds | | 6/18/1962 | 2 weeks | Sarah McLawler (or) Trio with Richard Otto (vn) | |
| 7/2/1962 | 2 weeks | Charles Bell's (p) Contemporary Jazz Quartet with Allen Blairman (d), Michael Taylor (b), and Donald Hanes (g) | | 7/2/1962 | 1 week | Red Prysock (ts) | |
| | | | | 7/9/1962 | 1 week | Daddy Bell Organ Combo | |
| | | | | 7/16/1962 | 1 week* | Jewel Brynner | |
| 7/23/1962 | 1 week | Rahsaan Roland Kirk (s, f) | *Domino* (Mercury, 1962) | | | | |

| Crawford Grill No. 2 | | | | Hurricane Bar and Grill | | | |
|---|---|---|---|---|---|---|---|
| Date | Length | Artist | Contemporary Recording | Date | Length | Artist | Contemporary Recording |
| 7/30/1962 | 1 week | Benny Golson (ts) and Art Farmer (t) Jazztet | *Big City Sounds* (Argo, 1961) | 7/30/1962 | 1 week | Gene Ludwig (or) | *The Educated Sounds of Gene Ludwig* (Travis Records, 1965) |
| 8/6/1962 | 2 weeks | Chico Hamilton (d) | | 8/6/1962 | 2 weeks | Jolly Jax | |
| 8/20/1962 | 1 week* | Al Grey (tb) and Billy Mitchell (s) Sextet | *Snap Your Fingers* (Argo, 1962) | 8/20/1962 | 2 weeks | Rhoda Scott (or) Organ Trio | *Hey, Hey, Hey* (Tru-Sound, 1962) |
| 9/3/1962 | 1 week* | Johnny Wright Quintet | | | | | |
| 9/10/1962 | 2 weeks | Les McCann (p) | | | | | |
| | | | | 9/17/1962 | 1 week | Chris Columbo (d) with Gil Askey (t) and Stan Hunter (or) | "Stranger on the Shore" / "You Can't Sit Down" (Battle, 1962) |
| | | | | 9/24/1962 | 1 week* | Hump Jones Organ Quintet | |
| 10/1/1962 | 1 week | Jimmy Giuffre (cl) | *Free Fall* (Columbia, 1963) | 10/1/1962 | 2 weeks | Frank Heppinstall's Allegros | |
| 10/8/1962 | 1 week | Chico Hamilton (d) Quintet | | | | | |
| 10/15/1962 | 1 week | Richard "Groove" Holmes (or) Trio | | 10/15/1962 | 1 week | Red Prysock (ts) | |
| 10/22/1962 | 1 week | Roy Haynes (d) Quartet | *Cymbalism* (New Jazz, 1963) | 10/22/1962 | 1 week* | Chris Columbo (d) | |
| | | | | 11/12/1962 | 1 week | Gene Ludwig (or) | |
| 11/19/1962 | 2 weeks | Charles Bell (p) Quartet | | 11/19/1962 | 2 weeks | Dayton Selby (or) and Willene Barton (ts) Organ Trio | *The Feminine Sax* (Design Records, 1957) |
| | | | | 12/10/1962 | 1 week* | Rhoda Scott (or) Trio | |
| 12/9/1962 | 2 weeks | Johnny Lytle (vib) | *Moon Child* (Jazzland, 1962) | 12/17/1962 | 3 weeks | Jolly Jax | |
| 1/1963 | 1 week* | Billy Kimes with Jimmy Reid | | | | | |

| | Crawford Grill No. 2 | | | | Hurricane Bar and Grill | | |
|---|---|---|---|---|---|---|---|
| Date | Length | Artist | Contemporary Recording | Date | Length | Artist | Contemporary Recording |
| | | | | 2/25/1963 | 2 weeks | Don Gardner and Dee Dee Ford Organ Quartet | "Don't You Worry" / "I'm Coming Home To Stay" (Fire, 1962) |
| | | | | 3/18/1963 | 1 week | Jewel Brynner | |
| | | | | 3/25/1963 | 1 week* | Frank Heppinstall's Allegros | |
| 4/6/1963 | 1 week | John Wright (ts) Quintet with Chuck Austin (t), John Heard (b), Roger Humphries (d), and Fred Tooks (p) | | | | | |
| 4/15/1963 | 1 week | John Coltrane (s) Quartet | Live at Birdland (Impulse, 1964) | | | | |
| 5/6/1963 | 1 week | The Three Sounds | | | | | |
| 5/13/1963 | 1 week | Al Grey and Billy Mitchell (ts) | | 5/13/1963 | 2 weeks | Jimmy Tyler Organ Trio | |
| 5/20/1963 | 1 week | Les McCann (p) | | | | | |
| 5/27/1963 | 1 week | John Wright (ts) Quintet | | 5/27/1963 | 1 week* | Johnny "Hammond" Smith (or) Jazz Organ Quartet | |
| 6/3/1963 | 1 week | Eric Dolphy (as) with Bobby Hutcherson (vib), Eddie Khan (b), and possibly Eddie Armour (t) | Conversations (FM, 1963) | | | | |
| 6/10/1963 | 1 week | Chico Hamilton (d) | | 6/10/1963 | 2 weeks | Rhoda Scott (or) Trio | "I Yi Yi Yi" (Tr· Sound, 1963 |
| 6/17/1963 | 1 week | The Jazz Crusaders with Joe Sample (p), Nesbert Hooper (d), Victor Gaskin (b) | Tough Talk (Pacific Jazz, 1963) | | | | |
| | | | | | | | |
| 6/24/1963 | 2 weeks | Belcastro Trio | | 6/24/1963 | 2 weeks | Sonny Warner (v) | "Precious Lo· and "Someth on Your Min· |

| Crawford Grill No. 2 | | | | Hurricane Bar and Grill | | | |
|---|---|---|---|---|---|---|---|
| Date | Length | Artist | Contemporary Recording | Date | Length | Artist | Contemporary Recording |
| | | | | 7/1/1963 | | Flip and His Flippers 7-Piece Entertainment Group | |
| 7/8/1963 | 1 week | Wynton Kelly (p) Trio with Paul Chambers (b) and Jimmy Cobb (d) | *It's All Right!* (Verve, 1964) | 7/8/1963 | 1 week | Dave Mitchell Quintet | |
| 7/15/1963 | 1 week | Max Roach (d) Quartet with Clifford Jordan (ts), Jymie Merrit (b) or Eddie Kahn (b), and Ron Mathews (p) | *Speak, Brother, Speak!* (Fantasy, 1963) | 7/15/1963 | 1 week | Jimmy McGriff (or) | *I've Got a Woman* (Sue Records, 1962) |
| 7/22/1963 | 2 weeks | John Wright (ts) Quintet | | 7/22/1963 | 2 weeks | Johnny "Hammond" Smith (or) | |
| 8/5/1963 | 1 week | Art Farmer (t) Quartet featuring Jim Hall | *Big Blues* (CTI Records, 1978) | | | | |
| 8/26/1963 | 2 weeks | Ramsey Lewis (p) Trio with El Dee Young (b) and Red Holt (d) | *Memphis in June* (Argo, 1962) | | | | |
| 9/9/1963 | 1 week | Gene Walker (ts) Quartet with Nelson Harrison (tb), Spencer Bey (p), and Sonny Nowlin (b) | | 9/9/1963 | 1 week | Jack McDuff (or) Trio with Joe Dukes (d), George Benson (g), and Harold Vick (ts) | *Brother Jack McDuff Live!* (Prestige, 1963) |
| 9/16/1963 | 1 week | Slide Hampton (tb) | | 9/16/1963 | 2 weeks | Freddie Roach Organ Trio | |
| 9/23/1963 | 2 weeks | Max Roach (d) and Abbey Lincoln with Eddie Kahn (b) and Clifford Jordan (ts) | *We Insist! Max Roach's Freedom Now Suite* (Candid, 1961) | | | | |
| | | | | 9/30/1963 | 1 week | Sammy Bryant Organ Trio | "He Know's How Much We Can Bare" (Checker, 1966) |
| 10/7/1963 | 1 week | Chris Columbo (d) | | 10/7/1963 | 1 week | Luther Randolph and Johnny Stiles Organ Trio | |

| Crawford Grill No. 2 | | | | Hurricane Bar and Grill | | | |
|---|---|---|---|---|---|---|---|
| Date | Length | Artist | Contemporary Recording | Date | Length | Artist | Contemporary Recording |
| 10/14/1963 | 1 week | Art Farmer (t) Quartet featuring Jim Hall (g) | | 10/14/1963 | 1 week* | Lyman Strong (or) Trio with J. Morgan (g), and A. Jones (d) | "Cross Roads" (Cameo, 1963) |
| 10/21/1963 | 1 week | Johnny Lytle (vib) | *Got That Feeling!* (Riverside, 1963) | 10/21/1963 | 2 weeks | Jolly Jax | |
| 10/26/1963 | 1 week | Chico Hamilton (d) with Charles F. Lloyd (as), Albert Stinson (b), and Gabor Szabo (g) | *Chico Hamilton* (Warner Bros. Records, 1976) | | | | |
| 11/4/1963 | 2 weeks | Johnny Lytle (vib) | | 11/4/1963 | 1 week | Kenny Burrell (g), Will Davis (p), Martin Rivera (b), and Bill English (d) | *Soul Call* (Prestige, 1964 |
| 11/18/1963 | 2 weeks(?) | Red Garland (p), Philly Joe Jones (d), and Joe Johnson (b) | *Can't See for Lookin'* (Prestige, 1963) | 11/11/1963 | 1 week* | Buddy Montgomery (vib) | *A Date with Th Mastersounds* (Fantasy, 196 |
| 11/25/1963 | 1 week | Bennie Green (tb) with John Wright (ts), Roger Humphries (d), John Heard (b), Fred Tooks (p), and Chuck Austin (t) | *Glidin' Along* (Jazzland, 1961) | | | | |
| 12/2/1963 | 1 week | Ramsey Lewis (p) Trio | | | | | |
| 12/9/1963 | 1 week | Charles Bell (p) Trio | | | | | |
| 12/16/1963 | 1 week | Wynton Kelly (p) Trio | | 12/23/1963 | 2 weeks* | Eddie Chamblee (ts) with Dayton Selby (or) and Al Davis (d) | |
| 12/23/1963 | 2 weeks | Rufus "Speedy" Jones (d) with Woody Shaw (t), Jimmy Manuel (p), Louis Morrel (b), and Bud Terry (ts) | | | | | |
| | | | | 1/6/1964 | 1 week* | Winston Walls Organ Group | *Boss of the B* (Schoolkid Records, 199 |

| Crawford Grill No. 2 | | | | Hurricane Bar and Grill | | | |
|---|---|---|---|---|---|---|---|
| Date | Length | Artist | Contemporary Recording | Date | Length | Artist | Contemporary Recording |
| | | | | 1/27/1964 | 1 week | Gene Ludwig (or) | "The Vamp" (Travis, 1965) |
| | | | | 2/3/1964 | 1 week* | Sammy Bryant Quintet | |
| | | | | 1/17/1964 | 1 week* | Jimmy Thomas and his New Allegros | "Make Someone Happy" |
| 2/10/1964 | 1 week* | Wynton Kelly (p) Trio | The Best Of (Vee Jay Records, 1964) | | | | |
| | | | | 3/9/1964 | 1 week | Butch Cornell (or) | Willis Jackson, Smoking With Willis (Cadet, 1965) |
| | | | | 3/16/1964 | 1 week* | Red Prysock (s) | |
| | | | | 3/30/1964 | 2 weeks | Sarah Lawler (or) and Richard Otto (vn) Trio | |
| | | | | 4/13/1964 | 1 week | Eddie Chamblee (ts) with Dayton Selby (or) | The Rocking Tenor Sax of Eddie Chamblee (Prestige, 1964) |
| 20/1964 | 2 weeks | Johnny Lytle (vib) Trio | | 4/20/1964 | 1 week | Dan Brown and the Dynamics | |
| | | | | 4/27/1964 | 1 week* | Jolly Jax with Humph Jones (or) | |
| 4/1964 | 1 week* | Horace Silver (p) Quintet with Carmel Jones (tr), Joe Henderson (ts), Arthur Harper (b), and Roger Humphries (d) | Song for My Father (Blue Note, 1965) | 5/18/1964 | 1 week | The Detergents Organ Quartet | |
| | | | | 5/25/1964 | 1 week* | Jimmy McGriff (or) | |
| 6/1964 | 1 week | Al Grey (tb) with Billy Root (s) | | | | | |
| | | | | 8/3/1964 | 1 week | The Detergents featuring Little Anthony | |

| Crawford Grill No. 2 | | | | Hurricane Bar and Grill | | | |
|---|---|---|---|---|---|---|---|
| Date | Length | Artist | Contemporary Recording | Date | Length | Artist | Contemporary Recording |
| | | | | 8/10/1964 | 1 week* | Stanley Turrentine (ts) featuring Shirley Scott (or) | *Soul Shoutin'* (Prestige, 1964) |
| 9/7/1964 | 1 week* | Johnny Lytle (vib) Trio | | | | | |
| | | | | 11/2/1964 | 1 week | Joe Thomas Quintet with Bill Elliott | |
| | | | | 11/9/1964 | 1 week* | Sammy Bryant Quintet featuring Sonny Harris | |
| | | | | 11/16/1964 | 1 week | Henry Green Organ Trio with Sheri Green | |
| 11/23/1964 | 10 days | Max Roach (d) with Abbey Lincoln (v), Julian Priester (tb), Gary Bartz (as), Ronnie Matthews (p), and Bob Cunningham (b) | *It's Time* (Impulse, 1962) | 11/23/1964 | 1 week* | Sarah McLawler (or) and Richard Otto (vn) Trio | |
| | | | | 11/30/1964 | 1 week | Stan Hunter (or), Floyd Smith (g) Organ Quartet featuring Dotti Clark | *Trip on the Stri* (Prestige, 196 |
| 12/14/1964 | 2 weeks | Johnny Lytle (vib) Trio | *Workin' Out* (Prestige, 1965) | 12/14/1964 | 1 week | Stanley Turrentine (ts) featuring Shirley Scott (or) | *Hustlin'* (Blue Note, 1965) |
| | | | | 12/21/1964 | | Eugene Barr (s) Organ Quartet with Uncle Dave (or), and Darrell Eubanks | |
| | | | | 1/4/1965 | | Red Prysock (s) with Boo Pleasant and Buster Smith (d) | |
| 1/8/1965 | 10 days | Horace Silver (p) | | 1/11/1965 | 1 week* | Andy and the Bay Sisters Quintet | |
| 1/25/1965 | 1 week* | Rufus "Speedy" Jones (d) | *Five on Eight* (Cameo, 1964) | | | | |

| | Crawford Grill No. 2 | | | | Hurricane Bar and Grill | | |
|---|---|---|---|---|---|---|---|
| Date | Length | Artist | Contemporary Recording | Date | Length | Artist | Contemporary Recording |
| | | | | 2/1/1965 | 1 week* | Eddie Chamblee (ts) with Dayton Selby (or) | *The Rocking Tenor Sax of Eddie Chamblee* (Prestige, 1964) |
| | | | | 2/22/1965 | 1 week | Billy Wooten (vib) Quartet | |
| | | | | 3/1/1965 | 1 week* | Don Patterson (or) Organ Trio with Pat Martino (g) and Billy James (d) | *Four Dimensions* (Prestige, 1967) |
| | | | | 3/29/1965 | 1 week | Little Anthony Mitchell and the Modern Detergents | "Don't Make Me Blue" / "Monkey Hips And Rice" (Luau Records, 1965) |
| 4/5/1965 | 5 days | Chico Hamilton (d) Quartet | *A Different Journey* (Reprise Records, 1963) | 4/5/1965 | 1 week* | Adolphus Bell and the Upstarts featuring 'Bama the Bluesman | "Black Eye Peas" / "Lafin Gas" (Satin Records) |
| 4/26/1965 | 1 week* | The Jazz Crusaders | | 4/26/1965 | 2 weeks | "Big Joe" Burrell Organ Trio | |
| 5/14/1965 | 1 week* | Horace Silver (p) Quintet with Carmell Jones (t), Joe Henderson (ts), Teddy Smith (b), and Roger Humphries (d) | *Song for My Father* (Blue Note, 1965) | | | | |
| | | | | 7/19/1965 | 1 week | Larry Frazier (g) Organ Quartet | "After Six" / "Before Six" (Impulse, 1962) |
| 7/22/1965 | 1 week | Johnny Lytle (vib) Trio | *The Village Caller!* (Riverside, 1965) | 7/26/1965 | 1 week* | Charles Earland (or) Organ Quartet | *Boss Organ* (Choice, 1969) |
| 8/2/1965 | 1 week | Jackie McLean (as) Quintet | *It's Time* (Blue Note, 1965) | 8/2/1965 | 1 week | Eugene Barr (s) Organ Quartet with Humph Jones (or), and Darrell Eubanks (v) | |
| 8/9/1965 | 1 week* | The George Green Quintet | | 8/9/1965 | 1 week* | Jack McDuff (or) Quartet with George Benson (g), Joe Dukes (d), and Red Holloway (ts) | *Silk and Soul* (Prestige, 1965) |

| Crawford Grill No. 2 | | | | Hurricane Bar and Grill | | | |
|---|---|---|---|---|---|---|---|
| Date | Length | Artist | Contemporary Recording | Date | Length | Artist | Contemporary Recording |
| 10/11/1965 | 1 week* | The Three Sounds | | 12/13/1965 | 1 week | The Elegants | |
| 12/13/1965 | 10 days | Johnny Lytle (vib) Quintet | | 12/20/1965 | 1 week* | Gene Ludwig (or) Trio with Jerry Byrd (g) and Randell Gillespie (d) | |
| 12/31/1965 | NYE | Horace Silver (p) | *The Cape Verdean Blues* (Blue Note, 1966) | | | | |
| 1/10/1966 | 1 week | Horace Silver (p) | | | | | |
| 1/17/1966 | 1 week* | Rufus "Speedy" Jones (d) Quintet | | | | | |
| 2/14/1966 | 1 week* | Walter Bishop Jr. (p) Trio with Louis McIntosh and Lennie McBrown (d) | *Bish Bash* (Xanadu, 1975) | | | | |
| | | | | 2/21/1966 | 1 week | Sonny Stitt (ts) and the Don Patterson (or) Organ Trio | |
| | | | | 2/28/1966 | 1 week | Al Morrell (s) Organ Trio | |
| 3/10/1966 | 10 days | Three Sounds | | 3/7/1966 | 1 week | Chuck Edwards | |
| | | | | 3/14/1966 | 1 week | Jolly Jax | |
| 4/4/1966 | | Kenny Burrell (g) | *The Tender Gender* (Cadet, 1966) | | | | |
| | | | | 4/11/1966 | 1 week* | Jack McDuff (or) | |
| | | | | 5/9/1966 | 1 week | Al Morrell (s) Trio with James Blackmore (d) and Don Molier (or) | |
| 5/16/1966 | 1 week | EPS Trio with Steve Novosel (b), Gabe Rush (p), and Jimmy Hopps (d) | | 5/16/1966 | 2 weeks | Sonny Stitt (ts) and the Don Patterson (or) Organ Trio with Billy James (d) | |
| 6/30/1966 | 3 days | Roger Humphries (d) Quartet | | | | | |

| | Crawford Grill No. 2 | | | Hurricane Bar and Grill | | | |
|---|---|---|---|---|---|---|---|
| Date | Length | Artist | Contemporary Recording | Date | Length | Artist | Contemporary Recording |
| | | | | 6/27/1966 | 1 week* | George Benson (g) Quartet | |
| | | | | 7/4/1966 | 2 weeks | Grant Green (g) Trio with John Patton (or) | Am I Blue (Blue Note, 1964) |
| 7/4/1966 | 1 week | John Hendricks | | | | | |
| 7/11/1966 | 2 weeks | Dick Morgan (p) Trio with Margie Day (v), Elgin Vines (b), and Jimmy Barber (d) | Settlin' In (Riverside, 1961) | | | | |
| 7/25/1966 | 1 week* | Jazz Messengers | | | | | |
| 8/4/1966 | 1 week | Max Roach (d) with Abbey Lincoln (v) | | | | | |
| 8/29/1966 | 1 week* | Richard "Groove" Holmes (or) with Gene Edwards (g), and George Randall (d) | | 8/29/1966 | 2 weeks | Sonny Stitt (ts) and the Don Patterson (or) Organ Trio with Billy James (d) | |
| 10/17/1966 | 1 week* | Johnny Lytle (vib) | The Loop (Tuba Records, 1966) | | | | |
| | | | | 10/24/1966 | 1 week | Rufus Harley (s, bagpipes) Quartet | Scotch & Soul (Atlantic, 1966) |
| | | | | 10/31/1966 | 1 week* | Jimmy McGriff (or) with Thornel Schwartz (g) | |
| | | | | 12/19/1966 | 1 week | Sonny Stitt (ts) and Don Patterson (or) Organ Trio with Bill James (d) | |
| | | | | 12/26/1966 | 1 week* | Red Prysock (s) with Boo Pleasant and Bob Smith (d) | |
| | | | | 1/16/1967 | 1 week | The John Bartel Quartet with Larry O'Brien (g), Lou Stellute (ts), and Jeff Martin (d) | The Jon Bartel Thing (Capitol Records, 1969) |

| Crawford Grill No. 2 | | | | Hurricane Bar and Grill | | | |
|---|---|---|---|---|---|---|---|
| Date | Length | Artist | Contemporary Recording | Date | Length | Artist | Contemporary Recording |
| | | | | 1/23/1967 | 1 week | Clarence "Gatemouth" Brown (g) | "The Grass Is Always Greener / "It's Alright" (Cinderella Records, 1965) |
| 1/30/1967 | 1 week | Dick Morgan (p) Trio with Margie Day (v) | | 1/30/1967 | 1 week | The King Ericson Organ Quartet with Jimmy McClendon | |
| | | | | 2/6/1967 | 1 week | The Elegants Organ Quintet | |
| | | | | 2/13/1967 | 1 week* | Orlando Smith Organ Quartet | |
| 4/1/1967 | 1 week* | Kenny Burrell (g) | | 4/3/1967 | 1 week | Jimmy McGriff (or) Trio with Larry Frazier (g) and S. Jenkins (d) | |
| | | | | 4/10/1967 | 2 weeks | Sonny Stitt (ts) and Don Patterson (or) Organ Trio with Bill James (d) | |
| 4/17/1967 | 1 week* | Ray Bryant (p) Trio with Jimmy Rowser (b) and Al Drears (d) | Slow Freight (Cadet, 1967) | | | | |
| | | | | 4/24/1967 | | Jimmy Jaye Organ Trio | |
| 5/15/1967 | 1 week | Booker Ervin (ts) Quartet with Mike Knock (p), Scotty Holt (b), and Lennie McBrown (d) | Structurally Sound (Pacific Jazz, 1967) | 5/15/1967 | 1 week | Red Prysock (s) Organ Trio | |
| 5/22/1967 | 1 week | Wynton Kelly (p) with Jimmy Cobb (d) and Ralph Flemming (b) | | 5/22/1967 | 1 week | Gene Ludwig (or) featuring Jerry Byrd (g) | |
| | | | | 6/5/1967 | 2 weeks | John Bartel Organ Quartet with Lou Stellute (ts), Larry O'Brian (g), and Jeffrey Martin (d) | |

| | | Crawford Grill No. 2 | | | | Hurricane Bar and Grill | |
|---|---|---|---|---|---|---|---|
| Date | Length | Artist | Contemporary Recording | Date | Length | Artist | Contemporary Recording |
| 6/19/1967 | 1 week* | Hazel Scott (p) Trio with Bob Hamilton (b) and Herbie Brown (d) | *Viens Danser* (Polydor, 1958) | | | | |
| | | | | 7/3/1967 | | Wild Bill Jennings (g) | |
| | | | | 7/3/1967 (?) | 1 week | The Jacky Hairston (or) Trio with Lou Schreiber (s), Harry Hunt (g), and Allen Landor (v) | |
| | | | | 7/10/1967 | 1 week | Lady Byron Organ Trio with Evelyn Childress (or) | |
| | | | | 7/17/1967 | 1 week* | Bob Craig Organ Trio featuring Wilma Randolph | |
| /17/1967 | 10 days | Quartette Trés Bien | *Where It's At* (Decca, 1967) | 8/7/1967 | 3 weeks | Bob Craig Organ Trio featuring Lorraine Rudolph | |
| /31/1967 | 10 days | Max Roach (d) and Abbey Lincoln (v) | | 8/28/1967 | 1 week | Sonny Stitt (ts) with Don Patterson (or) and Billy James (d) | |
| | | | | 9/4/1967 | | Jackie Ivory (or) with Wild Bill Jennings (g) | *High Heel Sneakers* (ATCO, 1966) |
| 21/1967 | 10 days | Ray Bryant (p) | | 9/18/1967 | 1 week | John Bartel Organ Quartet | |
| | | | | 9/25/1967 | 1 week | George Benson (g) Organ Quartet featuring Lonnie Smith (or) | *The George Benson Cookbook* (Columbia, 1966) |
| /1/1967 | 1 week* | Dick Morgan (p) Trio with Margie Day (v) | *Settlin' In* (Riverside, 1961) | | | | |
| 16/1967 | 2 weeks | Richard "Groove" Holmes (or) | | | | | |

| Crawford Grill No. 2 | | | | Hurricane Bar and Grill | | | |
|---|---|---|---|---|---|---|---|
| Date | Length | Artist | Contemporary Recording | Date | Length | Artist | Contemporary Recording |
| 11/22/1967 | 10 days | Louis Hayes's (d) Jazz Communicators with Joe Henderson (ts), Freddie Hubbard (t), Herbie Lewis (b), and Kenny Barron (p) | *Ichi-Ban* (Timeless Records, 1976) | | | | |
| | | | | 1/1/1968 | | Jon Bartel (or) and the Soul Masters | |
| | | | | 2/5/1968 | | Bill Heid (or) Quartet | *Wylie Avenue* (Doodlin' Records, 2009) |
| 2/9/1968 | 1 week* | Horace Silver (p) | *The Jody Grind* (Blue Note, 1966) | 2/12/1968 | 1 week* | George Benson (g) Quartet | |
| 2/19/1968 | 1 week* | Rufus Harley (bagpipes, f, s) | *A Tribute to Courage* (Atlantic, 1968) | | | | |
| | | | | 3/4/1968 | | Sonny Stitt (ts) and Don Patterson (or) Trio with Billy James (d) | *Parallel-a-Stitt* (Roulette, 1968 |
| 3/11/1968 | 1 week* | Horace Silver (p) | "Psychedelic Sally" / "Serenade to a Soul Sister" (Blue Note, 1968) | | | | |
| 3/18/1968 | 1 week* | Al Grey (tb) Quartet with Eddie McFadden (g) | *Shades of Grey* (Tangerine, 1965) | | | | |
| 4/4/1968 | Martin Luther King Jr. assassinated | | | | | | |
| 6/10/1968 | 1 week* | Max Roach (d) and Abbey Lincoln (v) | *Sounds as a Roach* (Joker, 1977) | | | | |
| 7/4/1968 | 10 days | Freddie Hubbard (t) and his Jazz Communicators | *High Blues Pressure* (Atlantic, 1968) | | | | |
| | | | | 9/16/1968 | | Jimmy McGriff (or) | *I"ve Got a Ne Woman* (Sol State Record 1968) |

| Crawford Grill No. 2 | | | | Hurricane Bar and Grill | | | |
|---|---|---|---|---|---|---|---|
| Date | Length | Artist | Contemporary Recording | Date | Length | Artist | Contemporary Recording |
| | | | | 10/7/1968 | | Sonny Stitt (ts) and Don Patterson (or) Trio | *Brothers* (Prestige, 1968) |
| | | | | 11/11/1968 | | Gene Ludwig (or) Trio | *The Hot Organ* (Time Records, 1966) |
| | | | | 11/18/1968 | | Little Samson & Delilah Organ Quartet (Formerly Little Anthony) | *Keep Me In Mind* (ABC Records, 1967) |
| | | | | 12/30/1968 | 2 weeks* | Samson & Delilah featuring Anthony and his Organ Trio | "There's A D.J. In Your Town" / "Time To Prove My Love To You" (Indigo, 1969) |
| /24/1969 | 9 days | Horace Silver (p) | "You Gotta Take a Little Love" / "Down and Out" (Blue Note, 1969) | 3/24/1969 | | Cleve Nickerson Organ Quartet | "F' Days" / "He's Coming Back Again" (Savoy, 1964) |
| | | | | 3/31/1969 | | Samson and Delilah | "Will You be Ready? / "Woman" (Red Cap Records, 1967) |
| | | | | 4/15/1968 | 1 week* | Jimmy McGriff (or) | |
| | | | | 5/12/1969 | 1 week | Jack McDuff (or) with Jerry Byrd (g), Joe Dukes (d), and Billy Phipps (s) | *I Got a Woman* (Prestige, 1969) |
| | | | | 5/19/1969 | 1 week* | Billy Wooten (vib) Organ Group | *Lost Tapes* (P-Vine Records, 2007) |
| | | | | 6/2/1969 | 1 week* | George Benson (g) | *Tell It Like It Is* (CTI, 1969) |
| 12/1969 | 9 days | The Three Sounds | | 6/9/1969 | 1 week | Al Dowe Quintet featuring Bobby O'Brown (v) | |
| | | | | 6/16/1969 | 1 week* | Lou Donaldson (ts) | *Say It Loud!* (Blue Note, 1969) |
| 4/1969 | 10 days | The Blu-Tones | | | | | |
| | | | | 4/18/1970 | | Hurricane Fire and Closure | |

| Crawford Grill No. 2 | | | |
|---|---|---|---|
| 1/16/1970 | 1 week* | Johnny Lytle (vib) | *Close Enough for Jazz* (Solid State Records, 1969) |
| 1/23/1970 | 1 week* | Richard "Groove" Holmes (or) | *Soul Mist* (Prestige, 1970) |
| 3/1/1970 | | Horace (or, p, t) and Mary Turner (d) Trio | |
| 4/23/1970 | 10 days | Stanley Turrentine (ts) and Shirley Scott (org) | *Common Touch* (Blue Note, 1968) |
| 5/4/1970 | 2 weeks | George Benson (g, v) | *The Other Side of Abbey Road* (CTI, 1970) |
| 5/18/1970 | 1 week* | Gene Harris (p) and His Three Sounds | *The Three Sounds* (Blue Note, 1971) |
| 8/3/1970 | 1 week* | Roy Ayers (vib) | *Ubiquity* (Polydor, 1970) |
| 8/10/1970 | 1 week* | Houston Person (ts) | *Truth!* (Prestige, 1970) |
| 8/20/1970 | 9 days | Horace Silver (p) | *In Pursuit of the 27th Man* (Blue Note, 1973) |
| 2/11/1971 | 9 days | Alvin Clark and the Soul Messengers featuring Miss Gigi | |
| 4/12/1971 | 1 week* | Roy Ayers (vib) Quintet | *Live at the Montreux Jazz Festival* (Polydor, 1972) |
| 4/19/1971 | 1 week* | Ruby and the Romantics | "Hurting Each Other" / "Baby I Could Be So Good a Lovin' You" (A&M Records, 1969) |
| 10/4/1971 | 1 week* | Roland Davis | |
| 10/11/1971 | 10 days | Clarence Wheeler and the Enforcers | *The Love I've Been Looking For* (Atlantic, 1971) |
| 11/5/1971 | 9 days | Grady Tate (v, d) | *She is My Lady* (Janus Records, 1972) |
| 11/5/1971 | Sundays | Gene Ludwig (or) & Bill Easley (s) Combo | *The Hot Organ* (Mainstream Records, 1965) |
| 11/11/1971 | 10 days | Arthur Prysock (v) featuring Red Prysock (ts) | *Unforgettable* (King, 1971) |
| 11/22/1971 | 1 week* | Samson and Delilah | "Move Over" / "Right There When You Need It" (C Records, 1971) |
| 12/23/1971 | 1 week | The Third World Creation featuring Sparky and David | |
| 1/8/1972 | 1 week | Richard "Groove" Holmes (or) | *American Pie* (Groove Merchant, 1972) |
| 2/19/1972 | 2 days | Tim Stevens (v) and Frank Cunimondo (p) Trio | *Echoes* (Mondo Records, 1971) |
| 3/18/1972 | 1 week | Gloria Coleman (v) and her Quartet | *Soul Sisters* (Impulse, 1964) |
| 3/31/1972 | 1 week | Arthur Prysock (v) featuring Red Prysock (ts) | "In the Rain" / "Thank Heaven for You" (Old Tow Records, 1973) |
| 4/27/1972 | 9 days | Gene Ammons (ts) | *Free Again* (Prestige, 1972) |
| 10/21/1972 | 1 week | Jimmy McGriff (or) | *Fly Dude* (Groove Merchant, 1972) |
| 5/11/1972 | 9 days | Grant Green (g) Quintet | *Live at the Lighthouse* (Blue Note, 1972) |
| 8/12/1972 | 1 week* | Opus IV | |
| 11/9/1972 | 9 days | The Wildman Steve Revue | |
| 12/23/1972 | 1 week* | The Piece Septet | |

| | | Crawford Grill No. 2 | |
|---|---|---|---|
| 6/28/1973 | 9 days | Chocolate Syrup | *Stop Your Cryin'* (AVCO Embassy, 1971) |
| 9/1/1973 | 9 days | Johnny Lytle (vib) | *People & Love* (Milestone, 1973) |
| 10/14/1973 | 1 week | Roy Haynes (d) | *Senyah* (Mainstream Records, 1972) |
| 10/22/1973 | 1 week | Gene Harris (p) and the Three Sounds | *Gene Harris of the Three Sounds* (Blue Note, 1972) |
| 11/24/1973 | 1 week | Arthur Prysock (v) | |
| 12/1/1973 | 1 week | Isaac "Redd" Holt (d) Unlimited | *Isaac, Isaac, Isaac* (Paula Records, 1974) |
| 3/21/1974 | 3 days | Richard "Groove" Holmes (or) | *New Groove* (Groove Merchant, 1974) |
| 4/11/1974 | 9 days | The New Day | |
| 4/25/1974 | 9 days | Johnny Lytle (vib) Quintet | *Everything Must Change* (Muse, 1978) |
| 5/9/1974 | 9 days | Samson and Delilah Revue | *Living in a World of Trouble* (King James Records, 1974) |
| ./27/1974 | 9 days | Joe Johnson Trio featuring Betty Carolle (v) | |
| ./24/1974 | 9 days | The Bill Doggett Quintet | |
| ./10/1974 | 9 days | Nate Evans (v) Sextet featuring Mean Green | "This Time with Feeling" / "The Look on Your Face" (DPR, 1972) |
| ./24/1974 | 9 days | Ruth Brown (v) | *The Real Ruth Brown* (Cobblestone, 1972) |
| ./28/1974 | 1 week* | The Johnny Gilliam (v) Sextet | "Tell Your Friend (It's Over)" / "Peace on Earth" (Cancer Records, 1973) |
| ./23/1975 | 9 days | Eddie Jefferson (v) and the Roy Brooks (d) Sextet | *The Free Slave* (Muse, 1972), |
| ./13/1975 | 9 days | Louis Hayes (d) Quartet featuring Dom Minasi | *Breath of Life* (Muse, 1974) |
| ./1/1975 | 10 days | Wildman Steve Gallon (comedian) | *Eatin' Ain't Cheatin!!!* (Laff Records, 1973) |
| ./31/1975 | 9 days | Chuck Jackson (v) and His Swinging Big Band | *Needing You, Wanting You* (All Platinum, 1975) |
| ./8/1975 | 2 days | Tim Stevens (v) with Bob Head (p), Jimmy Saunders (b), and Roger Humphries (d) | "Listen to Your Woman" / "And Now" (Stebro Records, 1973) |
| ./16/1975 | 10 days | Charles Earland (or), Abe Kamur Speller (d), Maynard Parker (g), Billy Colburn (b), Arthur Grant (s, f, v), and Jose Cheo (perc) | *Black Talk!* (Prestige, 1970) |
| ./28/1975 | 1 week | Don Patterson (or), Rusty Bryant (s), and Billy James (d) | *These Are Soulful Days* (Muse, 1974), *Movin' Up* (Muse, 1977) |
| ./18/1975 | 2 weeks | Houston Person (ts) and Etta Jones (v) | *Get Out'a My Way!* (Westbound Records, 1975) |
| ./1/1975 | 1 week* | Sheba Experience featuring Nelson Harrison (tb) and Joe Harris (d) | "At the Generation Gap" (Nelson Harrison and Elizabeth Davis) |
| ./8/1975 | 2 days | Tim Stevens (v) with Bob Head (p), Jimmy Saunders (b), and Roger Humphries (d) | |
| ./4/1976 | 5 days | Lonnie Smith (or) | *Afrodesia* (1975) |

| | | Crawford Grill No. 2 | |
|---|---|---|---|
| 5/21/1976 | 9 days | Tyrone Mitchell Sextet | |
| 6/3/1976 | 9 days | Sonny Stitt (ts) and Tim Stevens (v) | *My Buddy: Sonny Stitt Plays for Gene Ammons* (Muse, 1976) |
| 11/5/1976 | 2 weeks | Dayton Selby (or) | *Love Is the Key* (Emma Records, 1971) |
| 12/1/1976 | Matinees | Wendell Byrd (or) | |
| 12/13/1976 | 1 week | Irene Reid (v) | *Two of Us* (Glades, 1976) |
| 12/20/1976 | 10 days | Lonnie Youngblood (s) | *Sweet Sweet Tootie* (Turbo Records, 1973) |
| 1/19/1977 | 4 days | Samson and Delilah | "Got to Get Myself Together" / "Honey" (Match, 1977) |
| 5/21/1977 | 4 days | Samson and Delilah | |
| 6/9/1977 | 9 days | The Joneses | *Keepin' Up with the Joneses* (Mercury, 1974) |
| 7/8/1977 | 9 days* | Philly Joe Jones and his Grand Prix '77 Sextet | *Mean What You Say* (Sonet, 1977) |
| 5/27/1978 | | | *Bitches Brew* Theater Production |
| 3/1/1979 | 2 months | Kenny Clarke (d) Sounds of Togetherness with Pamela Johnson (v), James Johnson II (p), Jonathan Callis (t), Hideo Shimada (b), and Kenny Fisher (as) | *Kenny "To Day"* (Night and Day, 1980) |
| 5/18/1979 | 2 days | Slide Hampton (tb) and his World of Trombones | *World of Trombones* (West 54, 1979) |
| 11/16/1979 | 3 days | Lenwood Sloan's Three Black and Three White Refined Jubilee of Minstrels | "A Musical Tribute to Bert Williams" |
| 2/4/1982 | 3 days | Johnny Lytle (vib) with Joe Dukes (d), Dave Braham (or), and Mubutu (congas) | *Fast Hands* (Muse, 1980) |
| 4/30/1982 | 1 month (Fri./Sat.) | Tim Stevens and the High Energy Band | *Got to Be Free* (Pittsburgh International Records, 1981) |
| 7/29/1982 | 9 days | Johnny Lytle (vib) with John Mosley (t), Kenny Fisher (s), Roger Humphries (d), Leon Dorsey (b), and Mubutu (congas) | *Good Vibes* (Muse, 1982) |
| 8/9/1982 | 6 days | Leon Thomas (v) and Full Circle | *A Piece of Cake* (Palcoscenico Records, 1980) |
| 8/16/1982 | 6 days | Bobby Watson's (s) Great Reeds and Friends | *All Because of You* (Roulette, 1979) |
| 8/28/1982 | 6 days | Mickey Bass (b) featuring Carter Jefferson (ts), Steve Nelson (vib), and Mark Johnson (d) | *Sentimental Mood* (Chiaroscuro, 1982) |
| 6/18/1987 | 1 day | Lawrence Lucie (g) and the Carl Arter (p) Trio | *It Was Good . . . It Is Good* (Toy Records, 1982) |
| 3/30/1988 | 1 day | Mickey Bass (b) Quartet | *The Co-operation* (Early Bird, 1991) |
| 5/6/1988 | 2 days | Eric Johnson (g) | |
| 9/22/1988 | 3 days | Richard "Groove" Holmes (or) | *African Encounter* (Roots Record Company, 1988) |
| 6/19/1997 | 1 day | Harold Betters (tb) and George Green | |
| 6/20/1997 | 1 day | Mike Taylor (b) and the Territory Band | |

| Crawford Grill No. 2 | | | |
|---|---|---|---|
| 6/14/1999 | 1 day | Rodney McCoy (v) and Deep Pockets | *Deepockets* (RM Productions, 2006) |
| 6/15/1999 | 1 day | Gene Ludwig (or) Trio | |
| 6/16/1999 | 1 day | Flow Band | |
| 5/16/2000 | 1 day | Chuck Corby and Quiet Storm | |
| 5/17/2000 | 1 day | Suzy Sirnic and Tailor Made | |
| 4/22/2002 | 2 days | Sean Jones (t) Quintet featuring Tia Fuller (as) | |
| 0/31/2003 | 1 day | Roger Barbour Quartet, The Real Deal Band | |
| 11/1/2003 | 1 day | Tony Campbell Jazz Session, Colter Harper & Carolyn Perteete | |
| 7/24/2003 | 1 day | Crawford Grill Jazz Festival (outdoors): Max Kahen and Dave Pellow (b); Balance Band with Teresa Hawthorne; Don Aliquo Quartet; and Straight Ahead | |
| 7/25/2003 | 1 day | Crawford Grill Jazz Festival (outdoors): Roger Barbour Quartet; Gerald Hayman Quartet; Roger Humphries Big Band; and Sean Jones Quartet | |
| 7/26/2003 | 1 day | Crawford Grill Jazz Festival (outdoors): Hubb's Groove featuring Fred Pugh; Tony Campbell Quartet; Serious Inquiry; and Gerald Veasley | |

# NOTES

## Preface

1. Jazz at the Hill House took place in the Hill House Association's Kaufmann Auditorium. The Hill House was established as a nonprofit community organization in 1964 and primarily served the Hill District's African American population. The Auditorium was named after the Irene Kaufmann Settlement House, which had provided services to Jewish migrants in the first half of the twentieth century. Jazz at the Hill House began as a gathering of musicians in the Hill District home of music patron Frank "Geronimo" Battle. As interest grew, Battle and fellow Hill District natives Bill Blakey (cousin of the famed Pittsburgh drummer Art Blakey), former record store owner Travis Klein, and musicians Horace and Mary Turner approached the Hill House for support in organizing the event in a public venue that could accommodate a larger audience. James F. Henry was executive director of the Hill House Association during the time when Jazz at the Hill House was in operation.

2. Horace Turner attended Fifth Avenue High School and the Pittsburgh Musical Institute, where he earned a certificate in teaching and arranging. While his main instrument was trumpet, Turner developed the technique of simultaneously accompanying himself on the piano. Later, he learned to play guitar and the Hammond organ and led a band with his wife Mary Turner, who played drum kit ("Pittsburgh Musician is Regular One-Man Band," *New Pittsburgh Courier*, April 18, 1970, 13).

3. For a discussion of Black placemaking, see Marcus Anthony Hunter et al., "Black Placemaking: Celebration, Play, and Poetry," *Theory, Culture & Society* 33, no. 7–8 (December 1, 2016): 34, https://doi.org/10.1177/0263276416635259.

4. Stephen Kinzer, "Black Life, in Black and White; Court Ruling Frees the Legacy of a Tireless News Photographer," *New York Times*, February 7, 2001, Arts, https://www.nytimes.com/2001/02/07/arts/black-life-black-white-court-ruling-frees-legacy-tireless-photographer.html.

5. The Charles "Teenie" Harris Archive contains over seventy thousand photos, of which roughly sixty thousand have been digitized and made available through an online search engine. The image titles were generated by Carnegie Museum of Art archivists, who interviewed community members to identify people, places, and events. As a result, the titles are descriptive and also reflect the extensive and ongoing process of adding context to the mostly unlabeled negatives. Thirty-four of those have been included here and focus on jazz musicians and the clubs where they performed. "Charles 'Teenie' Harris Archive," Carnegie Museum of Art, accessed January 2022, https://cmoa.org/art/teenie-harris-archive/.

## Introduction

1. Chester L. Washington's weekly column "Up and Down the Avenue" first ran on December 31, 1938, and continued into the early 1940s.

2. Originally, the Herron Avenue Presbyterian Church, the building at 594 Herron Avenue, was purchased by the John Wesley African Methodist Episcopal Zion Church (AME Zion) in 1945. The Hill's first AME Zion Church, established in 1836, was home to one of the city's oldest African American congregations. It was AME church leaders who protested and subverted the Fugitive Slave Law, passed in 1850, and more than a hundred years later, hosted the NAACP's 1957 Fight for Freedom fundraiser featuring baseball player Jackie Robinson as speaker. See Richard J. M. Blackett, "'. . . Freedom, or the Martyr's Grave': Black Pittsburgh's Aid to the Fugitive Slave," *Western Pennsylvania History: 1918–2018*, 1978, 125.

3. *Wylie Avenue Days: Pittsburgh's Hill District* (Pittsburgh: QED Communications, Inc., 1991), film.

4. See Mumford (1997, xii): "In 1890 in Chicago only 14,000 of the city's more than 1 million residents were black; by 1930 nearly 240,000 black people lived in Chicago. Between 1910 and 1920 the black population of New York increased by 66 percent, and from 1920 to 1930 it expanded by 115 percent, from roughly 153,000 to more than 327,000 black residents." African American populations in Chicago in 1930 were 230,000 of a total population of 3,376,000. In New York City, the African American population was 327,000 of a total of 6,930,000 in 1930.

5. Peter Gottlieb, *Making Their Own Way: Southern Blacks' Migration to Pittsburgh, 1916–30* (Champaign: University of Illinois Press, 1996), 67.

6. Gabriel Winant, *The Next Shift: The Fall of Industry and the Rise of Health Care in Rust Belt America* (Cambridge, MA: Harvard University Press, 2021), 29.

7. Constance A. Cunningham, "Homer S. Brown: First Black Political Leader in Pittsburgh," *Journal of Negro History* 66, no. 4 (December 1, 1981): 314. From 1910 to 1930, Pittsburgh's Black population grew from 25,623 to 54,983, an increase from five to 9.2 percent of the city's total population. By 1930, 47.9 percent of the city's Black inhabitants lived in the Hill, while smaller African American communities continued to develop in East Liberty, Homewood-Brushton, and the Strip District.

8. Isabel Wilkerson, *The Warmth of Other Suns: The Epic Story of America's Great Migration* (New York: Random House, 2010), 270–71.

9. Laurence A. Glasco, ed., *The WPA History of the Negro in Pittsburgh* (Pittsburgh: University of Pittsburgh Press, 2004), 22. These population numbers are according to the according to the 1930 US Census. Also see https://explorepahistory.com/odocument.php?docId=1-4-125 for listings of Black population changes in Western PA between 1910 and 1930.

10. Glasco, *WPA History*, 25.

11. Chester L. Washington, "Deep Wylie," *Pittsburgh Courier*, July 20, 1929, 8.

12. Edward Murray East, *Mankind at the Crossroads* (Manhattan: Arno Press, 1924), 111.

13. Hazel Garland, "Pioneer Broadcaster Mary 'Dee' Leaves a Legacy," *Pittsburgh Courier*, April 4, 1964, 9.

14. John L. Clark, "Wylie Avenue," *Pittsburgh Courier*, December 24, 1955, 17.

15. This map uses the 1929 street grid depicted in Alexander Zerful Pittler's "The Hill District of Pittsburgh: A Study of Succession" (PhD thesis, University of Pittsburgh, 1930).

16. John L. Clark, "Wylie Avenue," *Pittsburgh Courier*, March 27, 1954, 16.

17. Bryan D. Palmer, *Cultures of Darkness: Night Travels in the Histories of Transgression* (New York: Monthly Review Press, 2000), 17–18.

18. Robin Kelley, *Race Rebels: Culture, Politics, and the Black Working Class* (New York: Simon & Schuster, 1994), 44.

19. Chester L. Washington, "Deep Wylie," *Pittsburgh Courier*, February 9, 1929, 7.

20. Len Barcousky, "Eyewitness 1943: Finding 'Pittsburghesque' in Wartime England," *Pittsburgh Post-Gazette*, March 11, 2018, https://www.post-gazette.com/news/portfolio/2018/03/11/Eyewitness-1943-Finding-Pittsburghesque-in-wartime-England/stories/201803110033. Charles Danver's "Pittsburghesque" first ran in the *Pittsburgh Post* in 1925 and continued in the *Pittsburgh Post-Gazette* from 1927 to 1964.

21. Charles Danver, "Pittsburghesque," *Pittsburgh Post-Gazette*, October 2, 1929, 10.

22. Danver, "Pittsburghesque," 10.

23. Charles Danver, "Pittsburghesque," *Pittsburgh Post-Gazette*, October 4, 1933, 10.

24. Washington, "Deep Wylie," February 9, 1929, 7.

25. John L. Clark, "Wylie Avenue," *Pittsburgh Courier*, October 27, 1923, 4.

26. Clark, "Wylie Avenue," 4.

27. Cecil Brooks II, interviewed by the author, November 19, 2008.

28. There is precedence in anthropology and sociology for employing photos in interviews as part of ethnographic research. John Collier, a photographer and researcher who worked for Cornell University in the mid-1950s, was instrumental in the development of photo-driven studies. In his paper "Photography in Anthropology: A Report on Two Experiments" (1957) and book *Visual Anthropology: Photography as a Research Method* (1967/1987), Collier formed a qualitative research methodology that moved beyond photos as purely illustrative material, employing them to shape the data gathered. The method of photo-centered interviews or "photo elicitation" was first outlined by cultural anthropologists and father and son team John and Malcolm Collier in their 1967 book *Visual Anthropology*. In this study, they argue that photo elicitation, as opposed to questionnaire-driven interviewing, aids in "decentering the authority of the author" and enriches the experience of the interviewee. More recent studies have brought the term "photo elicitation" into use to describe Collier's approach. Research published in journals such as *Visual Anthropology*, *Visual Studies* (originally *Visual Sociology*), and many other qualitative social science outlets has developed photo elicitation and other collaborative visual methods as a main component of visual methods. The specific use of historical photographs to elicit cultural memory was used by Douglas Harper in *Changing Works: Visions of a Lost Agriculture* (Chicago: University of Chicago Press, 2001), a study of agricultural history in upstate New York.

29. Ralph Lemuel Hill, "A View of the Hill—A Study of Experiences and Attitudes in the Hill District of Pittsburgh, Pennsylvania from 1900 to 1973" (PhD diss., University of Pittsburgh, 1973), 131.

30. Cheryl Finley, Laurence Admiral Glasco, and Joe William Trotter, *Teenie Harris, Photographer: Image, Memory, History* (Pittsburgh: University of Pittsburgh Press, 2011), xi.

31. Patricia Parker-Reid, interview by the author, September 6, 2007.

32. Nicole R. Fleetwood, *Troubling Vision: Performance, Visuality, and Blackness* (Chicago: University of Chicago Press, 2011), 64.

33. Eddie S. Meadows, *Jazz Research and Performance Materials: A Select Annotated Bibliography* (New York and London: Garland Publishing, Inc., 1995), 298. Martin Williams, *Jazz Masters of New Orleans* (New York: Macmillan Company, 1967); William Howland Kenney, *Chicago Jazz: A Cultural History, 1904–1930* (Oxford: Oxford University Press, 1993); Ross Russell, *Jazz Style in Kansas City and the Southwest* (Berkeley: University of California Press, 1971); Samuel B. Charters and Leonard Kunstadt, *Jazz: A History of the New York Scene* (New

York: Doubleday, 1962); Robert Gordon, *Jazz West Coast: The Los Angeles Jazz Scene of the 1950s* (London: Quartet Books Ltd., 1986).

34. Lars Bjorn, *Before Motown: A History of Jazz in Detroit, 1920–60* (Ann Arbor: University of Michigan Press, 2001); Clora Bryant et al., *Central Avenue Sounds: Jazz in Los Angeles*, New Ed edition, (Berkeley: University of California Press, 1999); Samuel Charters, *A Trumpet Around the Corner: The Story of New Orleans Jazz* (Jackson: University Press of Mississippi, 2008); Kurt Dietrich, *Wisconsin Riffs: Jazz Profiles from the Heartland* (Madison: Wisconsin Historical Society, 2018); Frank Driggs and Chuck Haddix, *Kansas City Jazz: From Ragtime to Bebop—A History* (Oxford: Oxford University Press, 2006); Benjamin Franklin, *An Encyclopedia of South Carolina Jazz & Blues Musicians* (Columbia: University of South Carolina Press, 2016); Jay Goetting, *Joined at the Hip: A History of Jazz in the Twin Cities* (St. Paul: Minnesota Historical Society Press, 2011); Sean J. O'Connell, *Los Angeles's Central Avenue Jazz* (Charleston, South Carolina: Arcadia Publishing, 2014); Elizabeth Pepin, *Harlem of the West: The San Francisco Fillmore Jazz Era* (San Francisco: Chronicle Books, 2006); Blair A. Ruble and Maurice Jackson, *DC Jazz Stories of Jazz Music in Washington, DC* (Washington, DC: Georgetown University Press, 2018); Mark Stryker, *Jazz from Detroit* (Ann Arbor: University of Michigan Press, 2019); Richard Vacca, *The Boston Jazz Chronicles: Faces, Places, and Nightlife, 1937–1962* (Belmont: Troy Street Publishing, 2012); Candice Watkins and Arnett Howard, *Ohio Jazz: A History of Jazz in the Buckeye State* (Charleston: The History Press, 2012); Christopher Wilkinson, *Big Band Jazz in Black West Virginia, 1930–1942* (Jackson: University Press of Mississippi, 2012); David Leander Williams, *Indianapolis Jazz: The Masters, Legends and Legacy of Indiana Avenue*, (Mount Pleasant, SC: Arcadia Publishing, 2014).

35. Several notable exceptions are William Howland Kenney's *Jazz on the River* (Chicago: University of Chicago Press, 2005), which examines Pittsburgh's place on the interwar riverboat jazz scene that filtered up the Mississippi from New Orleans, and the general interest publication *Smoketown: The Untold Story of the Other Great Black Renaissance* (Simon & Schuster, 2018) by journalist Mark Whitaker, which details the wide-reaching cultural and political impact of Pittsburgh's African American business, entertainment, sports, and media innovators.

36. Phyl Garland, "Musician Walt Harper Dubbed 'Prom King,' Musician Beats Odds to Make it in Hometown," *Pittsburgh Courier*, March 21, 1964, 13.

37. Linda Dahl, *Morning Glory: A Biography of Mary Lou Williams* (Berkeley and Los Angeles: University of California Press, 2001); Stanley Dance, *World of Earl Hines* (Lebanon, IN: De Capo Press, 1983); James M. Doran, *Erroll Garner: The Most Happy Piano* (New Jersey: Scarecrow Press and the Institute of Jazz Studies, 1985); David Hadju, *Lush Life: A Biography of Billy Strayhorn* (New York: North Point Press, 1996); Mike Hennessey, *Klook: The Story of Kenny Clarke* (London: Quartet Books Ltd.,1990); John Chilton, *Roy Eldridge: Little Jazz Giant* (New York: Bloomsbury Academic, 2002); Leslie Gourse, *Art Blakey: Jazz Messenger* (London: Omnibus Press & Schirmer Trade Books, 2002).

38. Dahl, *Morning Glory*, 37.

39. David Hajdu, *Lush Life: A Biography of Billy Strayhorn* (New York: North Point Press, 1996), 65.

40. Stanley Dance, *The World of Earl Hines* (New York: Da Capo Press, 1985), 31.

## Chapter 1: Racial and Sexual Politics of Black and Tan Nightlife

1. "Blame Late Hours for Nite Club Raid," *Pittsburgh Courier*, September 1, 1934, 6. *Pittsburgh Press* (August 28, 1934) and *Pittsburgh Post-Gazette* (August 29, 1934) also reported the same details of the raid.

2. "Nite Club Raid," 6.

3. William G. Nunn, "Favorite 'Hot Spot' of Celebs of Stage and Screen So-o-o Naughty It's Closed Forever," *Pittsburgh Courier*, March 30, 1935, 1.

4. "Down Our Way," *Pittsburgh Courier*, October 13, 1934, 5.

5. "Derby Dad's 'Harlem Jungle Club' Is Hot Spot for Nite-Lifers," *Pittsburgh Courier*, October 20, 1934, 19.

6. "Derby Dad's 'Harlem Jungle Club,'" 19.

7. Nunn, "Favorite 'Hot Spot,'" 1.

8. "License Lost by 'Hot Spot,'" *Pittsburgh Sun-Telegraph*, December 31, 1935, 4.

9. Nunn, "Favorite 'Hot Spot,'" 4.

10. Richard L. Hume and Jerry B. Gough, *Blacks, Carpetbaggers, and Scalawags: The Constitutional Conventions of Radical Reconstruction* (Baton Rouge: Louisiana State University Press, 2008), 1.

11. Millington W. Bergeson-Lockwood, *Race over Party: Black Politics and Partisanship in Late Nineteenth-Century Boston* (Chapel Hill: University of North Carolina Press, 2018), 12.

12. E. H. Henry, "Jackson Lore," *Clarion-Ledger*, October 22, 1911, 73.

13. Fanny Dolansky, "Celebrating the Saturnalia: Religious Ritual and Roman Domestic Life," in *A Companion to Families in the Greek and Roman Worlds* (John Wiley & Sons, Ltd., 2010), 488–503, https://doi.org/10.1002/9781444390766.ch29.

14. Black and tan factions of the Republican party began in the post-Reconstruction Era and continued to provide a basis for Black political representation until the 1960s. Historian Joshua Farrington noted that Democrats used the term to describe integrated southern Republican parties that "supported the northeastern wing of the party as delegates to national conventions, and in return, were rewarded with financial assistance and political appointments." Joshua D. Farrington, *Black Republicans and the Transformation of the GOP* (Philadelphia: University of Pennsylvania Press, 2016), 12.

15. Ralph E. Luker, *The Social Gospel in Black and White: American Radical Reform, 1885–1912 (Studies in Religion)* (Chapel Hill: The University of North Carolina Press, 1991), 259.

16. "A Matter of Taste," *New York Times*, May 3, 1908, 10.

17. "A Matter," *New York Times*, 10.

18. "The 'Black and Tan' Closed," *New York Times*, July 28, 1885, 2.

19. "'Black and Tan' Closed," 2. Early examples of reporting on black and tan saloons illustrate how interracial socializing was policed using wide-reaching legal powers such as common law restrictions on "disorderly houses," defined as places where "people promiscuously resort for purposes injurious to the public morals, or health, or convenience, or safety." Salon D. Wilson, "Disorderly Houses," *Criminal Law Magazine and Reporter* 10, no. 4 (1888): 514.

20. Dedicated to maintaining journalistic standards and using the *Courier* to fight racial discrimination in Pittsburgh and throughout the US, Vann instructed his staff to strike a balance between high-minded and salacious content: "I do not mean that we should by any means surrender our high standards and ideals by making the paper entirely yellow, but that more, or rather some, yellow matter should be printed each week." Patrick S. Washburn, *The African American Newspaper: Voice of Freedom* (Evanston: Northwestern University Press, 2006), 131–32.

21. "Police War on 'Immoral' Circuses, 'Hot Shows,'" *Pittsburgh Courier*, September 22, 1923, 1.

22. "Police War," 1.

23. When asked to explain the title of "Black and Tan Fantasy," Ellington mentioned that "black and tan" referred to nightclubs "where people of all races and colors mixed together for the purpose of fulfilling their social aspirations," a definition that implies a social space comprised of overlapping ambitions. Krin Gabbard, *Jammin' at the Margins: Jazz and the American Cinema* (Chicago: University of Chicago Press, 1996), 64. Cab Calloway, who replaced Ellington at the Harlem Cotton Club in 1931, offers a far terser definition of black and tan in his 1938 *Hepster's Dictionary*: "(n.): dark and light colored folks. Not colored and white folks as erroneously assumed." Andrew Clark, *Riffs & Choruses: A New Jazz Anthology* (London and New York: Continuum International Publishing Group, 2001), 351. Unlike Ellington's cryptic and open-ended description, Calloway's definition sets clear boundaries and limits on the social and economic function of the black and tan by occluding White patrons. His insistence on correcting perceived misperceptions was likely an attempt to de-emphasize inferences of racial harmony and to underscore the central role colorism played in marketing the performances to White Cotton Club patrons. As scantily dressed chorus girls, Black women with light complexions were the visual center of performances of exotic Blackness, serving White male desires and fantasies.

24. Kevin J. Mumford, *Interzones: Black/White Sex Districts in Chicago and New York in the Early Twentieth Century* (New York: Columbia University Press, 1997), 46.

25. "Black and Tan Editorial in Local Daily Misleading and Uncalled for," *Chicago Defender*, August 14, 1920, 12.

26. Chandler Owen, "The Cabaret—A Useful Social Institution," *The Messenger* 4 (1922): 461.

27. Sondra K. Wilson et al., *The Messenger Reader: Stories, Poetry, and Essays from the Messenger Magazine* (New York: Modern Library, 2000), 295.

28. Floyd G. Snelson, "Snelson Reviews 'Black and Tan' Craze in Metropolitan Centers as it Existed Twenty Years Ago," *Pittsburgh Courier*, March 5, 1932, A1.

29. Caroline Randall Williams, "You Want a Confederate Monument? My Body Is a Confederate Monument," *New York Times*, June 26, 2020, Opinion, https://www.nytimes.com/2020/06/26/opinion/confederate-monuments-racism.html.

30. Chad Heap, *Slumming: Sexual and Racial Encounters in American Nightlife, 1885–1940* (Chicago: University of Chicago Press, 2009), 209.

31. Heap, *Slumming*, 209.

32. Saidiya Hartman, *Wayward Lives, Beautiful Experiments: Intimate Histories of Riotous Black Girls, Troublesome Women, and Queer Radicals* (New York: W. W. Norton & Company, 2019), 219.

33. Hartman, *Wayward Lives*, 224.

## Chapter 2: Claiming a Place for Jazz: The Collins and Paramount Inns

1. Newspaper records show that the Little Paris (a basement venue located at the corner of Wylie and Fullerton Avenues) was opened in 1924 and closed in 1927 following a police raid, the Rathskeller (located at 1225 Wylie, on the ground floor of the Elite Hotel) was opened in 1924, and Frank Sutton's hotel (located at 518–20 Wylie Avenue) was opened in 1903 and closed in 1931 due to the economic downturn.

2. Ira De A. Reid, "Social Conditions of the Negro in the Hill District of Pittsburgh," 1930, 21, https://digital.library.pitt.edu/islandora/object/pitt%3A00afh9656m/viewer#page/20/

mode/2up. From 1900 to 1920, the Hill District's African American population grew from 260 to over 16,000, while the city's total African American population increased from 20,355 to 29,283. Pittsburgh's total population increased from 451,512 to 588,343 during the same time period.

3. John L. Clark, "Wylie Avenue," *Pittsburgh Courier*, July 14, 1951, 19.

4. "All Races, Creeds Mourn Death of 'Jimmy' Bates," *Pittsburgh Courier*, April 25, 1959, 2. Bates died in 1914, after which his younger brother Jimmy Bates took over his role as a political organizer and "committeeman" in the Hill District—a position he would have for thirty-eight years.

5. "Six Fifteenth Ward Lots Bring $15,000," *Pittsburgh Press*, April 24, 1911, 7. "Legal Notices," *Pittsburgh Gazette Times*, September 4, 1911, 10. *Pittsburgh Gazette Times*, September 16, 1911, 10. 1214 Wylie Avenue was located across the street from 1213 Wylie Avenue.

6. "Retail Liquor License Applications," *Pittsburgh Gazette Times*, February 16, 1918, 12.

7. "Wylie Avenue Building Sold," *Pittsburgh Gazette Times*, September 9, 1921, 9. "Retail License Applications," *Pittsburgh Press*, February 26, 1921, 11.

8. John L. Clark, "Black and Tan King of Prohibition Era Dies," *Pittsburgh Courier*, June 10, 1950, 1.

9. "Collins Tigers Known as 'Roughnecks,'" *Pittsburgh Courier*, February 24, 1962, 46.

10. Stanley Dance, *The World of Earl Hines* (New York: Da Capo Press, 1983), 132.

11. Dance, *The World of Earl Hines*, 29.

12. Abraham Epstein, *The Negro Migrant in Pittsburgh* (New York: Arno Press, 1918), 13, 23.

13. "A Brief Look at Pittsburg [*sic*] Cabaret Circuit Suggested," *Afro-American*, August 5, 1921, 8.

14. Earl Hines credits pianist Jim Fellman for improving his left-hand technique and teaching accompaniment patterns using the interval of the tenth. For further analysis, see Jeffrey Taylor, "Earl Hines's Piano Style in the 1920s: A Historical and Analytical Perspective," *Black Music Research Journal* 12/1 (1992), 57–77. John L. Clark wrote that Vivian Greenlee was the first African American woman to be featured on the radio in Pittsburgh (WJAS) and to perform in a black and tan club (the Collins Inn) (*Pittsburgh Courier*, January 18, 1941, 14). Russel Johnson's instrument is unlisted.

15. "A Brief Look at Pittsburg, Cabaret Circuit Suggested," *Afro-American*, August 5, 1921, 8.

16. "A Brief Look," 8.

17. "At Pittsburg—Cabaret Circuit Suggested," *Billboard*, August 13, 1921, 41.

18. Cary D. Wintz and Paul Finkelman, *Encyclopedia of the Harlem Renaissance: A–J* (London: Taylor & Francis, 2004), 435.

19. "Gilpin Banqueted Again," *Billboard*, November 12, 1921, 65.

20. John L. Clark, "Wylie Avenue," *Pittsburgh Courier*, March 8, 1924, 9.

21. Robert Gottlieb, *Reading Jazz: A Gathering of Autobiography, Reportage, and Criticism from 1919 to Now* (New York: Knopf Doubleday Publishing Group, 2014), 416.

22. Chester L. Washington, "Deep Wylie," *Pittsburgh Courier*, April 13, 1929, 9. In this column, Washington spells Charles Johnson's nickname as "Toadlow" rather than "Toadlo," as it is spelled in Hines's interview. In *The World of Earl Hines* (1983), Stanley Dance notes that arranger and bandleader Don Redman referred to the pianist as "Toodle-oo" Johnson (16).

23. Chester L. Washington, "Up and Down the Avenue," *Pittsburgh Courier*, January 14, 1939, 2.

24. Dance, *The World of Earl Hines*, 132.

25. Dance, 15.

26. Dance, 132.

27. Dance, 132.

28. Dance, 133.

29. "Latest Picture of 'Pittsburgh's Pride,'" *Pittsburgh Courier*, July 21, 1923, 1.

30. Linda Dahl, *Morning Glory: A Biography of Mary Lou Williams* (Berkeley: University of California Press, 1999), 33–34.

31. "Leader House Opens Upstairs Dining Room," *Pittsburgh Courier*, March 29, 1924, 5.

32. "Bill Page's Syncopators Coming Here," *Pittsburgh Courier*, October 4, 1924, 9.

33. Dennis C. Dickerson, *Out of the Crucible: Black Steel Workers in Western Pennsylvania, 1875–1980* (Albany: SUNY Press, 1986), 28.

34. Lynne Conner, *Pittsburgh in Stages: Two Hundred Years of Theater* (Pittsburgh: University of Pittsburgh Press, 2007), 89.

35. Conner, *Pittsburgh in Stages*, 89.

36. Conner, 71.

37. Conner, 96.

38. "Leader House," *Pittsburgh Courier*, March 29, 1924.

39. Geraldyn Dismond, "Rapid Rise of the Cabaret Seen as Social Marvel," *Pittsburgh Courier*, October 29, 1927, 14.

40. "Leader House Very Capably Managed," *Pittsburgh Courier*, July 28, 1923, 12.

41. "Musical Revue at the Leader House," *Pittsburgh Courier*, June 6, 1924, 10.

42. "Leader House," *Pittsburgh Courier*, March 29, 1924.

43. "Leader House," *Pittsburgh Courier*, September 8, 1923.

44. "Leader House Opens Upstairs Dining Room," *Pittsburgh Courier*, March 29, 1924, 5.

45. "Leader House," *Pittsburgh Courier*, April 26, 1924, 10.

46. Saidiya Hartman, *Wayward Lives, Beautiful Experiments: Intimate Histories of Riotous Black Girls, Troublesome Women, and Queer Radicals* (New York: W. W. Norton & Company, 2019), 399. Hampton, a "chorine, lesbian, working-class intellectual, and aspiring concert singer," is one of the historical figures created by Hartman from archival materials.

47. Hartman, *Wayward Lives*, 348.

48. Wintz and Finkelman, *Encyclopedia of the Harlem Renaissance*, 692.

49. Theophilus Lewis, "Theatre," *Messenger* 6 6, no. 1, January 1924.

50. Theophilus Lewis, "Theatre," *Messenger* 6, no. 5, May 1924.

51. Emmett G. Price III, Kernodle, Tammy L., and Horace J. Maxille Jr., eds., *Encyclopedia of African American Music* (Santa Barbara, CA: Greenwood Press, 2011), 958. The TOBA exclusively booked African American artists though it was run primarily by White and Jewish theater owners and managers. Milton Starr, the Jewish manager of Nashville's Bijou Theatre, was the organization's first president. Also see Athelia Knight, "He Paved the Way for T. O. B. A.," *The Black Perspective in Music* 15, no. 2 (1987): 153–81.

52. "TOBA Doings," *Chicago Defender*, June 4, 1921, 7.

53. James Austin, "The Stage," *Philadelphia Tribune*, April 3, 1920, 3.

54. "Sandy Burns," *Chicago Defender*, January 8, 1921, 4. "Going Good," *Chicago Defender*, January 29, 1921, 4.

55. Henry T. Sampson, *Blacks in Blackface: A Sourcebook on Early Black Musical Shows* (Lanham, MD: Scarecrow Press, 2013), 710.

56. Ted Gioia, *Delta Blues: The Life and Times of the Mississippi Masters Who Revolutionized American Music* (New York: W. W. Norton & Company, 2009), 38.

57. Wintz and Finkelman, *Encyclopedia of the Harlem Renaissance*, 958.

58. Dance, *The World of Earl Hines*, 25.

59. As sociologist Ira De A. Reid noted in his 1930 study of the Hill, domestic work was the "only field in which any number of Negro women find employment" while sex work remained

prevalent. He wrote, "One has only to walk along Wylie Avenue from Washington to Fullerton Streets any evening and glance through the side streets" to see brothels with Black sex workers (Reid, "Social Conditions of the Negro in the Hill District of Pittsburgh," 12, 61). In the context of Pittsburgh's growing African American population with increasing number of southern migrants, mobile and independent Black women became a source of anxiety and a target for moralistic commentators. *Courier* columnist John L. Clark wrote in 1923, "It is estimated that more than one hundred girls between the ages of 15 and 21 have come to the Third ward to live during the past year. Being reared in the [S]outh, they are not acquainted with social customs and practices of this section and don't seem to have much luck in finding the group to welcome them" (John L. Clark, "Wylie Avenue," *Pittsburgh Courier*, October 20, 1923, 4). Clark called on the Hill District Community House and YWCA to undertake the task of incorporating the girls into the neighborhood, with the implication that they were in danger of falling victim to predation. In black and tan cabarets, their sexualized image was central to their lives as performers, the popularity of the cabarets, and the associations of the venues with vice—a condition that was thought to be concomitant with Hill District nightlife in the city's struggle to enforce segregation in rapidly changing neighborhoods.

60. Hazel V. Carby, "Policing the Black Woman's Body in an Urban Context," *Critical Inquiry* 18, no. 4 (1992): 753.

61. "Ethel Waters to Appear at Star Theater," *Pittsburgh Courier*, October 27, 1923, 11.

62. Paul Slade, *Black Swan Blues: The Hard Rise and Brutal Fall of America's First Black-Owned Record Label*, PlanetSlade.com, 2014, 82.

63. "Bessie Smith to Appear at Star Next Week," *Pittsburgh Courier*, March 3, 1924, 10.

64. Jayna Brown, *Babylon Girls: Black Women Performers and the Shaping of the Modern* (Durham, NC: Duke University Press, 2008).

65. "Hardtack Jackson's '20th Century Wonders' a Hit at Gibson's Standard, Philadelphia," *Billboard*, February 12, 1921, 55.

66. Dance, *The World of Earl Hines*, 28.

67. Mary Lou Williams, "Mary Lou Williams Interview, Melody Maker, 1954," *Melody Maker*, June 1954, https://ratical.org/MaryLouWilliams/MMiview1954.html.

68. Williams, "Mary Lou Williams."

69. "Leader House," *Pittsburgh Courier*, July 14, 1923, 3.

70. "Leader House," *Pittsburgh Courier*, July 21, 1923, 3.

71. Dance, *The World of Earl Hines*, 28.

72. Dance, 28.

73. "Shufflin' Sam Goes Over Big at Niagara," *Morning Call*, December 10, 1926, 22.

74. "Shufflin' Sam," 22.

75. "Baby Hines and Trio Click in Cleveland," *Pittsburgh Courier*, September 30, 1933, 16; "Café Society," *Daily News*, November 11, 1942; "Shangri-La," *Philadelphia Inquirer*, January 21, 1946, 9; "Frolic Show Bar," *Detroit Tribune*, August 2, 1947, 10; "New York is My Beat," *New York Age*, January 21, 1956, 7.

76. "Charming Entertainer at New Cabaret Comes from Town Famous for Beauties," *Pittsburgh Courier*, July 25, 1924, 10.

77. "Charming Entertainer," 10.

78. "Charming Entertainer," 10.

79. Ross Laird, Brunswick-Balke-Collender Company, and Brunswick Radio Corporation, *Brunswick Records: A Discography of Recordings, 1916–1931* (Westport, CT: Greenwood Publishing Group, 2001), 9.

80. Sampson, *Blacks in Blackface*, 541.

81. "Leader House Has Special Act This Week," *Pittsburgh Courier*, May 17, 1924, 8.

82. "Leader House," 8.

83. "Four are Fined, 77 Freed After Jazzland Raid," *St. Louis Star and Times*, February 14, 1921, 1.

84. "Leader House," *Pittsburgh Courier*, August 4, 1923, 4; "Leader House," *Pittsburgh Courier*, September 1, 1923, 4.

85. "Blue Wednesday Cabaret," *Pittsburgh Courier*, August 25, 1923, 5.

86. "Elmore Theatre," *Pittsburgh Courier*, January 5, 1929, 10.

87. "Hill, City's Worst Plague Spot, Runs Wild Even as Probers' Light Advances," *Pittsburgh Daily Post*, August 6, 1926, 8.

88. Julien Comte, "'Let the Federal Men Raid': Bootlegging and Prohibition Enforcement in Pittsburgh," *Pennsylvania History: A Journal of Mid-Atlantic Studies* 77, no. 2 (2010): 167, https://doi.org/10.5325/pennhistory.77.2.0166.

89. Comte, "'Let the Federal Men Raid,'" 174.

90. Comte, 171.

91. "Retail License Applications," *Pittsburgh Press*, February 26, 1921, 11. The Court of Quarter Sessions legal body was established in the seventeenth century as part of the British colonies to try minor crimes and oversee licensing and infrastructure needs throughout Pennsylvania's counties. Stephanie Hoover, "Pennsylvania's Court of Quarter Sessions," accessed July 10, 2020, http://www.pennsylvaniaresearch.com/pennsylvania-quarter-sessions-court.html.

92. "Retail License Applications," 11.

93. "'Dry' Raiders Find Morphine," *Pittsburgh Gazette Times*, November 5, 1921, 2.

94. Comte, "'Let the Federal Men Raid,'" 170.

95. "Retail License Applications," *Pittsburgh Press*, February 25, 1922, 11.

96. "Cabaret Owner Freed, Music Held Not to Violate Law," *Pittsburgh Gazette Times*, July 23, 1922, 3.

97. "Police Head to Ask Court to Close 'Black and Tan' Cafe," *Pittsburgh Daily Post*, September 12, 1922, 1.

98. "War Upon Night Life Begun Here," *Pittsburgh Gazette Times*, September 12, 1922, 3.

99. "Agents Raid Seven Places," *Pittsburgh Gazette Times*, September 16, 1922, 7.

100. "Agents Raid," 7.

101. "Collins Inn License Revocation Is Asked by Safety Director—McCandless Accuses Proprietor of Violating Rules," *Pittsburgh Daily Post*, September 24, 1922, 2.

102. "Hearing Closed in M'Candless' Case Against Collins Inn—Witnesses Testify Place Is Properly Conducted," *Pittsburgh Daily Post*, November 10, 1922, 2.

103. "Hearing Closed," 2.

104. Kevin J. Mumford, *Interzones: Black/White Sex Districts in Chicago and New York in the Early Twentieth Century* (New York: Columbia University Press, 1997), 46.

105. "Night Life Resort Opens Legal Fight to Retain License," *Pittsburgh Press*, November 8, 1922, 17.

106. Peggy Pascoe, *What Comes Naturally: Miscegenation Law and the Making of Race in America* (Oxford: Oxford University Press, 2009), 166.

107. "Collins Inn License Revoked by Court," *Pittsburgh Gazette Times*, November 14, 1922, 3.

108. "Drug Crusaders Get Head of Collins Inn," *Pittsburgh Gazette Times*, October 24, 1922, 13.

109. "Owner Held, Agents Raid Collins Inn," *Pittsburgh Gazette Times*, October 25, 1922, 10. See Audrey Redford and Benjamin Powell, "Dynamics of Intervention in the War on Drugs: The Buildup to the Harrison Act of 1914," *Independent Review* 24, no. 4 (2016) for a discussion of the racialization of narcotics use in building support for passing the Harrison anti-narcotic law.

110. "Owner Held," 10.

111. "Witnesses Testify to Buying Narcotics," *Pittsburgh Gazette Times*, December 13, 1922, 18.

112. "Collins Narcotics Case Ends Today," *Pittsburgh Gazette Times*, December 14, 1922, 18.

113. "Harry Collins Gets Three to Five Years," *Pittsburgh Gazette Times*, February 17, 1923, 16.

114. "Harry Collins, Now in Prison, Seeks Parole," *Pittsburgh Courier*, November 22, 1923, 1.

115. John L. Clark, "Wylie Avenue," *Pittsburgh Courier*, November 17, 1923, 9.

116. "Harry Collins Freed," *Pittsburgh Courier*, August 16, 1924, 1.

117. Dance, *The World of Earl Hines*, 31.

118. "Harry Collins Offers New Idea in Sandwich Shoppe," *Pittsburgh Courier*, July 6, 1929, 6.

119. "Kid Welch Dies Two Hours After Witnessing Louis-Birkie Fight," *Pittsburgh Courier*, January 19, 1935, 1, 4.

120. Glasco, *The WPA History of the Negro in Pittsburgh*, 315.

121. "Kid Welch Dies.," 1, 4.

122. John L. Clark, "Wylie Avenue," *Pittsburgh Courier*, January 26, 1935, 6.

123. Rob Ruck, *Sandlot Seasons: Sport in Black Pittsburgh* (Champaign: University of Illinois Press, 1987), 138. Ruck cites *Pittsburgh Post-Gazette* journalist Charles Danver, who, in 1932, wrote a biographical sketch of Greenlee in his column "Pittsburghesque." Danver wrote that Greenlee "took that freight from Asheville, North Carolina, about 16 years ago because he didn't like school and had no taste for bricklaying like his father," a statement that places Greenlee's arrival in 1916 (*Pittsburgh Post-Gazette*, October 10, 1932, 8). However, Danver's investment in sensational and comical depictions of Hill District figures rather than critical or accurate commentary on Black life in Pittsburgh brings into question the reliability of his information.

124. Abraham Epstein, *The Negro Migrant in Pittsburgh* (New York: Arno Press, 1918), 8.

125. Epstein, *The Negro Migrant in Pittsburgh*, 12.

126. "Transfers Recorded," *Pittsburgh Daily Post*, August 17, 1924, 18. The inflation rate for $23,000 in 1924 was calculated on www.saving.org (accessed May 22, 2023).

127. "New Cabaret Is Modern in All Respects," *Pittsburgh Courier*, July 26, 1924, 10.

128. "Station WJAS Program," *Pittsburgh Press*, January 5, 1925, 37.

129. "Fletcher Henderson and His Famous Orchestra at Duquesne Garden Monday," *Pittsburgh Courier*, August 29, 1925, 9.

130. John L. Clark, "Wylie Avenue," *Pittsburgh Courier*, November 28, 1925, 3.

131. Clark, "Wylie Avenue," 2.

132. "Loendi Opening Game," *Pittsburgh Press*, November 8, 1925, 26.

133. Ruck, *Sandlot Seasons*, 127.

134. "Appearing at Re-Opening of Paramount Inn," *Pittsburgh Courier*, May 22, 1926, 8.

135. "Hubert Minor Mann," *Pittsburgh Courier*, June 12, 1926, 4.

136. Cotton Club dancer Howard "Stretch" Johnson notes that "skrontch" was slang for intercourse. Howard Eugene Johnson, *A Dancer in the Revolution: Stretch Johnson, Harlem Communist at the Cotton Club* (New York: Fordham University Press, 2014), 32.

137. Bill Coleman, *Trumpet Story* (London: Palgrave Macmillan, 2016), 47.

138. Thomas R. Pegram, "Brewing Trouble: Federal, State, and Private Authority in Pennsylvania Prohibition Enforcement under Gifford Pinchot, 1923–27," *Pennsylvania Magazine of History and Biography* 138, no. 2 (2014): 164.

139. "Cabarets Ordered Closed at Midnight—Nothing Said About Cleaning Up, However," *Pittsburgh Daily Post*, March 24, 1925, 1, 2.

140. "Cabarets Ordered Closed at Midnight," 1, 2.

141. "Cabarets," 1, 2.

142. "Cabarets," 1, 2.

143. "Cabarets," 1, 2.

144. "Mayor Closes Cabaret, Halts Dancing in Two Others—Gambling and Clubs Also Are Under Ban," *Pittsburgh Daily Post*, March 25, 1925, 1, 3.

145. "Revoke License of Paramount 'Inn': Dancing License Revoked," *Pittsburgh Courier*, March 28, 1925, 1, 2.

146. "Revoke License of Paramount 'Inn,'" 1, 2.

147. "Revoke License," 1, 2.

148. "Political War Grips City: 'Tired of Abuse and Brutality' Says Group," *Pittsburgh Courier*, July 4, 1925, 1, 2.

149. "Anti-Vice Group Formed to Request Cleanup Not to Map Course, M'Fall Says," *Pittsburgh Gazette Times*, August 6, 1926, 9.

150. "Here is Hill's Protest on Vice Sent to Mayor Kline and Clark," *Pittsburgh Gazette Times*, August 11, 1926, 2.

151. "Here is Hill's Protest," 2.

152. "Grand Jury Held Futile in Vice Drive," *Pittsburgh Gazette Times*, August 14, 1926, 1, 8.

153. "Gay Night Life Revels End at Leader House, Paramount Inn: Intermingling of Races Is Halted by Safety Head, Clancey Given Free Hand to Clean Up," *Pittsburgh Gazette Times*, August 13, 1926, 1, 5.

154. "Startling Exposures Promised by Safety Head," *Pittsburgh Daily Post*, August 7, 1926, 2.

155. "Startling Exposures," 2.

156. Marylynne Pitz, "Angel of the Hill District," *Old Pittsburgh Photos and Stories, The Digs* (blog), December 14, 2014, https://newsinteractive.post-gazette.com/thedigs/2014/12/14/angel-of-the-hill-district/.

157. "Gay Night Life," 1, 5.

158. "Gay Night Life," 1, 5.

159. "Gay Night Life," 1, 5.

160. "'Clean Up or Go!' Clark Is Warned by Crusaders," *Pittsburgh Daily Post*, August 14, 1926, 1, 3.

161. "Clark Launches Attack on Slot Machine Owners," *Pittsburgh Gazette Times*, August 14, 1926, 8.

162. "Clark Demands Five Cabaret Managers Explain Operations," *Pittsburgh Daily Post*, December 3, 1926, 1, 2.

163. "4 Policemen Post Bonds," *Pittsburgh Post-Gazette*, July 13, 1927, 1, 4.

164. John L. Clark, "Wylie Avenue," *Pittsburgh Courier*, April 9, 1927, 3.

165. Clark, "Wylie Avenue," 3.

166. Clark, 3.

167. "Disfranchised, Beaten Negroes Desert Polls in 'Thundering Third,'" *Pittsburgh Courier*, September 19, 1931, 1, 6.

168. "Disfranchised."

169. John L. Clark, "Wylie Avenue," *Pittsburgh Courier*, October 3, 1959, A1.

170. "The New Crawford Grill Opens with the Repeal Glory in 'New Ways and Wines' on Xmas Eve," *Pittsburgh Courier*, December 23, 1933, A6.

171. "New Crawford Grill," A6.

172. John L. Clark, "Wylie Avenue," *Pittsburgh Courier*, July 14, 1951, 19.

173. Ruck, *Sandlot Seasons*, 139.

174. "To Probe Baseball Status at Meet Here," *Pittsburgh Courier*, January 6, 1934, 14.

175. Strecker, Geralyn M. "The Rise and Fall of Greenlee Field: Biography of a Ballpark." *Black Ball: A Negro Leagues Journal* 2, no. 2 (Fall 2009): 37–67.

176. Marc Myers, *Why Jazz Happened* (Berkeley: University of California Press, 2013), 20.

177. John L. Clark, "Wylie Avenue," *Pittsburgh Courier*, May 12, 1934, 4.

178. John L. Clark, "Wylie Avenue," *Pittsburgh Courier*, March 13, 1926, 33.

179. "C. & G. Club Looms as Most Popular 'Hot Spot' On Hill," *Pittsburgh Courier*, March 30, 1935, A9.

180. "Slim Gaillard to Open Crawford Grill Fri. Night," *Pittsburgh Courier*, May 27, 1939, 21.

181. Hosea Taylor, interview by the author, December 16, 2008.

182. John Hughes, interview by the author, January 19, 2009.

## Chapter 3: Competing Visions of Modernity

1. Henri Lefebvre, *The Production of Space* (Hoboken, NJ: Wiley, 1992), 225.

2. George F. Brown, "Crawford Grill No. 2 Is Hailed as Prettiest Lounge in the East," *Pittsburgh Courier*, August 29, 1953, 19.

3. George F. Brown, "Crawford Grill No. Two's Grand Opening a Smashing Success," *Pittsburgh Courier*, September 5, 1953, 21.

4. Brown, "Crawford Grill No. Two's Grand Opening," 21.

5. Brown, 21.

6. Michael Weber, *Don't Call Me Boss: David L. Lawrence, Pittsburgh's Renaissance Mayor* (Pittsburgh: University of Pittsburgh Press, 1988), 168. Democrat David Lawrence served as Pittsburgh's mayor from 1946 to 1959. His support of concerns in Pittsburgh's Black communities is evident in his establishment of the Civic Unity Council in 1946 as well as his involvement in the election of Pittsburgh's first Black judge and councilman and appointment of the first Black magistrate.

7. Travis A. Jackson, *Blowin' the Blues Away: Performance and Meaning on the New York Jazz Scene*, (Berkeley: University of California Press, 2012), 60.

8. Jackson, *Blowin' the Blues Away*, 54.

9. Lefebvre, *The Production of Space*, 38.

10. Lefebvre, 38, 42.

11. Patricia Parker-Reid, interview by the author, September 6, 2007.

12. Mindy Thompson Fullilove, *Root Shock: How Tearing Up City Neighborhoods Hurts America, and What We Can Do About It* (New York: New Village Press, 2016), 11.

13. "Westerners Make Stop in Pittsburgh," *Pittsburgh Courier*, July 6, 1946, 5.

14. "Harlem in Frenzy of Joy at Knockout; Celebrants Rush from Radios into Streets for Crescendo Following Louis Victory Shrieks and Shouts Continue Louis Pennants Popular," *New York Times*, June 20, 1946, Archives, https://www.nytimes.com/1946/06/20/archives/harlem-in-frenzy-of-joy-at-knockout-celebrants-rush-from-radios.html.

15. Paul Barrett and Mark H. Rose, "Street Smarts: The Politics of Transportation Statistics in the American City, 1900–1990," *Journal of Urban History* 25, no. 3 (March 1, 1999): 416, https://doi.org/10.1177/009614429902500305.

16. Eric Avila and Mark H. Rose, "Race, Culture, Politics, and Urban Renewal: An Introduction," *Journal of Urban History* 35, no. 3 (March 1, 2009): 338, https://doi.org/10.1177/0096144208330393.

17. Dale Chapman, *The Jazz Bubble: Neoclassical Jazz in Neoliberal Culture* (Oakland: University of California Press, 2018), 158.

18. Mark Anthony Neal, *What the Music Said: Black Popular Music and Black Public Culture* (New York: Routledge, 1999), 39.

19. Neal, *What the Music Said*, 5.

20. bell hooks, *Yearning: Race, Gender, and Cultural Politics* (Boston: South End Press, 1990), 42. Rashad Shabazz in *Spatializing Blackness: Architectures of Confinement and Black Masculinity in Chicago* (Champaign: University of Illinois Press, 2015), links the daily negations of space and place within a racialized landscape in his discussion of "spatialized blackness" which "underscores how mechanisms of constraint built into architecture, urban planning, and systems of control that functioned through policing and the establishment of borders literally and figuratively created a prison-like environment" (2).

21. Marlon M. Bailey, *Butch Queens Up in Pumps: Gender, Performance, and Ballroom Culture in Detroit* (Ann Arbor: University of Michigan Press, 2013), 5.

22. Weber, *Don't Call Me Boss*, 228.

23. Weber, 275. Weber writes that the Pittsburgh Renaissance included sixteen projects taking place over one thousand acres.

24. Weber, 275.

25. Sara Blair and Eric Rosenberg, *Trauma and Documentary Photography of the FSA* (Berkeley: University of California Press, 2012), 30.

26. Constance B. Schulz and Steven Wright Plattner, *Witness to the Fifties: The Pittsburgh Photographic Library, 1950–1953* (Pittsburgh: University of Pittsburgh Press, 1999), 5. The Pittsburgh Photographic Library is currently housed in the Pennsylvania Room of Pittsburgh's main branch of the Carnegie Library.

27. References to Pittsburgh's urban redevelopment projects as a "Renaissance" appear in the *Pittsburgh Post-Gazette* as early as 1949 (See "City is Cited for New Look by Magazine," *Pittsburgh Post-Gazette*, September 22, 1949, 15). Later urban redevelopment projects under mayors Peter Flaherty (1970–1977) and Richard Caliguiri (1977–1988) became known as Pittsburgh's Renaissance II. See also George S. Duggar and International Union of Local Authorities, *Renewal of Town and Village III: Proceedings of the IULA Congress Belgrade, June 14th to 20th, 1965* (Dordrecht: Springer-Science + Business Media, B.V., 1966), 47. In this published lecture, Edward J. Magee, who served as the ACCD's director from 1959 to 1968, presents the story of "Pittsburgh's rebirth, starting with the close of World War II." The idea of "rebirth" was closely associated with the image of Pittsburgh as a "dying city" at the close of World War II.

28. Schulz and Plattner, *Witness to the Fifties*, 4.

29. Laura Grantmyre, "Visual Representations of Redevelopment in Pittsburgh's Hill District, 1943–1968" (PhD diss., University of Pittsburgh, 2014), 148–49, http://d-scholarship.pitt .edu/20304/.

30. Grantmyre, "Visual Representations," 151.

31. Schulz and Plattner, *Witness to the Fifties*, 50.

32. Gregory J. Crowley, *The Politics of Place: Contentious Urban Redevelopment in Pittsburgh* (Pittsburgh: University of Pittsburgh Press, 2005), 59.

33. Schulz and Plattner, *Witness to the Fifties*, 38.

34. Gottlieb, *Making Their Own Way*, 70.

35. Crowley, *The Politics of Place*, 35.

36. Pennsylvania General Assembly, "1945 Act 385," official website for the Pennsylvania General Assembly, 1945, http://www.legis.state.pa.us/cfdocs/Legis/LI/uconsCheck.cfm?txtType =HTM&yr=1945&sessInd=0&smthLwInd=0&act=0385.

37. Urban Redevelopment Authority of Pittsburgh, "Proposal for the Redevelopment of Redevelopment Area No. 3 in the 2nd and 3rd Wards of the City of Pittsburgh" (Pittsburgh: Urban Redevelopment Authority of Pittsburgh, 1955), 3.

38. Urban Redevelopment, "Proposal for the Redevelopment," 10.

39. William Howland Kenney, *Jazz on the River* (Chicago: University of Chicago Press, 2005), 169.

40. This map uses the 1929 street grid depicted in Alexander Zerful Pittler's "The Hill District of Pittsburgh: A Study of Succession" (PhD thesis, University of Pittsburgh, 1930).

41. Henri Lefebvre, *The Right to the City* (Paris: Anthropos, 1968), 24–25.

42. The Pittsburgh Bicentennial Association, *The Pittsburgh Bicentennial* (New York: Gilberton Co., 1959), 35, http://documenting.pitt.edu/islandora/object/pitt:31735051651556.

43. Lefebvre, *The Right to the City*, 64.

44. Urban Redevelopment, 10.

45. George Benson and Alan Goldsher, *Benson: The Autobiography* (New York: Hachette Books, 2014), 15.

46. Chuck Spatafore, interview by the author, September 10, 2008.

47. Fullilove, *Root Shock*, 10.

48. Fullilove, 14.

49. Fullilove, 10.

50. Roy Lubove, *Twentieth-Century Pittsburgh: The Post-Steel Era* (Pittsburgh: University of Pittsburgh Press, 1996), 154.

51. Chuck Spatafore, interview. In 1958, a group of parishioners formed to save St. Peter's Church. Their petition to the City Council, the court case against the URA and the City of Pittsburgh, and the direct appeal to Vatican officials yielded no results, and the church was demolished in 1960 (see Crowley, *The Politics of Place*, 86–89). The decision to save Epiphany Catholic Church was seen as an act of favoritism by Mayor David L. Lawrence, who was Irish Catholic like the church's parishioners.

52. Dan Fitzpatrick, "The Story of Urban Renewal," *Pittsburgh Post-Gazette*, May 21, 2000, http://old.post-gazette.com/businessnews/20000521eastliberty1.asp. "By 1960, Pittsburgh was one of the most segregated big cities in America."

53. Weber, *Don't Call Me Boss*, 273.

54. Derek G. Handley, "'The Line Drawn': Freedom Corner and Rhetorics of Place in Pittsburgh, 1960s–2000s," *Rhetoric Review* 38, no. 2 (April 3, 2019): 173–89, https://doi.org/10.1080/07350198.2019.1582239.

## Chapter 4: Life in the Jazz House:
## The Crawford Grill No. 2 and Hurricane Bar

1. The Pittsburgh Bicentennial Association, *The Pittsburgh Bicentennial* (New York: Gilberton Co., 1959), 35, http://documenting.pitt.edu/islandora/object/pitt:31735051651556.

2. Mindy Thompson Fullilove, *Root Shock: How Tearing Up City Neighborhoods Hurts America, and What We Can Do About It* (New York: New Village Press, 2016), xviii.

3. Derek G. Handley, "'The Line Drawn': Freedom Corner and Rhetorics of Place in Pittsburgh, 1960s–2000s," *Rhetoric Review* 38, no. 2 (April 3, 2019): 176, https://doi.org/10.1080/07350198.2019.1582239.

4. Gene Ludwig, interview by the author, March 3, 2006.

5. Tony Norman, "Anna Simmons Dunlap: Founder and Owner of Hurricane Club," *Pittsburgh Post-Gazette*, March 10, 1998, B5.

6. Bernard Holland, "Birdie Says Bye Bye to Hurricane, All That Jazz," *Pittsburgh Post-Gazette*, February 4, 1980, 18. The biographic details in the paragraph are drawn from both Holland and Ann Butler's articles on Birdie Dunlap.

7. In *Sandlot Seasons* (1987), sports historian Rob Ruck notes that Sellers McKee Hall was also a pitcher and manager of the Pittsburgh Giant's Negro League baseball team.

8. Ann Butler, "Birdie's Place," *Pittsburgh Press*, April 3, 1984, B7.

9. "New Hurricane Really Open; Ruby Young's Organ, 3 Stars," *Pittsburgh Courier*, October 31, 1953, 18.

10. George F. Brown, "Hurricane Sets Big Grand Opening Mon., Nov. 9," *Pittsburgh Courier*, November 7, 1953, 17.

11. Brown, "Hurricane Sets," 17.

12. Katrina Hazzard-Gordon, *Jookin': The Rise of Social Dance Formations in African-American Culture* (Philadelphia: Temple University Press, 1990), 143–44.

13. Bernard Holland, "Birdie Says Bye Bye to Hurricane, All That Jazz," *Pittsburgh Post-Gazette*, February 4, 1980, B7.

14. Patricia Parker-Reid, interview by the author, September 2007.

15. Chuck Austin, interview by the author, August 31, 2008.

16. George Thompson, interview by the author, December 11, 2008.

17. Tony Janflone Sr., interview by the author, January 6, 2009.

18. Janflone Sr., interview.

19. George Benson, interview by the author, May 28, 2020.

20. Ruby Younge Hardy, interview by Maurice Levy, Carnegie Library of Pittsburgh Oral History of Music in Pittsburgh, January 1, 1995.

21. Austin, interview.

22. "Air-Conditioned Jazz: Roy Eldridge Co-Stars this Week with Ruby Young 3 at Hurricane," *Pittsburgh Courier*, June 26, 1954, 19.

23. "Famed King Solomon 3 Wises Up Hurricane Jazz Lovers," *Pittsburgh Courier*, July 24, 1954, 19.

24. See this book's appendix for a list of artists who performed at the Hurricane Bar and Grill and Crawford Grill No. 2 during the 1950s and 1960s.

25. Hazel Garland, "Things to Talk About," *Pittsburgh Courier*, March 10, 1956, A21.

26. Garland, A24.

27. Janflone Sr., interview.

28. Neal, *What the Music Said*, 30.

29. Hazzard-Gordon, *Jookin'*, 173.

30. Harold Young, interview by the author, December 9, 2008.

31. Roger Humphries, interview by the author, December 5, 2008.

32. Humphries, interview.

33. Austin, interview.

34. Lou Stellute, interview by the author, December 1, 2008.

35. Janflone Sr., interview.

36. Phyl Garland, "Listening In: Swinging Organ Discs," *Pittsburgh Courier*, December 12, 1964, 13.

37. Joseph Christopher Columbus Morris performed under the name Crazy Chris Columbo, also spelled as Chris Colombo, Kris Kolumbo, and Kris Kolombo.

38. Bill Kent, "A Jazz-Age Survivor," *New York Times*, August 4, 1996, New York (section), https://www.nytimes.com/1996/08/04/nyregion/a-jazz-age-survivor.html.

39. "Jolly Jax . . . Held Over Through This Saturday," *Pittsburgh Courier*, June 18, 1960, 19.

40. "Jolly Jax Held Over Again at Hurricane," *Pittsburgh Courier*, October 31, 1959, 29.

41. "Jolly Jax Record Banned," *Pittsburgh Courier*, April 7, 1962, 28.

42. The band's end came in 1964 when Herman Hill was killed while taking flying lessons— a hobby prompted by his hope to overcome a fear of flying.

43. "Jimmy Smith Packing Hurricane," *Pittsburgh Courier*, July 14, 1956, 22.

44. George F. Brown, "New Hurricane Now Open For Biz; Ruby Young Plays," *Pittsburgh Courier*, October 24, 1953, 17.

45. "Jimmy Smith Packing Hurricane," 22.

46. "Progressive Organist Returns from Hollywood Stand: Hurricane Rocks with 'Incredible' Jimmy Smith," *Pittsburgh Courier*, December 15, 1956, A23. It is not clear whether Dunlap owned a Hammond organ, which was kept on site. Many photos from the Charles "Teenie" Harris Archive show custom-designed organs on the Hurricane stage, demonstrating that bands often traveled with their own organs.

47. "Jimmy Smith Rocking Hurricane," *Pittsburgh Courier*, December 29, 1956, A15.

48. "Heavy Drummer Blows into the Hurricane," *Pittsburgh Courier*, August 24, 1957, A20.

49. The opening date is listed as 1943 on the historical marker placed in front of the Crawford Grill No. 2 by the Pennsylvania Historical Society. The August 29, 1953, *Courier* article "Crawford Grill No. 2 Is Hailed as Prettiest Lounge in the East" covers the seven-year anniversary of the club that would place the opening date in late 1946. The Grill closed in 2003.

50. "Tom West Murdered in Grill," *Pittsburgh Courier*, July 27 *Pittsburgh Courier*, July 7, 1946, 1.

51. "Greenlee, City Sued by Woman," *Pittsburgh Courier*, August 26, 1950, 2; "Salesman Sues Greenlee for Injury to His Knee," *Pittsburgh Courier*, November 25, 1950, 6.

52. "Robinson-Greenlee's Grill No. 2 Drawing Satisfied Patrons," *Pittsburgh Courier*, June 15, 1946, 21.

53. "Leroy Brown Scores Big at Grill 2," *Pittsburgh Courier*, July 12, 1952, 22.

54. George "Duke" Spaulding, interview by the author, November 16, 2008.

55. Guidry, Nate, "A Life in Tune: Betty Brown Tells All about Her More than 50 Years of Living above Crawford Grill," *Pittsburgh Post-Gazette*, 2007, https://www.post-gazette.com/ae/music/2007/06/29/A-life-in-tune-Betty-Brown-tells-all-about-her-more-than-50-years-of-living-above-Crawford-Grill/stories/200706290272. Spaulding notes that the club catered to White clientele with Black patrons occasionally allowed to sit in the balcony, while the band was not allowed to interact with the audience and was required to go to a side room when they came off stage (George "Duke" Spaulding, interview). Spaulding remembers that Brown's band was able to break the color line because the Hollywood Showbar owners were "racketeers and had enough money that they weren't scared of Local 60." According to "US Files 154 Income Tax Liens" (*Pittsburgh Post-Gazette*, August 27, 1948, 15), the Hollywood Showbar was hit with a $1,400 tax lien in 1948. In "Two Arrested for Numbers" (*Pittsburgh Post-Gazette*, January 21, 1949, 1), it was reported that the Hollywood's manager Max Grant and bartender Sam Weinberg were arrested in a numbers racket raid and charged with operating an illegal lottery. Grant did not post bond and was quoted as saying that he "would rather go to jail as [he needed] a rest." The bar's license was suspended in May 1949, likely leading to its closing; "Board Suspends License of Showbar for 101 Days" (*Pittsburgh Post-Gazette*, May 17, 1949, 1).

56. "Leroy Brown Combo Makes Grill 2 Fun Rendezvous," *Pittsburgh Courier*, July 19, 1952, 22.

57. Guidry, "A Life in Tune."

58. "Leroy Brown Combo," *Pittsburgh Courier*, July 19, 1952, 22.

59. Hosea Taylor, interview by the author, December 16, 2008.

60. "Leroy Brown Held Over at Crawford Grill 2," *Pittsburgh Courier*, July 19, 1952, 22.

61. "Leroy Brown Hypos Music Appreciation," *Pittsburgh Courier*, August 2, 1952, 22.

62. "Walt Harper to Remain at Grill 2 to Labor Day," *Pittsburgh Courier*, August 21, 1954, 19.

63. "Walt Harper to Remain," *Pittsburgh Courier*, August 21, 1954, 19.

64. "Walt Harper Bids Farewell to Grill 2," *Pittsburgh Courier*, September 11, 1954, 19.

65. George E. Pitts, "After Hours," *Pittsburgh Courier*, March 17, 1956, A35.

66. Harold L. Keith, "Who Says Progressive Jazz is Doomed?" *Pittsburgh Courier*, May 5, 1956, 33.

67. Keith, "Who Says," 33.

68. Gillespie was the first jazz musician to tour as part of the US State Department's Jazz Ambassador's program.

69. Keith, "Who Says," 33.

70. Krin Gabbard, *Better Git It in Your Soul: An Interpretive Biography of Charles Mingus* (Berkeley: University of California Press, 2016), 55.

71. Gabbard, *Better Git It in Your Soul*, 56.

72. Scott Saul, *Freedom Is, Freedom Ain't: Jazz and the Making of the Sixties* (Cambridge, MA: Harvard University Press, 2003), 150.

73. Guidry, Nate, "Q&A with Horace Parlan," *Pittsburgh Post-Gazette*, November 5, 2006, https://www.post-gazette.com/uncategorized/2006/11/05/Q-A-with-Horace-Parlan/stories/200611050239.

74. George E. Pitts, "After Twelve," *Pittsburgh Courier*, March 31, 1956, 37.

75. "Charlie Mingus at Grill April 2," *Pittsburgh Courier*, March 31, 1956, 38.

76. Henri Lefebvre, *Rhythmanalysis: Space, Time and Everyday Life* (New York: Continuum, 2004), 73–74.

77. Charles Mingus, Liner Notes for *Pithecanthropus Erectus* (Atlantic 1237), 1956.

78. Lefebvre, *Rhythmanalysis*, 87.

79. Harold L. Keith, "Data 'Bout Discs," *Pittsburgh Courier*, September 8, 1956, 22.

80. "Obituary: Harold L. Keith / Ex-Editor of Courier, US Press Officer," *Pittsburgh Post-Gazette*, January 31, 2002, http://old.post-gazette.com/obituaries/20020131keith3.asp.

81. "Sax Ace, Paul Quinichette Next Attraction at Grill," *Pittsburgh Courier*, April 14, 1956, 35.

82. Alan Goldsher, *Hard Bop Academy: The Sidemen of Art Blakey and the Jazz Messengers* (Milwaukee: Hal Leonard Corporation, 2002), 2.

83. Cecil Brooks II, interview by the author, December 5, 2008.

84. "Art Blakey Moves into Grill on Nov. 25," *Pittsburgh Courier*, November 23, 1957, A13.

85. George E. Pitts, "Around the Theatrical World," *Pittsburgh Courier*, September 21, 1957, 20.

86. "W. Harper Explains Band's New Sound," *Pittsburgh Courier*, August 10, 1957, A23.

87. "It Happened . . . in Pittsburgh," *Pittsburgh Courier*, December 15, 1956, A1.

88. Chico Hamilton would compose for films including Roman Polanski's *Repulsion* (1965).

89. Nick Catalano, *Clifford Brown: The Life and Art of the Legendary Jazz Trumpeter* (Oxford: Oxford University Press, 2001), 185.

90. Mitch Berman and Susanne Wah Lee, "Max: Sticking Power: Jazzman Max Roach Has Kept Time for Mankind's Fastest 50 Years," *Los Angeles Times*, September 15, 1991, https://www.latimes.com/archives/la-xpm-1991-09-15-tm-3725-story.html.

91. *Time Out* and its single "Take Five" both sold more than a million copies, a first for a jazz artist.

92. "Max Roach Quintet Opens Two Weeks at Grill Feb. 16," *Pittsburgh Courier*, February 14, 1959, 18.

93. "Sidemen Serve Two Weeks' Notice—Max Roach 'Too Far Out,' Given His 'Walking Paper,'" *Pittsburgh Courier*, February 28, 1959, 3.

94. George E. Pitts, "'Miles Ahead' Or Miles' Head Is the Issue," *Pittsburgh Courier*, November 7, 1959, 16.

95. "'New' Max Roach Hypnotizes Awed Fans in Pgh.'s Grill," *Pittsburgh Courier*, July 27, 1963, 17.

96. Harold L. Keith, "'Social Awareness' Gives Max New Viewpoint on His Identity," *Pittsburgh Courier*, August 3, 1963, 17.

97. "Max Roach Has Tantrum, Throws Fiddle, Arrested," *Pittsburgh Courier*, August 13, 1966, 1A. "'Jazz Giant' Back, Intoxicated, Nabbed," *Pittsburgh Courier*, August 20, 1966, 1A, 4A.

98. "'Jazz Giant,'" *Pittsburgh Courier*, 1A, 4A.

99. "Grill No. 2 Books Ornette Coleman," *Pittsburgh Courier*, February 13, 1960, 16.

100. Harold Betters, interview by the author, November 12, 2008.

101. Sandy Staley, interview by the author, November 17, 2008.

102. Chuck Spatafore, interview by the author, September 10, 2008.

103. Valerie Wilmer, *As Serious as Your Life: Black Music and the Free Jazz Revolution, 1957–1977* (London: Allison & Busby Limited, 1977), 10.

104. Wilmer, *As Serious as Your Life*, 60.

105. Fred Moten, *Black and Blur* (Durham, NC: Duke University Press, 2017), 98.

106. Neal, *What the Music Said*, 32.

107. "Controversial Jazz Men in Appearance at Grill 2," *Pittsburgh Courier*, February 20, 1960, 22.

108. "Controversial Jazz Men," 22.

109. Wilmer, *As Serious as Your Life*, 88.

110. Phyl Garland's notable career as a journalist included being the first African American and woman to receive tenure at the Columbia School of Journalism (1981). Melissa Repko, "Phyllis Garland, Journalism Prof, Dies at 71," *Columbia Daily Spectator*, accessed April 24, 2020, columbiaspectator.com/2006/11/21/phyllis-garland-journalism-prof-dies-71/.

111. Phyl Garland, "Listening In: Experimenting in Jazz," *Pittsburgh Courier*, May 16, 1964, 17.

112. "Helicopter May Rescue the Beatles," *Pittsburgh Post-Gazette*, September 3, 1964, 23.

113. The 1965 Pittsburgh Jazz Festival, as advertised in *Pittsburgh Post-Gazette* (June 8, 1965, 22), lists the following performers: (Friday, June 18) Count Basie, Miles Davis, Modern Jazz Quartet, Thelonious Monk, Newport All-Stars including Rudy Braff & Bud Freeman, Tom McKinley; (Saturday, June 19) John Coltrane, Duke Ellington, Stan Getz, Earl Hines, Carmen McRae, Walt Harper; (Sunday, June 20) Dave Brubeck, Dizzy Gillespie, Woody Herman, Ahmad Jamal, Muddy Waters, Mary Lou Williams, Harold Betters. The ticket prices were $3, $4.25, and $5.50, which would amount roughly to $25, $35, and $46 in 2020.

114. Phyl Garland, "Listening In: Coltrane and the Concert," *Pittsburgh Courier*, July 3, 1965, 13.

115. Sandy Hamm, "Hill District Jazz Culture Revisited," *New Pittsburgh Courier*, June 19, 1993, 2.

116. Ludwig, interview.

117. Thaddeus Mosley, interview by the author, November 2, 2008.

118. Spencer Bey, interview by the author, January 1, 2009.

119. Guthrie Ramsey, *Race Music: Black Cultures from Bebop to Hip-Hop* (Berkeley: University of California Press, 2003), 77.

120. Parker-Reid, interview.

121. Mosley, interview.

122. Ann Butler, "Birdie's Place," *Pittsburgh Press*, April 3, 1984, B6.

123. Karen DeWitt, "CROSS BURNED HERE: Independence Day Chosen to Warn Negroes;" unidentified author, "Youth Slain by Cop Buried;" unidentified author, "Bombs Miss Auto of Teens," *Pittsburgh Courier*, July 11, 1964, 1.

124. Parker-Reid, interview.

125. Harold L. Keith, "Carl Arter, 'Bill' Powell Feuding over Union Policy," *Pittsburgh Courier*, March 9, 1957, 3.

Notes   291

126. Hazel Garland, "Things to Talk About," *Pittsburgh Courier*, March 17, 1956, A24. This excerpt appears as it originally was printed, including the use of ellipses.

127. Jack Smight (director), Will Lorin (story), Leonard Freeman (story), "Goodnight Sweet Blues," *Route 66*, aired October 6, 1961. *Route 66*, Herbert B. Leonard and Stirling Silliphant (creators), Herbert B. Leonard (executive producer), Lancer Productions, Sony Pictures Television (distributor), aired on CBS from October 7, 1960, to March 20, 1964.

128. The fictional band is comprised of veteran jazz musicians: drummer Philly Joe Jones, saxophonist Coleman Hawkins, and trumpeter Roy Eldridge, as well as actors Juano Hernandez and Bill Gunn.

129. Discussions of jazz and race continue to shape jazz discourse with writers grappling with racialized claims to the music. In *Where the Dark and the Light Folks Meet* (Lanham, MD: Scarecrow Press, 2010), trumpeter and writer Randall Sandke emphatically discounts narratives of jazz as a primarily African American expression. Sandke writes, "What most jazz texts don't reveal is the great degree to which Black musicians have benefited from and even depended upon the efforts of white presenters and the appreciation of white audiences. The more these dynamics are taken into account, the clearer it becomes that jazz has been an interracial phenomenon throughout most of its history" (139). Sandke continues with a laundry list of historical events that he uses to chip away at claims to jazz as distinctly Black rather than American music. Positive reviews by Joe C. Clarke and Rob Hoff support Sandke's revisionist history of jazz that aims to debunk "myths" that have excluded White contributions to jazz.

130. Parker-Reid, interview.

131. Stellute, interview.

132. Nelson Harrison, interview by the author, March 7, 2006.

133. Harrison, interview.

134. Humphries, interview.

135. Howard S. Becker, *Outsiders* (New York: Simon and Schuster, 1963), 108.

136. Don Aliquo, interview by the author, September 11, 2008.

137. Aliquo, interview.

138. "Jimmy Smith Still Swinging at Hurricane," *Pittsburgh Courier*, January 18, 1958, A10.

139. Jimmy Smith, *Live at the Village Gate*, Blue Note Records, 1963.

140. Harrison, interview.

141. Stellute, interview.

142. Lefebvre, *Rhythmanalysis*, 77.

143. Lefebvre, 96.


## Chapter 5: Civil Rights and the Musicians Union

1. James Baldwin, *The Fire Next Time* (New York: Vintage International, 1962), 101.

2. C-SPAN, "Howard University Commencement Address, C-SPAN.org," accessed February 24, 2020, https://www.c-span.org/video/?326895-1/president-lyndon-b-johnson-commencement-address-howard-university.

3. Martin Stokes, "Marx, Money, and Musicians," in *Music and Marx. Ideas, Practice, Politics* (New York/London: Routledge, 2002), 139.

4. Stokes, "Marx," 147.

5. Jesse Weaver Shipley and Marina Peterson, "Introduction: Audio Work: Labor, Value, and the Making of Musical Aesthetics," *Journal of Popular Music Studies* 24, no. 4 (2012): 400.

6. Shipley and Peterson, "Introduction," 405.

7. Jennifer Ryan, "Beale Street Blues? Tourism, Musical Labor, and the Fetishization of Poverty in Blues Discourse," *Ethnomusicology* 55, no. 3 (2011): 496–99.

8. Ingrid Monson, *Freedom Sounds: Civil Rights Call Out to Jazz and Africa* (Oxford: Oxford University Press, 2007), 283. Roger House is another scholar who examines African American musicians' roles in American culture and labor history with a focus on the period leading up to the Great Depression. He discusses how Black musicians established "occupational standards as working-class artists through individual training, family mentoring, and peer-group networking" (Roger House, "Work House Blues: Black Musicians in Chicago and the Labor of Culture During the Jazz Age," *Labor* 9, no. 1 [March 1, 2012]: 4). House's study of canonized jazz musicians as cultural workers struggling to control the conditions of their labor grounds their creativity in the material conditions of their lives.

9. Appendix A of Diane Delores Turner's 1993 study lists forty-eight Black locals that existed within the AFM (315).

10. David Gilbert, "Clef Club Inc.: James Reese Europe and New York's Musical Marketplace," *Journal of Popular Music Studies* 24, no. 4 (2012): 430–56.

11. Gilbert, "Clef Club Inc.," 436.

12. Glasco, *The WPA History of the Negro in Pittsburgh*, 293–332.

13. Leta E. Miller, "Racial Segregation and the San Francisco Musicians' Union, 1923–60," *Journal of the Society for American Music* 1, no. 2 (May 2007): 161–206. Chicago's Local 208 was chartered in 1902 and grew to be the largest AFM local founded by African American musicians. See Miller's Table 1 (page 194) for a detailed list of Black AFM locals.

14. "Sax Ace, Paul Quinichette Next Attraction at Grill," *Pittsburgh Courier*, April 14, 1956, 35. The meeting took place in the home of Benny B. Mitchell and included William A. Kelly, Albert Robinson, Charles Catlin, William S. Jones, Harry C. Waters, R. Dinguid, and R. Bush.

15. William Gould, Black Musicians of Pittsburgh et al., Plaintiffs-Appellants v. Local 60-471, American Federation of Musicians, AFL-CIO and American Federation of Musicians, AFL-CIO (Third Circuit 1977). The "Afro-American Agreement" was discussed during testimony for the *Black Musicians of Pittsburgh v. Local 60-471* court case.

16. Gould, at 34.

17. Glasco, 322. In 1835, Oberlin became the first US college to open enrollment to African American students.

18. "Afro-American Notes," *Pittsburgh Press*, April 17, 1921, 75.

19. "Coleman Industrial Home to Have Tag Day," *Pittsburgh Courier*, November 1, 1912, 1.

20. Sue Morris, "The Historical Dilettante: Forgotten History: Samuel and Luella Coleman, in a Class by Themselves," *The Historical Dilettante* (blog), February 9, 2019, http://historicaldilettante.blogspot.com/2019/02/forgotten-history-samuel-and-luella.html.

21. "Afro-American Notes," *Pittsburgh Press*, November 15, 1908, 23.

22. "Afro-American Notes," *Pittsburgh Press*, June 20, 1909, 29.

23. "Best Dance Orchestra in Pittsburgh," *Pittsburgh Press*, June 17, 1910, 31.

24. "Chemist," *Pittsburgh Courier*, June 29, 1929, 9.

25. "Death Ends Fine Career of Hawkins," *Pittsburgh Courier*, July 28, 1934, 1.

26. John L. Clark, "Wylie Avenue," *Pittsburgh Courier*, March 6, 1926, 3.

27. John L. Clark, "Wylie Avenue," *Pittsburgh Courier*, March 13, 1926, 3.

28. "Smoker and Dutch Lunch," *Pittsburgh Courier*, February 22, 1930, 8.

29. "Club," *Pittsburgh Courier*, September 1, 1923, 5.

30. James M. Doran, *Erroll Garner: The Most Happy Piano* (New Jersey: Scarecrow Press and the Institute of Jazz Studies, 1985), 33.

31. "'Death to Jazz,' Cries Union Musician Head in Pittsburgh," *Variety*, November 25, 1921, 6.

32. "'Death to Jazz,'" 6.

33. Dance, *The World of Earl Hines*, 24. For the Paramount Inn orchestra band listing, see "Station WJAS Program," *Pittsburgh Press*, January 5, 1925, 37.

34. Harold L. Keith, "Who's Who in Labor?" *Pittsburgh Courier*, November 30, 1946, 14.

35. Keith, "Who's Who in Labor?," 14.

36. African American classical musicians may have gravitated away from Local 471 due in part to the work of other local organizations. Pittsburgh had both the local chapter of the National Negro Association of Musicians as well as educator and opera singer Mary Cardwell Dawson, who established a music school in 1927 and the National Negro Opera Company in 1941 to advance classical music training for African Americans in the city.

37. Chuck Austin, interview by the author, August 31, 2008.

38. Lee A. Matthews, "Swingin' Among the Musicians," *Pittsburgh Courier* (November 8, 1941), 21.

39. Austin, interview.

40. Austin, interview.

41. Vincent Johnson, "This Jam Doesn't Go with Bread or Butter, but It's Still Good," *Pittsburgh Post-Gazette*, January 15, 1943, 24.

42. "At Musicians," *Pittsburgh Courier*, March 4, 1950, 22.

43. Ruby Younge Hardy, interviewed by Maurice Levy, January 1, 1995, Carnegie Library of Pittsburgh Oral History of Music in Pittsburgh.

44. "Fat Man, Leroy Brown at Musicians Sunday," *Pittsburgh Courier*, April 1, 1950, 20.

45. George "Duke" Spaulding, interview by the author, November 16, 2008.

46. George Thompson, interview by the author, December 11, 2008.

47. Hosea Taylor, *Dirt Street* (Pittsburgh: Arsenal Binding & Finishing, 2007), 143.

48. Joe Harris, interview by the author, November 21, 2008.

49. Harold L. Keith, "Who's Who in Labor: He Recalls Those Halcyon Days," *Pittsburgh Courier*, July 11, 1953, 6. "Musicians Move to Buy Building," *Pittsburgh Courier*, December 5, 1953, 1.

50. "Musicians Elect Entire New Slate," *Pittsburgh Courier*, December 12, 1953, 1.

51. "On Site of Old Famous Door: New Musicians Club Jumps All the Time; Harper Plays Friday," *Pittsburgh Courier*, January 23, 1954, 18.

52. Joe W. Trotter and Jared N. Day, *Race and Renaissance: African Americans in Pittsburgh since World War II* (Pittsburgh: University of Pittsburgh Press, 2010), 72.

53. Gould, at 70.

54. Gene Ludwig, interview by the author, March 8, 2006.

55. Harold L. Keith, "Who's Who in Labor?," 14.

56. "Musicians Member List of Local 471," University of Pittsburgh Library System, accessed March, 2020, http://www.library.pitt.edu/labor_legacy/MusiciansMemberList.htm.

57. Harris, interview.

58. Hosea Taylor, interview by the author, December 16, 2008. In 1962, Westray was elected as 471's president and moved the local's headquarters to the second floor of his own club called Westray's Plaza (Gould, at 70). Located at 915 Lincoln Avenue, Westray's Plaza served as a meeting place for 471 members and operated a bar downstairs. As Arter remembered, the new location of 471's headquarters did facilitate a place for socializing, though they discontinued running a club that featured live entertainment. This move away from operating the Musicians Club was likely in order to cut down on management and operation costs, though it remains unclear from available sources why the important tradition had been ended.

59. Walt Harper, interview by Chuck Austin, July 21, 1997, African American Jazz Preservation Society of Pittsburgh (AAJPSP) Oral History Project.

60. Harper, AAJPSP.

61. Harper, AAJPSP.

62. Thompson, interview.

63. Taylor, interview.

64. Thompson, interview.

65. Howard S. Becker, *Outsiders* (New York: Simon & Schuster, 2008), 82–83.

66. "Walt Harper's Band Plays Bartender Picnic, Sunday," *Pittsburgh Courier*, August 17, 1946, 23.

67. Roger Barbour, interview by the author, November 19, 2008.

68. Phyl Garland, "Musician Beats the Odds to Make It in Hometown," *Pittsburgh Courier*, March 21, 1964, 13.

69. Garland, "Musician Beats the Odds."

70. Cecil Brooks II, interviewed by the author, November 19, 2008. It should be noted that while Harper was not known as a bebop pianist, his recording of the songs "I Got the Blues" and "Body and Soul" (Hi-Lo Records, 1952) with vocalist Eddie Jefferson were pioneering for modern jazz. Here, Jefferson demonstrates the technique of "vocalese" in which lyrics are composed to a recorded instrumental solo. For more information on these and other jazz recordings in Pittsburgh, see Carlos Pena, *Pittsburgh Jazz Records and Beyond, 1950–1985* (master's thesis, University of Pittsburgh, 2007).

71. Hosea Taylor, interview by the author, December 16, 2008.

72. Joe Negri, interview by the author, December 17, 2008.

73. Harris, interview.

74. Cecil Brooks II, interview by the author, December 5, 2008.

75. Thompson, interview.

76. Scott Knowles DeVeaux, *The Birth of Bebop: A Social and Musical History* (Berkeley: University of California Press, 1997), 167.

77. Taylor, interview.

78. Thompson, interview.

79. Cecil Brooks and George Thompson, interview by the author, January 13, 2009.

80. Becker, *Outsiders*, 108.


## Chapter 6: Challenging Discrimination, Resisting Merger

1. "Musicians Continue to Fight Racism," *New Pittsburgh Courier*, February 2, 1974, 1. Also see the oral history project of the African American Jazz Preservation Society of Pittsburgh (AAJPSP), University of Pittsburgh archives (Box 4, Folder 11).

2. Everett Lee Refior, "The American Federation of Musicians: Organization, Policies, and Practices" (master's thesis, The University of Chicago, 1955), 59.

3. Miller, "Racial Segregation and the San Francisco Musicians' Union, 1923–60," 194. Miller states that in 1954, fifty-three of the 701 locals were Black. Miller's Table 1 compares membership numbers of Black and White locals in 1954. The total number of recorded unionized musicians in the fifty-three listed Black locals is 7,079 with an average of 134 per local. When excluding the two largest Black locals; Chicago's Local 208 (1,081 members) and Philadelphia's Local 274 (770 members), the average becomes 103.

4. Gould, *Black Musicians of Pittsburgh v. Local 60-471*, 59.

5. Gould, at 33–55.

6. Clark Halker, "A History of Local 208 and the Struggle for Racial Equality in the American Federation of Musicians," *Black Music Research Journal*, 1988, 214–15.

7. "Petrillo Favors 'Amalgamation' But His Musicians Are 'Anti,'" *Pittsburgh Courier*, May 4, 1957, A3.

8. Refior, "The American Federation of Musicians," 8.

9. "Executive Order #9346: Remembering Our Nation's Commitment to Equality During World War II," National WWII Museum New Orleans, accessed March 2, 2020, http://www .nww2m.com/2013/05/executive-order-9346-remembering-our-nations-commitment-to -equality-during-world-war-ii/.

10. "AFM's 'Jim Crow' Policy Is under Fire from NAACP; Test Looms in Barney Bigard Case," *Billboard*, January 1, 1944.

11. Harry Brooks, "In the Foreseeable Future? Locals 60 and 471 May Merge, But Past and Present Must Be Forgotten," *Pittsburgh Courier*, August 13, 1960, 4.

12. Gould, at 90.

13. Harold L. Keith, "Carl Arter, 'Bill' Powell Feuding Over Union Policy," *Pittsburgh Courier*, March 9, 1957, 3.

14. Keith, "Carl Arter," 3.

15. "Cafe Settles Union Dispute," *Pittsburgh Post-Gazette*, December 3, 1954.

16. Gould, at 77.

17. Harry Brooks, "75 Per Cent Clause Ignored by Federation: Will Musicians' Union Local 60 Provide 'Discriminating' Music for Fun Spots?" *Pittsburgh Courier*, July 30, 1960, 2.

18. Harold Keith, "Jazz World Mourns Demise of Pettiford Abroad in Copenhagen," *Pittsburgh Courier*, September 17, 1960, B6.

19. Harry Brooks, "Decision Rules Against Local 471, Then Reverses Decision; New Era Opening Now?" *Pittsburgh Courier*, August 6, 1960, 5. Kenin served as president of the AFM from 1958 to 1970 and was followed by Hal Davis.

20. Gould, at 97.

21. "Musicians Club Starts New Concert Band," *Pittsburgh Courier*, October 30, 1954, 1.

22. "Negro Band Cracks County Fair Barrier," *Pittsburgh Courier*, August 29, 1964, 2.

23. Harry Brooks, "Locals 60 and 471 May Merge, but Past and Present Problems Must Be Forgotten," *Pittsburgh Courier*, August 13, 1960, 4.

24. George E. Pitts, "Negro Musicians, Do They Really Want to Merge?" *Pittsburgh Courier*, December 5, 1959, 13.

25. George E. Pitts, "Pittsburgh Produced Some of Nation's Top Show Folk," *Pittsburgh Courier*, December 24, 1962, A17.

26. Harold L. Keith, "Complete Harmony Sets Tone for AFM Sessions," *Pittsburgh Courier*, June 16, 1962, 15.

27. F. Ray Marshall, *The Negro and Organized Labor* (Hoboken: Wiley, 1965), 103.

28. Clora Bryant et al., *Central Avenue Sounds: Jazz in Los Angeles*, New Ed edition (Berkeley: University of California Press, 1999), 389–93.

29. Bryant et al., *Central Avenue Sounds*, 396.

30. Peter B. Flint, "Hal Davis, 63, Head of Musicians Union," *New York Times*, January 13, 1978, Archives, https://www.nytimes.com/1978/01/13/archives/hal-davis-63-head-of-musicians -union-was-also-an-arts-council.html.

31. American Federation of Musicians, Local 60-471, Pittsburgh, PA Records, 1906–1996, AIS.1997.41, Archives & Special Collections, University of Pittsburgh Library System, 232.

32. Kenan A. Foley, "The Interpretation of Experience: A Contextual Study of the Art of Three Pittsburgh Jazz Drummers" (PhD thesis, University of Pittsburgh, 2007), 203.

33. Stanley Turrentine, interview by Chuck Austin, November 23, 1997, African American Jazz Preservation Society of Pittsburgh (AAJPSP) Oral History Project.

34. American Federation of Musicians, 232.

35. Gould, at 214.

36. American Federation of Musicians, 232.

37. American Federation of Musicians, 235.

38. Ruby Younge Hardy, interviewed by Maurice Levy, January 1, 1995, Carnegie Library of Pittsburgh Oral History of Music in Pittsburgh.

39. Chuck Austin, interview by the author, August 31, 2008.

40. Appendix K of Diane Delores Turner's 1993 study lists thirty-nine mergers of Black and White AFM locals between April 1, 1960, and January 1, 1971 (335).

41. Amy Absher, *The Black Musician and the White City: Race and Music in Chicago, 1900–1967* (Ann Arbor: University of Michigan Press, 2014), 129.

42. Absher, *The Black Musician*, 130.

43. Absher, 139.

44. Absher, 146.

45. Richard McRae, "Paying Their Dues: Buffalo's African American Musicians Union, Local 533, AFM," *Afro-Americans in New York Life and History* 20, no. 1 (January 31, 1996). The entire minutes of the meeting are included in McRae's study and detail the back and forth of questioning motives and methods of moving forward.

46. McRae, *Afro-Americans in New York*, 41.

47. McRae, 41.

48. McRae, 43.

49. McRae, 45.

50. William B. Gould, *Black Workers in White Unions: Job Discrimination in the United States* (Ithaca, NY: Cornell University Press, 1977), 416.

51. Diane Delores Turner, "Organizing and Improvising: A History of Philadelphia's Black Musicians' Protective Union Local 274, American Federation of Musicians" (PhD diss., Temple University, 1993), 240–41.

52. Turner, "Organizing and Improvising," 256.

53. Turner, 298.

54. Gould, *Black Musicians of Pittsburgh v. Local 60-471*, 2.

55. American Federation of Musicians, Local 60-471 Pittsburgh, PA, "Records of the American Federation of Musicians Local 60-471 (Pittsburgh, PA), 1906–1967, bulk 1911–1951," University of Pittsburgh Archives, 232.

56. Gould, at 238–39.

57. BMOP members later formed the African American Jazz Preservation Society of Pittsburgh, which conducted an oral history project from 1995 to 1999. The archive is currently housed at the University of Pittsburgh, and the organization continues to organize events. Available at http://www.aajpsp.org/, accessed March 2020.

58. Justia US Law, Black Musicians of Pittsburgh v. Local 60-471, Am. Fed. M., 375 F. Supp. 902 (W.D. PA 1974), Justia US Law, 1974, 3, https://law.justia.com/cases/federal/district-courts/FSupp/375/902/1669281/.

59. Fred A. Bernstein, "Derrick Bell, Law Professor and Rights Advocate, Dies at 80," *New York Times*, October 6, 2011, US (section), https://www.nytimes.com/2011/10/06/us/derrick-bell-pioneering-harvard-law-professor-dies-at-80.html.

60. William B. Gould IV, interview by the author, May 3, 2018. Gould explained the family connection between Bell and Childress as well as Gould's connection to Bell while teaching at Harvard Law School.

61. Justia US Law, *Black Musicians*, 375 F. Supp. 902, at 3.

62. Gould, *Black Musicians of Pittsburgh v. Local 60-471*, 8.

63. Gould, at 12.

64. Gould, at 14.

65. Justia US Law, Stamps v. Detroit Edison Co., 365 F. Supp. 87 (Dist. Court 1973).

66. Gould, at 321.

67. Justia US Law, *Black Musicians*, 375 F. Supp. 902, at 8.

68. Justia US Law, Black Musicians of Pittsburgh v. LOCAL 60-471, ETC., 442 F. Supp. 855 (D. PA 1977), Justia Law, 1977, 7. https://law.justia.com/cases/federal/district-courts/FSupp/442/855/2284967/.

69. Gould, at 12, McCune's Memorandum and Order.

70. See Fullilove's study *Root Shock: How Tearing Up City Neighborhoods Hurts America, and What We Can Do About It* (2009) for an analysis of the psychological effects of mid-century urban redevelopment on inner city communities.

71. Neal, *What the Music Said*, 102.

72. Neal, 102.

73. Bill Toland, "In Desperate 1983, There Was Nowhere for Pittsburgh's Economy to Go but Up," *Pittsburgh Post-Gazette*, December 23, 2012, https://www.post-gazette.com/business/business news/2012/12/23/In-desperate-1983-there-was-nowhere-for-Pittsburgh-s-economy-to-go-but-up/stories/201212230258.

74. Derrick Bell, *The Derrick Bell Reader* (New York: NYU Press, 2005), 120.

75. Robert Gorczyca, "Chuck Austin: Musician with a Mission," *Western Pennsylvania History: 1918–2016* 93, no. 4 (2010): 31.

76. Gorczyca, "Chuch Austin," 30.

77. Don Aliquo, interview by the author, September 11, 2008.

78. Gould, at 174–75.

### Chapter 7: Hill Nightlife in the Wake of 1968

1. The population of the Hill District reached 53,648 in 1950. It decreased to 42,777 in 1960, 29,372 in 1970, and 20,438 in 1980. In 2010, the neighborhood's population was less than one-fifth that of 1950. This data was derived from the 2000 report *Census: Pittsburgh, a Comparative Digest of Census Data for Pittsburgh's Neighborhoods*, compiled by the Pittsburgh Department of City Planning. Pittsburgh Department of City Planning, accessed March 16, 2021, https://web.archive.org/web/20070810193148/http:/www.city.pittsburgh.pa.us/cp/assets/census/2000_census_pgh_jan06.pdf.

2. Jane Jacobs, *The Death and Life of Great American Cities* (New York: Vintage Books, 1961), 402.

3. Susan Stoker and Cecilia Robert, *Hill District Community Plan* (Pittsburgh: Hill District Consensus Group, May 29, 1996), 4, https://ucsur.pitt.edu/files/center/HillDistrictCommunty Plan_May291996.pdf.

4. John F. McDonald, *Urban America: Growth, Crisis, and Rebirth* (Armonk, NY: M. E. Sharpe, 2008), 107.

5. Allen Dieterich-Ward, *Beyond Rust: Metropolitan Pittsburgh and the Fate of Industrial America* (Philadelphia: University of Pennsylvania Press, 2015), 149. Dieterich-Ward notes that Monroeville's population increased from eight to thirty-three thousand between 1950 and 1976. The growing number of jobs in the suburbs created further economic challenges for Downtown Pittsburgh as many opted to work and live outside the city rather than commute.

6. McDonald, *Urban America*, 69.

7. McDonald, *Urban America*, 183. This ranking is based on changes between 1970 and 1990.

8. McDonald, *Urban America*, 150.

9. Daniel Matlin, *On the Corner: African American Intellectuals and the Urban Crisis* (Cambridge, MA: Harvard University Press, 2013), 2.

10. Palmer, *Cultures of Darkness*, 436.

11. Baldwin, *The Fire Next Time*; Michael K. Honey, *Going Down Jericho Road: The Memphis Strike, Martin Luther King's Last Campaign* (New York: W. W. Norton & Company, 2011), 97.

12. United States Congress, *Congressional Record: Proceedings and Debates of the 90th Congress*, vol. 113 (Washington, DC: US Government Printing Office, 1967), 27815, https://books.google.com/books?id=RIfiNSj1JuEC&printsec=frontcover&source=gbs_ge_summary_r&cad=0#v=onepage&q&f=false.

13. Carl Morris, "The Black Mood in Pittsburgh." *New Pittsburgh Courier*, 1968, 1.

14. Morris, *The Black Mood*, 3.

15. Steve Mellon and Julian Routh, "The Week the Hill Rose Up," *Pittsburgh Post-Gazette*, April 2, 2018, https://newsinteractive.post-gazette.com/the-week-the-hill-rose-up/.

16. Interview by the author. I have omitted the interviewee name due to the topic of the quote.

17. Mellon and Routh, "The Week the Hill Rose Up."

18. Ralph Lemuel Hill, "A View of the Hill—A Study of Experiences and Attitudes in the Hill District of Pittsburgh, Pennsylvania from 1900 to 1973" (PhD diss., University of Pittsburgh, 1973), 160.

19. Tom Davidson, "Hill District Residents Lament Shop 'n Save's Closing," TribLIVE.com, February 22, 2019, https://triblive.com/local/pittsburgh-allegheny/as-hill-district-residents-lament-shop-n-saves-closing-officials-work-to-attract-another-store/.

20. Nelson Harrison, interview by the author, December 27, 2022.

21. Lou Stellute, interview by the author, December 1, 2008.

22. Sandy Staley, interview by the author, November 17, 2008.

23. Stellute, interview.

24. Bernard Holland, "Birdie Says Bye Bye to Hurricane, All That Jazz," *Pittsburgh Post-Gazette* (February 4, 1980), 19.

25. Holland, "Birdy Says Bye Bye," 19.

26. Holland, 19. The Hurricane was reported by the *Pittsburgh Press* (June 16, 1970, 15) to have suffered a fire in April 1970, leading one to believe that Birdie recalled the date incorrectly for the 1980 interview with Holland.

27. Hazel Garland, "Grill to Honor Birdie Dunlap," *New Pittsburgh Courier*, September 1, 1973, 20.

28. Hazel Garland, "Birdie Dunlap Has Her Night," *New Pittsburgh Courier* September 22, 1973, 17.

29. "Grill Owner Arrested," *New Pittsburgh Courier*, August 25, 1973, 4.

30. See "Chapter 2: Vice Wars on Wylie Avenue" for more context on the development of numbers running in Pittsburgh.

31. Matthew Vaz, "The Jackpot Mentality: The Growth of Government Lotteries and the Suppression of Illegal Numbers Gambling in Rio de Janeiro and New York City" (PhD diss., Columbia University, 2011), 55, https://doi.org/10.7916/D8B85G4C.

32. Thomas Burley, interview by the author, January 2006.

33. See the Appendix for a list of artists featured at the Crawford Grill No. 2.

34. James Johnson Jr., phone conversation with author, June 2021.

35. Greg Mims, "Prysock and the Grill, An Appealing Combination," *New Pittsburgh Courier*, November 24, 1973, 17.

36. John Hayes, "Johnny Lytle Cruises with Good Vibes," *Pittsburgh Post-Gazette*, October 11, 1991, 44.

37. Hazel Garland, "Crawford Grill Swings on New Courier Night," *New Pittsburgh Courier*, May 23, 1970, 16.

38. Hazel Garland, "Crawford Grill Swings," 16.

39. "Joe Robinson Honored at 'Appreciation Night,'" *New Pittsburgh Courier*, July 27, 1974, 17.

40. Ulish Carter, "Grill Still Tops After 50 Years," *New Pittsburgh Courier*, January 8, 1977, 1, 3.

41. University of Pittsburgh ULS Digital Collections, "Guide to the Bob Johnson Papers, 1949–2003 CTC.2014.03, Digital Pitt," accessed May 27, 2021, https://digital.library.pitt.edu/islandora/object/pitt%3AUS-PPiU-ctc201403/viewer#toc.

42. Bekka Rasul, "'Bitches Brew': Overdue Change for Pittsburgh," *New Pittsburgh Courier*, May 27, 1978, 17.

43. Rasul, "'Bitches Brew,'" 17.

44. Rasul, 17.

45. Bill Cleveland, "Episode 2: L. O. Sloan - A Gunrunner for the Arts (Pt. 1)," Change the Story, Change the World, accessed May 29, 2021, https://change-the-story-chan.captivate.fm/episode/l-o-sloan-a-gunrunner-for-the-arts-part-1. Commissioned by the de Young Museum, Sloan's musical was first staged in San Francisco as part of a 1976 American Bicentennial program.

46. Rasul, "'Bitches Brew,'" 17.

47. Lenwood Sloan, email correspondence with author, June 2021.

48. "Modern Twists on an American Theater Legend," *San Francisco Examiner*, December 17, 1978, 328.

49. Lenwood Sloan, email correspondence with author, June 2021.

50. Barry Paris, "A Tribute to Great Minstrel," *Pittsburgh Post-Gazette*, November 16, 1979, 21.

51. Paris, "A Tribute to Great Minstrel," 25. Though minstrelsy reached its peak in the second half of the nineteenth century, it continued to be a part of popular culture into the 1970s. It was not until 1978 that the BBC discontinued its immensely popular prime-time television program, *The Black and White Minstrel Show*, which was created in 1958 by Scottish entertainer George Mitchell and featured elaborate song and dance routines where the male characters performed in blackface makeup. Sloan dismissed *The Black and White Minstrel Show* as "horrible," not solely because of its overt racism but also because it defied "an old minstrel law" that held that performances draw on contemporary issues. As Sloan noted during his European tour, "That show is cast in an antiquated art form. It hasn't furthered the art form, or legitimized its style, [or] celebrated its beauty. They've perpetuated the stereotypes. They've sealed the taboo" ("Black Art," *The Guardian*, July 7, 1978, 8). While *The Black and White Minstrel Show* capitalized on minstrel performance as escapist, light entertainment, Sloan used *Three Black and Three White Refined Jubilee Minstrels* to delve into the ways White and Black gazes invested American popular culture with meaning.

52. Paris, "A Tribute to Great Minstrel," 25.

53. Malvin R. Goode, "Let's Build a Monument to Two Giants, *New Pittsburgh Courier*, December 10, 1983, 4.

54. Mike Kalina, "Crawford Grill Swings Back to Life," *Pittsburgh Post-Gazette*, April 30, 1982, 27.

55. "Grill Brings It Back Alive," *Pittsburgh Post-Gazette*, April 30, 1988, 27.

56. Michael A. Fucco, "Return of Glory: Hill District Determined to Regain Lost Greatness," *Pittsburgh Post-Gazette*, April 11, 1999, 1.

57. Louis Kendrick, "Crawford Grill #2—Institute of Jazz & Knowledge (July 4)," *New Pittsburgh Courier*, July 6, 2018, https://newpittsburghcourier.com/2018/07/06/crawford-grill-2-institute-of-jazz-knowledge-july-4/.

58. Rtmadminnpc, "Crawford Grill Purchased . . . Franco Harris Part of Investment Group," *New Pittsburgh Courier*, April 14, 2010, https://newpittsburghcourier.com/2010/04/14/crawford-grill-purchasedfranco-harris-part-of-investment-group/.

## Chapter 8: The Community Archive in Practice

1. Quotes are taken from "Jazz at the Hill House," a pamphlet printed in 1997 for the sixth anniversary of the event.

2. Bob Karlovitz, "An Education in Jazz," *Pittsburgh Press*, October 29, 1989, 97.

3. Sheila Venson, "Encore II: Keeping Jazz Alive in Pittsburgh," *New Pittsburgh Courier*, April 26, 1980, A5.

4. Henry Ward, "Market Square to Get New Supper Club," *Pittsburgh Press*, March 11, 1969, 30. While Harper was the face of the club, the business was co-owned between Harper, Pat Foy, Bill Millar, Jerry Cohen, and Alex Sweicke. "Walt Harper's 'Attic' Club Opens Friday," *Pittsburgh Press*, July 24, 1969, 12.

5. "Nightlife," *Pittsburgh Post-Gazette*, October 25, 1974, 28.

6. "Shadyside," *Pittsburgh Music History*, accessed May 26, 2021, https://sites.google.com/site/pittsburghmusichistory/pittsburgh-music-story/venues/shadyside. Harold Betters's record *At the Encore* (Gateway, 1962) was recorded Live at the Shadyside Encore with John Hughes (piano), Joe Ashliman (drums), and Al O'Brian (bass).

7. Venson, "Encore II," A5.

8. Venson, A5.

9. John Shannon, phone interview with author, June 2021.

10. Dan Wasson, personal interview with author, March 6, 2006.

## Epilogue: To Honor and Repair

1. Bruce Weber, "Jazz, Honors and Politics; A New Museum Pays Tribute to Musicians but Stirs Criticism," *New York Times*, January 5, 1998, Arts, https://www.nytimes.com/1998/01/05/arts/jazz-honors-politics-new-museum-pays-tribute-musicians-but-stirs-criticism.html.

2. Weber, "Jazz, Honors and Politics."

3. Dale Chapman, *The Jazz Bubble: Neoclassical Jazz in Neoliberal Culture* (Oakland: University of California Press, 2018), 28.

4. Chapman, *The Jazz Bubble*, 188.

5. Rtmadminnpc, "Crawford Grill Purchased . . . Franco Harris Part of Investment Group," *New Pittsburgh Courier*, April 14, 2010, http://newpittsburghcourier.com/2010/04/14/crawford-grill-purchasedfranco-harris-part-of-investment-group/.

6. Jeremy Boren, "Redevelopment of Civic Arena Site Hangs on SEA," *TribLIVE.com*, September 15, 2010, https://archive.triblive.com/news/redevelopment-of-civic-arena-site-hangs -on-sea/.

7. Boren, "Redevelopment of Civic Arena."

8. Rich Lord, "From the Hilltop to North Side, Black Flight Drives Population Change in Pittsburgh," *PublicSource*, News for a Better Pittsburgh, May 20, 2020, https://www.public source.org/from-the-hilltop-to-north-side-black-flight-drives-population-change-in -pittsburgh/.

9. Brentin Mock, "Pittsburgh: A 'Most Livable' City, but Not for Black Women," *Bloomberg*, September 20, 2019, https://www.bloomberg.com/news/articles/2019-09-20/how-pittsburgh -fails-black-women-in-6-charts.

10. Deesha Philyaw, "The Not-So Secret Lives of Black Pittsburgh Women," *Bloomberg News*, April 23, 2021, https://www.bloomberg.com/news/articles/2021-04-23/pittsburgh-is-not -a-livable-city-for-black-women.

11. Hill CDC, "Lower Hill Community Collaboration and Implementation Plan (CCIP), Hill Community Development Corp," 6, accessed May 19, 2021, https://hilldistrict.org/ccip.

12. Hill CDC, "Development Review Panel, Hill Community Development Corp.," accessed May 19, 2021, https://hilldistrict.org/drp.

13. Pittsburgh City Planning, "Planning Commission—May 4, 2021," streamed live on May 4, 2021, YouTube video, https://www.youtube.com/watch?v=5RHQ-g2fuBQ.

14. Pittsburgh City Planning.

15. Daniel Armanios, "Commentary: 3 Things Biden Can Do to Enforce More Equitable Infrastructure," *Fortune*, April 25, 2021, https://fortune.com/2021/04/25/biden-equitable -infrastructure-development-plan/.

16. Pittsburgh City Planning.

# INDEX

# ABOUT THE AUTHOR

Photo by Emmai Alaquiva

**Colter Harper** is an ethnomusicologist and musician whose creative and scholarly work explores jazz, American nightlife, and West African popular music. Harper is currently a teaching assistant professor of music at the University at Buffalo and has previously taught at the University of Ghana's Department of Music, where he served as both a Visiting and Fulbright Scholar. Harper has written articles for journals including *Jazz Perspectives*, *South African Music Studies*, *International Association of Sound and Audiovisual Archives*, and *African Performance Review*. As a guitarist and composer, Harper has recorded two albums as a leader and worked extensively as a sideman, including as a touring member of the rock band Rusted Root.

Printed in the United States
by Baker & Taylor Publisher Services